BODY DOUBLE

BODY DOUBLE

The Author Incarnate in the Cinema

LUCY FISCHER

RUTGERS UNIVERSITY PRESS
New Brunswick, New Jersey, and London

Frontispiece: *Swimming Pool* (2003)

Library of Congress Cataloging-in-Publication Data
Fischer, Lucy.
Body double : the author incarnate in the cinema / Lucy Fischer.
p. cm.
Includes bibliographical references and index.
ISBN 978-0-8135-5449-5 (hardcover : alk. paper) — ISBN 978-0-8135-5448-8
(pbk. : alk. paper) — ISBN 978-0-8135-5450-1 (e-book)
1. Motion picture authorship. 2. Auteur theory (Motion pictures) 3. Motion pictures
and literature. 4. Authors in motion pictures.   I. Title.
PN1996. F4553 2012
791. 43'657—dc23   2012009920

A British Cataloging-in-Publication record for this book is available from the British
Library.

Visit our website: http://rutgerspress. rutgers. edu

Manufactured in the United States of America

To my family—past, present, and future

CONTENTS

ACKNOWLEDGMENTS

As always, there are many people to thank for the genesis of a book. First, I gained much insight into the material through interaction with my graduate students in a seminar on Authorship and the Cinema at the University of Pittsburgh in 2006. Second, I had the opportunity to present my ideas at my Distinguished Professorship lecture to the university community in 2009. Third, I received helpful comments on my manuscript-in-progress from James Naremore (an outside reader for Rutgers University Press) and from Dan Morgan, a colleague at Pitt. I would also like to express my appreciation to Leslie Mitchner for encouraging me to write this book, offering her advice along the way, and helping to see it through to print. Murray Pomerance is to be thanked for giving me a tutorial on the capture of high-resolution frame grabs. I am grateful to the University of Pittsburgh School of Arts and Sciences for providing me with subvention funds to cover the cost of the numerous illustrations for the text. Katherine Coyle, my graduate student assistant at Pitt, worked with me throughout the manuscript's preparation—researching articles, proofreading, and formatting it for publication. Jennifer Florian, Film Studies administrative assistant, also helped in the book's completion. Finally, I continue to owe a great deal to my husband, Mark, and my son, David, for providing me with the love and support to see this project through.

A few sections of the work that follows were previously published in different forms. Part of chapter 2 appeared as "David Mamet's *Homicide:* In or Out?" in *Hollywood's Chosen People: The Jewish Experience in American Cinema*, edited by Daniel Bernardi, Murray Pomerance, and Hava Tirosh-Samuelson (Detroit: Wayne State University Press, 2012). Part of chapter 4 appeared as "Dancing through the Mine Fields: Passion, Pedagogy, Production, and Politics in *The Tango Lesson*," *Cinema Journal* 43. 3 (Spring 2004): 42–58. Part of chapter 7 appeared as "*Irezumi:* Tattoo, Taboo, and the Female Body," *Post Script* 18. 1 (Fall 1998): 11–23. And part of chapter 5 appeared in my book *Cinematerntity: Film, Motherhood, Genre* (Princeton, N.J.: Princeton University Press, 1996), 152–157.

BODY DOUBLE

INTRODUCTION
The Screen Author—Wanted: Dead or Alive

I was sorry to have my name mentioned among the great authors because
they have a sad habit of dying off.

—Mark Twain

AUTHORSHIP IN THE AGE OF DIGITAL REPRODUCTION

In 1968, the year of so many other cultural and political declarations, French critic Roland Barthes provocatively proclaimed "The Death of the Author" in an essay bearing that title. Privileging the text over its creator, Barthes saw the literary work as a place "where all identity is lost, starting with the very identity of the body writing."[1] As he stated: "It is language which speaks, not the author." Thus, as the act of writing begins, "the author enters into his own death." Taking his place is the "scriptor," who "is born simultaneously with the text," neither "preceding nor exceeding the writing."[2]

What Barthes actually sought to bury here were traditional notions of authorship that treated the writer as the godlike authority on his work. As he observed: "To give a text an Author is to impose a limit on that text, to furnish it with a final signified, to close the writing" (and, moreover, the reading).[3] Barthes also decried approaches that assumed a rather transparent relationship between the poet and his creation; he questioned biographical studies, which sought seamlessly to link the author's life to the fates of his characters, or naively to equate the work's narrator with its creator. Thus for Barthes, as Colin MacCabe has noted, the concept of the author "obscured the form of the work at every level."[4] T. S. Eliot apparently agreed, once having said, "Honest criticism and sensitive appreciation is directed not upon the poet but upon the poetry."[5] Finally, Barthes's revision of the author concept sought to eradicate notions of pure originality, seeing the literary text as primarily "a tissue of quotations" from preexisting sources.

As though to render Barthes's theoretical work (and its themes of authorial erasure, plagiarism, and stylistic conventionality) in fiction, one chapter of Italo Calvino's *If on a Winter's Night a Traveler* takes the perspective of novelist Silas Flannery, who muses upon his craft: "How well I would write if I were not here!

If between the white page and the writing of words and stories . . . there were not interposed that uncomfortable partition which is my person!"[6] Rather than describe his composition process in the first person ("*I write*"), he wishes he could say, "*It writes*" (my emphasis). This is because "the author of every book is a fictitious character whom the existent author invents to make him the author of his fictions." One day, Flannery's translator warns him of unauthorized editions of his work circulating in Japan. In fact, the volumes in question are not even his. As he learns: "A firm in Osaka has managed to get hold of the formula of [his] novels, and . . . to produce absolutely new ones." Curiously, Flannery "feel[s] . . . a timid attraction for these fakes, for the extension of [him]self that has blossomed from the terrain of another civilization." Dupery is taken even one step further when a reader complains of having purchased two copies of his book "identical on the outside but containing two different novels." Flannery responds with a witticism: "The only books I recognize as mine are those I must still write.' "[7]

Despite such fantasies of self-annihilation, reports of the author's death have been greatly exaggerated, and the topic has done anything but expire. As Sean Burke has noted (in *The Death and Return of the Author*), "Like cosmology [authorship] remains a source of fascination for believers and non-believers alike."[8] This continued interest has also marked the field of cinema, as evidenced by the recent spate of books on the topic: some twelve volumes since the year 2000, not to mention the horde of monographs released on individual directors.[9] But film studies has always had an ambivalent relationship to claims of the author's erasure, since the idea that a film might have an author at all was largely contested in the first half of the medium's existence — when movies were often known by their producers, studios, or stars. It was not, in fact, until the late 1950s that the so-called "auteur" theory of cinema gained credence in France (asserting the director as a film's creative force) — and not until the 1970s that this notion achieved prominence in the United States. But the question arises as to why the subject continues to haunt film studies today — some forty years later.

First, one might observe, authorship is currently a vital and ubiquitous topic within the broader culture. This, of course, results from the dawning of the "Digital Age." A 2011 article by James Gleick in the *New York Times* regrets that books are being digitalized and refers to how their material remnants are fast becoming "fetish objects."[10] In the same publication, Bill Keller notes how "for years now the populist prophets of new media have been proclaiming the death of books, and the marketplace seems to back them up. Sales of print books in the U.S. peaked in 2005 and have been in steady decline since."[11]

Established writers like the late John Updike have seen authorship itself compromised by the disappearance of books. As he notes: "The printed, bound and *paid-for book* was — still is, for the moment — more exacting, more demanding, of its producer and consumer both. It is the site of an encounter, in *silence, of two minds*, one following in the other's steps but invited to imagine, to argue, to concur on a level of reflection beyond that of personal encounter" (my emphasis).[12] Here

Updike attacks free literary downloads (which he sees as reducing the reader's commitment to the author), but one might counter that many digitalized works are sold just like traditional books. However, his focus on silence still stands in light of the proliferation of audio books. In them, a writer's words are vocalized (usually by an actor, not the creator)—adding another voice to the reading process and interrupting its acoustic serenity. But, perhaps, Updike's most insistent complaint is with the fragmentation (into "snippets," paragraphs, and pages), of the unified text encouraged by digital technology. Having charted the author's decline, however, he ironically sees his rebirth in the form of the celebrity book tour star. As he remarks: "In my first 15 or 20 years of authorship, I was almost never asked to give a speech or an interview. The written work was supposed to speak for itself, and to sell itself, sometimes even without the author's photograph on the back flap. As the author is gradually retired from his old responsibilities of vicarious confrontation and provocation, he has grown in importance as a kind of walking, talking advertisement for the book." Updike takes no pleasure from this turn to embodiment because of its consumerist thrust. As he wryly comments: "Authors, if I understand present trends, will soon be like surrogate birth mothers, rented wombs in which a seed implanted by high-powered consultants is allowed to ripen and, after nine months, be dropped squalling into the marketplace." So, in this futurist view, the author, once again, fades away.

Copyright (which implies authorial ownership of a text) is also highly debated in the current era, with countless articles being written about the rise of plagiarism especially among students (ostensibly made easier by the "cut and paste" rhetoric of digital text).[13] Concerns of this kind have also entered the rarefied literary scene, where there was a dispute around the publication of *Axolotl Roadkill* (2010), a German novel by Helene Hegemann. It was hailed as a triumph, and then revealed to have incorporated sections of another's fiction. Despite this, it was chosen as a finalist for the Leipzig Book Fair award, with the selection panel aware of the charges made. In fact, one jury member saw plagiarism as merely "part of the concept of the book."[14] In the response to Hegemann's novel, one senses a change from the 2006 controversy around author Kaavya Viswanathan, a Harvard sophomore who was severely chastised for having repurposed the writing of others in her novel, *How Opal Mehta Got Kissed, Got Wild, and Got a Life*. She was forced to issue a public apology and was denigrated by her publisher (Crown), whose representative called her behavior "nothing less than an act of literary identity theft."[15]

Moreover, in the realm of criticism, one recalls the publication of David Shields's *Reality Hunger: A Manifesto*, about 50 percent of which is quotes by others, with sources noted only in an appendix. There, Shields asserts that plagiarism, in fact, is "a major focus of the book." According to Luc Sante, "The decision to identify the authors of the appropriated texts was . . . not [Shields's] but that of his publisher's lawyers, and [Shields] suggests that readers might want to scissor out those nine pages of citations."[16] Jonathan Lethem was evidently inspired by Shields's work to issue his own "pilfered" essay, "The Ecstasy of Influence," in which "every single line derives from [the writing of] other authors."[17]

Finally, there have been several recent high-profile cases of journalistic plagiarism. In February 2010, *New York Times* reporter Zachery Kouwe was forced to resign, reminding everyone of the 2003 scandal around Jayson Blair at the same institution.[18] Even more recently, the *Washington Post* suspended reporter Sari Horowitz for incorporating (without sourcing) material from another newspaper in her coverage of the shooting of Gabrielle Giffords in Tucson, Arizona.[19] One story of journalistic plagiarism was even made into a movie—the case of Stephen Glass, a writer for the *New Republic*—dramatized as *Shattered Glass* (2003).

The introduction of hypertext has also problematized authorship, since, as one apprehends such copy, she is presented with a network of "topics and their connections," including paths to other documents (some not composed by the original creator). Furthermore, with all these "detours," each person's reading experience will be different.[20] Thus, as Jay David Bolter notes, such a text has "no univocal sense" or "fixed order." "It can remain a multiplicity without the imposition of a principle of domination" by its writer.[21]

Authorship of visual media has recently been complicated as well. As for hypertext, there are now digital versions of film classics that purposefully "interrupt" the cinematic narrative in a didactic fashion to provide viewpoints other than ones sanctioned by the original filmmaker. "Griffith in Context" is a CD-ROM designed by Ellen Strain and Gregory VanHoosier-Carey that provides a "bifocal" approach to *The Birth of a Nation*. On one level, it presents a hypermedia filmstrip constituting a condensed version of D. W. Griffith's original work. On another level, it offers links to audio lectures on the film by scholars, touching on such issues as film technique, historical background, racial representation, and literary origins. It also provides visual and print artifacts (e.g., posters and stills) and other original documents. Finally, it allows the user to reedit scenes of the original movie (which is in the public domain). Clearly, none of these add-ons are part of a viewing experience that Griffith would have endorsed, and certainly much of the scholarly material included severely critiques his ideological point of view.

There are other ways in which digital media impinge on cinematic authorship. First, there is the wholesale violation of copyright through the illegal duplication of DVDs, especially in Asia. Second, there are ways in which, as Kevin Kelly notes, "an emerging set of cheap tools is now making it easy to create digital video[s] . . . many [of which] are mash-ups of existing video material."[22] Here (as in the reediting of *The Birth of a Nation*), not only can authorial rights or intent be abrogated, but the initial work is changed or attached to others. Henry Jenkins talks of this kind of textual "poaching" in the realm of fan culture whose "art lies in transforming 'borrowed materials' from mass culture into new texts. A fan aesthetic centers on the selection, inflection, juxtaposition, and recirculation of ready-made images and discourses . . . emphasizing borrowing and recombination as much or more as original creation and artistic innovation."[23]

Conversely, the omnipresent availability of new technology has lead the vanishing author to make a dramatic reappearance, though not as the singular, renowned genius—but as a member of the masses. As Denis G. Pelli and Charles Bigelow note, due to the proliferation of written text through social media outlets like blogs, Facebook, and Twitter, "nearly universal authorship will shape tomorrow's [world]."[24] The observation applies equally to original works of visual media, which now routinely are created for and circulated on YouTube.

CREATION AND CINEMA

Aside from debates about authorship in the larger culture, the topic still compels film critics and theorists. Here, it is interesting to note that the political climate of Paris 1968 that spawned Barthes's essay on the subject was, in part, a result of an event specifically tied to film.[25] According to Simon Hitchman:

> It began when Henri Langlois, who had set up and nurtured the *Cinémathèque Française*, was fired as its head by the Minister of Culture Andre Malraux....
>
> The firing sparked protests among Parisian film students who continued to receive much of their education through screenings at the *Cinémathèque*, as well as New Wave directors like Truffaut, Godard, Rivette, and Resnais, who proudly proclaimed themselves "children of the Cinémathèque."[26]

But beyond this historical footnote, there continue to be reasons why film authorship warrants heated discussion. First, there are some issues particular to the cinema that have not yet been given adequate attention (despite the medium's one-hundred-plus-year history). Prior to the age of the Romantics (when authorship became linked to original and inspired genius), it was often associated with the act of imitation, and, as Sean Burke notes: "The mimetic picture accords very little significance to authorial inventiveness."[27] What changed in the nineteenth century was that "the power newly assigned by the romantics to individual consciousness in the creation of a world" diminished the respect for merely mirroring or representing it.[28] This view still obtains, and as Scott Hess remarks: "It is . . . because our society is still constructed in terms of the possessive individualism of the capitalist marketplace, that . . . Romantic ways of reading continue to exercise such power today."[29] Clearly, this perspective has had particularly troubling implications for the film artist whose conventional tool has been photography—a fundamentally mimetic art. As Barthes has written (hyperbolically) in *Camera Lucida:* "A specific photograph, in effect, is never distinguished . . . from what it represents, or at least, not immediately or generally."[30] Thus, in cinema (barring special effects, transforming lenses, filters, and mattes)—the act of filming (be it chemical or digital) is essentially a replicative one. Rather than work hard to make their medium imitative (as must the crafters of words), filmmakers must work hard to make it otherwise. Hence, such artists' "inventiveness" (a *sine qua non* of Romantic conceptions of the author) might be seen as a battle against their métier. Filmmaker Maya Deren realized this when, in 1946, she commented ironically: "The use of the camera as a utilitarian instrument for recording remains such a fertile field of activity that a completely creative use of it will remain, both to potential producers and to potential audience, a rather superfluous excursion."[31] Working in another medium, René Magritte invoked this enigmatic relation between realistic art and base reality in "The Human Condition" (1933), which plays on the confusion (and similarity) between the painter's canvas and the view outside the window that it depicts. Similarly, in Peter Greenaway's *The Draughtsman's Contract* (1982), the spectator sees a view of a landscape that an artist will draw through an open picture frame divided into sixteen equal squares—a tool he employs to segment the panorama into workable sections to sketch. Thus, in a sense, the drawing and its subject are thereby merged. Here, one also thinks of Roland Barthes's remark in *Camera Lucida* that "the Photograph belongs to that class of laminated objects whose two leaves cannot be separated without destroying . . . both: the windowpane and the landscape."[32]

But there is another aspect of the cinema that has made it resist tidy ascriptions of authorship. As a highly collaborative art, generally based on the work of scriptwriters, cinematographers, editors, art directors, and actors, one can rarely identify a single individual as a film's inventive force. If, on the other hand, one believes that such an attribution is possible, arguments erupt around naming one or another of the craftspeople as the true cinematic mastermind (as in the famous debate over whether the authorship of *Citizen Kane* [1941] belongs primarily to director Orson Welles or screenwriter Herman Mankiewicz; while Pauline Kael championed the latter as prime mover of the project, Robert Carringer [whose research scholars have deemed more credible] favored the director).[33] As Colin MacCabe has noted: "The importance of the director as author finds considerable backing in the industrial realities of a film set. When a shot is finished all eyes, the actors, the camera crew, wardrobe, props, hair and make-up turn to the director to see what the shot was as wanted or whether another take is required. To ignore the importance of the individual in the determination of the text required a willed ignoring of every reality from commercial to common sense about how a film set functions."[34]

Despite this, continuing conflicts play out between the Directors and Writers Guilds as to whether or not the former should have the right to claim onscreen that a film is "by" a particular cineaste (a notation deemed by some a "vanity" or "possessive" credit). For many writers such markers are insulting. As John Wells has said: "The idea that a film is by one person denigrates the contribution not only of the writer but all the artists and craftspeople who collaborate on a film."[35] Evidently, the desire for such ascriptions dates back to the time of D. W. Griffith and Cecil B. DeMille, but in 1966 the practice was halted by the Writers Guild in negotiations with producers. By 1970, however, the Directors Guild had filed a suit against the injunction and threatened to go on strike, so the order was eventually rescinded.

Rarely in commercial cinema, however, is there just one writer to vie with a director for prestige. The film *Tootsie* (1982), for example, had six of them.[36] What is ironic about such disputes is that, while cinematic practice is treated here as anomalous in terms of its collective authorship, many scholars have shown that, historically, collaboration has been routine (if not always acknowledged) in the making of art—for example, the use of assistants in famous painters' studios (like that of Rembrandt).[37] What makes such debates seem more hermetic is that the legal situation of motion picture authorship is rarely mentioned in the annals of film criticism.[38] In fact, with movies considered "works for hire" the official author is almost never an artist but, instead, a producer.[39] As Randall Larsen writes: "Corporate interests have increasingly embraced the romantic notion of the author as a hegemonic discourse to press their interests as intellectual property owners against the interests of artist creators."[40] The situation differs in Europe. As Paul Goldstein notes:

> Commentators regularly cite the doctrine of an author's moral right [in Europe] and its rejection in the United States, as evidence of a profound and pervasive division separating two cultures of copyright. . . . The European culture of copyright places authors at its center, giving them as a matter of natural right control over every use of their works that may affect their interests. . . . (Indeed, many European countries call their statutes protecting literary and artistic works, not 'copyright' law at all, but 'author's rights' laws—*droit d'auteur* in France. . . .) By contrast, the American culture of copyright centers on a hard, utilitarian calculus that balances the needs of copyright producers against the needs of copyright consumers, a calculus that appears to leave authors at the margin of its equation.[41]

No wonder the notion of cinematic authorship was born in France.

When theorists allow (as do many Europeans and Americans) that the director is the author of a movie, discussions resume as to what constitutes a cinematic signature or creative marker: does it reside within the script (with the director as its requisite author) or in the mise-en-scène (in some noteworthy brand of design, camera movement, or lighting)? Does it inhabit the realm of theme (as in a focus on spirituality) or genre (as in a penchant for westerns or musicals)? Does it attach only to the independent filmmaker who works outside the system, or also to the commercial director who overcomes the constraints of studio production? Again, such questions ignore the fact that, on a legal basis, the very notion of an authorial signature in cinema was long denied, based on the medium's mechanical nature. For as André Bazin once put it, with photography the world seems "formed automatically without the creative intervention of man."[42] Thus, for years, copyright law refused to sanction artistic "labor . . . connected to machines," which was thought to bear no human autograph.[43] Interestingly (given claims of the death of the author), Burke finds a connection between authorial signature and fatality as though the former's utility was as preparation for the artist's demise. As he notes:

"The primary ethical function of the signature is to set up a structure of resummons whereby the author may be recalled to his or her text. As with the legal signature, the textual mark is addressed to the future, *to mortality and the afterlife of the written sign*" (my emphasis).[44]

If, for the moment, we take the notion of signature quite literally, however, we find that, in certain cases, directors have given it special emphasis. The credit sequence of Abel Gance's *La Roue* (1923) depicts a long shot of the filmmaker followed by an extreme close-up of his countenance, an image that takes the authorial signature at "face value." This is followed by an insert (signed and penned by the director's hand) that dedicates the film to his recently departed love, Ida Danis. Employing a different practice, avant-garde artist Stan Brakhage quite literally scratches his name, frame-by-frame, into the filmic emulsion, making it appear as if written before our eyes. Here, we think of Béatrice Fraenkel's notion that signatures derive their power not only "from the written name that evokes the identity of a specific author, [but] from the trace of the physical gesture made by the hand attesting to an individual's presence."[45] She also remarks that, as personal handwriting developed historically, the signature became "endowed with a special expressive function."[46]

Other artists have employed different strategies for lending their mark to a film, as when the credits for *The Merry Widow* (1925) boast that the film was "*personally directed by Erich von Stroheim.*" In some instances, the director's name forms a

FIGURE 1. Abel Gance's self-portrait opens *La Roue* (1923).

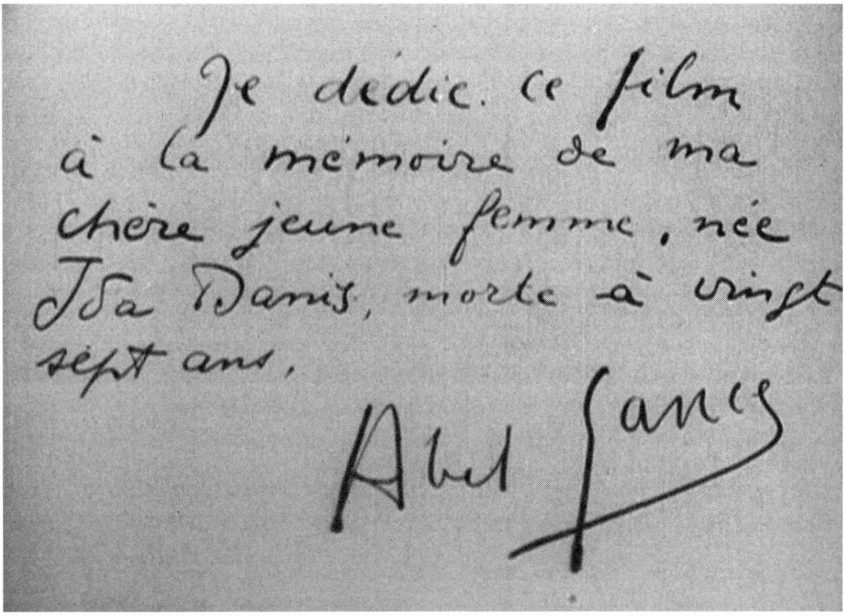

FIGURE 2 (*top*). The author's hand pens a dedication for *La Roue* (1923).
FIGURE 3 (*bottom*). Experimental artist Stan Brakhage scratches his signature into his films.

part of the film title (as in *David Cronenberg's Naked Lunch* [1991], which distinguishes it from William Burroughs's).[47] Alternately, some directors embrace the literary author whose work they adapt. In *La Bête Humaine* (1938), after the credit for Jean Renoir, we see an image of Émile Zola (who wrote the original novel) along with his signature. Some filmmakers invoke the authorial body by literally showing their hand in the act of writing, as did cartoonist Winsor McCay in 1911, when he drew for the camera (as preview to his animated film *Little Nemo* [1911]), or the Fleischer Brothers in their "Out of the Inkwell" series (1918–1929). The animator's arm in the silent film frame reminds us of Barthes's description of the author's hand, "cut off from any voice, borne by a pure gesture of inscription," or of the desire of Calvino's novelist to be "only . . . a severed hand that grasps a pen and writes."[48] Of course, some directors have taken the notion of bodily signature even farther by making cameo appearances in their films. On some level, we can say that this practice started in a most dramatic way with the nude appearance of Eadweard Muybridge in his human motion studies, but it has been carried on (more demurely) by creators like Alfred Hitchcock.

Of course, some film authors have sought to have their signatures removed from the screen (when ashamed of the product), which was forbidden by the Directors Guild until the faux generic name "Alan Smithee" was chosen as a viable credit substitution. Interestingly, this "death of the author" was authorized in 1968, the very year of Barthes's famous article. Until the practice went into disuse

FIGURE 4. Erich von Stroheim puts his authorial mark on *The Merry Widow* (1925).

FIGURE 5. The hand of filmmaker Winsor McCay appears in a shot in *Little Nemo* (1911).

around the year 2000, many films bore Smithee's name, including *Death of a Gun-fighter* (1969), *Twilight Zone: The Movie* (1983), and *Woman Wanted* (2000). In 1997, Arthur Hiller directed a comic movie about this very situation—*An Alan Smithee Film: Burn Hollywood Burn*. It concerns a film editor *actually* named Alan Smithee who thinks he has gotten the chance of a lifetime when he is hired to direct a major production featuring three stars. He soon realizes that he has no control over the picture and that it will be a bomb. He cannot use the conventional fake name of Alan Smithee for the movie's credits, since that is his real name. He therefore steals the only print of the film and tries to pressure his producers to allow him final cut.

Even when questions of authorial signature are settled, quarrels immediately break out about who does or does not rise to true auteur stature (as in the famous ranking of directors by Andrew Sarris—the American popularizer of the auteur theory). Ironically, he wrote his book the very year that Barthes declared the author "dead" and that Alan Smithee (the ersatz author) was born. While, for Sarris, some filmmakers enter the pantheon (Charles Chaplin, Robert Flaherty, John Ford), others are left below—deemed "lightly likable" (Michael Curtiz, Busby Berkeley, Alexander Korda), "oddities and one-shots" (Lindsay Anderson, Ben Hecht and Charles MacArthur) or (perish the thought) "less than meets the eye" (John Huston, Elia Kazan, David Lean). Only one woman, Ida Lupino, is mentioned in the book (in the "oddity" category), thus ignoring the career of Dorothy Arzner, the major female director in the classical Hollywood era. Clearly, in forming his canon, Sarris was following in the dogmatic footsteps of the French New Wave critics. François Truffaut, for instance, once said: "To anyone who would reject [directors Howard Hawks and Nicholas Ray], I make so bold as to say this: stop going to the cinema . . . for you will never know the meaning of inspiration, of a viewfinder, of poetic intuition, a frame, a shot, an idea, a good film, the cinema."[49]

Given that the field of Cinema Studies has tended to shadow the older discipline of literature, it was inevitable that eventually film theorists would not only attack the film author, but the "auteur theory" itself. As early as 1973, Ed Buscombe wrote in *Screen:*

> The test of a theory is whether it produces new knowledge. The *auteur* theory produced much, but of a very partial kind, and much it left totally unknown. What is needed now is a theory of the cinema that locates directors in a total situation, rather than one which assumes that their development has only an internal dynamic. This means that we should jettison such loaded terms as "organic," which inevitably suggest that a director's work derives its impetus from within. All such terms reveal often unformulated and always unwarranted assumptions about the cinema; a film is not a living creature, but a product brought into existence by the operation of a complex of forces upon a body of matter. Unfortunately, criticism which deals with only one aspect of the artistic object is easier to practice than that which seeks to encompass the totality.[50]

As though to make a joke of artist-centered film criticism, a 1999 murder mystery movie entitled *The Auteur Theory* (directed by Evan Oppenheimer) concerns a group of filmmakers competing in a festival who are killed off one by one by a fellow contestant. Significantly, in order to find the perpetrator, a detective (serving as a pseudo-critic) must interpret the work of the surviving directors for signs of homicidal tendencies.

Film scholars have also considered how viewers engage with a screen author in terms of their selection and reception of movies—reminding us of Michel Foucault's focus on the author's name, which he sees as oscillating "between the poles of description and designation."[51] Thus, as Colin MacCabe has noted, for Foucault, "authorship obscured the institutions that produced the author as category." In watching Steven Spielberg's *ET* (1982), then, a spectator may recall that director's earlier sci-fi work, *Close Encounters of the Third Kind* (1977)—since the artist's moniker "describes" a certain *oeuvre* and generic focus. Long before Foucault, however, back in the 1950s, E. M. Forster had questioned the importance of an author's name. As he mused: "Do you like to know who a book is by? . . . Do we gain more or less pleasure from it when we know the name of the poet?"[52] Interestingly, he concludes that texts of pure "information" (e.g., histories, newspaper reports) require a signature since they are purported to be true and require someone to blame if they are not. On the other hand, works of "atmosphere" or imagination need no authorial imprimatur as they are of limited "use." Citing one example, he remarks that "while we are reading 'The Ancient Mariner' we forget our astronomy and geography. . . . Do we not also forget the author? We remember him before we begin the poem and after we finish it, but during the poem nothing exists but the poem." Forster admits that when one analyzes literature, the author's name and "personality" may become important: "Then we are no longer reading the book, we are studying it and making it subserve our desire for information." Nonetheless, he feels that "while the author wrote he forgot his name" and "while we read him we forget both his name and our own." Thus, literature "wants not to be signed."[53]

Film critics have also examined the marketing power of authorship as a kind of brand name in its ability to sell a film (much as does a star). Thus, a film "by James Cameron" alerts the viewer to expect an impressive blockbuster in the vein of *Titanic* (1997) or *Avatar* (2009). Clearly, Cameron's "logo" is different from Guy Maddin's, which connotes a more experimental cinematic mode. A final approach to screen authorship has involved the tendency (borrowed from traditional literary studies) to investigate a film author's influences (be they biographical or artistic). Thus, one might see the film style of Satyajit Ray as, in part, derived from that of Jean Renoir, with whom he worked on *The River* (1951). Or, one might link Alfred Hitchcock's obsession with terror to having been (allegedly) sent once by his father to the local police station when he misbehaved.[54]

THE AUTHOR ONSCREEN

While all these perspectives on authorship are compelling, I approach the matter in another way—both by drawing on an element of auteur studies that has been underplayed, and by utilizing it to lead me to *film texts that are themselves treatises on the subject.* I start by going the etymological route. One of the sources of the word "author" is the Latin word "autor," which, according to the *Oxford English Dictionary*, derives from a verb that means to "originate." However, the term later became confused with the word "auctor," which meant "actor." Of course, Barthes drew on this conflation by conceiving the literary text as reaching "that point where . . . language acts [or] '*performs*'" (my emphasis).[55] Although I know that the terms *act* and *perform* can be taken in a variety of ways, I draw on their theatrical valences, since those are the ones most relevant to cinema—largely, a dramatic art. I also shift the concept of performance from language back to the writer, a stance that is familiar to us from the work of Jorge Luis Borges. In the famous meditation entitled "Borges and I," he remarks: "The other one, the one called Borges, is the one things happen to. . . . I know of Borges from the mail and see his name on a list . . . in a biographical dictionary. I like hourglasses, maps, eighteenth-century-typography, the taste of coffee and the prose of Stevenson; he shares these preferences, but in a vain way that turns them into the *attributes of an actor*" (my emphasis).[56] In pursuing my meditation on cinema and authorship I wish to track this *parallel between the author and the player*, looking not only for the creative figure who stands outside the text, but the one who stands within it as a corporeal presence.

Cinema, of course, provides us with numerous cases in which the two figures merge. Orson Welles has long been recognized as one of the great cinematic auteurs in his role as director. But in *Citizen Kane* he is also, of course, the lead actor —one who, conveniently, plays a writer—specifically a journalist/publisher. At certain points in the narrative, we confront his writing—the most interesting instance being when Kane's employee Jed Leland (Joseph Cotten) gets drunk while authoring a scathing review of an opera starring Kane's talentless wife. Finding Leland comatose at his typewriter, Kane usurps his role as theater critic and completes the notice himself. But, rather than draft a positive piece in his own voice, he pens the kind of vitriolic column he knows Leland would have submitted, signing the latter's name to the article instead of his own. This split in Kane's personality (reflecting the rift between Welles the actor and Welles the author) is further highlighted in a sequence in which Kane's guardian, Mr. Thatcher, criticizes him for lambasting the Manhattan Transfer Company in his muckraking newspaper. Kane responds by saying: "The trouble is, Mr. Thatcher, you don't realize you're *talking to two people* [my emphasis]. As Charles Foster Kane, who has 82,631 shares of Metropolitan Transfer . . . I sympathize with you. . . . On the other hand, I am [also] the publisher of the *Inquirer*. As such, it is my duty . . . to see to it that the decent, hardworking people of this city are not robbed blind by a group of money-mad pirates."

Citizen Kane also raises (through "News on the March," a faux documentary on the magnate's life) a question that has always plagued (and, for Barthes, perverted) author studies: What is the relation between the writer and his biography? Finally, *Citizen Kane*, with its famous retrospective structure that moves from the present back through earlier moments of Kane's existence, makes us think of Barthes's statement about the temporality of authorship. As he notes: "The Author, when believed in, is always conceived of as the past of his own book: book and author stand automatically on a single line divided into a before and an after."[57]

If *Citizen Kane* highlights our sense of authorial doubling, it is an issue on which Barthes has also commented. As he notes (referring to himself in a distanced third person): "His (sometimes acute) discomfort—mounting some evenings, after writing the whole day . . . was generated by his sense of producing a double discourse."[58] This disquietude also surfaces in Borges's 1939 piece "Pierre Menard, Author of the *Quixote*," in which a contemporary novelist essentially tries

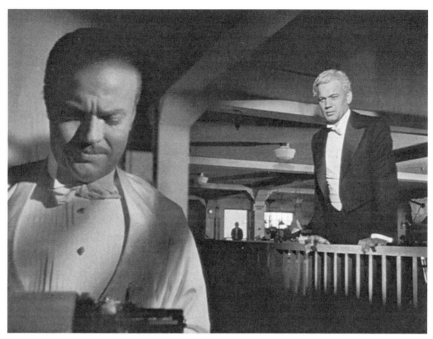

FIGURE 6. Charles Foster Kane (Orson Welles) writes Jed Leland's (Joseph Cotten) opera review in *Citizen Kane* (1941).

to "become" Cervantes by rewriting his masterpiece. As Borges muses: "Pierre Menard did not want to compose *another* Quixote, which surely is easy enough —he wanted to compose *the* Quixote."[59] Once more Barthes's notion of literature as "a tissue of quotations" is highlighted (albeit ironically) since Menard's "goal was never a mechanical transcription of the original; he had no intention of *copying* it. His admirable ambition was to produce a number of pages which coincided —word for word and line for line—with those of Miguel de Cervantes." Similarly, in Calvino's novel, the author/protagonist faces writing block and so begins to copy "the first sentences of a famous novel, to see if the charge of energy contained in that start is communicated to [his] hand, which, once it has received the right push, should run on its own."[60] He ends up transcribing nearly all of *Crime and Punishment* in an attempt to channel Dostoevsky.

As the filmic examples presented thus far begin to indicate, in my consideration of cinema and authorship, I plan to ask the question: *What have films themselves (as narrative, aesthetic, and theoretical texts) taught us about this issue through their inscription of the author into the narrative?*—a figure that we might deem (using Hollywood terminology) the film creator's "body double"—a version of him- or herself personified onscreen. Here, I am reminded of Jonathan Auerbach's insight that film "as a medium of incarnation . . . seems at once totally obvious and yet frustratingly difficult to articulate."[61] Of course, the identification of an author figure onscreen does nothing to resolve the dilemma of who its offscreen counterpart might be: director, writer, craftsperson, or all of the above. Here, we are reminded of the Magritte painting *The Uncertainty Principle*, in which a figure paradoxically casts a shadow on the wall that is strangely dissimilar to it.

In a famous article from 1948 that heralded the cinematic "auteur theory," French critic Alexandre Astruc predicted that film would soon break free from the tyranny "of the narrative" to fashion "a means of writing just as flexible and subtle as written language." He called this new development "the age of the *caméra-stylo* [or] (camera-pen)," one in which "the film-maker/author [would] writ[e] with his camera as a writer writes with his pen."[62] In the spirit of Astruc's words, rather than examine the onscreen author in the guise of the filmmaker (as in works like Truffaut's *Day for Night* [1973] or Jean-Luc Godard's *Contempt* [1963]), I pursue Astruc's metaphor more literally and look for the filmic author in the image of the *onscreen writer*—a kind of "displaced person" as it were—standing in for the cinematic auteur. For Astruc and many of his New Wave counterparts, there was, in fact, an equation between the director and the writer, since they felt that only the writer-director was a genuine auteur. As Astruc observed, true cinematic creativity "implies that the scriptwriter directs his own scripts; or rather, that the scriptwriter ceases to exist, for in this kind of film-making the distinction between author and director loses all meaning. Direction is no longer a means of illustrating or presenting a scene, but a true act of writing."[63] While Astruc gets all the credit for this viewpoint, in truth, Maya Deren said something similar a few years earlier. In "Cinema as an Art Form" (1946), she wrote: "When the day comes that the camera—the visual element—ceases to be thought of as an annoying complication by 'film writers' who concern themselves with cinema not out of an appreciation of it as a medium, but because the film industry provides the most lucrative employment for 'writers,' cinema as an art form will begin to come of age."[64] And later, Agnès Varda would adapt this idea into her notion of *cinécriture*—a process that combines verbal and visual composition. As she notes: "A well written film is also well filmed, the actors are well chosen, so are the locations. The cutting, the movement, the points-of-view, the rhythm of filming and editing have been felt and considered in the way a writer chooses the depth of meaning of sentences, the type of words, number of adverbs, paragraphs, asides, chapters which advance the story or break its flow, etc. In writing it's called style. In the cinema style is cinécriture."[65]

In examining the author's filmic "body double," I highlight works that I deem to be self-reflexive (whether intentionally or not)—ones that simultaneously tell a plausible story while contemplating the conditions of their making. According to András Kovács, such films establish "a hole . . . in the texture of the fiction," allowing a direct communication between author and viewer "which is not mediated by the conventions of the fiction itself."[66] Through such strategies, authors "may say something not only according to the aesthetic rules of a genre but also about the rules themselves." Finally, such works "never [constitute] a simple play with *trompe l'oeil,*" but rather evince a "critical attitude" that comments on and theorizes their production. In focusing on the act of writing in the cinema, a rather ineffable linguistic activity, there are perhaps parallels to Garrett Stewart's consideration of the "scene of reading" in painting (to be discussed more fully in chapters 6 and 8). If ekphrasis is the rendering of the plastic arts in verbal terms, for him, "reverse" *ekphrasis* is the representation of reading in pictorial discourse.[67] Perhaps the latter also pertains to the depiction of writing in the cinema.

Having argued here for the importance of the topic of authorship and cinema, the eight chapters of the book approach the subject in numerous ways, demonstrating (1) the manner in which the issue is omnipresent, not only in film theory, but in movies themselves, specifically in the vision of the onscreen writer; (2) the varied and complex subthemes that the topic entails (involving gender, age, health, writing mode, readership, criticism, etc.), and (3) the manner in which many such works play in intricate ways with elements of cinematic style, including tensions between word and image, two major components of film form. In each chapter, while certain films are analyzed in depth, others are noted in passing, in order to give the reader a sense of how numerous are such works. In fact, the number of films (over the course of film history) that concern the writer are staggering —indicating that authorship, in one form or another, has always been a central interest of the movies. While, as it turns out, many of the films I examine have been based on literary properties (as is the case with much of cinema), they have not been selected for that reason. Furthermore, I do not treat them as "adaptations," though, occasionally, I make reference to the texts that preceded them. Rather, the films are approached as original works of cinema, yet it is noteworthy (though predictable) that so many novels and short stories take writers and writing as their subject. What is more remarkable is that those works (focusing on this rather uncinematic topic) have been adapted to film.

Chapter 1 ("Typecasting the Author") concentrates on the icon of the typewriter, which traditionally (and even in the computer age) stands as the prop signifying authorship. Here, I examine numerous literary works about or featuring the typewriter (including an essay by Paul Auster and several fantasy tales about supernatural writing machines). I then investigate the typewriter as the subject or material of visual art, and close with a discussion of a film in which the machine plays a central role—*Naked Lunch* (1991). Chapter 2 ("Beyond Adaptation: The Writer as Filmmaker") examines the careers of three prominent American authors who have also made films: novelist Paul Auster, playwright David Mamet, and essayist/comic Woody Allen. In all cases, I move away from the familiar terrain of adaptation studies to examine films by these men that did not preexist as literary or theatrical texts. The discussion of Auster focuses on the movie *Smoke* (1995), which concerns a stalled writer, while that of Mamet highlights *Homicide* (1991), a *policier*. Here I argue for parallels between the detective (a figure that fascinates all three authors) and the writer. The examination of Allen concentrates on *Deconstructing Harry* (1997), a work in which he (as star) plays the role of a literary author plagued by visions derived from his fiction. Chapter 3 ("The Author at the Dream Factory: The Screenwriter and the Movies") first considers the historical role of the American screenwriter, then surveys a series of films in which he or she figures as protagonist (including *The Bad and the Beautiful* [1952], *Boy Meets Girl* [1938], etc.). While most such works use the scriptwriter as a mere character type, others, like Billy Wilder's *Sunset Blvd.* or Nicholas Ray's *In a Lonely Place* (both 1950), establish some intriguing formal link between plot and style. Finally, *tour de force* films like Spike Jonze's *Adaptation* (2002), the Coen brothers' *Barton Fink* (1991), and Xiaolu Guo's *How Is Your Fish Today?* (2006) self-consciously highlight the writing of a screenplay within the movie itself. I close the chapter with an examination of an experimental film, Hollis Frampton's *Poetic Justice* (1972), the reductio ad absurdum case for incorporating the screenplay into the cinema. Chapter 4 ("The Authoress: Sexuality and Textuality") confronts the fact that the woman writer is far less frequently cast as a character within fiction film ("biopics" aside) and, in a similar manner, has largely been excluded from the male canon of film auteurs. After briefly surveying a series of pedestrian works in which she appears (including *My Dear Secretary* [1949], *Romancing the Stone* [1984], and *Basic Instinct* [1992]), I concentrate on two complex dramas that foreground issues of eroticism. In François Ozon's *Swimming Pool* (2003), the writer is a rather repressed woman, frustrated in her sexual and authorial endeavors, whose voyeuristic encounter with a young girl's sexuality (and homicidal impulse) seems to liberate her creativity. The heroine of Sally Potter's *The Tango Lesson* (1997) —a filmmaker/writer—is also blocked in her artistic work until she merges the realms of body and mind through studying dance and wooing her instructor. Chapter 5 ("Writing Pain: The Infirm Author") deals with the ubiquitous figure of the sickly author. Three of the films considered focus centrally on the writer. In the case of Dennis Potter's *The Singing Detective* (1986), he is suffering from psoriasis and hospitalized for his skin disease. In the case of Julian Schnabel's *The Diving Bell and the Butterfly* (2007), he is a mute and paralyzed stroke victim who can dictate his memoir only by blinking his eyes. In the case of Alain Resnais's *Providence* (1977), he is an old man heading toward death, spending a restless night imagining his next novel. Three other works discussed split attention between writer and caretaker. In Percy Adlon's *Céleste* (1980), we find the asthmatic Marcel Proust tended by his loyal servant. In Rob Reiner's *Misery* (1990), we encounter a crippled writer hostilely "nursed" by an irate fan who holds him hostage. Finally, in Stanley Kubrick's *The Shining* (1980), a writer who slips into madness stalks and abuses his helpmate-wife. Chapter 6 ("*Cinécriture*: Word and Image") examines films in which the viewer must actively and repeatedly read words on the screen (beyond the intertitles of silent films and the subtitles of foreign ones). I consider the urtext of this genre, Robert Bresson's *Diary of a Country Priest* (1951), which is the story of a curé who keeps a daily journal that records his struggles, doubts, and ailments. I also examine an entirely different kind of work—Shari Springer Berman and Robert Pulcini's *American Splendor* (2003), which is based on a series of comics and graphic novels, two forms that utilize the conjunction of pictures and words. Chapter 7 ("Corpus and Oeuvre: Authorship and the Body") investigates films concerned (quite literally) with instances of "writing on the skin." *Irezumi* (1982), directed by Yoichi Takabayashi, is about a woman who gets tattooed to satisfy her lover, while *The Pillow Book* (1996), directed by Peter Greenaway, portrays a woman obsessed with being carnally "inscribed." Both raise questions about writing and embodiment. Chapter 8 ("Stealing Beauty: The Reader, the Critic, and the Appropriation of the Authorial Voice") examines the manner in which both readers and critics have been figured in cinematic works as "foils" to the author. In Michel Deville's *La Lectrice* (1988), for instance, the heroine is someone who reads aloud great works of literature to her clients. In *Starting Out in the Evening* (2007), directed by Andrew Wagner, a young graduate student of literature befriends an elderly author whom she is studying but then takes advantage of him. In Sophie Fiennes's *The Pervert's Guide to Cinema* (2006), an actual theorist, Slavoj Žižek, stars as critic at large, speaking of the likes of Alfred Hitchcock and David Lynch. Ultimately, I argue that, in contemporary textual studies, the critic has overtaken his authorial subject—casting himself in the void that remains. In the Afterword, I examine two more works by Hollis Frampton: *Zorns Lemma* (1970) and *(nostalgia)* (1971). I choose Frampton because he is a filmmaker who doubles as a critic/scholar (given his numerous published philosophical essays, and the highly theoretical nature of his creative work). Beyond that, he is a cinematic master of word and image. Finally, like all authors discussed in this volume, he manages to inscribe several "body doubles" into his work.

In a recent *New York Times Book Review*, illustrator Grant Snider presented a nine-frame cartoon entitled "Behind Every Great Novelist Is . . ." in which he listed (and pictured) the following traits: "childhood trauma, miserable job, moments of self-discovery, episode of debauchery, pathologic ambition, loyal pet, neglected spouse, personal demons, and years of boring hard work."[68] Clearly, all such qualities are stereotypes of the authorial biography and are meant to be taken ironically. But, in fact, in the course of this volume, we encounter nearly all of these clichés (debauchery in *Naked Lunch*, self-discovery in *Diary of a Country Priest*, a neglected spouse in *The Shining*, a miserable job in *American Splendor*, boring hard work in *Céleste*, pathological ambition in *Deconstructing Harry*, childhood trauma in *The Pillow Book*, and personal demons in *Adaptation*). In this vision of the martyred writer, all that is missing is the compensatory "loyal pet."

Later in the volume, I quote critic Georges Poulet as saying that books, being "made of paper and ink . . . lie where they are put until the moment someone shows an interest in them."[69]

Dear Reader—I trust that someone is you.

1 TYPECASTING THE AUTHOR

Typewriting is dead, but its ghosts still haunt us. Even in our image-saturated culture, the iconic value of the typewriter looms large. Artfully grainy, sepia-toned close-up photos of its quaint circular keys grace the covers of tastefully matte-laminated paperbacks, announcing yet another volume extolling the virtues of the writing life.

—Darren Wershler-Henry, *The Iron Whim*

The act of writing is not a compelling cinematic event—hence the difficulties of portraying authors onscreen. (As the aforementioned Grant Snider cartoon makes clear, they engage in "years of boring hard work.") Such characters either pick up a pen or pencil and move implement to paper, or sit at a keyboard and type—both largely static occurrences. Perhaps that is why in *The Shining* (1980), novelist Jack Torrance (Jack Nicholson)—riffing on a cliché nursery rhyme—declares himself a "dull boy." No "cinema of attractions" here. For this reason the very tools of writing often stand in, synechdochically, for the larger (and boring) composition process, and thereby achieve iconic status.

In the broad history of cinema, the emblem (and, perhaps, fetish object) in question has been the typewriter—though, in recent years, the computer has begun to challenge its dominance (less than one might suppose). Here, the typewriter is like the arcane film reel standing in for the contemporary non-celluloid cinema. It is important that the typewriter is a machine—and was popularized in approximately the same era as photographic and filmic technology, the mid- to late nineteenth century. In this regard, we are reminded of some ironic advice by Carrie Hoffman and Rusty W. Spell on "How to Make a Movie about a Writer": " (Important note: Do not—do *not*—give the writer a computer. In fact, make the typewriter particularly old-fashioned. Writers are old-fashioned people who detest technology.)"[1] We also think of the cover for *Best of American Splendor* by Harvey Pekar (an anthology of his comics that we later discuss in its filmic adaptation). It depicts a perspiring Pekar sitting at a computer with a thought-bubble emerging from his head: "@*!!!*!! Why can't I learn to work a *!! Computer!?! I been usin' this thing for ten months now an' I still have no idea when I push a button what's gonna happen!"

Of course, we find typewriters in films set or made in eras earlier than the digital age (for instance, *Barton Fink* [1991], which takes place in the 1930s, or *Laura* [1944] and *His Girl Friday* [1940]), but we also find them in contemporary works set in the present like *Misery* (1990), *The Shining*, or *Smoke* (1995). So in some respects, the typewriter constitutes another character in the drama of the author on-screen and occasionally functions as the latter's "double."

TYPEWRITER FICTIONS

This is certainly how Paul Auster (the co-writer/director of *Smoke*) feels about his own typewriter (and why the author-character in that film still uses one in the electronic era). Auster, in fact, has written a book called *The Story of My Typewriter* (illustrated by Sam Messer). In it, he describes the "death" of one machine in 1974 and his purchase of another—the one he presently owns and to which he has become inordinately attached. Having no money, he buys a used 1964 Olympia portable from a friend. As he tells us, "since that day . . . every word I have written has been typed out on that machine"—including, we suppose, the very ones we are reading.[2] As years go by, he considers an electric model (the then-new, cutting-edge technology) but eschews it: "I didn't like the noise that those contraptions made: the constant hum of the motor, the buzzing and rattling of loose parts, the jitterbug pulse of alternating current vibrating in my fingers." He prefers the "stillness" of his present machine. As Auster's narrative progresses, he begins to anthropomorphize his machine, talking about the "serious trauma" it suffered when his son snapped off its carriage return "arm" (an accident that was not the machine's "fault"). Describing its eventual repair, he notes: "There is a small scar on that spot now, but the operation was a success." As more time passes, computers are an option, but Auster has heard too many "horror stories about pushing the wrong button and wiping out a day's . . . or a month's work . . . or [about] sudden power failures that could erase an entire manuscript in less than half a second." So he sticks with old technology. He asserts that it "was never [his] intention [in the book] to turn [his] typewriter into a heroic figure." He claims that the blame for this belongs to artist Messer, "who stepped into [Auster's] house one day and fell in love with a machine." Auster observes that, through his drawings, Messer "has turned an inanimate object into a being with a personality and a presence in the world."[3] Thus, the Olympia "has moods and desires now, it expresses dark angers and exuberant joys, and trapped within its gray, metallic body, you would almost swear that you could hear the beating of a heart." Auster finds all this "unsettling."

Clearly, in Auster's refusal to use a computer there is a certain wistfulness for the bygone age of the typewriter (here, we wonder if Auster's preference for a quiet manual over a raucous electric one is like early film theorists' preference for silent film over sound—a question interesting to contemplate given that the end of *Smoke* plays out for us as a silent movie in black-and-white). Auster knows that eventually he will not find ribbons for his outdated machine, so he orders a horde of them in advance, cornering the market, hedging his bets. As Darren Wershler-Henry asks: "Why do people persist with all of this picking, gutter-sniping and scavenging for pieces of the typewriter? The answer, in a word, is nostalgia."[4] For him, the effect of nostalgia is cinematic; it is "like a thick smear of Vaseline on the lens of a movie camera, blurring our objectivity."[5] Beyond this, he sees the typewriter as representing a particular moment of the past associated with "unalienated modernist writing": "[It] has become the symbol of a non-existent sepia-toned era when people typed passionately late into the night under the flickering light of a single naked bulb, sleeves rolled up, suspenders hanging down, lighting each new cigarette off the smoldering butt of the last, occasionally taking a pull from the bottle of bourbon in the bottom drawer of the filing cabinet." Of course, in earlier days, it would have been handwriting that was the mark of an authentic writer. As Martin Heidegger observed in 1942–1943: "Mechanical writing deprives the hand of its rank in the realm of the written word and degrades the word to a means of communication. In addition . . . it conceals the handwriting and thereby the character."[6]

Interestingly, the opening of a recent film about an author, *My Effortless Brilliance* (2008), articulates a survey of writing technologies, past and present. As the movie begins, we view a man sitting before a window at dusk. When the camera circles around, we find him writing on a laptop whose illuminated screen is visible (though the words are not). When we come upon him the next morning he is sleeping in a lounge chair with the closed computer on his lap—signaling unproductivity. After a few close-up shots of him in pensive poses, we discover him composing in longhand, accompanied by the sound of a pencil scratching the page. Soon, he drops the implement and leaves his papers on the desk. We then hear offscreen tapping sounds and cut to him at a manual typewriter; he sprays the keyboard to eliminate dust—implying that it has not been used recently. Abruptly, he puts the machine away and exits the scene. It is here that we get the title of the film, printed on a book cover in his office. Clearly, though each writing technology has its own mystique and allure, none is sufficient to the task—demonstrating that authorship is never "effortless" and rarely "brilliant."

Wershler-Henry also discusses the nostalgic sale of typewriters on eBay—making clear that it is now a valued "collectible."[7] According to a recent *New York Times* article there is now a "typosphere"[8]—a community of typewriter aficionados who communicate on such websites as "Adventures in Typewriterdom" and go to "type-ins" in bars and bookstores where people can be found "tapping out letters to send via snail mail and competing to see who can bang away the fastest." Beyond this, one finds hundreds of typewriter videos on YouTube. Some merely visualize an item being sold, while others proudly demonstrate an owner's prized machine.[9] Finally, there are numerous illustrated websites on typewriter history (e.g., "The Virtual Typewriter Museum"). Rather than cherish typewriters, however, some have mocked their irrelevance in a computer age. One YouTube video is entitled "Typewriter—The Ultimate Wireless Laptop"—and depicts a college

student bringing said machine to class to take lecture notes. As he loudly strikes the keys, students turn around and laugh, and eventually the instructor asks, "What is that?" and sighs, "Oh dear." In a similar fashion, there is a humorous moment in an episode of the TV show *Scrubs* in which a character enters numbers on a typewriter and is nonplussed when the machine fails to compute the sum.[10]

Through the paintings of Sam Messer in Auster's *The Story of My Typewriter*, the machine becomes a pictorial object—and the volume approximates an illustrated children's book. In the movies, the machine (when part of the mise-en-scène) is, by definition, visualized—be it placed on a writer's desk in long shot (as in *Smoke*) or poised for close-up (as in *Barton Fink*, where we see its brand name—Underwood). In certain very special cases (read: musicals), however, the typewriter can take on gargantuan proportions and function as the center of a film set. In *Ready, Willing and Able* (1937), we have a formulaic backstage story involving a group of people who wish to "put on a [Broadway] show." When the play finally opens, one of its revue numbers is entitled "Too Wonderful for Words" —which utilizes a famous song from 1929.[11] As is common for such musical episodes, it begins with a prologue. This one is set in a large office where a series of showgirls (wearing white halters and short skirts) sit on library ladders leaning against bookshelves. The boss (Ross Alexander) is dictating a letter to his assistant (Wini Shaw). He tells her he is writing to someone in order to "land a contract for life." We realize that the epistle will be sent to the girl he hopes to marry. The boss first uses the salutation "My dear prospective wife," but his assistant tells him to avoid language resembling a "statistician's treaty." The two then begin to sing the title song, which concerns trying to find the proper phrase to fully describe the love object—playing with common words like *rapturous, glamorous*, and *amorous* but then reaching for more rarefied epithets like *tintinabulous, euphemistical*, and *eulogistical*.[12] As Anderson and Shaw sing, the chorus girls sit at typewriters and push the keys with choreographed hand movements while the machine sounds function as a percussive musical beats. With the letter finished, we see a close-up of the envelope that dissolves to it being viewed by its recipient (Ruby Keeler). She then walks to a typewriter to answer her beau and we observe the page she is composing.

Through an optical effect, we pull back to find a huge printed sheet in a giant typewriter where the legs of chorus girls (lying down, limbs raised and extended) "strike" the page to imprint letters (accompanied by metallic noises). Later, Keeler and Lee Dixon dance on the machine's keys with their tap shoes making rhythmic sounds (here we can't help but think of Auster's mention of "the jitterbug pulse" of electric typewriters—even though this one is a manual).

What we have seen is a rather average production number (staged by Bobby Connolly); we can only imagine what Busby Berkeley would have made of the opportunity. Nonetheless, if we give it a bit more attention than it deserves, it proves an interesting (if fundamentally silly) text. The lyrics are about the impossibility of language to represent the loved one who is much too "'very very' to ever be in

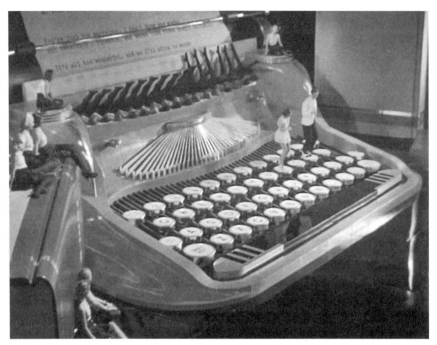

FIGURE 7. A couple (Ruby Keeler and Lee Dixon) dances on a typewriter in *Ready, Willing and Able* (1937).

Webster's dictionary." And some of the words that fail the writer are essentially ones that reference visuality, like "glamorous." All the while, we (the viewers) can see (in a space separate from the letter-writer [Alexander] and unavailable to his vision) the pretty, vibrant, and graceful Ruby Keeler, whose image we grasp without the need for verbal discourse to characterize it—proving that a picture can be worth a thousand words.

Three decades later, the film *Bombay Talkie* (1970) imitates this sequence within the context of a movie about an author. As the film opens, British writer Lucia Lane (Jennifer Kendel) is visiting an Indian film studio. The musical number being staged there involves a giant typewriter on which chorus girls and, eventually, the lead actor Vikram (Shashi Kapoor) dance and sing. When a studio writer, Hari (Zia Mohyeddin), introduces Lucia to Vikram, the star is asked if he knows her work; he admits he does not. Hari caustically says that Vikram "can't read" and informs him that the title of her last novel was *Consenting Adults*. Vikram says that he "saw it," at which point Hari snidely remarks: "It was a book before it was a film. People write them you know—*write*." The movie's director then approaches the group and comments on how the typewriter set is called the "fate machine." As he notes: "The typewriter keys represent the keys of life and we human beings dance on them. As we press down the keys the story that's written is our fate." Lucia remarks that this is all "very symbolic." (Interestingly, William Burroughs [whom we discuss later] thought of the typewriter as a metaphor for God, calling it the "Control Machine"—one that "writes people into being and regulates their behavior.")[13] Eventually, Lucia "mounts" the typewriter keys for a group photo and has trouble balancing, as the keys go up and down like a trampoline.

Again, this rather trivial scene (in a bad movie) has some interesting implications for word and image. Though a typewriter forms the major object in the decor, we understand that movie people do not read and, while Hari writes for the cinema, he is entirely contemptuous of the medium, favoring serious poetry. Furthermore, Lucia—who has, ostensibly, come to India for authorial inspiration —fails to write at all as she is enamored with the gorgeous movie idol, Vikram. Hence she becomes as "unbalanced" in life as on the typewriter keys—perhaps linking the "fate machine" to her unhappy romantic future.

The notion of the typewriter as controlling destiny (or at least having a mind of its own) is a popular one in fiction, dating back to the time of the technology's inception. In John Kendrick Bangs's *The Enchanted Typewriter* (1899), the narrator discovers in his attic a typewriter that produces a novel on its own. As he notes: "The following pages has [*sic*] evolved itself . . . proceeding directly from a type-writing machine standing in the corner of my library, manipulated by unseen hands."[14] When the narrator attempts to write his own name with the machine, he finds that of "William Shakespeare printed there in its stead"—a joke, perhaps, on the vagaries of the Bard's authorial status.[15] The narrator can even have conversations with the typewriter. When he calls the latter a machine, it objects, and claims that it is a person.[16] Here, we are reminded of Wershler-Henry's observation that "writers not only attribute souls to their machines, but . . . attribute *someone or something else's soul* to their machine." In other words, most typewriters are possessed."[17] As the narrator notes in the novel's opening chapter: "The magic

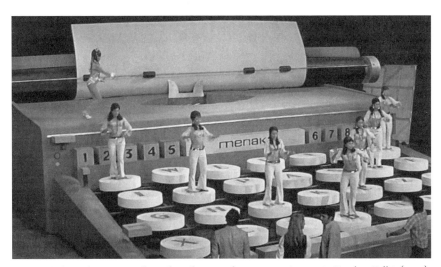

FIGURE 8. A production number takes place on a huge typewriter set in *Bombay Talkie* (1970).

qualities of the machine were made known to me, and out of it the following papers have grown."[18]

A supernatural typewriter also figures in Salomo Friedlaender's *Gray Magic* (1922), in which a machine telepathically receives the thoughts of its maker (Dr. Sucram) and transcribes them into print. Here is how the process is described: "The doctor ... put a metal helmet on his head; fine wires connected the helmet to the keyboard of the typewriter. Without any movement on the doctor's part, the levers of the machine started moving. It was a ghostly sight to behold."[19] Here, we think of Friedrich Nietzsche's observation that "our writing tools are also working on our thoughts."[20] In *Gray Magic*, however, the dynamic is reversed: a man's thoughts are working on his writing tools.

In 1940, L. Ron Hubbard published *Typewriter in the Sky* in two installments in the sci-fi magazine *Unknown*. It concerns an author of swashbuckling pirate stories who, in describing the narrative of his next novel to his publisher, includes the name of his friend as its villain. His recitation of the drama is overheard by the friend, who suddenly feels ill: "Even as he reached out with [his] hand it was disappearing! From fingertips to wrist to elbow! Vanishing! With a quiver, he shifted his fading gaze to his other hand, but it, too, was missing. And his legs were missing and his shoulders were missing—There wasn't anything left of him at all!"[21] We soon learn that he has been transported into the writer's tale where, periodically, he hears a "faint whir, reminiscent of a typewriter, which seemed to come out of the sky"—clearly that of the novelist who continues to craft his fiction.[22]

More recently, in *Still Life with Woodpecker* (1980), Tom Robbins invests his typewriter with creative agency. As he notes in the prologue: "If this typewriter can't do it, then fuck it, it can't be done. This is the all-new Remington SL3 ... [and] I sense that the novel of my dreams is in it."[23] In an epilogue, Robbins again comments on his machine: "I have to hand it to the Remington SL3, it hung in there."[24] He vows, however, that he'll "never write another novel on an electric typewriter" and decides to "pull its plu-ug-ggg."[25] He continues writing in longhand (which is reproduced in facsimile version on the page). He taunts the machine as though it were a person: "Ha! What's the matter, Rem, got a speech impediment?"[26]

Around the same time, Frank Darabont wrote the novella *Walpuski's Typewriter*.[27] Interestingly, Darabont is primarily known as a screenwriter/director (e.g., *The Shawshank Redemption* [1994] and *The Green Mile* [1999]). The narrative concerns a penniless LA author, Howard Walpuski, who brings his IBM Selectric into a shop for repair. As Howard tells the reader, using anthropomorphic rhetoric: "It had self-destructed with an oily belch of smoke and a prolonged death-rattle."[28] The proprietor of the shop is strange and seems to know that Howard is poor. He offers to repair the machine for five dollars and 10 percent of all Howard's "earnings from his first three published novels." Howard agrees and follows the man into the basement where the latter dons a ceremonial robe and draws a pentagram on the floor around the Selectric. As Darabont describes it: "A bulge was growing in the floorboards next to Howard's typewriter, pressing upward as if something beneath it were doing its damnedest to break through. The wood began to smoke and char, the boards splinter and give way." Soon a demon springs forth with "a stubby segmented tail tipped with a fat scorpion stinger." The proprietor then consigns the demon to Howard's Selectric. Howard tries to escape without the machine but it follows him home. Though he bolts the door, the next morning it appears on his desk. He attempts to write a commissioned piece, but when he types the opening words, others appear. When he mutters, "What the hell is this?" the Selectric answers (in type): "The first line of your novel." It tells him that its name is Lucius (reminding us of the devil). When the Selectric demands more and more paper, Howard must devise a roller to continuously feed it. Soon, however, its "appetite" changes and it demands food—specifically meat. A hamburger patty he feeds it "disappeared with an unholy sucking sound" as "the front and back of the typewriter . . . moved together and apart in a monstrous parody of chewing."[29]

As a side note, it is interesting to observe that, recently, this kind of fiction has begun to take the computer as its subject. In 1983, Stephen King published a short story entitled "The Word Processor," in which a writer discovers that, by erasing mention of his enemies in his digitally produced manuscript, he can eliminate them in the real world and insert himself in their place.[30]

TYPEWRITER ART

But literary fiction is not the only realm in which the typewriter has had a significant cultural presence; it has also achieved iconic status within the contemporary visual arts. In a 1966 project, artist Ed Ruscha took a Royal Model X typewriter (first produced in 1914) and jettisoned it from the window of a speeding car on US Highway 91, outside of Las Vegas. Photographer Patrick Blackwell documented the event and his images became part of a book, *Royal Road Test* (1967). The nihilistic tone of the venture (fitting for the 1960s) is summarized in the volume's epigraph: "It [the typewriter] was too directly bound to its own anguish to be anything other than a cry of negation; carrying within itself, the seeds of its own destruction." On the one hand, we might view the demolition of the Royal X as a sign that electric technology had made it obsolete (the IBM Selectric having come on the market in 1961). But Wershler-Henry sees it otherwise: "The typewriter [in Ruscha's work] itself was only ever a symbol of something much larger . . . how Western cultures performed the act of writing, but also of how we organized work, play, and even education and production of 'useful' members of society, for two and a half centuries."[31] Significantly, Ruscha is also known as "a painter of words" —so his interest in the typewriter seems fitting.[32] As Alexandra Schwartz notes, "even among a generation of artists for whom verbal language was a particular concern . . . his consistent and inventive use of words in his art stands out for its nuanced dissection of everyday communication." The cinematic ramifications of this are especially apparent in two of his canvases: *Eight Spotlights* (1962), which depicts the Twentieth Century-Fox logo, and *Back of Hollywood* (1977), which portrays the famous Hollywood sign from the rear (with letters reversed).

On first glance, Leopoldo Maler's flaming typewriter (*Hommage* [1974]) seems to represent another attempt to annihilate the machine. However, it takes the opposite position in that, here, the typewriter is heroic and fire stands for the subversive force of words. According to the Hess Collection catalog, "[Maler's] uncle, a well-known Argentinean writer, is believed to have been killed for the inflammatory content of his political essays. The old Underwood Typewriter [*sic*] that now emits flames in the place of words is of the same style that Maler's uncle used during his esteemed career." There is certainly an uncanny quality to Maler's work, which also characterizes Robert Arneson's *Typewriter* (1966), a ceramic piece with nail-polished fingers as keys; appropriately, it was featured in the 1968 MoMA exhibit "Dada, Surrealism, and Their Heritage."

As already noted, in fiction, there is often an association between the typewriter and a person. In *The Enchanted Typewriter* the machine has a name, and in *Gray Magic* it receives human thoughts. In the field of contemporary art, Jeremy Mayer has become known for creating life-sized human sculptures made entirely out of typewriter parts. Each scale figure makes use of some forty deconstructed typewriters and takes about twelve hundred hours to assemble; and in putting them together, Mayer does not solder, weld, or glue the elements. Of his own work, Mayer says, "I think of the typewriter as a product of nature. . . . Though it is cold metal created by human hands, the typewriter is just as much a natural material as stone or wood. I concentrate on bringing this fascination with the raw material and interest in science and science fiction together in the subtleties of the human form."[33]

Beyond being manipulated by artists (set on fire, fragmented and reconstructed), "pristine" machines have been exhibited in art museums as instances of premier contemporary design. A red Valentine Portable Typewriter (1969) is part of the Museum of Modern Art's permanent collection, and a 1961 IBM Selectric is displayed at the Indianapolis Museum of Art.[34] While here and in the work of Messer, Maler, and Arneson it is the housing of the machine that fascinates, and in the work of Mayer its interstices, in the work of Paul Smith it is typewriter function that is central. What Smith achieves is to sketch using strokes of typewriter keys so that what we ultimately see is not letters or symbols but pictorial subjects: landscapes, animals, human portraits. A victim of cerebral palsy, Smith received no formal education but trained himself to "draw" with the typewriter, largely utilizing the characters at the top of the number keys: @ # $ % ^ & * ( ) _.

While the typewriter has had a significant role within the visual arts, it also has had a place in modern music. Perhaps most famous is the composition "The Typewriter" (1950) by Leroy Anderson, which utilizes the machine as a percussion instrument. It is this piece that accompanies a mime sequence in *Who's Minding the Store?* (1963), in which Jerry Lewis, an inept store clerk, sits at an empty desk (next to one at which a secretary is typing) and pretends to type (based on the noise emitted from her machine). As a sign that this musical composition still fascinates, it appears in many YouTube videos. Some are amateur reenactments of Lewis's bit, while others present someone playing an old version of the piece (e.g., on an antiquated 78 rpm record).[35] Significantly, typing sounds are also integrated into the musical score for *Atonement* (2007), a film about a novelist. Likewise, there is a YouTube video that simply depicts someone typing on an old machine —apparently for the acoustic pleasure of the noise it emits.[36]

Finally, both sound and image are at play in a contemporary artwork that brings together the technologies of the typewriter and the cinema. In Rodney Graham's installation *Rheinmetall/Victoria 8* (2003), an old 35mm movie projector is placed in a gallery running a film loop that depicts a typewriter as it is gradually covered with snow. Here is how the piece is described:

> A 1930s German Rheinmetall typewriter is the subject of a silent film projected by a 1961 Victoria 8 film projector, once considered the "Rolls Royce" of projectors. Views of the typewriter are presented in a series of long, slow, silent, static shots.... Close-ups reveal the inner workings—the hammers and the keypads—and unexpected beauty of the obsolete technology. Over the course of the short film, snow begins to fall, casting an icing sugar-like dust over the keys. . . . As the film progresses, the typewriter becomes completely engulfed and begins to resemble more a stormy snow-covered landscape. In the film's denouement, a final dump threatens to bury the contraption, but stops short. The last scene depicts a frontal view of the snow-covered typewriter. Then the film, installed on a looper, begins again.[37]

Here, the sound of the old projector substitutes for the missing noise of the typewriter, leading to a productive coalescence of the machines through a-synchronization.

In the image of a typewriter covered with snow we of course get resonances of *Citizen Kane* (1941) and the sled that is slowly buried by a storm. But it also seems to signify the passage of time and the onset of obsolescence. The brilliance of Graham's piece is to link typewriter to film projector—both pieces of equipment that (like Kane) have lost their childhood and are facing "death." But, as Wershler-Henry has noted, though technologies perish and get "consigned to the dustbin of history . . . their ghosts are everywhere"—like the author's.[38]

DRUGS AND BUGS

> In my writing i am acting as a map maker, an explorer of psychic areas . . . as a cosmonaut of inter space, and i see no point in exploring areas that have already been thoroughly surveyed.
> —William Burroughs, "Statement"[39]

While typewriters are common props in most films about writers, they often function only as banal pieces of the mise-en-scène—objects with which authors

FIGURE 9. The writer William Lee (Peter Weller) in *Naked Lunch* (1991).

can interact or that signify her profession. In one film, however, the typewriter takes a lead role and, thereby, reveals aspects of the composition process—David Cronenberg's *Naked Lunch* (1991)—inspired by the 1959 novel by William Burroughs. Cronenberg, in fact, admits that he was reading *Naked Lunch* when he made his first commercial horror film.[40] Had the typewriter been prominent in Burroughs's original work, Cronenberg's movie would be of less interest. But, in truth, it was the film director who gave the "writing machine" the status of a star.[41]

Cronenberg's *Naked Lunch* draws not only on aspects of Burroughs's novel (hereafter referred to as *NL*), but also on his other works (for example, *Queer*, which discusses his homosexuality)· In particular, the film borrows from one of his short stories, "Exterminator!" based on a job that Burroughs once held. *Naked Lunch*, in fact, opens with a scene of writer William Lee (Peter Weller), Burroughs's frequent alter-ego, on an extermination assignment—spraying insecticide in wall crevices, behind wallpaper, and on moldings in an apartment until some huge and repulsive cockroaches emerge and expire. This is our first sign that insects will take on a heavy burden of symbolization in the film—here, as that which is hidden, abject, and to be purged. In large part, this choice of imagery reflects Cronenberg's imaginative obsession, since Burroughs rarely mentions insects in his writing.[42] As evidence of the film director's fascination, we recall *The Fly* (1986), in which a mad scientist becomes fused with an insect as a result of an experiment with teleportation. Cronenberg has said that, in part, his interest in insects relates to his authorial activities: "When I write at night with the light on, insects come and land on the page" (shades of Stan Brakhage's *Mothlight* [1963]).[43] Clearly, in "Exterminator!" Burroughs must deal with insects. One passage, for instance, reads: "I have spotted a brown crack by the kitchen sink put my bellows in and blow a load of the precious yellow powder. As if they had heard the last trumpet the roaches stream out and flop in convulsions on the floor."[44] Elsewhere, he describes the fumigation of a mattress for bedbugs.[45]

Such creatures, however, function in other ways in *Naked Lunch*, since Lee, a heavy drug user, is addicted to "bug powder," the substance used to kill them. In "Exterminator!" the narrator does invoke this topic when he expresses his preference for "a pyrethrum job to a fluoride [job]," and one scene describes the owner of the pest control company ingesting bug poison: "The boss has a trick he does every now and again assembles his staff and eats arsenic been in that office breathing the powder in so long the arsenic just brings an embalmer's flush to his smooth grey cheek."[46]

When, in *Naked Lunch*, Lee returns to his apartment, he finds his wife, Joan (Judy Davis), shooting up bug powder (which makes her breath poisonous enough to kill the creatures). As we will see, this concoction is only one of many chemicals Lee and his acquaintances use to get high; others include "black meat" (made from ground centipedes) and "jism"—a fluid emitted from Mugwumps (fictional sinister beings that appear in a variety of Burroughs's writings). Cronenberg admits that most of these substances are not mentioned in Burroughs's work.[47] But the writer was an admitted addict and Cronenberg wanted to represent this part of his life without referencing actual drugs. For Cronenberg, the fact that Lee uses toxic substances to get stoned is a metaphor for what drugs do to the lives of writers who believe that they need such potions to be creative.

It is in this section of the story that we also get the first instance of a talking insect. Two detectives (figures from *NL*) round Lee up on drug charges and take him to their office. He claims the powder he possesses is only for extermination purposes. To test this theory, they open a box from which a giant and hideous beetle emerges. They place it in the powder and leave the room. The insect then begins to converse with Lee from a fleshy opening at the center of its carapace, claiming to be his "case officer" who reports to Lee's "controller." It tells him to kill his wife (who is allegedly some kind of "agent") and asks him to rub some powder on its "lips," which resemble an anus. When Lee does so, the creature moans in ecstasy. Throughout the encounter, it makes a rustling, twittering, sound, which adds to its general repugnance. Cronenberg says that the creature's oral cavity is a representation of Burroughs's notion of the "talking asshole"—a trope that would never have survived censorship if rendered literally. For Burroughs, this imaginary orifice tells us what we are too afraid to hear, what society censors. Lee is so disturbed by the bizarre creature that he takes off his shoe and smashes it to a disgusting pulp. In reality, Cronenberg used his own hand to do the dirty deed. His DVD commentary also informs us that no CGI was used for these or other special effects in the film; they were all done through on-set puppetry. For Cronenberg, such physicality is crucial (versus the ethereality of CGI), since he sees himself as a very tactile director. Peter Weller actually performed with these synthetic beings as offscreen actors voiced their lines.

The film's narrative also depicts a tragic incident in Burroughs's life (related to the beetle's command): his alleged accidental killing (while intoxicated) of his wife, Joan, as the two played a "William Tell Routine," in which he fired a gun at a glass on her head (and missed). This act is repeated in *Naked Lunch* (though not in *NL*) because Cronenberg was interested not so much in the literal text of the work as in the man behind it (and the Life of the Author). Thus, *Naked Lunch* is not an adaptation of *NL* but a film about the person who wrote it. Burroughs's criminal incident is especially important here because he has said: "I am forced to the appalling conclusion that I would never have become a writer but for Joan's death and to the realization of the extent to which this event has motivated and formulated my writing. I live with the constant threat of possession, and a constant need to escape from possession, from control. So the death of Joan brought me in contact with the invader, the ugly spirit, and maneuvered me into a lifelong struggle in which I have had no choice except to write my way out."[48] In the film, the crime forces Lee to escape from the United States to the "Interzone" (a play on the International Zone)—a locale that resembles North Africa. Again, Cronenberg is drawing upon Burroughs's biography, since he lived in Morocco in 1953 and wrote a collection of pieces entitled *Interzone*.

Once there, an addict's paradise, Lee is frequently high, a fact that is signaled by the hallucinatory imagery that ensues—some of which, again, involves the grotesque insect first encountered in New York. (In his essay "International Zone," Burroughs writes: "Hashish is the drug of Islam. . . . No effort is made to control its sale or use in Tangier, and every native café reeks of the smoke.")[49] Before leaving for the Interzone, Lee had hocked his gun for a "Clark Nova" typewriter in a local pawnshop—a swap that seems to equate writing with violence and, in this case, Lee's murder of his wife (a link admitted by Burroughs). Once "abroad," we see him typing in an Interzone café. A paper in the carriage reads: "Report on the Assassination of Joan Lee by Outside Forces" (a phrasing consonant with Burroughs's admission of having felt "possessed").

We next find Lee in his apartment, eyes closed, slumped before his typewriter —clearly in a trance. The machine begins to type on its own (reminding us of *The Enchanted Typewriter*). Soon it morphs into a huge, revolting beetle/typewriter hybrid. Thus, the world of the Interzone is again repellent. Here Cronenberg borrows from some of Burroughs's characterizations of Tangier, where "you see filth, poverty, disease, all endured with a curiously apathetic indifference" or where one encounters "a man, barefooted, in rags, his face eaten and tumescent with a horrible skin disease."[50] The vision of the writer in contaminated Tangier also reminds us of Burroughs's statement that "language is a virus."[51]

The typewriter tells Lee (via its obscene mouth) that "homosexuality is the best all-around cover an agent ever had." It orders him to type more forcefully and not be a "pansy"—to "hurt" it. As Lee pounds away, the machine moans blissfully, at which point he flees his apartment. Certainly, this strange imagery equates writing with venting repressed material (e.g., one's sexual proclivities), an issue that can only be voiced by a nauseating "talking asshole." It also establishes a decidedly erotic relation between artist and instrument. Furthermore, in its mention of "agents," it bespeaks the paranoia first uttered by the beetle in New York —imagining a world of case officers, reports, and controllers. As Burroughs once said: "Sometimes paranoia's just having all the facts."[52]

On another level, this and later weird renditions of the typewriter seem to embody the "invader, [or] the ugly spirit" with which Burroughs has "struggled" since the death of his wife, that he can only banish by "writ[ing] [his] way out." It also reminds us of his suggestive statement that "every man has inside himself a parasitic being who is acting not at all to his advantage."[53] Finally, the Clark Nova's demonic aura and its insect status remind us of the machine in *Walpuski's Typewriter*, which takes the form of a malevolent scorpion.

The next time we see the typewriter follows a conversation Lee has about being queer with Interzone ex-pat Yves (Julian Sands). We find Lee stoned at his machine, which bears a page reading: "I shall never forget the unspeakable horror that froze the lymph in my glands when the baneful word seared my reeling brain." We know from the previous discussion that the word is "homosexual." As Burroughs notes in "International Zone," Tangier was a haven for such men. He speaks of "the perverts sitting in front of the cafes looking over the boys, [and] the boys parading past."[54] He also talks of how "male prostitutes [were] everywhere . . . and solicit[ed] openly in the streets."[55] After the scene of Lee typing, there is a cut to his bathroom where a huge centipede crawls on the tile wall. He blows on it and the creature drops to the floor (as when Joan breathed deadly bug powder on insects in New York). Though here the typewriter is not an insect, it is associated with one—specifically, the revolting creature that serves as the source of a popular Interzone drug.

On several occasions, Lee meets two other writers in a café: Tom (Ian Holm) and Joan Frost (in "International Zone," Burroughs talks of Tangier as populated by émigré authors hoping to "write a best seller").[56] The latter is played by Judy Davis, the same actress who portrays Lee's wife; so she is her literal "double" (in more than her first name). In fact, the couple is based on Paul and Jane Bowles, authors that Burroughs met in North Africa. In one such encounter Tom gives Lee the drug "majoun" and also suggests that he try his "Martinelli" typewriter. We next see Lee at home with two typewriters on his desk (his and Tom's). He is shivering in some sort of compromised state and the words on the typed page speak of his being "addicted to something that doesn't exist." He takes to bed and awakens to offscreen shouts. When he looks at his desk the typewriters have become two huge, warring beetles, with the Clark Nova scolding Lee for having given the Martinelli "access to [his] innermost vulnerabilities." In the midst of the carnage, the Clark Nova orders Lee to seduce Joan Frost, whereupon the writer obeys and scurries to her apartment. Here, the writing machine seems an artist's jealous lover, treasuring the secrets he reveals to it alone. At the same time, it seems to warn the artist against admitting clandestine thoughts in the first place.

At the Frosts,' Lee learns that Joan writes in longhand. Evidently (and stereotypically) she's "not good with machines," which "intimidate her." He confesses that he's broken Tom's typewriter while suffering from "sporadic hallucinations." She reveals that Tom has another machine, a "Mujahideen" that types in Arabic. (Interestingly, the name means "guerrilla warriors engaged in jihad"—thus writing is equated with terrorism.) When asked if he intends to break that too, Lee responds: "Only in self-defense. I knew writing could be dangerous but I didn't realize the danger came from the machinery."[57] Of course, since Lee's machines are as informed by his fantasies as by industrial design, the perils of writing seem to be largely internal.

Lee and Joan put the Mujahideen on a desk and, after sampling some majoun, she begins to type. As the machine prints Arabic letters, Joan tells Lee that the text is "erotic," "uncivilized," "filthy." The machine seems to melt and bend. It opens up to reveal its bloody, fleshy, "vaginal" interstices into which she places her hands, ultimately licking her fingers. Its "bellows" expand and a huge, penile projection emerges and grows in size. Here, in the machine's gross corporeality, we are reminded again of Walpuski's typewriter, which eats meat "with an unholy sucking sound," its "front and back . . . mov[ing] together and apart in a monstrous parody of chewing."[58] After Lee and Joan make love, we return to the machine, which has become a giant, disgusting, flesh-toned centipede, with a buttock-like rear end. Later, when it is chased out a window, it smashes on the ground and "becomes" a broken typewriter. On the one hand, this writing machine is the most erotic of all we have seen and seems to embody both male and female sexual organs. On the other, it is a monstrous and revolting being that must be banished from human space.

We later find Lee retrieving Frost's broken typewriter from the street and placing its parts in a bag; in the scene that follows, he lies dazed on the ground. There, he is met by two of his New York writer buddies, Martin (played by Michael Zelniker as a stand-in for Allen Ginsberg) and Hank (played by Nicholas Campbell as a stand-in for Jack Kerouac). Not expecting to see them, Lee says, "I must be hallucinating," and he later tells them, "Everybody blacks out in the Interzone" (in "International Zone," Burroughs wrote: "Here fact merges into dream, and dreams erupt into the real world").[59] They ask him what is contained in the sack and he responds: "The remains of my last writing machine." When the two men (and the viewer) peer into the bag, however, all that is seen is a mass of medicine vials and hypodermics—which equates the typewriter with an addictive drug. The two men have come to the Interzone to help Lee publish the novel NL as, in truth, did Ginsburg and Kerouac.

After Lee sends Hank and Martin home, he is picked up by a beautiful Interzone boy, Kiki (Joseph Scoren), who takes him to a place where "they can fix anything that is broken." There, Kiki pours the typewriter parts from Lee's pack into

FIGURE 10. The carnal "Mujahideen" typewriter in *Naked Lunch* (1991) opens up to show its interstices.

an open furnace and what emerges is a huge, molten Mugwump head. We next find Lee in his apartment, typing on the monster's skull, his hands in its mouth. Worm-like projections top its cranium and squirm around. One of them bends and emits a viscous fluid, making the protrusion seem more penile. Lee later "milks" it for juice to drink. So here, the writing machine not only requires one to be drugged but produces drugs itself. Lee's interaction with the machine also evokes fellatio, as though that, too, were a requisite for writing.

Lee packs up the "Mugwriter" and takes it to Tom's home, asking him to return the Clark Nova. He tells Tom it "dispenses fluid when it likes what you've written," so here drugs seem to be a writer's critic and reward (in addition to his stimulus). Frost gives him the machine and Lee opens its case on the street. The grotesque beetle machine tells him that "a writer lives the sad truth like anyone else; the only difference is he files a *report* on it"—giving new meaning to Lee's prior use of the term and turning all creative output into an undercover account of adversity. Shortly thereafter the machine begins to smoke and immolate (shades of Maler's *Hommage*), being replaced by a regular typewriter.

Lee then joins Joan in a Mugwump den where the creatures are hung from hooks so that people can suck out their jism. She holds a notebook in which she has written, "All is lost," demonstrating that the pen is no more sanguine an instrument than the typewriter. We next find the couple driving down a road in an old tank on the way to "Annexia" when they are stopped by a border guard asking for papers. Lee says he's a writer and, when proof is demanded, he holds up his pen, now his only "writing device." The soldier balks that this is "not good enough" and asks him to write something as further evidence. He turns to the back of the tank where Joan is sleeping. He tells her it's time for their William Tell Routine again and shoots her dead. So the film ends where it began—with murder as the only true impetus for writing (and proof of authorship) and with the malign typewriter replaced by the primitive pen.

While no beetle-, Mugwump-, or centipede-typewriters appear in Burroughs's work, he does, at times, represent the writing device in imaginative ways. In *NL*, for example, he talks of how "time jumps like a broken typewriter."[60] In *The Ticket That Exploded*, he speaks of "the soft typewriter" that holds "thin transparent sheets on which is written the action from birth to death."[61] Here we get some sense of the machine as quasi-organic, as more body-like than mechanical—a vision extended in Cronenberg's film. Finally, in *Nova Express* Burroughs speaks of "The Man at the Typewriter" and of a "liquid typewriter."[62] He also again invokes the Soft Typewriter, which can't "create anything" and "can only repeat your instructions." Certainly, this seems at odds with the Clark Nova in *Naked Lunch*, which writes on its own and barks commands at its owner. But as the typewriter is Lee's hallucination, its instructions ultimately come from the artist himself. Finally, in commenting on writing with the "soft machine," Burroughs compares the process to a photomontage, which "makes a statement in flexible picture language."[63] This image is evocative of cinematic editing and seems to presage the visual construction of Cronenberg's *Naked Lunch*.

It is important to note that certain shots in *Naked Lunch* (and other films about the writer) hit us with a sense of what Barthes has deemed the "punctum" of the photographic experience—images that pierce our being with some unexpected and intangible insight or apprehension. The ones in question are those in which written or typed words are shown to the viewer. In a sense, such shots (of words converted to image) remind us that, by making a film about a writer, Cronenberg has found a way to articulate the intermedial nature of cinema, and by imaginatively envisioning the author's writing machine, he has tapped his *own* perverse sensibility—all this in the Interzone between realism and fantasy, film and literature, typewriter and camera.

2   BEYOND ADAPTATION
The Writer as Filmmaker

> The time has long passed when popular fiction was almost inevitably filmed
> by Hollywood and when, as in the 1940s, seven of the 10 Best Picture Oscar
> winners were based on novels.
>
> —Richard Corliss, "Books vs. Movies"

In the last chapter, we ended our examination of the typewriter icon
with a discussion of a film by David Cronenberg inspired by William Burroughs's
Naked Lunch. In truth, however, the relationship between cinema and literature
has been an uneasy one. In 1942, Soviet filmmaker Sergei Eisenstein wrote an
essay entitled "Dickens, Griffith and the Film Today," in which he credited the
great English novelist with forging literary prototypes of such visual devices as
the close-up and montage. Clearly looking for validation for his nascent art (one
linked to low culture), Eisenstein wrote: "I have always derived comfort from repeatedly telling myself that our cinema is not entirely without an ancestry and
a pedigree, a past and traditions . . . from earlier epochs."[1] Similarly, it does not
seem accidental that when post–World War II French and American critics were
looking for a way to legitimize the role of the film director they chose the epithet
"author"—a designation previously associated with the creator of poetry, prose,
and drama. In fact, they were drawing upon the work of French essayist and filmmaker Alexandre Astruc, whose 1948 article advanced the idea of the *camera-stylo*
or the camera-pen.

In later years, as film criticism (drawing upon semiotics, structuralism, and psychoanalysis) developed its own critical discourse, comparisons to literature were
often seen as retrograde in that they anchored the cinema to a prior medium rather
than allowing it to be understood on its own terms. Here, adaptation studies suffered in particular—given that they conceived the literary work as source and the
movie as derivative. What, after all, could the critic do but endlessly catalog the
changes from open-ended novel to time-constrained film—alterations that would
necessarily truncate or simplify the predecessor? At best, aesthetic proclamations
might be made that essentialized each medium, asserting that literature allegedly "could do" one thing while cinema another. In recent years, there has been

a return to adaptation studies with more sophisticated theories emerging—with critics formulating various paradigms for the process (be it translation, performance, dialogue, recycling, ventriloquizing, or decomposing).[2] No matter how one imagines the practice, however, it is trapped in the vice of a binary—between original and copy. Though, of course, sometimes that relationship is reversed, as when there is a "novelization" of a previously made film that was not based upon a literary property (as in the case of *2001, A Space Odyssey* [1968]).[3]

Here, however, I want to offer a more original means of affiliating literature and film—the case of the artist who works in both media in a manner that moves "beyond adaptation." We should not be surprised at this, since, as André Bazin once wrote, "there is nothing absurd in trying to write a novel on film, to concern oneself—like a filmmaker or a novelist . . . with the idea of unfolding a real world."[4]

Clearly, it is not unusual for a writer to pen the screenplay for a film that is based on his or her work but directed by another. This is the case for *Daniel* (1983), directed by Sidney Lumet with a scenario by E. L. Doctorow derived from his novel *The Book of Daniel* (1971). It is also not uncommon for a writer to be employed as a screenwriter for a property that is independent of his own literary pursuits. Harold Pinter, for example, wrote the scenario for *The French Lieutenant's Woman* (1981), a work based on a 1969 novel by John Fowles.

The instance I have in mind, however, marks a more oblique link between writer and motion picture—the case of the author who composes for both media but generally avoids adapting his own prior work. Those who accomplish this form a rather elite club including Marguerite Duras, Alain Robbe-Grillet, and Pinter. Not surprisingly, over time, some of these artists have become film directors, often bringing original scenarios to the screen. Hence Duras's *Nathalie Granger* (1972), *Woman of the Ganges* (1974), or *India Song* (1975) never existed as novels. To my mind, however, the most intriguing figure of this group is Paul Auster (mentioned in the previous chapter). He wrote the original screenplays for *Smoke* and *Blue in the Face* (both 1995), which he co-directed with Wayne Wang, as well as one for a film he made himself—*Lulu on the Bridge* (1998).[5]

PAUL AUSTER

> Working on . . . films has been a terrific experience, and I'm glad it happened. . . . But enough is enough. It's time for me to crawl back into my hole and begin writing again. There's a new novel calling out to be written, and I can't wait to lock myself in my room and get started.
>
> —Paul Auster, "Making of *Smoke*"

Smoke was Auster's first scenario, and he admits that his only preparation for the task was "a lifetime of watching movies."[6] He confesses to having written "scripts" for silent movies as a young man—strange for someone born in the sound era. As he recalls: "They were very long and very detailed, seventy or eighty pages of elaborate and meticulous movements, every gesture spelled out in words. Weird, deadpan slapstick." Unfortunately, they are lost. Auster also comments on the difference between composing a screenplay and a novel. While the latter is "long . . . slow and very grueling," it is an "organic process" that mostly "happens unconsciously." The former, however, is "more like a jigsaw puzzle." As he notes: "Writing the actual words [of a script] might not be very time-consuming but putting the pieces together can drive you crazy." Furthermore, in cinema, one must think in "dramatic . . . rather than narrative terms." Auster also speaks in a stimulating way about the editing process (in which he participated)—making comparisons between imagery and language: "You're stuck with the footage you have, and that limits the possibilities. You're like a novelist trying to revise his book, but fifty percent of the words in the dictionary are not available to you. You're not allowed to use them."[7]

While a champion of the cinema, some of his views express a rather retrograde opinion of the medium. He assumes that people watch movies "passively" and that "in the end they wash right through" them. Literature, however, requires something more: "You have to work, you have to use your imagination. And once your imagination has been fully awakened, you enter into the world of the book, as if it were your own life." Furthermore, while in cinema we encounter a two-dimensional universe, in literature we "find . . . a three-dimensional world."[8] Although theorists would of course argue with Auster's notion that cinema inherently requires little intellectual activity from the spectator or is two-dimensional, his view leads him to prefer "directors who emphasize telling stories over technique," who "are not in love with the image for its own sake." I beg to differ.

Beyond being a novelist who works in cinema, one of the central themes of Auster's fiction is the process of writing (and, by extension, reading). *Leviathan* (1992), for instance, concerns two writer friends—one who kills himself and one who inherits the task of reconstructing the deceased's life. A similar structure is evident in *Invisible* (2009), in which a dying writer contacts an old college friend (now a novelist), asking the latter to read and complete his memoir. In "Ghosts," one segment of *The New York Trilogy* (1985–1986), a man is hired to spy on another and compile notes on what he observes. Another part of the volume ("City of Glass") involves a former mystery writer, and a third ("The Locked Room") depicts a magazine author who must take over the project of his writer friend. Finally, in *Travels in the Scriptorium* (2007), an old man awakens imprisoned in a room with no recollection of how he got there; he finds a manuscript on a table (written by someone else) left for him to read.

Thus in many of Auster's works one writer merges with another. In *Leviathan*, for instance, one author autographs the work of another without letting people know that the signature is a forgery (an ironic take on the notion of the individual artist).[9] To some extent, a form of authorial fusion took place in the making of *Smoke* as well. Though normally screenwriters disappear from the scene once filming begins, Auster remained on the set—collaborating with Wang on casting, art direction, and editing. As Auster notes: "Wayne and I forgot to pay attention to the rules. It never occurred to either one of us to part company then. I was the writer, Wayne was the director, but it was *our* film, and all along we had considered ourselves equal partners in the project. I understand now what an unusual arrangement this was."[10]

Beyond focusing on writing, many of Auster's works are peppered with resonant film allusions. (As Auster has said: "I've always been drawn to [movies]. . . . It's the rare person in this world who isn't.")[11] *The New York Trilogy* mentions *The Wizard of Oz* (1939) and *It's a Wonderful Life* (1946), as well as such screen clowns as Buster Keaton, Harry Langdon, Harold Lloyd, and Laurel and Hardy.[12] Several of the characters are shown going to the movies and one (we are told) has written on the subject.[13] But the preponderance of citations cluster around works of *film noir*, specifically *Lady in the Lake*, *Dark Passage*, and *Out of the Past* (all from 1947 —significantly, the year of Auster's birth).[14] These references are not surprising given the gritty urban locale of the *Trilogy*, the murderous impulses of its characters, the femmes fatales and detective figures who populate the bleak, enigmatic narrative.[15] In a highly self-reflexive gesture typical of Auster, the narrator notes that one of his characters knows everything he does about crime "from books [and] films."[16]

Cinema also figures prominently in *Leviathan* (the novel Auster was working on prior to penning *Smoke*).[17] Its protagonist, Benjamin Sachs, is a failed Hollywood screenwriter, and the novel makes reference to *Citizen Kane* (1941), *Clair's Knee* (1970), and *Phantom of Liberty* (1974).[18] Similarly, the title of Auster's *Book of Illusions* (2002) seems to conjure up film magic. The work concerns a college professor who has suffered the devastating accidental death of his wife and children. While recuperating from his loss, he happens to catch an old movie clip on television and becomes inexplicably obsessed by the career of its obscure maker, Hector Mann—a silent film comedian (recalling Auster's fascination with Keaton, Lloyd, and Langdon). While such filmic citations run throughout Auster's novels, they go largely unnoted in reference texts that seek to categorize his myriad citations, for example *A Paul Auster Sourcebook* (2001), by Carsten Springer.

If cinema continually and productively crops up in Auster's writings, writing crops up in Auster's films. *Smoke* concerns yet another traumatized widower, Paul Benjamin (William Hurt)—significantly, a writer whose name is identical to Auster's first and middle ones and is a moniker he employed as his *nom de plume* for his first novel, *Squeeze Play* (1982). Furthermore, Benjamin lives in Brooklyn and has writer's block, both details from Auster's biography. Finally, like a book, the film is divided into five chapters—each identified by a character's name and introduced with an intertitle.[19] Auster speaks of the attention he paid to assisting set designer Kalina Ivanov in making Paul's apartment look genuine—both as a New York City dwelling and as a writer's studio. It was, in fact, the only set constructed for the film (the rest being shot on location). As Auster notes: "We talked about everything: the books on the shelves, the pictures on the walls, the precise contents of the clutter on the desk. . . . The little coffee-cup rings on the table, the postcard of Herman Melville over the desk and the unused word processor sitting in the corner."[20] Given our discussion of Auster's love of typewriters, the last detail should come as no surprise.

Aside from Paul, there are two other artist-figures in *Smoke*—both of whom work in visual media. One is Rashid (Harold Perrineau), a young black boy whom Paul befriends when the teenager saves him from being run over on the street.[21] Rashid, who grows up fatherless, learns that his dad, Cyrus (Forest Whitaker), moved back to the New York area and owns a gas station in Peekskill (significantly, the hero of *Out of the Past* owned such a business and, like Cyrus, was fleeing his personal history). Rashid arrives at the filling station, unannounced, and situates himself across the road, sketching the building's exterior. He leaves the drawing for the proprietor, who has no idea that its creator is his son. Clearly, here, Rashid's artwork seems to help him come to terms with his paternal loss and its potential restoration.

While Rashid's father initially rejects him, Paul seems to adopt him in a parental fashion—allowing him to crash in his apartment for a while—until the boy's presence begins to upset his "writing schedule." His concern with a timetable seems entirely unfounded since, as we learn, Paul has failed to compose anything since the death of his wife. When, later, Rashid reappears on Paul's doorstep (attempting to escape from some thugs who are hounding him), Paul is more open to being involved with the boy and becomes his mentor. It is as though counseling Rashid stands in for Paul's creative work, reminding us of Roland Barthes's notion that "the Author . . . is in the same relation of antecedence to his work as a father to his child."[22]

The second and more relevant visual artist in the film is Auggie (Harvey Keitel), an unlikely personage, given that he is the manager of a cigar shop. It is significant (considering Auster's fascination with cinema) that Auggie is an amateur photographer who takes daily snapshots outside his store on precisely the same corner at exactly the same time each day (8 A.M. in the morning). In this respect, Auggie is similar to the character of Maria in *Leviathan*, who follows random people on the street and photographs them. She deems her subject "the eye, the drama of watching and being watched," and claims that her "camera [i]s no longer an instrument that record[s] presences, it [i]s a way of making the world disappear, a technique for encountering the invisible."[23] The theme of voyeurism shows up elsewhere in Auster's work. In *The New York Trilogy* there is a veiled reference to *Rear Window* (1954), a film about a photographer forced to amuse himself by staring out his apartment window while recuperating from a broken leg. In a segment of Auster's book, a character called Blue is employed to write reports on a person named Black (shades of the "agents" in Cronenberg's *Naked Lunch*). He lives in an apartment whose window faces that of his subject and through which he can observe the man's every move—which includes the act of writing.[24] At some point, however, Blue realizes that, as he reports on Black, the latter is reporting on him. Here,

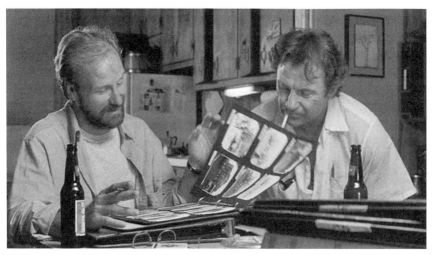

FIGURE 11. Paul (William Hurt) looks through Auggie's (Harvey Keitel's) photograph album (*Smoke*, 1995).

perhaps, Auster was influenced by Italo Calvino, who in *If on a Winter's Night a Traveler* describes a novelist who has an idea for a story: "Two writers living in two chalets on opposite slopes of the valley, observe each other alternately."[25]

In *Smoke*, Auggie's voyeuristic documentary act has led him to accumulate an album of some 4,000 exposures of people on the street—which means he has taken pictures for some ten and a half years. While Paul (steeped in the word) sees nothing but similarity in these views, Auggie (immersed in the image) sees subtle differences in light, weather, and characterization. He tells Paul that unless he slows down, he will see nothing at all. (This is reminiscent of a line in *The New York Trilogy:* "Books must be read as deliberately and reservedly as they were written . . . the trick is to go slowly.")[26] Clearly, in urging Paul toward extended reflection on the single frame, Auggie's perspective is that of a still versus motion picture photographer, since the latter medium is temporally preprogrammed to move along quickly. Though Auggie sees variety in his formulaic snapshots, he also admits to a certain monotony. Drawing upon great literature, he remarks: "You know, 'Tomorrow and tomorrow and tomorrow creeps at this petty pace . . .'"

As Auster has commented: "Auggie was photographing time . . . both natural time and human time and he was doing it by planting himself in one tiny corner of the world and *willing it to be his own, by standing guard* in the space he had chosen for himself" (my emphasis).[27] It is noteworthy how Auster's language implies a desire for possession in the photographic impulse, one that seems reflected in the colloquialism "capturing" an image. Furthermore, in speaking of Auggie as "standing guard," Auster, perhaps, subtly references the sense of the photograph as both bespeaking and warding off fatality—a quality that Roland Barthes has discussed in *Camera Lucida* (1981). As Barthes notes: "Each photograph always includes th[e] imperious sign of [our] future death."[28] This theme is emphasized when Paul (now going slowly) finds, in Auggie's album, an image of his deceased wife crossing the street on her way to work some years back—a vision that, with its faux "presence," shocks him again with her true absence ("Look at my sweet darling," he declaims in tears). Perhaps, this is what Maria in *Leviathan* has meant by calling photography "a technique for encountering the invisible." The snapshot also testifies to the role of contingency in life and art, and it seems no coincidence that one of Auster's novels is entitled *The Music of Chance* (1990). Interestingly, Maya Deren once observed that photography, in particular, is a medium "of the 'controlled accident.'"[29]

Paul's wife died in the random gunfire of an urban robbery, and Auggie muses that had she lingered longer in his store that day she might have been saved. Ironically, what Paul has not been able to accomplish in his writing (which has faltered with his grief over his wife's tragic demise), Auggie manages to achieve unintentionally through the photographic medium—through his routinized, quasi-automatic taking of images. He has shot Paul's wife (so to speak) before she was fatally shot—thus reviving her from the dead—retrieving her from "Out of the Past."

The conjunction of the literary and cinematic merge most forcibly at the end of the film when Paul stops in to Auggie's shop and tells him that the *New York Times* has commissioned him to write a Christmas tale but that he lacks inspiration for it.[30] Auggie says that he has a good story idea and will tell it to Paul over lunch. The two sit down in a deli and, as the camera moves progressively closer to Auggie's face, he relates a yarn about what happened to him years back when a young kid named Roger Goodwin stole some magazines from his shop. In absconding, Roger dropped a wallet in which Auggie finds an ID card and some family snapshots, which personalizes the kid and quells Auggie's anger. He decides to return the wallet and when he arrives at the indicated address, he is greeted by a blind, elderly black woman, Goodwin's Granny Ethel, who assumes that Auggie is Roger paying her a surprise Christmas visit. Rather than correct her error, Auggie (who is lonely himself), feels sorry for Ethel and plays along with the ruse, sharing a holiday meal with her, becoming Roger's "double." But he also comprehends that Ethel is duping him: "It was as if we both decided to play this game." When, having drunk some wine, Ethel falls asleep on the sofa, Auggie goes to the bathroom and finds a stash of cameras that he assumes Roger has stolen and stored there. Impulsively, he steals one and leaves the apartment with it. It is *this* apparatus (found by chance, while impersonating another, and pilfered) with which he has subsequently accomplished his photographic "life's work."

What this incident foregrounds (among other things) is the theme of theft that has run throughout the work. First of all, photography (in its voyeuristic/proprietary stance) can be seen as stealing people's images (and in some cultures, their souls). Second, Rashid is involved in having taken some funds that a gang of crooks dropped in fleeing a crime scene. Third, when Rashid appears at his father's garage, the former thinks he's a thief casing the joint. Fourth, we are led to believe that Paul "steals" Auggie's Christmas vignette in order to fulfill his commission from the *New York Times*. And finally, in utilizing that published piece as the basis for a film, we might ask if Auster is not stealing from his own writing to create cinema—casting the very act of adaptation in a new light. In all these instances, Auster would seem to endorse Roland Barthes's notion of the text as "a tissue of quotations," "a multidimensional space in which a variety of writings, none of them original, blend and clash."[31] He would also seem to approve Pablo Picasso's sense that "bad artists copy" but "good artists steal."[32] Interestingly, in *Leviathan*, a writer says that he takes as his own "figures stolen from the pages of other novels."[33]

What is especially interesting from the cinematic perspective is that, following Auggie's verbal recounting of his Christmas anecdote, we see a black-and-white film rendition of it (which contrasts to the rest of the color movie). The tone here connects to Auggie's photographs that are likewise in monochrome. It also engages the racial theme of the film, which understands "black and white" in social terms. The final segment is also without diegetic speech or sound effects, so it proceeds like a silent picture, setting it off from the sound film in which it is embedded. Clearly, the roots of this sequence are in the silent movie scripts that Auster penned as a young man. The segment is also strangely reminiscent of one from *The Fatal Glass of Beer* (1933), a W. C. Fields spoof of melodrama in which, as a man tells his story of downfall in the wicked city, we see the scene unfold in wordless images onscreen.

The muteness of *Smoke*'s final sequence also highlights its refusal of language (though the characters' lips move)—the very medium used for Auggie's original narrative. This lack is somewhat qualified by the lyrics of a Tom Waits song that accompanies the sequence. Though refusing verbal dialogue, the segment starts by depicting printed words on a piece of paper in Paul's typewriter—establishing what follows as both a visual translation of Auggie's aural chronicle and of Paul's written story.

Several things are important here. First, we get an illustration of the historically common practice of film adaptation as, before our eyes, a verbal text is transformed into a cinematic one. Second, the sequence highlights our differing expectations of the verbal versus the photographic sign. While the veracity of the word (a symbolic form) must, in general, be taken on faith, until recently (with the advent of computer generated imagery) the truth of the photograph was sacrosanct and tied to its indexical status—giving it the force of evidence. Here, there are parallels between Auster's sense of photography and his reverence for language in its Ideal, prelapsarian status. As one character muses in *The New York Trilogy:*

> Adam's one task in the Garden had been to invent language, to give each creature and thing its name. In that state of innocence, his tongue had gone straight to the quick of the world. His words had not been merely appended to the things he saw,

they had revealed their essences, had literally brought them to life. A thing and its name were interchangeable. After the fall, this was no longer true. Names became detached from things; words devolved into a collection of arbitrary signs; language had been severed from God. The story of the Garden, therefore, records not only the fall of man, but the fall of language.[34]

To mix up the verbal/visual registers further in *Smoke*, just before the filmed rendition of Auggie's tale, we focus on extreme close-ups of Auggie's mouth talking and Paul's eyes watching him—despite the fact that it is Paul who is associated with the word and Auggie with the image. Interestingly, Auster has said that he sees the film as moving slowly from long shot, through medium shot, to close-up. He also mentions that the latter shots are meant to shock the spectator. "The viewer is not at all prepared for it. It's as if the camera is bulldozing through a brick wall, breaking down the last barrier against human intimacy."[35] In particular, the attention to Paul's vision at the end of the film seems doubly ironic since the narrative Auggie recounts involves the motif of blindness, and the music attached to the film's final credits is "Smoke Gets in Your Eyes." Thus, at the end of the work (as in *Naked Lunch*), the viewer is suspended between two signs (word and image), two media (literature and film), and two poles of belief: avowal and disavowal.

The particular lyrics of Waits's song ("You're Innocent When You Dream") are also highly suggestive. Their focus on reverie parallels the surreal aura of the black-and-white footage. The song's refrain, which speaks of stealing memories, elicits the theme of theft that runs throughout the narrative. Waits's song also references notions tied to Paul's traumatic reaction to the image of his dead wife in Auggie's album. Thus, the lyrics mention graveyards and friendship-until-death—highlighting the film's recurrent theme of mortality. Again, this motif has both verbal and visual dimensions. At one point Paul tells Rashid an anecdote about a young skier who dies in a mountain avalanche and whose son, decades later, climbs the same mountain only to find his father encased in ice—fully preserved at the moment of expiration. Ironically, the son is now older than his father was at the time of his demise (seeming to reverse the chronology of parent-child relations). Interestingly, Auster has borrowed this anecdote from *The New York Trilogy*—thereby "plagiarizing" himself, and, like the skier, returning to a frozen past.

Here again, in this tale within a tale that visualizes a man's ice-bound "suspended animation," *Smoke* evokes a filmic metaphor for fatality and the passage of time. For as André Bazin famously noted (using mummification rather than cryogenics as the operant symbol): "If [cinema] were put under psychoanalysis, the practice of embalming the dead might turn out to be a fundamental factor in [its] creation."[36] Just before Auggie finishes his Christmas fable (and the film comes to a close), he says to Paul: "And that's the end of the story." For Auster, it is not only the literary or cinematic tale that bears a requisite "sense of an ending," but the photographic image—which implies (within its very frame) the termination of the life it seems to promise.[37] The title of the film also seems to highlight this theme. As director Jim Jarmusch says in *Blue in the Face:* "Cigarettes are sort of a reminder of your mortality. Each puff is like a passing moment, a passing thought; you know, you smoke; smoke disappears, it reminds you that to live is also to die." Smoke is also associated with the destruction of the creative object in the film, since a story Paul tells Rashid about Mikhail Bakhtin involves the theorist using his manuscript as cigarette paper—destroying it rather than giving up his "habit."

Auster's invocation of death in *Smoke* as well as its associations with the cinema seems reiterated in a passage from his novel *Invisible,* whose very title is suggestive of the trope. There, a character watches Carl Theodore Dreyer's *Ordet* (1955), and is deeply affected by its conclusion: a funeral scene in which the brother of a deceased woman (who thinks he is Jesus) orders her body to arise—and it does. While at first the character in Auster's novel who is viewing *Ordet* thinks the cinematic sequence is supposed to be a hallucination, he eventually concludes that the scene is to be taken as real: the woman has been "fully restored to life."[38] Significantly, the character viewing *Ordet* lost his brother in childhood and the screening seems to have "washed out some of the poison that ha[d] been building up inside [him]." We might say the same of Paul in *Smoke* who, like the protagonist of *Invisible*, is "stunned" by Auggie's photograph of his dead wife seemingly "restored to life." Like the novel's hero, "something changes in [him] after that" and makes the narrative we have witnessed in *Smoke* possible. (Alternately, it is precisely the death of Burroughs's wife that serves as the catalyst for his creativity.)

It also seems important that the scene Auster's character finds so affecting in *Ordet* occurs at the end of the Dreyer film. We might say the same of the denouement of *Smoke* when the verbal tale that Auggie has recounted is illustrated on-screen. Here, something that has been visually "null" (narrated only in words) comes "alive" in an unexpected fashion. As the fictional viewer of *Ordet* opines: "It is the end that counts, for the end does something to you that is wholly unexpected, and it crashes into you with all the force of an axe felling an oak." Clearly, even here, death is not far from Auster's mind.

DAVID MAMET

> Not only the search for truth, but long hours and avoidance behaviour make fictional policemen kindred spirits with their authors.
> —R. N. Morris, "The Writer as Detective"

To my mind, Paul Auster is the most fascinating case of the filmmaker/writer, given his relentless focus on authorship and cinema. One aspect of his fiction in particular leads us to consider another author—playwright David Mamet. While he is known primarily as a dramatist for such works as *American Buffalo* (1975), *Speed-the-Plow* (1984), and *Glengarry Glen Ross* (1988), he has also directed several films that are independent of his previous writings, for example *Heist* (2001) and *Spartan* (2004). Two other texts, however, are of greatest concern here. *State and*

Main (2000) is a self-reflexive movie about the making of a film, whose protagonist is an author—specifically the screenwriter of the work being shot. But it is not *State and Main* that is most relevant to our discussion of Mamet, despite its featuring a writer and taking cinema as its subject. Rather, it is a work of another sort that is most intriguing: *Homicide* (1991), a cop film that focuses on a detective's unraveling of an anti-Semitic plot.

But why is it of interest? To answer this, we must first return to the work of Paul Auster. Aside from being preoccupied with the writer, Auster is fixated on the detective. In the "City of Glass," the hero of writer Daniel Quinn's mystery novels is private eye Max Work. In "Ghosts," Blue is a detective who has trained with another named Brown. In "The Locked Room," Fanshawe is said to have written detective fiction.[39]

What is especially noteworthy about Auster's fascination with the detective is the manner in which that figure is related to the author. While it has been common to liken the reader of a novel to a sleuth who must piece together clues, Auster likens the figure to a writer.[40] As he notes in "City of Glass": "The detective is one who looks, who listens, who moves through this morass of objects and events in search of the thought, the idea that will pull all these things together and make sense of them. In effect, *the writer and the detective are interchangeable*" (my emphasis).[41] Similarly, in "Ghosts," as Blue watches Black, he speculates on the nature of his subject's life story, and on the reason White has hired him to follow the man:

> Of Black, of White, of the job he has been hired to do, Blue now begins to advance certain theories. More than just helping to pass the time, he discovers that *making up stories can be a pleasure in itself*. He thinks that perhaps White and Black are brothers and that a large sum of money is at stake: an inheritance, for example, or the capital invested in a partnership. . . . Another theory that Blue puts forward has White and Black as rivals, both of them racing toward the same goal: the solution to a scientific problem, for example. . . . Day by day, the list of these stories grows. . . . As the days go on, Blue realizes there is no end to the stories he can tell. For Black is no more than a kind of blankness, a hole in the texture of things, and one story can fill this hole as well as any other.[42]

In the same way, a story can fill a blank sheet of paper. Blue also begins, defensively, to hypothesize that White has tricked him and is actually watching *him*: "This would make White *the real writer* then—and Black no more than his stand-in, a fake, an actor with no substance of his own" (my emphasis).[43]

If, according to Auster, the detective is an ersatz writer, then we can use that notion to look at Mamet's *Homicide* in a new way. This would not be the case if it were simply a routine genre picture, but it is a highly original work (an "art film" *policier*), in which word and image play central roles. *Homicide* concerns Jewish Baltimore police detective Robert Gold (Joe Mantegna), who, as the film opens, is involved in a major case involving an African American drug dealer. By chance, he gets sidetracked from that assignment when he stops at another crime scene, a murder of an elderly white variety store owner in a black ghetto. The proprietress-victim is a Jewess (as we learn from a Star of David pendant around her neck), and her family is convinced that her death is a hate crime. As her son, Dr. Klein (J. S. Block), says upon arrival at the bloody scene: "It never stops." There is some immediate evidence that his conjecture might be true, since an African American neighborhood kid calls the dead woman "a Jew broad," and asserts that she had a "fortune in her basement" (tapping into stereotypes of Jewish wealth). Gold (an agnostic and assimilated Jew whose very name speaks to the associations of Jews and money) dismisses this theory and tries to dump the seemingly insignificant case he has inadvertently stumbled upon.

He fails, however, and later that day is told that Dr. Klein has reported gunshots on the roof of his apartment building; Gold is sent to investigate. Clearly, he thinks that the Klein family is hysterical and has heard automobile backfire. Dr. Klein, sensitive to Gold's condescension, responds: "When the fantasy is true, when we've been killed, then you say 'what a coincidence.' . . . That at the same time we were being paranoid, someone was coincidentally trying to hurt us." While at the Kleins,' Gold receives a phone call from headquarters and leaves the doctor to retreat to another room, complaining to his caller: "I'm stuck here with my Jews . . . buncha' high-strung fuckin' bullshit, they pay so much taxes . . . Fuck 'em." Clearly, his refusal to identify as a Jew has turned into outright hatred of the group. He continues: "You tell me. Ten more bucks a week they're making lettin' her work down there? Not . . . 'my' people, baby. . . . Fuck 'em, there's so much anti-Semitism, last four thousand years, they must be doin' *something* bring it about." Here, we find Gold accepting notions of the Jew as greedy (sending old ladies to work for a few dollars more). We also recognize parallels between his statement about racial hatred and a line from one of Mamet's plays (*The Disappearance of the Jews*) in which a Jewish character relates a comment someone made to him: "If you've been persecuted so long, eh, you must have brought it on yourself."[44]

While, on the one hand, this scene in *Homicide* positions Gold as divorced from Jewish self-identity, on the other, it is here that his feelings start to change. He is overheard complaining by Dr. Klein's daughter (Rebecca Pidgeon, Mamet's second wife). She realizes he is Jewish and asks him if he is not ashamed for saying what he has. "Do you hate yourself that much . . . do you belong nowhere?" she inquires. He apologetically promises to pursue her grandmother's killer.

At this point, however, a second explosion is heard in the apartment and, when Gold looks out a window, he sees a man running on the roof. Now taking Klein's claim more seriously, he sprints upstairs, but the stranger gets away. He surveys the scene and finds a pigeon coop as well as a folded paper scrap on the ground that reads GROFAZ. When he returns to the Kleins' apartment (still unconvinced he heard a gunshot), he begins to explore some photographs of the murdered woman (in her youth) on the wall. As he straightens one hung crookedly, another snapshot drops down from behind it. It pictures the same woman (probably in the

1940s) holding a rifle and smiling. He picks up a magnifying glass and sees that, at the woman's feet, is a box of guns.

This piques his curiosity enough for him to return to the crime scene where he notices some posters taped to a building that blame Jews for ghetto poverty. When he descends into the variety store basement, he finds an empty crate that once contained "tommy guns." He locates an invoice in it, dated 1948, as well as a list of Semitic names (ostensibly customers for the munitions). We assume that he is beginning to connect old Mrs. Klein's past with the rise of the Jewish state in the late 1940s and with Irgun soldiers who fought on its behalf. Hence, Gold's initial certainty that Dr. Klein is paranoid about anti-Semitism becomes more tenuous as he connects the dots and rewrites the story.

What Gold finds in the basement leads him to reconsider the explosions heard by the Kleins as well as to ponder the meaning of the word GROFAZ on the crumpled paper. He therefore goes to a Jewish library to investigate. He learns that, rather than being nonsensical, the term was once used at the end of World War II to signify Adolf Hitler as "the greatest strategist of all time." He asks the librarian to get the file on this topic. As he waits for the information, another researcher stares at him intently. Gold assumes the man is troubled by his gun and explains that he is a police detective. The scholar, however, responds that what upsets him is actually Gold's badge—a five-pointed star. He says: "The pentagram . . . it is identified as a star, but it is not the symbol of heaven. It is the symbol of earth . . . the Mogen David is the intersection of the opposites and can be deconstructed into heaven and earth, but the pentagram cannot be deconstructed." He then asks Gold if he is a Jew, implying that, if he is, his allegiance should be to the Mogen David and not the police badge—to the spiritual realm versus the state. About to show Gold the text he is reading, the scholar asks if he knows Hebrew. When Gold says no, the scholar chides: "You say you're a Jew and you can't read Hebrew? What are you then?" Again, Gold is shamed for his decision "to be nothing," to be what Mamet has elsewhere deemed an "ex-Jew." As Mamet asks in *The Wicked Son* (2006): "Why would anyone who possessed a heritage, racial, cultural, or otherwise, prefer to 'just be nothing'? Can one simply choose to embrace a negative, and must not such a choice be, effectually, a repudiation? Why would assimilated Jews (Jews by race or cultural heritage) choose to repudiate a culture, a history, and a religion about which they knew nothing?"[45] Mamet also mocks those Jews who want to select certain elements of their religion and culture while rejecting others. Such a Jew "feels that, rationally, a person . . . may be free to choose, to opt out of any inconvenient association, free of debt, and so of guilt. But he may not and is pursued by an unquenchable sense of loss. He may identify this loss as a desire for justice, for redress, for equality, for freedom. The sense of loss will persist. His guilt and anxiety are not for the unfortunate state of the world but for his identity. This identity cannot exist outside the tribe."[46] No wonder Gold feels alienation and anomie.

When the librarian informs Gold that the file on GROFAZ has been borrowed by someone else, the detective sneaks a look at the individual's address and sets out to go there. What he finds upon arrival is an underground Jewish cell, comprising elderly veterans of the Israeli war of independence as well as younger, radical fighters against contemporary anti-Semitism. He tells them he wants to help and hands them a photocopy of the list of individuals found in the rifle box at the variety store (assuming that it is an important document). But the group wants the original. Gold explains that it has already been entered as official evidence and that he cannot violate police rules by removing it. They throw him out—mocking his lack of commitment to the cause. One of them tells him, "Be a Jew!" and shouts: "Where are your loyalties? You want the glory, you want the home, [but] you are willing to do nothing."

As he leaves the building, he reencounters Chava (Natalija Nogulich), a woman whom he had encountered at the Kleins' apartment—again connecting the issue of anti-Semitism to old Mrs. Klein's death. He tells Chava that he wants to help the cause, and the two sit in a diner and talk. It is here that Gold confesses hurtful elements of being a Jew on the police force. He feels he has been made a hostage negotiator because he is seen as an outsider. His assignment also reflects stereotypes of the Jews as good "talkers" versus actors (his partner Sullivan [William Macy] calls him "the orator"). He reveals that he has been called a "pussy" all his life (tapping into notions of Jewish male effeminacy), and that it was said that one might as well send in a "broad" as a Jew to do violent police work. We recall that Sullivan had asked Gold why he always strives to be the first one in the door at a police raid and we realize that this has been a compensatory act. Gold calls the Jewish men he has just met "heroes" and wonders what it is like to "have your own country," not to work for someone else, a question he, more than others, might well ask since he works for the state. He begs to assist Chava in her fight and we surmise (since she is carrying a suspicious black suitcase) that she intends to plant a bomb at a store that fronts a neo-Nazi group responsible for the anti-Semitic posters we have previously seen. Gold insists that he be the one to detonate it (thus entirely abnegating his role in law enforcement). His allegiance to the six- versus five-pointed star is seemingly complete.

Significantly, the store that Gold blows up is a train hobby shop and, when he enters it, we see numerous models, some in dioramas replete with toy soldiers. Clearly, trains have a charged history in events of the Holocaust since they were used to transport Jews to the camps. Realizing this, Gold smashes some of the displays. In order to find the neo-Nazi heart of the shop, Gold must go through a series of doors. In the stockroom, he finds a brown shirt with a swastika. Opening a second door, he locates a printing press and a Nazi flag. The camera pans over a series of anti-Semitic tracts, one of which reads: "The admixture of Jewish blood into the clan's White Race is a crime against humanity." He sets off the bomb, escapes, and drives with Chava back to the diner. There, however, some of the men from the Jewish cell appear once more demanding the original list of names found in the rifle box. When he refuses, they produce photos of him blowing up the

FIGURE 12. Detective Robert (Bobby) Gold (Joe Mantegna) discovers a secret Nazi print shop in *Homicide* (1991).

hobby shop and it is clear that they intend to blackmail him. This is the first sign that Gold's turn to Jewish identity may not be entirely benign—that it is fraught with its own problems, that no group is exempt from bad behavior.

The negative ramifications of his act grow even stronger when Gold realizes that he has missed an assignation with Sullivan who is still involved in the drug case. By the time Gold arrives on the scene, Sullivan has been shot and soon thereafter dies. Hence, Gold's allegiance to one star has caused the death of a beloved partner associated with the other. To avenge Sullivan, Gold singlehandedly pursues the fugitive drug dealer and, though the latter is eventually arrested, Gold is seriously wounded in the process.

The film ends with Gold returning to the detective squad some months later (ostensibly after medical leave), still showing signs of injury. His fellow cops treat him coldly and his superior tells him that they have solved the case of the variety store murder. We then see the African American kids who had been present at the crime scene emerge from an office and state that they killed Mrs. Klein for her alleged stash of money. Finally, someone hands Gold a file folder and, when he opens it, he learns that the paper on which GROFAZ had been written is actually a fragment of a bag for GROFAZT feed (i.e., grow fast), a pigeon food that was likely used for the birds in the rooftop coop. As the camera pulls back, we leave Gold sitting stunned on a chair in the police station corridor, with his story in need of another revision. Like Blue in Auster's "Ghosts," he has learned that one's subject of inquiry "is no more than a kind of blankness, a hole in the texture of things, and one story can fill this hole as well as any other."[47]

Several things are noteworthy about the film. First, in the figure of Gold puzzling out the narrative of Mrs. Klein's death, we see an illustration of Auster's notion of the detective as storyteller—someone who sequentially constructs various versions of a tale, with alternate motives, trajectories, and denouements. Initially, Gold posits that the woman's demise is simply the result of ghetto crime; then he believes that it is part of an anti-Semitic plot. The latter theory has diverse accounts of good guys and bad. On the one hand, the members of the Jewish cell are heroes; on the other, they are villains. By the end of the narrative, he is back to where he started, with the woman's death fueled by common greed.

Second, the creation of Gold's story line involves the interpretation of both alphabet and image in an attempt to crack a code. He dismisses Dr. Klein's theory of a hate crime until he sees the photo of Mrs. Klein as a young woman in the 1940s holding a gun—one that alerts him to her former role in the fight for Jewish independence. Having put his faith in the image, he then becomes retrospectively curious about the relevance of a verbal clue he has found and previously dismissed: the nonsensical word GROFAZ written on a scrap of paper. This, of course, leads him to the Jewish library where he learns that the term (an acronym) signifies Hitler. While this is not wrong, it turns out to be irrelevant, since the particular paper fragment he has obtained is merely part of a label for GROFAZT pigeon food. Thus, his reading of a photograph has led to his misreading of a word. Photography trips him up in yet another way, since it documents his bombing of the hobby shop and provides a means to blackmail him. Thus, neither word nor image has provided him truth.

Other visual and verbal signs are relevant to his investigation of the crime. In the Jewish library, a scholar interprets for him two visual icons: the pentagram (a symbol of the state) and the Mogen David (a symbol of ethnic/religious identity). Furthermore, when he breaks into the hobby shop, he is greeted by three pictorial emblems that strengthen his resolve to detonate a bomb: a brown shirt, a swastika, and the Nazi flag. He also encounters a series of inflammatory words in the form of anti-Semitic tracts that have been duplicated on an arcane printing press, which, strangely, resembles a medieval torture device. Since his terrorist act leads to his entrapment by extortionists, his reading of verbal and visual signs has again failed him, despite the fact that he has seemingly read them correctly. Significantly, his literacy has been challenged earlier, when a scholar in the library is shocked to learn that the Jewish detective cannot read Hebrew. Finally, in the Jewish cell's puzzling insistence on Gold producing for them the actual list of names he found in Mrs. Klein's basement, we get a discourse on questions of the original versus the copy—which reminds us of Barthes's statement that literature is always a version of prior texts.

Ultimately, given Mamet's interest in Jewish issues, one wonders how to interpret the denouement of the film. On the one hand, Gold seems to have made a transition toward cultural identity that the author would applaud. On the other hand, Gold's foray into Jewish consciousness leads to his taking a wrong turn in a murder case and to fatally failing his partner. So Gold's Jewish quest ultimately seems as negative as it is positive. Perhaps that is why Mamet has commented: "I am neither expecting people to call the film anti-Semitic, nor will I be surprised if they do."[48] There is another possible reading of the film that is less dismissive of Gold's pursuit. If one believes that the neo-Nazi group that he uncovers is real (and not, as some have argued, an elaborate fiction to maneuver him into being blackmailed), then we have learned that even when one makes mistakes in investigating anti-Semitism, one will simply uncover yet another (and perhaps unrelated) case of the same phenomenon.[49] In other words, no matter where one looks (on the correct or incorrect trail, to word or image), one will hit the mark.

There is yet a final aspect of the film's conclusion that bears consideration and relates to Mamet's thoughts on writing. In 3 Uses of the Knife — On the Nature and Purpose of Drama (1998), he discusses his reservations about the so-called "problem play" which he calls "a melodrama cleansed of invention" that infantilizes the spectator.[50] It presents a "false struggle," gives the spectator a sham sense of power, tells her what she already knew, and offers indignation "undergone in safety."[51] Worse yet, it is unsatisfying: the viewer's concern about the problem reasserts itself the moment she leaves the theater.[52] To the extent that Homicide fits this genre (a film about the problem of religious/cultural identification and difference), Mamet seeks to pull the rug out from under us, disabuse us of the notion that all will be settled at the end, that we will have gleaned a clear message. Rather, Mamet prefers Tragedy, which avows human powerlessness, involves heroes "unfit for the journey they must take." As he notes, referencing the audience: "I'm not going to give them what they want if what they want is a lie."[53]

There are also formal aspects of the film that are interesting in and of themselves and have ramifications for its complex theme. The film starts in medias res with a group of armored, hooded, gun-toting FBI enforcers in a tenement house, sneaking upstairs for a raid on (what we later learn) is a drug dealer's apartment. Since they are trying to be quiet, they only mime to one another and do not talk. This conforms to Mamet's theory of filmmaking, which stresses the visual over the verbal. As he comments: "Basically, the perfect movie doesn't have any dialogue. So you should always be striving to make a silent movie" (as the youthful Paul Auster once did).[54]

Homicide is also a "police procedural," a genre in which the reader follows a law enforcement professional as he goes through the codified steps of cracking a case and, as we have seen, inventing a series of stories in the process, replacing one with the other as circumstances dictate. In a sense, Mamet also sees the task of filmmaking as requiring a systematic set of rules. As he writes: "The film is directed in the making of the shot list. The work on the set is simply to record what has been chosen to be recorded. It is the plan that makes the movie."[55] For Mamet this is not an empty or merely conventional dictum but a means of liberating the imagination. As he remarks: "*The purpose of technique is to free the unconscious.* If you follow the rules ploddingly, they will allow your unconscious to be free. That's true creativity. If not, you will be fettered by your conscious mind. Because the conscious mind always wants to be liked and wants to be interesting. The conscious mind is going to suggest the obvious, the cliché, because these things offer the security of having succeeded in the past." (emphasis in the original).[56] When Gold abandons the logic of the detective's rulebook, his unconscious is likewise unshackled. But, rather than the creativity of art, he finds the confusion of paranoia as well as its flip side—the lesson that even paranoids have enemies.

WOODY ALLEN

> I believe there is something out there watching us. Unfortunately, it's the government.
> —Woody Allen

While paranoia is frightening in *Homicide*, in the work of Woody Allen it becomes comic. But pithy *bons mots* are not the only literary products for which Allen is known. Though he is viewed primarily as a filmmaker, he has always had considerable renown as a writer. He began, of course, by providing jokes for comics like Sid Caesar and Art Carney, as well as writing for such humorous television programs as *Candid Camera*, *The Ed Sullivan Show*, and *The Tonight Show*. Later in his career, he penned his own stand-up comedy routines and then became famous for droll and sophisticated belles lettristic short stories and essays for such magazines as *The New Yorker*, *Playboy*, and *The Evergreen Review*. He also succeeded as a Broadway playwright. *Don't Drink the Water* premiered in 1966 and *Play It Again, Sam* in 1969. While the latter was adapted as a film, it was not directed by Allen but by Howard Morris. Allen eventually did, however, direct and star in a television version (in 1994). He has also written several one-act plays (e.g., *Writer's Block*, *Riverside Drive*, *Central Park West*, and *Old Saybrook*).[57]

Interestingly, in relation to the oeuvre of Auster and Mamet, several of Allen's short stories have involved detectives—specifically, "The Whore of Mensa," "Mr. Big," and "Match Wits with Inspector Ford."[58] More intriguingly, though, much of Allen's literary output has been about apocryphal writers and writings. Thus, if Auster saturates his published work with references to the movies, Allen steeps his with references to literature. "The Metterling Lists," for instance, purports to be reprints of the laundry lists of a famous author. "The Schmeed Memoirs" presents itself as the published recollections of Hitler's barber. "Conversations with Helmholtz" alleges to be passages from a book about a contemporary of Freud. "Viva Varga!" claims to be excerpts from the diary of a revolutionary. "The Irish Genius" stands as selections from the annotated poems of (the fictional) Sean O'Shawn. "Fabulous Tales and Mythical Beasts" proposes itself as extracts from a forthcoming book of world literature. "Fine Times: An Oral Memoir" alleges to be

selections from the published reminiscences of Flo Guiness (an invented personage). Finally, "By Destiny Denied" masquerades as "notes from an eight-hundred-
page novel" that never existed.[59]

Moreover, one of Allen's essayistic pieces, "But Soft . . . Real Soft," humorously
tackles authorship head on. Here, he discusses the fact that many scholars think
that Shakespeare was not the individual who wrote the plays and poems attributed to him. Most recently, Allen notes, it is Christopher Marlowe whose name
surfaces as the true auteur. But, as he inquires, "If Marlowe wrote Shakespeare's
works, who wrote Marlowe's?" Furthermore, he concludes: "Under the new theory, it is actually Marlowe who was married to Anne Hathaway, a match which
caused Shakespeare no end of grief, as they would not let him in the house."[60]
Allen then goes on to allege that "Marlowe's young wife took up the pen and continued to write the plays and sonnets we all know and avoid today." The subterfuge
of authorship spins even further out of control. As Allen continues: "In an effort to
conceal Marlowe from Shakespeare, should they prove to be the same person, [Sir
Francis] Bacon had adopted the fictitious name of Alexander Pope, who in reality
was Pope Alexander, head of the Roman Catholic Church."

In this context, it is interesting to consider the film *Deconstructing Harry* (1997),
one of Allen's works about a writer-protagonist (played by the director himself).[61]
Even the use of the word "deconstructing" in the film's title (with its reference to
lofty academic theories) indicates that Allen sees himself among the literati. Like
Paul in *Smoke*, the hero of the film is a novelist, and, as ever, is frequently pictured
before his arcane typewriter. Similar to many works of this kind (*Paris When It
Sizzles* [1964] and *How is Your Fish Today?* [2006], discussed in chapter 3, or *Providence* [1977], in chapter 5), the film mixes sequences of the artist at work with
those of his novelistic visions — not a highly original technique. But, occasionally,
Allen manages to give the strategy some innovative twists.

He begins the drama without letting on that it is about a writer or that we are
actually "within" one of his fictions. The scene is a lovely country barbecue (like
an American version of the picnic in Ingmar Bergman's *A Lesson in Love* [1954]).
Ken (Richard Benjamin) annoys his wife Janet by remaining in the house to watch
a baseball game rather than joining the group outside. Soon her sister Leslie (Julia
Louis-Dreyfus) goes into the house as well. The two (who are clearly having an
illicit affair) begin to make love by a window, but Ken's desire is thwarted when
he catches sight of his wife outside. The scene turns farcical when a blind, elderly
relative enters the room and is completely unaware that the couple is having sex.

The scene then cuts to an entirely unrelated event: a woman (Judy Davis) exits
from a cab on a city street (as presented in a repetitive and visually disjunctive
manner). She arrives at writer Harry Block's (Woody Allen) apartment. Livid,
she reads to him a passage from his newest books that resembles the sequence
we have just watched, making clear that he and she (Lucy) were the real lovers
on which it was based. She claims that her family has recognized her in his fiction
and that, consequently, they know that she betrayed her sister, then Harry's wife.

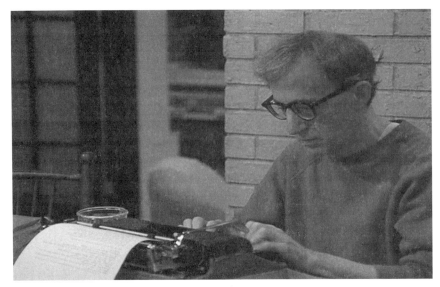

FIGURE 13. Writer Harry Block (Woody Allen) works at his typewriter in *Deconstructing Harry* (1997).

He counters that the story was only "loosely based" on their liaison and justifies this by mentioning the blind grandmother (who was made up). In arguing, the two of them keep confusing the names of the actual and fictional individuals: she calls her sister Janet (instead of Jane) and he calls her Leslie (instead of Lucy). She accuses him of being a "black magician" who turns the misery of others into gold. Finally, she aims a gun at him and shoots. Thus the film begins with the (almost) Death of the Author. It also draws on a technique that Luis Buñuel used in *That Obscure Object of Desire* (1977) of two actors playing the "same" part—here, ones that are imagined (Leslie and Ken) and others that are real (Lucy and Harry). Clearly, this tactic also makes apparent, in a tangible way, the manner in which the author (here a fictional one) draws upon his biography (while transforming it)— a fact to which auteur critics attend but their opponents ignore. We will have more to say about this process in our later discussion of *Providence*.

Throughout the drama, we shift between these two worlds—actual and imagined—in a dizzying relay of characters whose reality status leaves us confused. Not only is the real author Allen doubled by Harry (who shares his body), but he is secondarily duplicated by Ken, Harry's fictional stand-in. As the film progresses, however, it prepares us more (and rather obviously) for the moves between levels of "fidelity." In one scene, for instance, Harry sees his shrink and discusses his anxiety about returning to the college from which he was expelled on the occasion of its honoring him. Here, we have a second reference to Ingmar Bergman (perhaps another alter ego for Allen/Ken)—specifically to *Wild Strawberries* (1957), in which an elderly academician travels to a university to receive a medal. Sensing his patient's angst, the psychiatrist reminds Harry of a story he once wrote. When the scene switches to a new and unrelated locale, the viewer realizes that she is watching a visualization of that whimsical tale. The vignette it presents is also noteworthy from a cinematic perspective. It concerns an actor, Mel (Robin Williams), who is on a film set when the cinematographer looks through the lens and finds Mel "soft," or out of focus. At first he thinks that something is wrong with the camera, but then he realizes that Mel's body is the problem. When Mel returns home, he appears out of focus to his family, who assume he is ill. They take him to a doctor, who, rather than solving Mel's corporeal irregularity, gives his family corrective eyeglasses so that they will view Mel normally and not get "seasick." For the latter part of this sequence, Allen's voiceover narration is heard—a further nod (beyond his status as a star of the picture) to his authorial position. Harry's psychiatrist sees his patient's story as indicating that he wants others to adjust to his personality "distortions" rather than change himself. The issue of existential blurriness resurfaces later in the film when Harry arrives at the college that is celebrating him. Now he (the writer versus his character) becomes "out of focus"—a sign of fiction infecting reality as well as of his neurotic panic at being unworthy of tribute.

There are other productive collisions between the author and his characters in the film, with both types incarnated onscreen. At one point, Harry meets Ken (his fictional self) in an amusement park (like the old academician and his younger self sharing the frame in *Wild Strawberries*). He fails to recognize him (though we do) until Ken says: "I'm you, thinly disguised" (ironic since he is far more handsome than Harry). When Ken tells him to think about the past, Harry looks through an arcade peep-show machine and (through a matte, mimicking the eyepiece) we witness (in color more muted than present-day sequences) a scene between Lucy and her sister Jane (Amy Irving), in which the latter talks of the dissolution of her marriage to Harry.

While most of the scenes that represent Harry's fictional fantasies look realistic, this one is more interesting since it has the whimsical, far-fetched quality of some of Allen's literary pieces. Here, for example, one thinks of "The Kugelmass Episode," about a college professor who is unhappily married and longs for new love and romance.[62] He is so desperate that he consults a magician, The Great Persky, who tells him to step into a Chinese cabinet. Persky says: "If I throw any novel into this cabinet with you, shut the doors, and tap it three times, you will find yourself projected into that book." Kugelmass decides that he wants to have a French lover and chooses *Madame Bovary*. Sure enough, before long: "He appeared in the bedroom of Charles and Emma Bovary's house at Yonville. Before him was a beautiful woman, standing alone with her back turned to him as she folded some linen. I can't believe this, thought Kugelmass, staring at the doctor's ravishing wife. This is uncanny. I'm here. It's her." On numerous occasions he returns to Persky's place and asks to reenter Flaubert's novel, telling the magician: "Make sure and always get me into the book before page 120. . . . I always have to meet her before she hooks up with this Rodolphe character." With Kugelmass's insertion into Flaubert's narrative, its storyline changes as well, with Emma Bovary asking her new lover about O. J. Simpson, the Academy Awards, *A Chorus Line*, and Jack Nicholson. A Stanford professor is perplexed by these alterations of Flaubert's work. He muses: "Well, I guess the mark of a classic is that you can reread it a thousand times and always find something new." Emma even leaves the space of the novel (France), migrating to Kugelmass's New York City: "Savoring each moment, [Kugelmass] and Emma went to the movies, had dinner in Chinatown, passed two hours at a discotheque, and went to bed with a TV movie. They slept till noon on Sunday, visited SoHo, and ogled celebrities at Elaine's." Eventually, however, Kugelmass needs Emma to disappear back into the novel so that he can resume his regular life. As he tells the magician: "I'm a married man, and I have a class in three hours. I'm not prepared for anything more than a cautious affair at this point." Unfortunately, Persky's attempts to make Emma vanish fail. Kugelmass stashes her at the Hotel Plaza, but she soon grows bored and discontent. She complains: "Get me back into the novel or marry me. . . . I want to get a job or go to class, because watching TV all day is the pits." Eventually, Persky solves the "transmission" problem and returns Emma to the novel, and Kugelmass vows that he has learned a lesson. But, before long, he is back at Persky's door, asking to be transported into Phillip Roth's *Portnoy's Complaint*. This time, however, Persky's magic fails and Kugelmass ends up trapped in the textbook *Remedial Spanish*.

Clearly, this tale anticipates Allen's later film *The Purple Rose of Cairo* (1985), in which a spectator enters a film and a movie character escapes to the real world. But it is the more indirect parallels to *Deconstructing Harry* that I want to pursue since, as we have seen, some of its "stories-within-stories" are equally fanciful and border on moral parables. One such tale (taken from Harry's writings, and based on his first marriage) concerns a shoe salesman who has tired of his wife. His colleague advises him to hire a prostitute to fulfill his sexual desires. To do so, he borrows a friend's apartment for the tryst—that of Mendel Birnbaum, who has recently been hit by a car and hospitalized. Unfortunately on this particular day, Death (a black-hooded figure with a scythe, straight out of Bergman's *The Seventh Seal* [1957]) has come for Birnbaum and happens upon the shoe salesman instead. Though the former tells Death that he is not the person being sought (more mix-ups with characters and their doubles), he is taken anyway.

Another fanciful sequence follows Harry's panic attack upon arrival at his alma mater. He mentions that he is composing a tale about hell and we suddenly find him in an elevator descending to levels of the Inferno. As he passes various floors, he sees people there who are nude and chained, positioned in pornographic poses. He encounters his father who is there for being a bad parent; all the patriarch wants is to go to a Chinese restaurant (an obvious Jewish joke). Ultimately, Harry meets the devil in the form of Larry (Billy Crystal), in real life a romantic rival for Harry's girlfriend. Hell seems quite a wonderful place—air-conditioned (so as to damage the ozone layer), and filled with background jazz music.

The film ends with another flight of the imagination. The college award festivities begin but are interrupted by the entrance of Harry's irate ex-wife (Kirstie Alley), who accuses him of kidnapping their son (whom he has snatched from school to attend the ceremony). To the strains of Richard Rodgers's "I Could Write a Book," all of Harry's literary characters appear and applaud him. He responds by telling them that they "saved his life," since he can only function in art.

Whereas in the story of Kugelmass, the mixture of real and fictional personae leads to disaster, here it offers a means to survive. But ultimately, this is not a satisfying ending. First, it appears too obvious. Second, it seems imitative of yet another European director—Federico Fellini—whose *8 ½* (1963) ends with all the characters a film director has imagined for his movie joining him on the beach. Third, it seems too "uplifting." Fourth, it feels overly narcissistic. Fifth, its autobiographical overtones are too blatant. It is important here to recall the context in which the film was made. On some level, Allen's career had hit a plateau since he was getting too old to play the comic romantic lead in his own movies. Furthermore, he had been embroiled for five years in a scandal around his sexual relationship with partner Mia Farrow's adopted daughter Soon-Yi Previn, thirty-five years his junior. In fact, he married Soon-Yi two weeks after *Deconstructing Harry* was released.[63] Due to the tabloid uproar, he had also become estranged from his only biological child, son Satchel Ronan O'Sullivan Farrow (whom he transposes into Harry's child in the film). Thus, at a time when Allen lacked as many real supporters as he may have wished, he trots out a loyal cast of thousands of his own making. Rather than closing with the ironic cynicism that characterized his best literary pieces (Kugelmass stuck in a Spanish textbook instead of *Portnoy's Complaint*), Allen ends *Deconstructing Harry* with forced (and, we suspect) faux optimism.

As noted, the narrative of *Homicide* emphasizes the difference between original and copy, since the Jewish cell members that Gold encounters insistently reject his offer of a photocopied replica of the paper he has found in Mrs. Klein's gun box. Imitation, here, will not do (though the viewer has no idea why).

In a sense, the refusal to repeat themselves or to present "facsimiles" of their literary work characterizes the films discussed here by Auster, Mamet, and Allen. Mamet was, of course, eventually to break this rule with his own direction of his adapted stage play *Oleanna* in 1994. But original works of cinema that distinguish themselves from a writer's novelistic, essayistic, or theatrical *oeuvre* still constitute the most exciting relation between literature and film—releasing us from the poles of source and derivative, allowing us to observe how an artist works creatively "from scratch"—on a *tabula rasa*—moving from one medium to another.

3 THE AUTHOR AT THE DREAM FACTORY
The Screenwriter and the Movies

BEHIND THE SCREEN

> Hollywood has always had a hate-hate relationship with the writer.
> —Desson Thomas, in Boon, *Script Culture*

It comes as no surprise that when the figure of the author is represented in movies, it is often the screenwriter portrayed. Here, of course, we have a far more direct invocation of the film auteur than in works about the novelist. Almost always, the scenarist is male—and either a cad, a neurotic, a misfit, a miscreant, or a womanizer (and sometimes all five) who is generally cynical about his profession. Before examining such fictional protagonists, however, it would be well to say a few words about the historical position of the screenwriter in Hollywood.

As soon as the movies shifted from the "cinema of attractions" to storytelling, literature played a central role in filmmaking. Often, producers in need of material turned to established sources—be they biblical (*From the Manger to the Cross* [1912]) or classical (*A Midsummer Night's Dream* [1909]). When a film was to be set in the contemporary era, narratives were sometimes "ripped from the headlines." The first screenplays were mere scene lists. Kevin Alexander Boon credits some of the earliest such texts to Georges Méliès (for *Trip to the Moon* [1902]) and Edwin Porter (for *The Great Train Robbery* [1903]).[1] In 1904, the first screenplay was copyrighted (listed as a "dramatic composition"): Frank J. Marion's *The Suburbanite*.[2] Thus, as Boon comments, "the origin of the screenplay proper is primarily a legal issue." As the "scenario" (as it was called) developed through the 1910s, it came to have four requisite sections: synopsis, cast of characters, scene plot (a list of sequences taking place at each location), and continuity (story elements arranged in cinematic form).[3] The final segment most resembles the modern screenplay. By the mid-1920s, the screenplay had become "a literary form in its own right."[4]

Of course, traditionally, New York City had been the mecca for writers, and the 1920s was a period of "unparalleled prosperity in the literary marketplace."[5] But more and more, Hollywood required original stories as the rate of film production grew and demands on film quality escalated. Responding to this need, many East Coast authors left for points west—novelists, playwrights, and newspaper journalists. Sometimes writers could participate in the industry from afar when their literary works were adapted for the screen. While their contributions were noted, they were not necessarily intimately involved in the process.

Soon "story departments" were formed at many Hollywood studios and the role of "scenarist" became a career; appropriately, onscreen film credits began to take cognizance of this job. If a writer were not the author of a script, she might, instead, be employed to compose intertitles—a distinct skill of its own. Some producers prided themselves on attracting prestigious talent. Samuel Goldwyn, for instance, created the Eminent Authors program in 1919 and hired renowned scribes such as Mary Roberts Rinehart, Elinor Glyn, Elmer Rice, and Rex Beach. Such artists were given a percentage of box office receipts as well as a regular salary. While the program had successes, it also had failures, and it was disbanded in 1923. Some of its writers had long given up on the program. As Glyn notes: "No one wanted our advice or assistance, nor did they intend to take it. All they required was the use of our names to act as shields against the critics."[6] While most screenwriters in the silent era were male, some women (aside from Glyn and Rinehart) assumed this position, for instance Jean Gauntier, June Mathis, and Jeanie Macpherson.

With the coming of sound, film drama became more urbane and there was a greater call for sophisticated screenwriters (frequently culled from the theatrical world). Furthermore, the Depression, which followed on the heels of the introduction of sound, hit the New York publishing world hard. Thus, many East Coast authors (including Ben Hecht, Lawrence Stallings, Clifford Odets, Herman Mankiewicz, F. Scott Fitzgerald, and Nathanael West) went to California. While most were male, some East Coast women also made the change: Sonya Levien, Lillian Hellman, and Dorothy Parker. Fueling this exit was the added fear that the "talking picture" might kill stage drama. For many, however, Hollywood remained the "Great Destroyer," with F. Scott Fitzgerald (who first arrived there in 1927) viewed as its most notorious casualty. As S. J. Perelman once commented: "The mere mention of Hollywood induces a condition in me like breakbone fever. It was a hideous and untenable place when I dwelt there, populated with few exceptions by Yahoos."[7] Similarly, Robert Nathan said that when first offered a job in the movie capital, he never dreamed of accepting it.[8]

Alternately, certain East Coast authors spoke positively of their experience in the movie capital and were grateful to receive regular wages in an era of unemployment. Irwin Shaw remarked: "Hollywood only ruins those who want to be ruined." And James Cain gushed: "The capacity of a studio to make life agreeable to you, indeed, savors almost of the magical."[9] Even Nathan finally changed his tune:

"I found that I really loved the whole motion picture life—the studio, the sound stages, and all the excitement."[10]

As Richard Fine has observed in his book *Hollywood and the Profession of Authorship*, many emigrant writers found the authorial cultures of East and West radically different: "A writer's talent was not under attack in Hollywood so much as the *profession of authorship* as he had known it. . . . In short, working in Hollywood inevitably challenged, and in some cases shattered, many of the traditional notions about the nature of the professional writer's trade and life" (my emphasis).[11] In the New York literary world, writers held considerable power and had strong bonds with their publishers. As Fine comments: "A handful of ambitious, anti-traditionalist young publishers played an important role in nurturing [a] belief that American literature had finally come of age." One of these was Horace Liveright, who worked with such figures as Eugene O'Neill, Theodore Dreiser, Sherwood Anderson, Robinson Jeffers, Hart Crane, Ezra Pound, and E. E. Cummings. While a publisher certainly had the right to a profit or to recoup his losses, if a book thrived it was understood that "both author and publisher should share equally in that success." Furthermore, while publishers were consulted on such decisions as choice of title, jacket design, advertising copy, and typography, they "were loath to interfere with a writer's creative process." A similar ethic obtained in the theater world, where the playwright was generally more famous than the stage director.[12] Hence, on the East Coast, the writer had the sense of being a valued and respected intellectual.

In Hollywood, however, writers were often viewed by producers as "an independent lot, often irreverent toward studio policy and potentially troublesome."[13] However, according to Nathan, a writer's treatment by executives "depended on how much money [he] made." One was more likely to be respected "if [he] were not really dependent on motions pictures" for his income.[14] Writers were frequently warned of the "gap between reading and viewing public[s]" and made to feel like elitist intellectuals. Jack Warner notoriously asked of a script: "Will it play in Peoria?"[15] The screenplay, rather than being viewed as a literary work, was seen as a mere production blueprint. Moreover, writers were unwelcome on the set once filming began. There were often tensions between authors and the staff of the scenario department over story ideas. Writers were shocked at their own lack of creative control and the fact that (if on contract) they were assigned to projects they disliked. Often they were typecast for genres, limiting their imaginative range. Furthermore, censorship constrained the type of material with which they could deal (e.g., extramarital romance, pregnancy, homosexuality, drugs, and radical politics). Sometimes, a favored script they had written failed to be produced. Finally, in some studios (e.g., Columbia and Warner Bros.), writers were expected to work a nine-to-five day in the office and produce a minimum number of pages per week.[16] As Fine summarizes the situation: "Many Eastern writers refused to conform to the studio system; many others did so only under the greatest protest; and still others, with little success, sought ways to circumvent the system and re-establish the writer's traditional prerogatives."[17] The formation of the Screenwriter's Guild (later called Writers Guild of America) in 1933 helped to provide them a forum in which to vent their views, complaints, and demands. Nonetheless, as Ronald Davis remarks: "Writers in the big studio era consistently felt underpaid and far less respected than directors and producers."[18]

Apparently, things have not changed much in the ensuing decades. In March 2011, Dana Goodyear wrote in the *New Yorker* about Barry Michels, a psychotherapist who caters to beleaguered Hollywood screenwriters:

> In the hierarchy of Hollywood . . . the writer . . . [is] a pasty loser, whose suggestions are constantly being ignored or overruled. "No one looks to the writer to make the decisions," one of Michels's writer patients said. "You're trying to fulfill everyone's expectations. They think of you almost as an arm to do their thoughts." "We're like carnies, always out there trying to sell some idea," another writer, who sees Michels . . . told me. It can be a frustrating, demoralizing job; scripts are bastardized to the point of being unrecognizable, if they get made at all. According to Michels, "Writers always feel beaten up. They always feel like an underclass. How do you maintain a sense of self in this environment?"[19]

The academic Film Studies field also demeaned the screenwriter, with the director more frequently being viewed as the true auteur. Conversely, a few critics have championed the writer. We have noted how, weighing into a famous controversy, Pauline Kael in *Raising Kane* gives major credit to scenarist Herman Mankiewicz (over "helmer" Welles) in the making of *Citizen Kane* (1941). On the other hand, Robert Carringer (whose view is widely accepted) has strongly countered that claim.[20] And in two other books, *Hollywood Screenwriters* (1972) and *Talking Pictures* (1974), Richard Corliss celebrates the careers of numerous writers and their contributions to the medium.

DRAMATIS PERSONAE

> Out of the thousand writers huffing and puffing through movieland there are scarcely fifty men and women of wit or talent.
>
> —Ben Hecht

This Side of Paradise

Historically, there have been a host of movies that cast the screenwriter as a major character. In most cases, they are pedestrian works that make no attempt self-consciously to mirror the craft of the profession within the style of the film. Lloyd Bacon's *Boy Meets Girl* (1938), for example, is a banal Warner Bros. comedy that begins with a close-up of a "final script" as pages turn to show the film's credits. It concerns two writers, Robert Law (James Cagney) and J. C. Benson (Pat O'Brien), who work at Royal Studio in Hollywood. They make a career of shirking their duty and loafing on the job. While a "Do not disturb" sign hangs on their door, typing noise wafts through it, but the sound is emitted from a phonograph record (as a ruse) and not the writing machine. Law is a self-proclaimed "hack" who claims to have almost won a Pulitzer Prize. Benson is saddled with a spendthrift wife who keeps billing him for her latest Beverly Hills shopping spree. Throughout the movie, the two men run roughshod through the studio, creating chaos, invading sets, and interrupting shoots with their shenanigans. When a studio waitress is revealed to be pregnant, they hatch a harebrained scheme to produce a series of pictures about a cowboy and a baby, which (when actually made) is, surprisingly, successful. Throughout the film, names of real-life Warner stars are dropped: Joan Blondell, Dick Powell, and Bette Davis—so the work serves as a form of self-promotion.

The Bad and the Beautiful (1952), directed by Vincente Minnelli, is a prestigious, star-studded MGM melodrama that uses the screenwriter as a mere plot device. The narrative focuses on film producer Jonathan Shields (Kirk Douglas) and the negative effect he has had on the careers of several other Hollywood notables—actress Georgia Lorrison (Lana Turner), director Fred Amiel (Barry Sullivan), and writer James Lee Bartlow (Dick Powell). All three have been called to the office of studio executive Harry Pebbel (Walter Pidgeon), who tries to convince them to work with Shields again. Each individual relates a tale of harm by the producer—flashbacks providing the drama. When Bartlow relates his "backstory," he talks of once having been a satisfied college writing professor and author of a best-selling book. When Shields inquires about adapting it for the screen, Bartlow initially rejects the idea, but his wife, Rosemary (Gloria Grahame), is intrigued with going to Hollywood. Once there, she continually distracts Bartlow from work. Shields finally suggests that Bartlow retreat to a mountain cabin. Meanwhile, he hires a handsome actor to escort Gloria around town while her husband is away. Tragically, the two run off together and are killed in a plane crash. Bartlow eventually learns of Shields's role in his wife's tryst and death, and this marks the bitter end of their relationship.

Every now and then, however, a film is made that attempts to use the conceit of the screenwriter in a noteworthy fashion. One such work is *In a Lonely Place* (1950), directed by Nicholas Ray, which tells the tale of a film professional within the context of a *noir* frame. It is based on a 1947 novel by Dorothy B. Hughes, which is actually not about a screenwriter, but a displaced World War II soldier, Dix Steele, who stalks women in LA, raping and murdering them (his masculinity issues make us wonder if his name is a pun on "steel dick"). In the film version, Steele (Humphrey Bogart) is a film writer suspected of a woman's murder but ultimately innocent. On one level, *In a Lonely Place* reflects the dismissive attitude toward the screenwriting profession that many Hollywood practitioners have described. As Dana Polan notes, "As a screenwriter Dix is immediately caught up in a nexus of power that means he is never really able to be his own man."[21] Steele mentions that he never sees the pictures he has written, underscoring his contempt for his profession. When a cloakroom girl displays naiveté about a novel she is reading, his agent says: "Remember, *she's* your audience." When offered an assignment he disdains, Steele tells the director that he won't work on a project he doesn't like and is quickly reminded that, given his paucity of recent hits, he can't be "choosy." He retorts by calling the filmmaker a "popcorn salesman" who makes the same movie repeatedly. Thus, *In a Lonely Place* is "a depiction of a whole subculture and its mores"—an unattractive one at that.[22] When the subject of adapting a novel comes up, Steele is told that it requires merely "following the book" —making light of the creative labor entailed. This comment is especially ironic given that the scenarist and adapter of the film we are watching (Andrew Solt and Edmund H. North) did not take that easy route.

What is especially intriguing about the film's script, however, is the way in which it establishes a similarity between authorship and police detection—the very parallel we found in Auster's writing and in Mamet's *Homicide*. Steele is suspected of murdering the aforementioned coat check girl, Mildred Atkinson (Martha Stewart), whom he met the night of her demise. When he encountered her in a restaurant, she was reading a book (*Althea Bruce*) that a director had left with her for Steele to consider adapting. She tells Steele that she has only a few pages left and asks to finish it while he and his friends have a drink. When she later returns the volume, he asks if she will come to his apartment and summarize the plot for him (since he is too lazy to read it). She does so and recounts the narrative, which he clearly scorns. He then gives her taxi money and sends her home. So his tryst with the murder victim has involved the act of storytelling (and nothing more).

After having been questioned by the police, Steele has dinner with his friend on the force, Brub Nicolai (Frank Lovejoy), and his wife Sylvia (Jeff Donnell). Steele's experience as an author leads him to dispute the police theory of the crime and he asks Sylvia and Brub to act out his version of the heinous deed, placing himself in the position of writer/director. When Steele's girlfriend Laurel Gray (Gloria Grahame) later becomes suspicious of Steele and asks Sylvia about his behavior that evening, the latter says, "We were very impressed with his imagination." In conversations with people, Steele often makes macabre statements that relate murder to writing. On one occasion, he says: "I've killed dozens of people in pictures." On another (referring to plotting deaths in fiction), he says, "We so-called creative artists have a great respect for cadavers."

Sylvia becomes convinced that Steele is abnormal and Laurel, too, finds him frightening and "strange." Furthermore, we witness instances where his violent streak is out of control. In one scene, Steele is driving to a bar when his car idles by another vehicle, and one of its passengers recognizes him and begins to talk. Her husband becomes jealous and the two men barely avoid a brawl. Then, having arrived at the bar, another fight erupts and a woman remarks, "There goes Dix again!" Later, angry at Laurel for speaking with the police, Steele speeds off in a car, almost crashing into another vehicle. When its irate driver emerges from his automobile and yells at him, Steele beats the man up, almost pummeling his skull with a rock. We learn that Steele has a criminal record for fighting and drunken behavior. While Atkinson's boyfriend (whom Steele believed to be the murderer from the start) eventually confesses, we are left with the sense that Steele is "guilty" nonetheless, at least of pathological aggression. We also wonder whether there is some relation between this trait and the hardboiled screenplays he fashions—as though the latter contaminates the former.

Billy Wilder's *Sunset Blvd.* (1950) is another intriguing work about the screenwriter—one which uses that plot device to influence storyline and style. It concerns a down-and-out Hollywood scribe, Joe Gillis (William Holden) who, at the outset of the narrative, is heavily in debt and fleeing the "repo" men who wish to commandeer his car. In dodging them, he veers into the driveway of an old mansion. Though his arrival there is accidental, a morose butler (Erich von Stroheim) appears at the front door and ushers him in as though he were expected. Evidently, he has been mistaken for an undertaker who has been summoned to remove the remains of the resident's pet monkey. The house is old and decrepit but clearly was once a grand Los Angeles residence. Gillis soon learns that the person who resides there is former silent screen star Norma Desmond (Gloria Swanson), once a great beauty but now a haggard and eccentric matron—still wearing clothes and makeup from the 1920s.

When she learns that he is a screenwriter, she becomes interested in him and reveals that she is at work on a script for a comeback picture based on the biblical story of Salome (with herself in the lead role). She insists that Gillis read it immediately, and, as he does (his thoughts about it rendered in voiceover narration), she watches him like a predator. He finds the script dreadful and the idea of her playing Salome ludicrous, but realizes that he has stumbled onto a lucrative gig, since she wants to hire him to revise the text. He takes the job, moves in to an apartment on the grounds, and the two set to work. Periodically she "treats" him to screenings of her old movies (which we learn were directed by her butler), and what is interesting is that the shots we see are actual footage of Gloria Swanson in Stroheim's *Queen Kelly* (1929). So fictional and real worlds intersect, both in the casting of the film and the images onscreen. This connection is made even more direct when Norma makes a long-delayed return visit to Paramount Studios and encounters Cecil B. DeMille (played by the director himself).

Before long, Desmond has fallen in love with Gillis and he senses that he is more a gigolo than a script doctor. At times he escapes her clutches and hangs out with his young writer friends, among them Betty Schaefer (Nancy Olson), with whom he falls in love and secretly collaborates on a screenplay. When Norma learns of the affair, she shoots Gillis dead and is taken off by the police. Famously, she mistakes her arrest as a call to the set and exits by exclaiming that she is "ready for her close-up" (which will soon be her mug shot). Aside from its self-reflexive use of Swanson, von Stroheim, and DeMille—and its invocation of the difference between silent and sound cinema—the film is of interest in terms of screenwriting since it actually opens with the end of the drama, with Gillis floating dead in

Desmond's pool. It is, in fact, Gillis's voiceover (as from the grave) that narrates the story that follows in an impossibly posthumous flashback. Thus, not only do we have a drama about a screenwriter, but we also have a script that innovates screen story and style.

In the previous chapter we have mentioned David Mamet's *State and Main* (2000), about a film crew that invades a small Vermont town as a production site. One of the characters is screenwriter Joe White (Philip Seymour Hoffman), about whom we said very little. Though relatively youthful, White seems to be an old-fashioned writer who is tied to his typewriter. In the beginning of the film, he is upset because his machine has been lost in transit and he goes in search of purchasing a new one. Of course, since Waterford is a postcard New England town (presented in a tongue-in-cheek fashion), there is a bookstore that sells old machines. Later on, he even hires a typist so that he can dictate his ideas—another traditional practice uncharacteristic of the computer age.

In the bookstore, he meets owner Ann (Rebecca Pidgeon), a smart, witty, down-to-earth woman with whom he falls in love. It is she who helps him through his writer's block to discover that his screenplay is really about the "quest for purity" (clearly a cliché that Mamet is lampooning and an unlikely theme in the context of Hollywood production). White is further satirized since the key line of his screenplay and the film-in-progress ("The only second chance you get is to make the same mistake twice") is one he "steals" from the conversation of two townsmen (demonstrating Roland Barthes's point that writing is a "tissue of quotations"). The issue of "purity" ironically invades the world of production when White observes the film-to-be's handsome lead actor Bob Barrenger (Alec Baldwin) emerge from a wrecked car with a teenage girl (with whom he has obviously had a liaison). When a town lawyer decides to prosecute Barrenger for statutory rape, the producer and director pressure White to lie when questioned in court. He does so but immediately regrets his decision, only to learn that Ann (suspecting he needed a "trial run") used her amateur theatrical skills to stage his deposition. When the real court date arrives, he decides to tell the truth (and be "pure"), but the prosecutor has been bribed by the producer to drop the case. Hence, White has had a second chance not to "make the same mistake twice," but the opportunity conveniently disappears. Ultimately, Truth and Love triumph in the form of the requisite Happy Couple. While *State and Main* is exceedingly clever in its barbed but affectionate burlesque of film production and in its matching of fictional scenario details to the lives of its characters, it does so on the plane of narrative and not on the level of discourse.

The Anxiety of Influence

Paris When It Sizzles (1964), directed by Richard Quine, is more ambitious in this regard.[23] It concerns screenwriter Robert Benson (William Holden), who is in France leading a dissipated life while unable to finish a commissioned screenplay. His producer is about to arrive to read the nonexistent script, so Benson hires typist Gabrielle Simpson (Audrey Hepburn) to help him complete the project. To do so, she will live in his apartment. Here we recognize the familiar movie theme of male writer and female office assistant that we also find in films such as *My Dear Secretary* (1949).

Where *Paris When It Sizzles* attempts to distinguish itself is in its technique of intermixing Benson's verbal descriptions of the story he crafts (as he dictates it to Simpson) with cinematic visualizations of the tale onscreen, as though it were a finished picture. To further the requisite romance that must ensue between Benson and Simpson, we see the writer's screenplay depicted with Holden and Hepburn in the roles of its lead characters, Rick and Gaby (the trailer for the film foregrounds the actors' dual star power by highlighting the letter "H" that begins both of their names). Of course, some fourteen years earlier, Holden also played a screenwriter in *Sunset Blvd.*

It would seem that the impetus for self-reflexivity in *Paris* issues from its status as an American film made in the shadow of the European New Waves (hence, perhaps, its Parisian setting as well). Significantly, it was written by Julien Duvivier, a French director and scenarist at the end of his career.[24] By 1964, such experimental European films as *Breathless* (1960), *Hiroshima mon amour* (1959), *Cleo from 5 to 7* (1962), and *Shoot the Piano Player* (1960) had been released in France, and such cutting edge works as *L'avventura* (1960), *La notte* (1961), *L'eclisse* (1962), and *8 ½* (1963) in Italy. It is the last (already mentioned in relation to *Deconstructing Harry* [1997]) that is most relevant to *Paris*, as it concerns the making of a film.

The lead character of *8 ½* is Guido Anselmi (Marcello Mastroianni), a film director who is artistically "paralyzed" while shooting his latest project. He seeks a rest cure but, at the spa, is harassed by producers, actors, job-seekers, lovers, church officials, and troubling memories from his past. The dramatic events of the film, while always otherworldly and theatrical, slip between ostensible "real" occurrences (though deformed by Guido's consciousness), reminiscences, and outright fantasies. For instance, a scene occurs between Guido and his wife Luisa (Anouk Aimée) who has come to visit, only to find her husband's mistress in tow. It is highly realistic (and involves them arguing in bed about their marriage). A few scenes later, however, we have a totally fantastic sequence that imagines Guido simultaneously residing with all the women in his life. While Luisa (now dressed as a traditional Italian wife in head scarf) happily cooks and cleans, Guido's myriad paramours parade around, including one dressed like a feathered Folies Bergère showgirl and another who plays the harp. When the showgirl is banished "upstairs" because she is too old (twenty-six), the women turn on Guido (who has just been bathed as though a little boy), complaining that he is a sexist Lothario. Other scenes take us to the terrain of memory (versus hallucination). In one such sequence, we see the young Guido and his schoolboy pals visit La Saraghina (Eddra Gale), the town whore.

What is especially interesting here is that, in the figure of Guido, we see the problem of assigning authorship to a work of cinema. While he is the film's director, he is treated as the creator of its overall narrative shape. Hence, people continually ask him whether he has decided what the film is about. He has already ordered a faux rocket launching pad to be constructed as a set, but he appears unsure of how to use it. Thus, Guido seems responsible for the movie's "story" while, perhaps, others craft its screenplay. So, who is the true author here? The film says Guido—since other writers are entirely absent. His position clearly mirrors that of Fellini in formulating *8 ½*. He and Ennio Flaiano get credit for the "story" while several others for the "screenplay." Furthermore, it is widely known that the plot of *8 ½* borrows heavily from Fellini's life.

Numerous lines in *Paris When It Sizzles* make reference to the vital, European filmmaking scene. Simpson talks of having worked for a "New Wave director" who makes very "avant-garde" films and believes that the only important action onscreen is what doesn't happen. One of that director's films, *The Scrabble Game Will Not Take Place*, is about people who assemble to play a game but decide not to; his next film *Blow Out No Candles* will reputedly be about a birthday party that is canceled (here, we think of Andrew Sarris's clever pseudonym for Antonioni: Antoni*ennui*). Ultimately, Benson tells Simpson that he is more of an "Old Wave man." Later, he advises her to stop going to "art theaters" and to watch more "American family pictures."

Paris employs a variety of techniques to announce its cleverness (the very enunciation of which tends to negate its wit). When Simpson arrives and asks about the picture Benson is writing, he pulls a ridiculous title out of thin air (*The Girl Who Stole the Eiffel Tower*) and then begins to relate the story we have already witnessed onscreen (a young girl living in Paris comes to work for a debauched playboy-author). Simpson then eagerly sits down at the typewriter as Benson dictates; his discourse is peppered with cinematic terms like "Fade In, Exterior Day." For the first time, we zoom into Benson's face as he speaks and begin to see a version of what he is imagining onscreen. Periodically, he says "No!" indicating that he does not like the direction his tale is taking, and we return to Benson and Simpson in the apartment working. Sometimes, his dictation leads to in-jokes, as when he describes a scene in which Marlene Dietrich will emerge from a Paris cab —which is followed by a shot of the actress just so. When, in the film-within-a-film, Tony Curtis takes the role of Gaby's boyfriend, he acts (in an over-the-top fashion) the part of a beatnik and hipster (and self-proclaimed "New Wave stud"), but he also comments on his supposed Method acting skills and on breaking the "fourth wall." Later, one character interrupts the story to tell Curtis that he is getting very low billing in the film, and another denigrates his part by calling it "a literary convenience." At one point, Benson describes someone in his film as driving a Rolls Royce (which we see onscreen), but then he decides that the automobile should be a Bentley. Like magic, the vehicle depicted is transformed. Later, when Benson revises his script, his voiceover describes the opening of the film he imagines—how the title will appear, what the theme song will be, and who will sing it. As he mentions Frank Sinatra, the crooner's voice is heard.

Often as Benson narrates (and we watch the film-to-be onscreen), we hear the sound of Simpson's typewriter in the background (making clear that the work we are watching is an illustration of the dictated/transcribed text). Benson often speaks in terms of narrative clichés (and says he will soon pen a screenwriting textbook). Thus, he mentions plot "switches," "conflicts," "the other man," "boy meets girl," and "the mysterious stranger." Numerous times, the tale that is spun is entirely outrageous (as when someone morphs into a vampire). When Benson invokes such optical devices as a freeze-frame, reverse motion, or fade, the screen complies—doing precisely what the script-in-progress commands. And, at the end of the film, when the couple embraces, the printed words "kiss" and "fade out" actually appear onscreen (as though lifted from the script). In one instance, Benson dictates how a dissolve should follow a love scene between Gaby and Rick that we are watching. When the film cuts back to the apartment, Simpson asks Benson whether he'll "get away" with the sequence (referencing Hollywood's response to potential censorship), to which he replies, "We dissolved, didn't we?" In another scene in the film-to-be, Gaby is shown pointing a revolver at Rick (as the genre turns to *policier*). When we return to Benson's apartment, her hand is pointing toward him in a mimed, gun-like pose as she asks, "What happens next?" The fact that one of the myriad story lines of the film-to-be entails cops and robbers (with Rick a suave thief/race-car driver/piano player who deals with microfilm and Interpol) reminds us that, by 1964, two of the British James Bond movies had been made and proven popular: *Dr. No* (1962) and *From Russia with Love* (1963) —more European films with which Hollywood had to compete.

Other parodic moments ensue. After Simpson has spent her first night in Benson's apartment (chastely, in a spare room) and she emerges in the morning, he takes her head lovingly in his hands and, suddenly, on the sound track, we hear Fred Astaire singing "That Face." Benson also mimes a viewfinder with his fingers to frame her visage. Suddenly the couple begins to dance, after which Benson comments how it is unfortunate that he's not writing a musical. What is doubly ironic about this moment is that, in 1957, Hepburn had appeared in the musical *Funny Face* with Astaire playing a fashion photographer (hence the mimed viewfinder). Other movie references emerge in *Paris*. At one point, Simpson observes that the film Benson is crafting is a lot like *My Fair Lady* (1964)—a work, starring Hepburn, that would be released some seven months after *Paris* premiered (and about which the public would have known).

The gender politics of the film are what one might expect of the mid-1960s (before second-wave feminism and the sexual revolution prevailed). Holden walks around his apartment with his shirt open, muscles and chest hair visible, as though to assert that, while he is forty-four years old (and Hepburn thirty-three), he is still a fitting romantic lead. While Simpson is ostensibly a mere typist, she clearly collaborates on the screenplay. (The subject of uncredited female labor is discussed in chapter 5 in relation to the film *Céleste* [1980].) At one point Benson speaks of "*our* fabulous prose," and at another it is Simpson's voiceover we hear narrate the would-be drama as we watch it unfold onscreen. Moreover, in one scene, Benson taps her response for the female audience reaction. Finally, by any standard, his romantic behavior (kissing her, making her work in his bedroom) is clearly sexual harassment. Simpson is primly dressed in designer suits and at one point tells him that she is "not that kind of girl." Quickly, however, as though to update her comment for the New Wave age, she remarks that she hates women who say that.

Despite what seems like wit in *Paris*, the film is unsuccessful—mainly because the self-referential techniques are obvious and seem to be underlined to ensure we get the joke. While attempting to compete with the New Wave, *Paris* does not live up to the movement's off-beat, quirky originality. A *Variety* review speaks of "Paris When It *Fizzles*" (my emphasis) and calls the film "contrived," complaining of the "artificiality of the shell in which the takeoffs are encased." A *Time* review comes to the same conclusion, calling it a cinema "flame out": "*Paris When It Sizzles* is a multimillion dollar improvisation that does everything but what the title promises. It fakes, falters and fidgets."[25] A December 1965 *New York Times* article about Holden by Peter Bart calls *Paris* a "bomb."[26] The column also makes clear that the actor (like Benson) has lived abroad in recent years and has been linked to a series of "international *femmes fatales*." Furthermore, like Benson, Holden is entirely cynical about the Hollywood scene, where he finds "no breathing room." As he says: "I don't give a damn about my image. My only obligation to the public is my performance—what they see on that screen. That's all the public should ask of me. Anyway, that's all I'm giving." Apparently, however, in *Paris When It Sizzles*, that was not enough. The trailer for the film (which seems to sell it entirely on the star power of Holden and Hepburn) tries to pique the viewer's interest by bragging that the movie contains spies, beatniks, monsters, and a girl who stole the Eiffel Tower. It asks: "What kind of a picture is this?"—which seems to admit, in advance, that the work misses the mark.

TOURS DE FORCE

> Talking about dreams is like talking about movies, since the cinema uses the language of dreams.
>
> —Federico Fellini

Barton in Wonderland

More recently, there have been several extraordinary works about the screenwriter that take the subject matter and use it to transform the film's stylistic discourse —often abandoning the terrain of realism. One such work is *Barton Fink* (1991), directed by Joel Coen from an original screenplay co-authored with his brother, Ethan.[27] Set in pre–World War II America, it concerns a New York City playwright (in the socially engaged tradition of Clifford Odets) who goes to Hollywood to become a screenwriter.[28] In so doing, the plot invokes the tension discussed

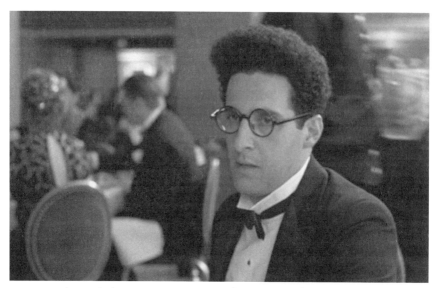

FIGURE 14. Playwright/screenwriter Barton Fink (John Turturro) in *Barton Fink* (1991).

earlier between East and West Coast authors—the former being viewed as the literati and the latter as the sell-outs.

The film begins with one of Fink's working-class dramas opening on Broadway to rave reviews. At a post-theater party, an associate reads the laudatory newspaper headlines, which deem Fink (John Turturro) "the toast of Broadway" and a "tough new voice" in the theater. Fink's fellow celebrants are high-toned, affected WASPs, a strong contrast to the Semitic and earnest artist. (Odets was Jewish as well.) It is on this evening that Fink's agent informs him that he has received an offer from Capitol Pictures for a great deal of money. When Fink says he wishes to remain in New York to create "a new living theater for the common man," his agent assures him that the common man will still be there when he returns, and that perhaps there are a few of them in Hollywood.

When the high-minded Fink arrives in Los Angeles, he encounters crass studio head Jack Lipnick (Michael Lerner), who claims that the writer is "king" at his studio, the "proof" being in his paycheck. He brags that he has "horse sense" and that he is "bigger and louder than any other kike in town" (a clear reference to the roots of the studio system in Jewish immigrants). Clearly, the man is a strong contrast to the effete eggheads with whom Fink has previously circulated. Lipnick assigns Fink to a "wrestling picture" starring Wallace Beery—both a genre and actor Fink knows little about. (Capitol, we are told, has already produced such great fight dramas as *Devil on a Canvas* and *Blood, Sweat, and Canvas*.) Lipnick wants Fink to invest the script with the "poetry of the street" without, however, making it "fruity" —and to include in the story an orphan or a dame, requisite characters for the genre. Here formulaic demands come up against artistic individuality.

In a scene that follows, Fink meets producer Geisler (Tony Shaloub), who mistakes him for an actor auditioning for a western. When Fink reveals that he is a scenarist, Geisler says: "Writers come and go. We always need Indians." He also tells Fink that he has been assigned to a B-picture (despite Lipnick's claim that none are made at Capitol). When later Fink refuses to share his script ideas with Lipnick, the executive's assistant reminds him that he is a "contract employee" whose ideas are "owned" by the studio—thus highlighting the writer's role as a laborer rather than a thinker. When Fink finally delivers a manuscript, Lipnick hates it and makes clear that the writer is dispensable: "Do you think you're the only one who can give me that Barton Fink feeling?" Clearly, the unique genius does not exist in the Hollywood world. Fink's individuality is a dime a dozen. In his plight, we are reminded of the writer in Italo Calvino's novel *If on a Winter's Night a Traveler*, who learns that a Japanese publisher has mastered the "formula" to his novels and produced new ones without him.[29]

For most of the movie, Fink is so blocked in writing the wrestling picture that he rarely gets past sketching out the opening scene, whose text (as typed on paper) reads: "Fade in: A tenement building on Manhattan's lower east side. Early morning. Traffic is audible." (Interestingly, the Coens were evidently stalled in completing the script for *Miller's Crossing* [1990] when they began working on *Barton Fink*.)[30] The author in Calvino's novel also faces this impasse. As he notes: "You start writing in a rush, anticipating the happiness of a future reading, and the void yawns on the white page."[31] Later, he conceives the idea of "writing a novel composed only of beginnings."[32]

Finally, Fink succeeds in adding another image to his script: "A big man in tights" (ostensibly the fighter, but a phrase reminding us of Lipnick's directive not to be "fruity"). Among the only other words we see him type (and simultaneously question) are "dame?" and "orphan?"—more requisite stereotypes. In fact, Fink is so overwrought that, at one point, when he opens a page of the hotel room Bible, he imagines the words of his scenario imprinted on it. Significantly, he has opened to a section of Genesis, the story of another kind of creation. The above shots are instances in which words are seen onscreen as images themselves—privileged moments (as we have noted) in movies about writers. What is ironic, however, is that here they are taken from a screenplay—where words are meant to be translated into visible action. While Fink, the artist, is stalled in the process of composing, Geisler's secretary is not. Frequently we cut to her hands rapidly hammering on typewriter keys accompanied by harsh, repetitive, mechanical sounds. While art stands still, commerce presses on.

Had the Coen brothers' film remained in this mocking vein, it would have been one among many acerbic (but somewhat accurate) portrayals of Hollywood as a world of crude capitalism, mindless mass entertainment, and creative prostitution.[33] The name of Fink's hotel—the Earle—is, after all, an approximate anagram for the word "real." As for the film's jaded view of the film colony, Fink encounters Mayhew (John Mahoney), a drunken, degenerate, racist Southern literary figure

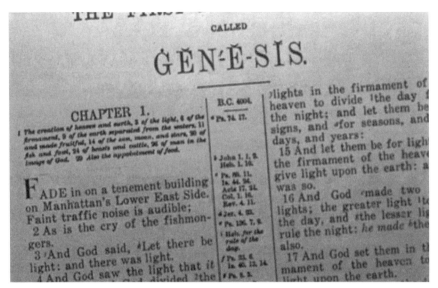

FIGURE 15. The Bible morphs into a screenplay in *Barton Fink* (1991).

who clearly stands in for William Faulkner, who did spend time in LA.[34] Mayhew batters his secretary/lover, Audrey (Judy Davis), who, we learn, is probably the true author of his recent work. But the movie goes beyond the realm of burlesque to invoke the grim mental world of Fink as he is plagued by his milieu and gradually sinks into a morass of despair—all without any clear demarcation between the spheres of distanced disdain and subjective terror.

First, the Hotel Earle (despite its aristocratic name) is strange, tawdry, and gloomy, far from the kind of glamour associated with studio-era Hollywood. (Fink has chosen it himself to avoid the profligate luxury of the film colony.) Its décor is drab, its hallways are tunnel-like, and its elevator man seems insensible; Fink's room is infested with mosquitoes and, for no apparent reason, its wallpaper slowly peels off, oozing a repulsive, viscous fluid (shades of *Naked Lunch*). Furthermore, Fink's next-door neighbor, Charlie Meadows (John Goodman), is a bizarre and menacing character. He claims to be an insurance salesman (selling "peace of mind") but turns out to be a serial murderer (whom the police know as Mad Man Munt). Before Fink realizes this, he and Meadows (one of the "common men" that Fink embraces) have numerous chats in which Meadows brags about the countless "stories" he could tell—but Fink, a narcissist, never inquires further. Rather, he goes on endlessly about the job of "plumbing the depths" of the soul, about the pain of a "life of the mind."

Meadows's sociopathology begins to surface when one morning Fink awakens and is shocked to find Audrey (with whom he has had a sexual tryst) lying dead in his bed. Not suspecting his neighbor, he calls on Meadows to help dump the body. Shortly thereafter, Meadows abruptly announces he will leave town and gives

Fink a box that we fear contains Audrey's head (a true "Monster in a Box," to bor-row Spalding Gray's term for a manuscript-in-progress). Mad Man Munt, we later learn, decapitates his victims, which makes it all the more disquieting when he tells Fink that they must remain calm and "keep their heads." Finally, when Mead-ows later sets the Earle on fire (turning it into a demonic inferno), he runs through the flames chanting: "I'll show you the life of the mind!" When Fink asks Mead-ows why he has caused the conflagration, he yells, "Because you don't listen!" He mocks Fink further by shouting: "You think you know pain? You're a tourist with a typewriter. I live here."

Hence Fink, the champion of the common man, has had no understanding of Meadows (whom he deems an "average working stiff"). Moreover, he has failed to hear Meadows's "stories"—consumed as he has been with his own creative burden. "We all have stories," he tells Meadows rather than learn those that the man might tell. Instead of the virtuous plebeian figure that Fink imagines him to be, Meadows is an evil mass-murderer. He counters Fink's "life of the mind" with "peace of mind" delivered not by the insurance he peddles, but by slaughter (a new twist to *Death of a Salesman*). Given such developments, it is no surprise that a tag line for the movie reads: "Between Heaven and Hell There's Always Hollywood."

On one level, in sequences depicting the Earle, it is as though we have left the world of Fink's alienated screenwriter to enter the kind of screenplay he could never have written—a Hollywood Gothic. On another level, the specific type of horror Fink encounters tends to literalize various metaphors about writing—an activity emphasized by repeated shots of Fink (the camera closing in on him) sit-ting motionless at his Underwood typewriter (a brand name that hints at under-taking in the funereal rather than the tasking sense). If as a writer Fink is "burnt out," the blaze in his hotel literalizes this notion. If as an intellectual Fink has claimed that "the life of the mind" is painful, the phrase has a macabre sense when he receives the dismembered head. If we think of someone (like Fink) who loses his mind as becoming "unglued," we remark that this is precisely what happens to the wallpaper in his room. If in Hollywood Fink is surrounded by capitalistic bloodsuckers, they are incarnated in the mosquitoes that haunt him at night. In chapter 6 we discuss Noël Carroll's claim that tropes like these (that draw linguis-tic phrases to mind) can be called "verbal images."[35]

Furthermore, there is another odd element of the mise-en-scène that seems to stand for both the artistic and filmic process. On the wall of Fink's hotel room (above his typewriter) is a picture of a beach scene that depicts a woman sitting on the sand as seen from the rear. Throughout the film, Fink continually and in-explicably stares at this painting (as does the viewer) seemingly hypnotized, and it consequently takes on the uncanny import of artworks in certain novels by Alain Robbe-Grillet.[36] At the end of the narrative, with no resolution of the sur-real events that have hitherto unfolded, Fink suddenly appears by the ocean with the monstrous box in hand and passes a beautiful woman on the beach positioned much like the figure in the painting. He asks her if she's "in pictures"—meaning the movies. However, this question seems ironic given that she is a double for the woman in the hotel's framed scene. Thus, in finding her, it is as though Fink has walked into the picture—into the fiction, into the screen, through the looking glass. As evidence of the picture's fantastic status, the first time Fink regards it in his room, he mysteriously hears the sound of waves. In the next shot, he awakens from a dream as though the picture has been part of it. Taking another view, R. Barton Palmer sees Fink's arrival on the shore as a triumph of reality over the "meditation of representation," as well as evidence that he "completes the journey from the East Coast . . . to the West."[37]

Finally, it is noteworthy that a novel Mayhew autographs for Fink is entitled *Nebuchadnezzar*; in signing it, he pens a note about "sojourn[ing] among the Philistines" (meaning Hollywood). Nebuchadnezzar was the Babylonian king who sent the Jews into exile. Much later on, Fink opens the hotel room's Bible to a page from Daniel that reads: "And the King, Nebuchandnez, answered and said to the Chaldeans I recall not my dream; if ye will not make known unto me my dream, and its interpretation, ye shall be cut in pieces and your tents shall be made a dunghill." Since we have already seen a drama about people "cut in pieces" set in a film colony that resembles a "dunghill," we can only assume that the full interpretation of the Coens' dreamlike film will ultimately elude us, no matter how much we strive to make sense of it. Appropriately, when the woman on the beach asks Fink what's in the box he is carrying, he replies, "I don't know"—and ultimately neither do we.

Double Indemnity

A second challenging work about the screenwriter (that raises discursive questions beyond thematic ones) is *Adaptation* (2002)—written by Charlie Kaufman and directed by Spike Jonze. Here, the onscreen embodiment of the author is highlighted by the creation of a central character (played by Nicolas Cage) that is named Charlie Kaufman (like the actual scenarist). Furthermore, reminiscent of the trope of "Borges and I" (discussed in the Introduction), said screenwriter is himself split into two, since Cage also plays Charlie's twin brother, Donald (another aspiring scriptwriter). Here, perhaps, we also have a wry homage to famous twin Hollywood scenarists: Julius and Philip Epstein, the authors of *Casablanca* (1942). To make matters more comical, in one scene Donald "impersonates" Charlie (while all the time both are played by Cage). So the tropes of incarnation and body doubling that are central to this study are literalized here—facilitated by cinema's special effects.

If Barton Fink was arrogant, the fictional Kaufman (from here on called Charlie) is insecure—both about his literary skills and status as a man. Thus, in the opening sequence, through voiceover narration, we hear what he is thinking while we view a black screen: "Do I have an original thought in my head? My bald head? . . . Today is the first day of the rest of my life. . . . I'm a walking cliché." While Charlie is sensitive and romantically challenged, Donald is boorish and

FIGURE 16. Twin screenwriter brothers Charlie and Donald (both played by Nicolas Cage) in *Adaptation* (2002).

considers himself a dude. In a scene that ostensibly takes place on the set of one of Kaufman's prior screenwriting successes—*Being John Malkovich* (1999), also directed by Jonze—Donald (an interloper) flirts with the make-up girl while Charlie (a high-level crew member) hides in the background. To make matters worse, Charlie is told by the cinematographer that he is "in the eyeline" and must leave the set. The status of the image in this sequence is immediately in question: is the footage documentary material from the shooting of *Malkovich* in "Summer 1998," or is it a faux restaging of it in 2002?

While Charlie is a creative guy, his twin is a dull conformist. When Donald decides to pursue screenwriting (in crass imitation of his brother), his technique and goals are anathema to Charlie, who has gone the independent, experimental route. While Charlie believes in the uniqueness of the artwork, Donald aspires to copy past moneymakers. Hence, he takes a course with Hollywood guru Robert McKee (a real author of screenwriting how-to books, here impersonated by actor Brian Cox). So the proliferation of writer doppelgangers continues. To make the trope denser, Donald's hackneyed screenplay involves a character with multiple personalities (which he signifies by a cracked mirror—part of his "image system"). Explaining how he would "pitch" the screenplay (using Hollywood lingo), he deems it "*Sybil* meets *Dressed to Kill*."

In a scene in which the fictional McKee (Cox) delivers a lecture to a room full of screenwriter wannabes (laying out formulas of the commercial script), notions of authorship and originality are mocked. As a defeated and desperate Charlie sits in the audience (having been reduced to attending the kind of "how-to" seminar he despises), his voiceover narration reveals his self-loathing at the precise moment that McKee says: "And God help you if you use voiceover narration!" The more discouraged Charlie feels about his own work, the more he begins to consider using McKee's well-worn paradigms. Furthermore, much to Charlie's chagrin, Donald is able to sell his trite scenario, while he is blocked on a far more worthwhile project.

We actually also have a third writer in *Adaptation*—*New Yorker* columnist Susan Orlean (again a real author, here played by Meryl Streep). She has published a book about an orchid cultivator (a volume that exists outside the film). When it is optioned for a movie, Charlie's agent gets him the screenwriting commission. Hence (as the film title indicates) the movie we are watching is not only about screenwriting, but also about the specific and contested process of adaptation. What makes this both a comic and resonant practice in the film is that the literary property involved, Orlean's *The Orchid Thief* (1998), is wildly unsuitable for conventional cinema (as Charlie bemoans: "I can't make flowers fascinating"). Consider the following passage from the actual book: "Many wild orchids don't like to live away from the woods. They will usually flourish and produce seeds only if they are in their own little universe with their favorite combination of water and light and temperature and breeze with the perfect tree bark and the perfect angle and with the precise kind of bugs and the exact kind of flotsam falling on their roots and into their flowers."[38] As the real Kaufman proclaims in an interview: "[*The Orchid Thief*] seemed not to be a movie, which intrigued me."[39] Orlean concurs: "The story . . . seemed too subtle and convoluted for movie-making."[40]

Ironically, however, despite Charlie's protestations, the film we are watching has managed to do the impossible as when, in an earlier scene, it responds (in visual imagery) to an existential question he poses. He wonders (in acoustic interior monologue): "I've been on this planet for 40 years and I'm no closer to understanding a single thing. Why am I here? How did I get here?" His voice then ceases and we see images and hear sound effects associated with the following things (sometimes superimposed or rendered in time-lapse photography): molten lava (labeled "Hollywood CA. Four Billion and 40 Years Ago"); fiery eruptions, transformations of earth, particles and microbes; a lizard crawling on the rocks; oceans drying; vegetation sprouting; a bug crawling through grass; a plant blooming; dinosaurs walking; an explosion; earth shifting; a fox decomposing; a crater opening; Cro-Magnon Man rising; an aerial view of LA; a vagina with a baby's head crowning; the baby born; the baby's face; adult Charlie in a restaurant. Clearly, in this sequence (imagined by Charlie or presented by the filmic narrator), we get an answer to Charlie's philosophical query in the form of an absurdly compressed, abstract timeline of the development of our planet, the beginning of life, the movement from sea creature to mammal, the evolution of humanity, the settling of Los Angeles, and the birth of Charlie. Hence, Kaufman and Jonze accomplish, in a filmic joke, the very kind of discourse that cinema is ostensibly denied.

Confronting Orlean's work, a discouraged Charlie muses (in voiceover): "How can a screenplay be about flowers? How can one create a script without a love

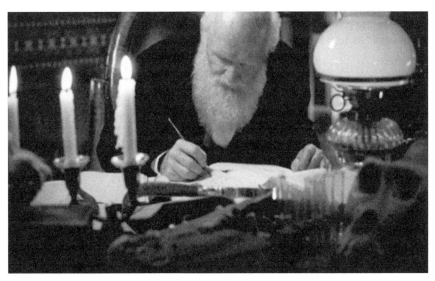

FIGURE 17. Charlie's (Nicolas Cage) vision of Charles Darwin for his screenplay-in-progress in *Adaptation* (2002).

story, drugs, guns, or action? How can one convert to visual imagery literary passages about Charles Darwin, ecology, and the evolution of the species?" Here, the practice of screen adaptation morphs toward evolutionary adaptation at the very moment that Charlie attempts professional adaptation. In a later sequence, however, he feels he has made a breakthrough. Standing in his bedroom, he thinks (in voiceover narration) how he must "dramatize" the flower, show its "arc." As he muses: "How did this flower get here? What was its journey?" He looks at horticulture books on his desk and then at *The Portable Darwin*. Suddenly we cut to a black-and-white sequence (in what has been a color film) labeled "England 139 Years Earlier." An old man (presumably Darwin) sits at a desk philosophizing about evolution. Returning to Charlie in the present, we see him grab a voice recorder and start dictating: "The film will open with life beginning on earth, will move to organisms, then creatures crawling out of the sea, then dinosaurs, then monkeys, then an asteroid crashing into the planet, etc." Moments later, however, Charlie listens to what he has recorded with a depressed expression on his face, realizing that it is unfilmable drivel. We, however, recognize it as precisely the successful sequence we have seen earlier cued in by Charlie's existential query: "Why am I here?"

The process of adaptation is also referenced in the film through its intricate point-of-view structure. While for the most part we are identified with Charlie and often hear his thoughts, when he begins to read Orlean's work her voice sometimes takes over. In these sequences, it is never entirely clear whether we are directly witnessing dramatizations of Orlean's memoir or of Charlie reading it. In one particularly intriguing moment, his and her consciousnesses converge. We watch Charlie at an orchid show trying to learn about the flowers. At first we hear Orlean's voiceover (ostensibly from her book) describing various types of blooms (which are pictured onscreen). Soon, however, as Charlie's mind wanders, her voice morphs into his, categorizing kinds of women—as the image displays females in the crowd. At one point later on (as Orlean listens to a tape of *The Origin of Species*) we even hear a surrogate form of Charles Darwin's voice.

Ironically, adapting *The Orchid Thief* has not only been the task of the fictional Charlie but the actual Kaufman, a problem the latter solved by writing a screenplay about the problem of writing a screenplay (which turned into the film we are watching). Perversely, Charlie chides himself for writing a script that includes himself, calling it narcissistic, solipsistic, and pathetic—clearly, charges that could be launched at Kaufman himself. The film also comments on the tense dynamic between the author of source material and its adapter. At moments, Charlie imagines conversations between himself and Orlean (which the spectator also hears from inside Charlie's head). At one point he even fantasizes making love to her (imagining adaptation as a form of "copulation"). Above all, however, he is afraid of disappointing her since he finds her work beautiful.

In response to this, the film takes a U-turn in the weird spirit of *Barton Fink* (Orlean calls Kaufman "a master practitioner of non-linear, eccentric storytelling").[41] We already have experienced an intricate narrative involving a book-within-a-film, fractured point of view, doppelgangers, and puzzle-like temporality (in which we suddenly [as in *Un Chien Andalou* (1929)] get titles like "three years earlier" or "two years later"—as though we can follow the confusing timeline). Then, gradually, the film we are watching (about Charlie's screenwriting problems) shifts into one based on the kind of script that McKee would have sanctioned (and Charlie abhorred), as an unlikely love story blossoms between Susan Orlean and the orchid-grower and they become involved in the drug trade that ultimately leads to a shootout involving the three writers (a comic twist on the macho Western gunfight). Again, we leave the world of ostensible reality to enter a fictional world of a second order, in a vertiginous *mise-en-abyme*. Thus, in the Darwinian universe of Hollywood, the survival of the fittest has led to the triumph of Donald and McKee over Charlie—the hacks over the geniuses. Of course, this pertains only to the narrative fiction since the work we are watching, *Adaptation*, is anything but a pedestrian text. Ironically, by having his protagonist-self follow the codes of commercial production, the real Kaufman has escaped their constraints, crafting an entirely original artwork. At the close of the film, the two worlds self-reflexively collide as Charlie is seen driving down a street. On the sound track we hear his thoughts (as voiceover monologue) musing: "I know how to finish the script. It ends with him driving home thinking he knows how to end the script." The music that accompanies the shot is "Happy Together," a relentlessly upbeat, corny, pop rock tune that Donald had planned for his own movie. As Charlie smiles we realize that he has had the requisite epiphany for a movie's end (learning that "it is more important to love than to be loved") and that this change (following convention) has come "from within." Clearly, in such mockery, Kaufman has managed to have his cake and eat it too.

East Meets West

Thus far, we have been discussing American works in our examination of the screenwriter persona in fiction film (with brief mention of some post–World War II European art movies). There is, however, a fascinating example of the "author incarnate" in film made in 2006 and set in China. *How Is Your Fish Today?* (*Jin tian de yu zen me yang?*), by female director Xialou Gou, follows scriptwriter Hui Rao (the actual co-scenarist of the film) as he tries to write a screenplay. The drama makes reference to Rao's having written previous scripts, and during the course of the film we see him host a television program that shows officially approved foreign movies to the public. But we have no assurance that this TV show is "real" or that his career as a screenwriter extends beyond the film we are watching. Indeed, a check of his listing in the Internet Movie Database suggests that it does not.[42] Though the narrative takes place in various actual Chinese locales, and the film is produced by the British *Documentary* Foundation, it is by no means a conventional nonfiction work. In fact, the screenplay (whose crafting the film records) is dramatized within the work itself (as though it were completed, and not just being written), lending the film a fictional, temporally complex element that conforms to the dimensions of the writer's imagination.

The work's experimental style is signaled at its opening, since it begins *in medias res* on a train to Mohe, the northernmost Chinese town, located on the Siberian border. Some offscreen unidentified individual is interviewing passengers about their vision of the place, which has a mythic valence in Chinese lore. Here is how *China Daily* writer Tiffany Tan describes it: "Imagine a place where snow blankets the earth for more than half the year, where -35 C is considered a 'warm' winter day and where the sun begins its descent at 3 P.M. Mohe county in Heilongjiang province is so cold you can feel icicles form around your nostrils with each breath. . . . Even so, China's northern frontier has a raw beauty. . . . All Chinese learn about Mohe in their elementary geography classes, but only a handful ever set foot on it."[43] Then, accompanying a black screen, we hear a man's voice (which we learn in the credits is Rao's), talking of how he will write a script about a man who voyages to Mohe. We next cut to a proleptic image of Rao's protagonist-to-be (identified as Lin Hao [Zijiang Yang]) arriving at the snow-covered, mythic landscape. Rao's voiceover says that he does not yet know what Hao's destiny will be. As he inquires: "Will he save or end his life? I'll let him decide." Hence, we already know that this "documentary" will visualize Rao's imaginative acts as he conceives the screenplay (which is simultaneously visualized for us as though it were finished). Furthermore, we sense that Rao is not in control of the drama. He does not yet know what will happen (perhaps, his characters will decide), and later we learn that events he has initially formulated will have to be revised.

Entering yet a third dramatic level (beyond the real train ride and the imagined story), we see images of the exterior of a huge Beijing apartment bloc where Rao ostensibly lives. Eventually we move inside his flat as he tells us about a screen-writing commission he received and in preparation for which he studied Holly-wood genre pictures (e.g., *The Fugitive* [1993]). He tells us that he has finished the script (no writer's block here), which concerns Lin Hao, a young man who has killed his lover and fled southern China for the North. Obviously, Rao is toying with the plot of *The Fugitive*, about a surgeon who escapes from police after being accused of murdering his wife. But *How Is Your Fish Today?* is as far away from an American thriller as Hollywood is from Beijing. Rao's producer seems to have agreed and (we are told) rejected the scenario. In fact, the first time we see Rao typing on his computer keyboard, his voiceover calls his script "cliché" and asserts that he must start over.

We get further double-layered sequences involving Rao composing his story-line along with visions of what that story might be (much in the manner of *Paris When It Sizzles*). He goes to a restaurant where he often writes and, as his voiceover discusses how his protagonist might look, we are shown faces of various male customers—candidates for Lin Hao's corporealization. Rao's thoughts also begin to link his protagonist to himself, as he notes: "I think Lin Hao is like me, from a small village in the South, like this [one] in Guang Xi Province." As he mentions the locale, a town is pictured onscreen as though to help us visualize Hao's birthplace. Rao suggests that Lin Hao is bored living there, after which the camera reveals a man leaning languorously against a wall. Rao's voiceover proclaims (as though he sees the image too): "That's him. That's Lin Hao . . . I think he has never seen snow. I want him to head north." We learn later that Rao thinks himself differ-ent from Hao—more sedentary (like a "plant"). Clearly, his fictional double will embark on an adventure that Rao has been too timid to undertake—"compensat-ing" for the author's limitations.

The rest of the film consists largely of an alternation of two types of scenes, representing both tiers of the drama. Live-action sequences in color depict screen-writer Rao in Beijing: at his gym, in his apartment, driving through the city, typ-ing on his computer, shopping for clothes, etc. Conversely, abstract segments (either shot in blurry, bleached color or comprising tinted still images linked by dissolves) portray the imaginary Lin Hao and his journey to Mohe: his nights in hotels, his train rides, his stops in towns (e.g., Wu Han, Chang Chun, Shen Yang), and his liaison with a young woman named either "Mi Mi or Sha Sha or Li Ying" (played by director Guo Xiaolu). These latter sequences almost never involve syn-chronous dialogue (so Hao remains largely a silent figure). Even when he meets the young woman, we are told by Rao: "There are no words between them." Ac-companying the imaginary scenes of Lin Hao are ambient sounds and electronic music, the latter helping us to identify the shifts between "reality" and the fictional "story-within-a-story."

The self-reflexivity of the film is heightened at certain points. In one sequence, we find Rao in his apartment playing cards with friends from the film industry as others film them. He tells his pals that he has "thought about making a documentary about a screenwriter" and, in response, one of them inquires whether the film being shot now is the one he has mentioned. At other times, as we follow the exploits of Lin Hao onscreen, Rao's voiceover points to the mechanics of plot construction. For example, when Hao meets the young woman, Rao's voiceover says that he (the author) "needs" Hao to meet a woman because she is the one who will bring him to Beijing (a location he has deemed necessary for his drama). The fact that Hao stops in Beijing before going on to Mohe is also important as this brings him to the author's own home turf (we almost expect them to pass on the street). Again, what this corporealization of author and character makes clear is the manner in which the latter is often the alter ego of the former. It is shortly after bringing Hao to Beijing that Rao tells us that he doubts his character killed his girlfriend after all (a total change in the plot line). Now he believes that Hao simply has "gotten lost" and can only find himself through the people he meets on his journey. Interestingly, this portion of voiceover (augmented by typing sounds) is accompanied onscreen with images of Rao's film books on a shelf. Rao then informs us that his Zen master once told him that all people's stories are alike—you live, you die—which reminds us of Barthes's notion that literary works lack originality and, by definition, draw on prior texts. Rao wonders why he is struggling to fabricate something "different."

Several aspects of director Guo's theoretical writings are relevant to the formal structure of her film. In "Notes toward a Metaphysical Cinema Manifesto," she decries conventional storytelling: "Narrative is important to us, but its function is negative . . . [We] us[e] narrative as a tool, not as an end."[44] Rather than aiming for seamless story construction, she is interested in "time and space in fragments." She also denigrates the notion of the author's total power over the drama (demonstrated by Rao's inability to direct his plot line). Instead, she favors a "controlled abandon, a sober pandemonium." She continues: "To engage in metaphysical cinema is to . . . [use] poetic tools that project us beyond the comforts of control. . . . Gone [is] the camera of absolute control, the idea that precedes the hand and eye moving through the world. Our way of filming and editing is a kind of trust in accident." She also talks of cinematic practice in a manner consonant with her use of Rao's voiceover narration. As she remarks: "We say no to . . . a voice [that] is no longer a subjective voice; where a voice ends up as a non-reflective, unexamined manipulation of a God's Eye view." Furthermore, certain statements she makes seem to gesture toward her use of the "double": "Instead of looking at the object in the scene, we look to the shadow it casts. The shadow is the more basic reality." Likewise, she seeks "a mosaic, reflective, plural-voice narrative." Moreover, in relation to Guo's refusal to let Hao speak, we think of her statement that "the appearance of life . . . is a kind of silence . . . an eloquent silence, which bursts forth from a crack in narrative structure." Finally, for Guo, metaphysical cinema is dialogic and heteroglossic, taking in "documentary and TV footage, fictional conventions, text, home video, photos, tape recording, archives." We recognize many of these elements in the narrative assemblage that constitutes *How Is Your Fish Today?*

In the same manner in which Lin Hao visits Beijing, Hui Rao travels to Mohe —forcing character and author to cross paths again. Rao talks of having learned about the northern village as a schoolchild and having always wanted to see the Northern Lights that are visible there. Here we are reminded of a movie reference dropped earlier in the narrative. We are told that Rao regularly teaches a film class in Beijing and that, in one session, he has screened *The Green Ray* (1986) for his students. That film also involves a character's journey and a magical kind of light that illuminates the sky.

Gradually, we begin to see the parallels between Rao and Hao: both are lonely, both smoke too much, both are from the south, and both are preoccupied with Mohe. We are therefore not surprised when Rao opines: "I want [Hao] to do the things I am not doing with my life." After he scripts Hao's arrival in Beijing, Rao notes that he does not wish for his character to get "stuck" there (perhaps like him). As we watch Hao running down the street escaping, Rao is seen driving a car, enumerating various statistics about Beijing that mark it as an inhospitable megalopolis: 2.5 million cars, 3,587 people named Lin Hao in the phonebook, and so on.

When Hao boards a train to Mohe, Rao's voiceover announces: "I got on the same train to see it with my own eyes." We then cut to a shot of the author sitting in the vehicle, reflected in his compartment window—doubling our sense of his being doubled. Like Hao, he is voyaging to see "the green ray"—something miraculous that will ameliorate the banality of ordinary life. Here the story of the two figures (author and subject) fuses for the final time. Both arrive in Mohe. After a single shot of Hao in this locale, we leave him to follow Rao as he explores the town. We are then presented with a mini-documentary of the place: its generator plant, its school, its store, its Christian church, the hostel in which Rao spends the night. The next day his host takes him ice fishing along the Russian border —which involves puncturing the frozen surface to hoist up nets (now full of fish) that were dropped there the previous spring. Earlier, we had heard a parable about how, in Mohe, both Russian and Chinese fishermen meet on the border and inquire of each other "How is your fish today?" In traveling to Mohe in search of his protagonist, Rao has crossed such a boundary, though one of an artistic kind. But the image of fish has also been invoked earlier in the film when Rao informs us that his Feng Shui master told him to get a pet fish for good luck (which he did, naming it Belle de Jour, ostensibly in honor of Buñuel).

As Rao and his host unpack their nets on the icy river, we see dead fish flopping around, gasping for air. Significantly, it is at this point that Rao muses, "I wish to encounter Lin Hao here." Almost immediately, he finds his fictional hero Hao lying "breathless on the snow" (like a dead fish) as a shot reveals the scene to us as well. He wonders if Hao died trying to cross the border. Rao approaches Hao's body (author and character finally in the same frame—overcoming the barrier of existential and montage separation), then passes it by, informing us: "That's when I decided to stop writing Lin Hao's story." Rao confesses that he needed Hao to take him on this journey and help him learn that, in place of extraordinary visions, there is "nothing to see."

In an epilogue, we view a black screen and hear Rao's voice telling us that, while he has resisted returning to his family's village for five years, he now misses the place. Thus, you *can* go home again. The failure of the film to reach a conventionally satisfying epiphany (Rao merely learns that there is nothing to see) is in line with director Guo's theoretical pronouncements. As she notes, cinema's "addiction to meaning carries with it a kind of death. Meaning, or living the search for meaning, is one in which reality is obscured. . . . Life carries on with or without meaning. A rock lies on the ground with or without meaning. A life looking for meaning goes on with or without meaning"—as does Rao's.[45]

Unlike *Adaptation* and *Barton Fink*, which eschew a clear gap between the life of the screenwriter and the scenario he is composing (having one "bleed" into the other), *How Is Your Fish Today?* makes clear the separation of the two—all without eliminating the mysterious and enigmatic sense of their collision and comingling. Once we catch on to Guo's "system," we always know when we are watching Hao or Rao. Furthermore, the film matches the embodiment of the writer with the corporealization of his character—making clear the symbiotic relation between the two. In fact, the narrative implies that, in writing his scenario about Hao's voyage to Mohe, Rao is actually telling his own story—hence, the two figures "meet" in the final scene (an impossibility)—and one must perish so the other can survive. Thus, with the Death of the Character comes the Life of the Author. In this way, the film argues for the central role of the text in a writer's life: it is Hao's fictional trip to legendary Mohe that propels Rao to actually journey there and to purge himself of visions of this phantom locale. Hence, by the end, fiction has allowed Rao to accept life: suddenly, he even misses home. Writing is a kind of "cure," or hallucinatory therapy, like psychodrama—by which one embraces a fiction in the hope of "getting a life."

EPILOGUE: REDUCTIO AD ABSURDUM

> A screenplay is not a finished product; a novel is. A screenplay is a blueprint for something—for a building that will most likely never be built.
>
> —Nicholas Meyer

While all the films discussed thus far posit fictional screenwriters who stand in for the cinematic author, the experimental work *Poetic Justice* (1972), by Hollis Frampton, simultaneously highlights the scenarist's role while erasing him entirely from the scene. If, as I have asserted, the image of words onscreen is the *punctum* of the writer film genre, this is the tour de force work of that form.

Frampton pens a "faux" screenplay (really a modernist parody thereof) that he never intends to dramatize or shoot. He films each page of the script as a separate shot—without ever showing us the images imagined by the written discourse. Hence *Poetic Justice* is a literal movie of a screenplay (rather than the usual adapted form). Here, he mockingly supports David Mamet's view that a "film is directed in the making of the shot list"—that it "is the *plan* that makes the movie."[46] In fact, aside from successive sheets of paper and the words upon them, the only objects we regularly see in *Poetic Justice* are a table—and the script, coffee cup, and cactus that it holds. Thus the screenplay *is* the film in a direct (vs. mediated) sense; no "performance" of it is undertaken (or is ever meant to be). Here Astruc's notion of the "camera stylo" seems humorously realized—with Frampton subsuming writing into the film. Interestingly, he also released *Poetic Justice* as a flipbook—a volume that animates images as one riffles its pages, thus blurring the distinction between cinema and literature.

But the film is far more complex than this.[47] First, while refusing to visualize the events implied on the printed page (e.g., "a zoom shot of a lilac seen outside a window," "a hand picking up a photograph," "a couple making love in bed"), *Poetic Justice* depends on the fact that the spectator *will* visualize them—thus highlighting the active mental role of the viewer in watching films (or the reader in processing text). Essentially, as we watch *Poetic Justice* on the screen, we simultaneously run the movie it describes in our heads, creating both cognitive overload and paradox (Frampton was a great fan of Jorge Luis Borges). Second, there are moments when the film we are watching and the one imagined in the screenplay overlap and intersect, as when Shot #4 describes "A small table below a window. A potted cactus. A coffee cup"—the very things we are seeing.[48] Second, the four "tableaux" the screenplay comprises involve a love story (and perhaps a love triangle) —the favored subject of mainstream cinema from its inception till the present. As Bruce Jenkins has noted, the film described in *Poetic Justice* (which itself is without sound) is also lacking auditory cues and hence may be an homage to the silent cinema (the word *tableau* also seems antique and was commonly used in that era).[49] Third, despite the fact that the interior narrative mimics the standard love story, bizarre occurrences are noted in the script. Thus as the couple makes love in bed, strange things are seen outside an open window: eggs hatching baby turtles (Shot #176), grizzled drovers herding sheep (Shot #175), a crystal of pure nicotine (Shot #165). Here, of course, Frampton is hailing both Surrealism and scientific cinematography as well as the possibility of cinema to use special effects like matting (in addition to the standard dissolves he mentions frequently as shot transitions). Fourth, unlike traditional cinema, which attempts to erase the producer from audience consciousness (to make the spectator feel that she is watching an unstaged occurrence), *Poetic Justice* underscores the act of filming and the role of the filmmaker in the script itself. First, there is the fact that the words on successive sheets of paper describing each shot are handwritten—thereby containing an authorial mark. Then, already in Shot #7 we get the following text: "My hand places a color photograph of your face on a table" (shades of the bodily presence of Winsor McCay or the Fleischer Brothers). Later, in Shot #179, we read: "Bedroom. Love Making. Outside the window, I am aiming a camera" (shades of Dziga Vertov and the opening of *Man with the Movie Camera*). The use of the pronouns "my" and "I," and the fact that some situations involve forms of image making, leads us to believe that this narrator/character is the director-surrogate—usually an invisible participant in screen drama. A later shot (#239) mentions "a still photograph of my own face"—thus "embodying" and revealing more about this phantom figure. Other "characters" in the implied drama (designated as "you" and "your lover") also are said to have cameras or photographs in their hands—though the use of the second person also, of course, hails the viewer. Thus while *Poetic Justice* for the most part only pictures text, other filmed imagery is continually referenced and conjured.

At the end of the film its self-reflexivity and conundrums become even more vertiginous. Shot #237 tells us: "Your lover's hand is holding a still photograph of my hand writing this text." Shot #238 then says: "Your lover's hand is holding a still photograph of myself, filming these pages." Hence, both the writing of the screenplay and its transfer to cinema are embedded in the film script itself. Furthermore, in the text's reference to a photographic self-portrait, it also calls to mind Frampton's (*nostalgia*) (1971), discussed in this volume's Afterword. Finally, following our view of the last page of text (Shot #240), we see a blank page, and then Shot #240 is repeated ("My hand covers a still photograph of my own face"). Next, unexpectedly, a rubber glove drops onto the page—the only real filmed action in the movie and its final image. In the reference to a *covered* still photograph of *my own* face, we get a sense of the author in hiding—his usual place within the text. However, in the glove that drops onto the page, we get an object that potentially touches the author's hand—and, in a humorous, unromantic, and corporeal fashion, stands in for it—just as the artwork concludes. The glove seems more reflexive when we realize that Frampton was also a photographer who may have had to use it in developing film. Furthermore, it reminds us of a Surrealist painting by Giorgio de Chirico (*The Song of Love* [1914]), in which a rubber glove hangs on a wall next to a sculpted bust.

In *Script Culture*, Kevin Alexander Boon complains that, historically, the screenplay has never been taken seriously as an art form, and that it is entirely ignored once the film on which it is based has been shot. In Frampton's work the script takes its revenge (as does the word) over the pictorial image. Poetic justice, indeed.

4   THE AUTHORESS
Textuality as Sexuality

An omnipresent metaphor [has] equated women with the white sheet of
nature or virginity onto which a very male stylus could then inscribe the glory
of its authorship.

— Friedrich Kittler, *Gramophone, Film, Typewriter*

THE UGLY TRUTH

It comes as no surprise (given literary history) that most films about the fictional
writer center on a man (a fact that previous and subsequent chapters of this book
amply demonstrate). As Sandra Gilbert and Susan Gubar noted in their seminal
text *The Mad Woman in the Attic* in 1979: "It is no wonder that women have historically hesitated to attempt the pen . . . authored [as they are] by a male God and
by a godlike male." Engaging in word play, they ask, "If the pen is a metaphorical
penis, with what organ can females generate texts?"[1]

While, in recent decades, attention to the existence of female writers has certainly transformed the academy (in both literature and creative writing departments), this shift has not substantially altered the world of feature film. The one
area in which there has been considerable progress is in the portrayal of historical authors (whose existence cannot be denied). Hence we have seen "biopics"
of such figures as Janet Frame, Jane Austen, George Sand, Beatrix Potter, and Iris
Murdoch (to rival those of Truman Capote, Charles Bukowski, C. S. Lewis, and
Marcel Proust).[2] Beyond that, there have been numerous high prestige adaptations
of works by canonical female writers—for instance, a cottage industry of movies
based on Jane Austen novels, and several derived from those of Edith Wharton.

But when fictional author characters have been created for the screen, they have
been predominantly male—be they newspaper reporters, novelists, or screenwriters. (Even female director Xialou Gou picks a male protagonist for her film about
a writer.) There are exceptions, of course. In the category of journalists, one thinks
of newswoman Hildy Johnson (Rosalind Russell) in *His Girl Friday* (1940)—but,
of course, she struggles with competing roles of wife/mother versus professional,
and considers leaving her post. Ultimately, it seems only her romantic attachment

to charismatic editor Walter Burns (Cary Grant) keeps her on the job. In the category of novelists, one thinks of *My Dear Secretary* (1949), a romantic comedy in which Kirk Douglas plays Owen Waterbury, an established author who lectures to a class of aspiring writers that includes Stephanie "Steve" Gaylord (Larraine Day). Attracted, he hires her as his new secretary, and she gives up a promising job with publisher Charles Harris (Rudy Vallee). Waterbury seems to be cavalier about his work and continually whisks her off for various adventures (e.g., gambling). One day he takes her to his beach house and dictates a story about a writer who meets a girl while lecturing and falls in love with her (obviously Stephanie). The two marry, but Owen soon experiences problems writing, and when he submits his latest book to his editor, he receives negative feedback. Secretly, Stephanie takes both his manuscript and her own to Harris. He thinks Stephanie's work is fantastic and Owen's mediocre, but she refuses to publish hers for fear of hurting her husband's ego. Owen misunderstands her meeting with Harris and becomes jealous. After a tumultuous argument, the two separate. Stephanie's book is released and is a smash success. Owen realizes that he has misjudged his wife and, upon hearing that she needs a secretary, he "applies" for the job. Mirroring the earlier episode, she dictates to him a scene that makes clear her continuing love for him. We assume that he will not remain her employee for long. Like *His Girl Friday*, this 1940s film places a woman's professional ambition below her role as wife and angel of the house. Furthermore, for the sake of her mate, the authoress must suppress her own desire for success (even if she is more talented than he).

Since the rise of second-wave feminism, there have been more films about female novelists (some directed by women) that (at least) give lip service to progressive conceptions of the authoress. Most, however, are stylistically conventional and fail to utilize their subject matter in an innovative or reflexive fashion. *My Brilliant Career* (1979) takes place in the Australian bush in the 1890s and concerns a plain, poetic, and spirited young woman, Sybylla Melvyn (Judy Davis), who aspires to be a writer but grows up in a poverty-stricken, rural family. Fortunately, she is sent to live with her wealthy grandmother and there meets the handsome Harry Beecham (Sam Neill), who falls in love with her and proposes marriage. Though he is a "good catch," and from a class far above her own, she rejects his offer, claiming that she must "find herself" first. When her father falls further into debt, Sybylla is brought home to teach the children of a lower-class neighbor to whom he owes money. Harry pursues her but she, again, refuses his betrothal in order to pursue her dreams as a writer. At the end of the film, we see her mail her manuscript (a memoir that ostensibly tells the story we have just witnessed). While the movie was applauded as a work by a female director (Gillian Armstrong) and for its vision of a strong, unconventional woman who chooses career over domesticity, its focus on authorship is minimal—more a rationale for Sybylla's ambition than a full-fledged depiction. Only in the opening of the film do we hear (through Sybylla's voiceover) any words from her book, and only a few times in the drama do we briefly see her with notebook and pen in hand.

Significantly, the only words we actually see her compose are "Dear Harry" in a letter to Beecham.

Romancing the Stone (1984), directed by Robert Zemeckis, concerns best-selling novelist Joan Wilder (Kathleen Turner). It opens with (what we retrospectively learn) is a visualization of a passage from a book that she is composing at a typewriter. Set in the old days of the Wild West, it depicts an outlaw robbing and menacing a gorgeous young woman who manages to kill him. As she escapes, she is pursued by the outlaw's brothers, but is soon saved by a handsome man on horseback. When we leave the cliché scene for present-day reality, we find that Joan lives in New York City with a cat named Romeo, with whom she dines by candlelight. In exiting her apartment one day, she passes an old female neighbor (her future?) who hands her an envelope, commenting, pitifully, that she hopes it is a love letter. Instead, it is a treasure map that her sister Elaine has sent from Colombia. She is being held hostage there and she asks Joan to fly down in order to help set her free. When Joan tells her publisher that she will go, he reminds her that she gets airsick and says, "You're not up to this," but she goes anyway. Once in Colombia, she is followed by several people—a fact she fails to realize. She gets on the wrong bus, which eventually crashes into a truck. That vehicle's owner is Jack Colton (Michael Douglas), who is dressed in a manner that resembles Indiana Jones. She pays him to help her find and rescue her sister. They set off walking—Joan dragging a large suitcase and wearing high heels. When it begins to rain, she recalls that she has brought along no umbrella. When a flash flood carries them both downhill, Jack lands with his head between her legs. Later, as they trek through high foliage, Jack cuts them a path with his knife. When they find a skeleton in a crashed plane, she screams and runs into his arms. Following that, he saves her from a snake. The two decide to look for the treasure themselves. Many car chases ensue (in which Joan looks terrified). When they stop in a field she picks flowers, and her dress, torn by brambles, looks seductive—conveniently off the shoulder at the bodice and slit at the thigh. Eventually, they find the treasure (a huge green stone)—aided by the brand of logic Joan has used in plotting her romance novels. In fighting off the bandits, she begins to show her moxie and strength. With her sister safe and the bad guys defeated, Jack bids her goodbye and Joan is clearly upset. In a coda to the film, we find her back in New York. As she returns to her residence one day, Jack is there (with his yacht parked on the street), ready to take her on a sail around the world. Clearly, the film condescendingly depicts an authoress who writes adventure novels but fails at real-life escapades. Furthermore, while her narratives are awash in heterosexual romance, her day-to-day Romeo is a cat. She gets sick on airplanes, does not pack walking shoes or umbrellas when she travels, gets easily lost, and is afraid of skeletons and snakes. She requires a heroic man as her guide—a valiant, storybook lover. Hence, her writing has been compensatory, bespeaking pure wish fulfillment.

Whereas the films just discussed feature the authoress as lead character, in *She-Devil* (1989) she is a secondary one. The heroine is Ruth Patchett (Roseanne

Barr), the homely wife of accountant Bob (Ed Begley Jr.). At a business gala, Bob ignores Ruth when he encounters famous romance writer Mary Fisher (Meryl Streep), with whom he begins an affair. Fisher (who is portrayed in burlesque fashion) pens Harlequinesque novels aimed at women—selling outlandish stories of fairytale love in a world where men are hyper-masculine and women are frail and subservient. She lives in a pink house and dresses like a southern belle. When Ruth decides to take revenge on her for stealing Bob away, Mary is revealed as a phony. We learn that she was a teenage slut who bore an illegitimate child and that her father was a kosher butcher. By the end of the film both Mary's and Bob's lives are destroyed, though the former emerges as a newly serious writer who authors a memoir entitled *Trust and Betrayal*. Like *My Brilliant Career*, *She-Devil* is directed by a woman (Susan Seidelman), but rather than romanticize the authoress it treats her with feminist irony.

Another work that scripts a female writer as a secondary character is Paul Verhoeven's *Basic Instinct* (1992). The film's hero is Nick Curran (Michael Douglas), a San Francisco police detective who is assigned to the ice-pick murder case of an ex-rock and roller. On the night of his death, the musician had been seen with crime novelist Catherine Tramell (Sharon Stone). When questioned by police, it is clear that she is not only beautiful and sexy, but hard-nosed—claiming only to have "fucked," not dated, the victim. In a famous scene, as she is interviewed by male officers, she spreads her legs slightly to reveal that she is wearing no underwear. From the onset, she flirts with Nick, seeming to know a lot about him (e.g., that criminal charges were once pressed against him for shootings in the line of fire). She becomes a prime suspect for the musician's murder since her last book (written under the pen name of Catherine Woolf [animal? or Bloomsbury writer?]) concerns one killed with an ice pick. Her other novels also have strange connections to notable deaths. Seducing Nick, she now claims to be writing a novel about him.

One day, in arriving at her house, Nick sees her manuscript being printed out. One page narrates the death of the fictional cop's partner. Sure enough, in the next scene Nick's real one dies. On the one hand, all signs point to Catherine's guilt (as a classic femme fatale); on the other, she spins a web of suspicion around other individuals, including one of Nick's ex-lovers. While *In a Lonely Place* absolves the male writer of blame for murder, *Basic Instinct* leaves us questioning Catherine's innocence. For in its final sequence, we find her and Nick making love in her bed; the camera pans away from the couple to frame an ice pick on the floor nearby. While a marvelous thriller, *Basic Instinct* utilizes Catherine's authorial status as a mere plot point, and we never see her in the act of writing.

So far, we have examined works in which the female reporter or novelist was depicted in the movies. As for female screenwriters, examples are almost nonexistent. *I Could Never Be Your Woman* (2007) skirts the issue by focusing on Rosie (Michelle Pfeiffer), a forty-ish television writer and single mother. Rather than dealing with her craft (penning a popular teen show), or on the tensions of being a working parent, the film is a generic romcom whose major "problem" is whether the gorgeous Rosie is too old for her suitor Adam (Paul Rudd)—the average-looking twenty-nine-year-old actor appearing in her series. Though written and directed by a woman (Amy Heckerling), the film is far from progressive.

While all these are entirely conventional films of almost no stylistic interest, one recent work about the authoress plays modestly with form. *Stranger Than Fiction* (2006), directed by Marc Forster, attempts the convoluted complexity of *Adaptation* but fails—nonetheless raising some noteworthy points along the way. It concerns a repressed tax auditor, Harold Crick (Will Ferrell)—a "nowhere man" —who suddenly begins to hear a woman's voice in his head, narrating his every action; her words are audible to the audience as well. Through this discursive strategy, the spectator experiences simultaneously and in a palpable way the difference between an imagistic rendering of a scene (that which we see onscreen) and its verbal description (that which we hear). While Harold's co-workers and shrink think he is schizophrenic, he soon comprehends that he is a character in someone else's story (the tagline for the film reads: "He's not crazy. He's just written that way"). We learn the truth of this when the scene shifts to writer Karen Eiffel (Emma Thompson)—whose novel-in-progress, in fact, concerns Harold.

But what does the film say about female authorship? First, the use of a female voiceover in the classical cinema has been rare (though it also appears in *My Brilliant Career* and *She-Devil*, significantly, works by women directors). The female voiceover in *Stranger Than Fiction*, however, is conduited through a man's head. Furthermore, Karen almost drives her male character crazy. Moreover, she intends to kill him off, so he must resist her pernicious clutches in order to stay alive (as Nick Curran must resist Catherine Trammel's). Beyond that, at points Karen seems to be quasi-suicidal herself. In imagining deaths for Harold, we view her teetering on the edge of a tall building, realizing, only retrospectively, that she is merely standing on her desk, fantasizing the scene and placing herself in her character's position. Finally, Karen belongs to the group of neurotic authors (like Barton Fink or Charlie Kaufman): she suffers writer's block, and is both a chain smoker and a nervous wreck. Ultimately, of course (in a manner consonant with the Hollywood happy ending), Harold's dilemma leads him to "learn how to live life fully" (the kind of epiphany mocked in *Adaptation*). But he accomplishes this largely through lessons taught him by a male literature professor he consults, rather than through the insights of Karen.

SWIMMING POOL: THE RETURN OF THE REPRESSED

As we have seen, even when the female writer appears onscreen, it is not necessarily the case that she does so in a film worthy of her skills. Most such movies use the authoress merely as a character type (and a none-too-progressive one at that), failing to engage her profession in the formal structure of the film. This is decidedly not the case in *Swimming Pool* (2003), directed by François Ozon and written by

Ozon and Emmanuèle Bernheim. The film concerns middle-aged mystery writer Sarah Morton (Charlotte Rampling), who is famed for her Inspector Dorwell series. Thus she takes on a subject not unlike that of Catherine Tramell. She is a rather cold and aloof individual who lives with her elderly father. In a sequence occurring in the office of her publisher (and former lover) John (Charles Dance), she reveals that, although the Dorwell series has been hugely profitable, she is fed up with murder stories and wants to work on something new. He suggests that she retreat to his vacant summer home in France to work in peace and quiet.

When Sarah arrives in France at John's lovely, old stone house, the first thing she does is to open the window and heartily breathe in the country air; the second is to remove a crucifix from the wall of her bedroom. Her third act is to take from the armoire a burnt orange floral-patterned robe (a contrast to her conservative, monotone garb) and hold it up to herself in a mirror. Her fourth act is to take out her laptop and plug it in. All these moves will prove important within the filmic narrative.

Sarah settles into country life and frequents an outdoor café tended by a handsome young waiter, Franck (Jean-Marie Lamour)—choosing tea over spirits. At home, she eats nothing but plain yogurt. On numerous occasions, we see her working: staring at a notebook, looking at a blank computer screen, typing on a keyboard, printing out pages, reading them. When John telephones to ask how Sarah is doing, she calls his home a "paradise," but is disappointed when he fails to respond to her query about visiting her.

What this narrative exposition has established is, first, that Sarah is a serious writer. Ozon has called the film "a self-portrait" of "the way [he] work[s]." As he notes: "I show the writing process in its most concrete form, [and] talk about the little habits we may have before starting to write."[3] We can see this in his screenplay's description of Sarah arranging her workspace: "[Sarah] must now set up her desk. She pushes a nightstand against the window, places a small lamp on it and takes her laptop, her printer, a power strip, an adaptor, sheets of paper and a small pencil case out of a big bag. She meticulously places each object where it belongs, the printer on the floor, the laptop at the center of the table."[4] Second, the exposition makes clear that Sarah is not only socially remote, but reclusive. Third, the repeated shots of her deeply breathing country air suggest that she lacks vitality. Fourth, her choice of tea (over liquor) and yogurt (over solid food) hints at asceticism. Finally, her interactions with John propose that she is a lover manquée. One of the first times we see her working at her computer, something interesting happens. As she turns her head left (looking offscreen) the camera pans to what appears to be a modern marble, egg-shaped sculpture on a bureau. Its surface is transected by demarcated lines positioned in a geometric fashion. It is not clear whether they are simply elements of design or breaks that allow the piece to come apart and be reassembled. We will return to it later.

In classic dramatic fashion, having set up a situation of equilibrium, the narrative takes a drastic turn when a chaotic element enters the scene in the form of an unexpected guest. John's daughter Julie (Ludivine Sagnier) shows up without prior notice, caustically asking Sarah if she is his father's "latest conquest." The contrast between the two women could not be greater. Julie is youthful, seductive, and beautiful, whereas Sarah is middle-aged, handsome, and restrained. Julie is messy (leaving clothing, liquor bottles, and dirty dishes around the house), while Sarah is tidy and orderly. But the greatest "affronts" to Sarah's sensibility come in regard to Julie's sexual demeanor. She walks around topless and swims naked. Moreover, she has a series of one-night stands (her behavior bordering on nymphomania), culminating in loud, raucous sex. Sarah calls John to complain, but he is not there.

Sarah's response to Julie is also telling. She is frequently seen observing the girl (often through her bedroom windows), and her penchant for watching Julie's antics has the taint of voyeurism—positioning the girl as sexually liberated and Sarah as repressed, but curious. This is shown most dramatically in a scene in which Sarah stumbles on Julie and her date nude in the living room making love. As Sarah peers through a paneled glass door, we see the couple's reflection in it, superimposed over her own. At one point, through a rack focus (but still in a reflective shot), Julie looks up, defiantly making eye contact with Sarah. A sense of Sarah's erotic unease is also signaled by her wearing earplugs to drown out the sounds of Julie's lovemaking (interestingly, the sound is muffled for the audience as well, identifying us with Sarah's acoustic point of view). Likewise, her reticence is suggested in one scene that positions Julie's bare breasts uncomfortably close to Sarah's body when the latter sunbathes. In the same scene, we get a close-up of Julie's navel as though from Sarah's point of view. If one is extremely perceptive, she may notice a small scar on Julie's belly.

Not surprisingly, the swimming pool of the title figures heavily into the drama. When Sarah first arrives at John's house, a plastic sheet covers the water, with leaves littering its surface. After Julie arrives, the pool is uncovered and the young woman swims in it naked or bikini-clad. When Julie asks Sarah if she wants to take a dip, the writer responds that she "loathes" pools, which are "cesspools of living bacteria." Again, we sense that Sarah is repulsed by biological contact.

Hearing that Sarah is a writer, Julie assumes that she pens romances (like Joan Wilder or Mary Fisher), a mistake that the author snidely corrects. Retaliating, Julie calls her Miss Marple (a fictional matron and amateur detective in numerous Agatha Christie novels). When Sarah is annoyed by a loud telephone conversation that Julie is having, the latter calls her an "English bitch with a broom up her ass" (an allusion to witches). On a later occasion, she calls her an "old maid."

Though Sarah clearly despises Julie's behavior, the young woman begins to influence her. Although she rejects Julie's offer to share her *foie gras*, when the young woman departs Sarah raids the refrigerator and sneaks some of her pate and salami. We also see her swig some of Julie's wine straight from the bottle. Sarah begins to swim in the pool (in a tasteful one-piece suit), sunbathe, and engage in pleasant conversation with Franck at the town café. On one occasion, it is implied

FIGURE 18. Sarah (Charlotte Rampling) and Julie (Ludivine Sagnier), contrasting figures, sit on the patio in *Swimming Pool* (2003).

that she has an erotic dream about him. In this sequence we suddenly (with no motivation) see an image of a man's torso standing over Julie, who is sunbathing on a chaise longue. The camera pans sensuously down his body to the young woman, who begins to masturbate as the man watches. Suddenly, we cut to Sarah in bed at night, her eyes abruptly opening. Offscreen, we hear Julie's real sexual moans (with no indication of whom she is with). This time, Sarah reaches for her earplugs but does not insert them. The suggestion is that she continues to listen. Later on, there is a shot of Sarah sunbathing in a chaise. A man's torso is seen beside her (as in her dream), but when the camera pans up it is only the old gardener (Marc Fayolle). Clearly, there is a difference between Sarah's sexual fantasies and her reality.

Significantly, the morning after her dream of Franck and Julie, as Sarah sits at her computer screen, she opens a new folder entitled "Julie" (next to one called "Dorwell on Holiday"). She smiles a bit as she types at a faster pace than usual —clearly energized. Later, however, when she encounters Julie downstairs, she scolds her for the noise made the previous night. Julie snaps, "Yes, mother," and accuses Sarah of being a "frustrated English woman who writes about dirty things but never does them."

Ironically, this fight with Julie seems to have cemented Sarah's interest in her (both personal and literary). The next day she goes into Julie's room and finds a diary. We then get an over-the-shoulder shot of Sarah reading the handwritten tome. Inserted into the volume is a photograph of a woman who looks (from her age) as though she could be Julie's mother. Back in Sarah's room, the camera pans from Julie's diary to Sarah's fingers on her computer keyboard, typing.

After this, Sarah's behavior toward Julie drastically changes. She expresses concern when the girl does not return one night, then asks her out for dinner. At the restaurant, the conversation turns to Julie's mother, whom the girl claims John abandoned. Sarah interrogates Julie further and learns that her mother is a writer who burned her autobiographical novel when John denigrated it.

In a sequence that resembles Sarah's earlier exploration of Julie's bedroom, Julie now sneaks into Sarah's and searches her desktop and drawers. When she examines a folder, she looks upset, reads it voraciously, gasps, and stares at the camera. We assume it is the file entitled "Julie" and that she has learned that Sarah is studying her for novelistic purposes. Later, when Sarah returns home, she is puzzled that the crucifix has been repositioned over her bed, but she does not take it down. Here and in many other scenes, *Swimming Pool* is reminiscent of Ingmar Bergman's *Persona* (1966), which places two women (Elisabeth [Liv Ullmann], a psychiatric patient, and her nurse, Alma [Bibi Andersson]) in a country home. Slowly, the two become close, until the nurse opens a letter that the patient has written and learns that the woman has been studying her—letting her confess secrets only to find them banal and amusing. At that point, the nurse takes revenge by leaving a piece of broken glass at a location where the barefoot patient is sure to walk. The film is infused with a discourse of character doubling.

In a similar fashion, Julie plans her reprisal for the unsuspecting Sarah's breach of trust. Having noticed the writer's interest in the town waiter, Franck, she brings him home one night as her "date" in order to make Sarah jealous. All three share a drink and Julie offers a sardonic toast to Sarah's book. Sarah excuses herself and goes to her bedroom, where we see her typing furiously and smoking, as seen reflected in the room's window. When she hears a splash outside, she goes to the balcony and observes the couple taking a nude swim. Franck tries to leave, but Julie grabs him and begins to engage in fellatio, almost as an act of rape. Sarah then picks up a stone and throws it down at the water, expressing her annoyance. Hearing the splash, Franck commands Julie to stop and pushes her in the water. As he dresses to leave, Julie gets out of the pool and yells at him. A loud argument ensues.

We next see Sarah awakening the following morning, startled. She finds Julie asleep alone. Suspicious of a bulge under the pool cover, she cranks it open, as though expecting to find a body below. When only a pool float is revealed, she hurries to the café to look for Franck. It is closed because he has not shown up for work. She returns to the house and notices bloodstains on the poolside concrete. She goes to Franck's house, only to find it empty.

When Sarah returns home, convinced that Franck is dead, she discovers Julie in bed, frantic and hysterical: "I thought you abandoned me," she cries, and calls Sarah "Mommy." Significantly, Sarah has learned that Julie's mother died in an accident and is not alive, as the girl implied. Finally, Julie confesses to killing Franck. When asked why, she responds: "For you, for the book." Strangely, Sarah does not react to this startling statement and we next see her open a shed door to find Franck's body. As she leans on a wall catching her breath, a flashback ensues. Some of it represents moments we have seen, but others we have not: Julie fellates

Franck; Sarah throws a rock down from her balcony; Franck tries to flee from Julie; an argument occurs; Sarah removes her ear plugs; Julie smashes Franck's head with a rock. Her groans, in so doing, mimic the sounds she has made in love-making. What is implied here is that this is Sarah's recollection and that, in fact, she has overheard the crime. Hence she awakens with a start the following morning, "knowing" (on some level) that a murder has taken place. Furthermore, it is her rock-throwing (which foreshadows Julie's assault on Franck) that initiates the latter's retreat and the argument that follows, so in some sense she bears "guilt" for what happened—especially since we have sensed that she has feelings for Franck.

Following Julie's admission of the crime, Sarah takes charge—their roles finally reversed—the older woman now in control (like Mommy). Here, she is a far cry from Joan Wilder, who writes romances but has no flair for real-life adventure. Rather than report the murder as we might have assumed, Sarah helps Julie bury the body on the house grounds. When Julie tells Sarah that she should burn her manuscript since it could be used as evidence, Sarah looks horrified (now realizing that Julie has read it). Julie covers over this, saying, "I didn't read it, but I can just imagine." Julie also asks whether Sarah is helping her because she writes about murder, and Sarah replies: "Absolutely." When Sarah returns to her room, she takes down the cross that has been repositioned over her bed.

Sarah orders Julie to act as though nothing has happened and continue her day-to-day existence to avoid suspicion. When the old gardener arrives and seems suspicious of the soil under which the women have buried Franck, Sarah (wearing the loud orange robe) calls him to her bedroom as a means of distraction. For the first time, the camera pans Sarah's naked body as his hands stroke her leg. Surprisingly, a close-up reveals her contented face.

Julie announces that she will soon leave and Sarah promises to say nothing about the murder to her father. She asks Julie a final question about how she got the scar on her stomach. The girl answers that it was "a car accident" and we suspect that it may be from the same mishap that killed her mother. After Julie departs, Sarah finds a large envelope on her bed. Julie's voiceover (standing in for the note Sarah is reading) informs us that it contains her mother's manuscript, which she is giving to Sarah. In the next scene, the camera pans from pages of the manuscript to Sarah's hands typing.

An abrupt cut takes us to John's publishing house in London, where he is expressing puzzlement and dismay at Sarah's latest work, entitled *Swimming Pool*. She retorts slyly: "Shall I burn it?" She tells him it is her finest work and that another press will publish it. She leaves a signed copy for his daughter. As Sarah departs the office (through glass-paned swinging doors), a young girl enters. The secretaries call her Julia and, after she asks for her father, we see her greet John. She is young and blonde, but not the girl we have seen in France—more of a chubby adolescent with braces. Sarah peers at her, though she does not look surprised. The film ends with an unexplained (and dreamy) cut back to the French country house. Sarah is on her balcony slowly waving; a young woman is down below by the pool (seen from behind) waving back. When we cut to a frontal close-up of her, we first see Julia's face, then a second later, Julie's.

This film has required an elaborate and lengthy description because it is a highly complex work. But how is it of interest in relation to the female writer? And how does that subject wend its way not only into the film's action, but into its very style? On the one hand, it seems to present the authoress in an old-fashioned mode—as a reserved "spinster"—a variation on the stereotypical depiction of the middle-aged professional woman. This is precisely the image that Ozon sought. As he notes misogynistically: "I enjoy the personality of these strictly dressed women, these generally unpleasant, sex-deprived spinsters who write stuff that looks nothing like them."[5] Clearly, the term (in signifying an unmarried/childless female) has negative connotations. As Suzette Henke notes: "The spinster is, by definition, 'de trop'—a supplement to traditional community organization and an outsider whose disruptive and subversive behavior might, indeed, make her an outcast, a rebel, or a bohemian artist."[6] The last characterization (artist) relates to another meaning of the term: "a woman whose occupation is spinning"—thus Sarah's vocation as novelist is especially apt. As Henke comments: "Often alone and sometimes defenseless, [the spinster] continues to spin wheels and words, webs and visions, fantasies and frustrations—all collected in the marginal spaces allotted to the out-cast curiously at odds with contemporary society's prominent domestic center."[7] Henke's mention of the spinster's isolation reminds us that Sarah's father has warned her not to be alone. But seclusion is part of her work method, a point he ignores. As Victoria Boynton remarks: "In a capitalist culture that depends on constant attention to social relations and discourages sitting still and keeping one's own company—especially for women—many of th[e] negative terms [associated with solitude] point to feelings of being ostracized, disconnected, depressed. . . . This retreat is characterized as either pitiable or pathological."[8] Disagreeing with this view, Virginia Woolf famously commented on the need for seclusion in writing. As she notes, "At a certain moment [the writer] must leave the company and withdraw, alone, to that mysterious room."[9]

As part of her spinster portrayal, Sarah is repressed, lacking libido, doing (as Julie taunts) in her books what she cannot do in life (thus, having "uptight morals"). She barely eats, cannot tolerate the sounds of lovemaking, and is an obsessive housekeeper. The title of her last book, *Inspector Dorwell Wears a Kilt*, makes Julie and Franck laugh. Kilts, of course, are known (correctly or not) for being worn without underwear—so the image stands as a quaint and modest metaphor for Sarah's veiled interest in the opposite sex. Furthermore, when she fantasizes about Franck, she needs to imagine Julie as her surrogate (masturbating as Franck stands above); so Sarah's desires are triangulated or deflected.

It is worth mentioning that the idea of the artist sublimating sexual desire through creative work has a long history in criticism, originally based on the theories of Sigmund Freud. In "The Relation of the Poet to Day-Dreaming," he asserts that literature derives from the transposition of fantasies into writing. He argues that "happy people never make phantasies [*sic*] only unsatisfied ones," thus implying that the artist is dysphoric. Furthermore, those fantasies can be divided into "two principal groups." "Either they are ambitious wishes . . . or they are erotic," though sometimes the two are "united." Moreover, for women, "erotic wishes dominate . . . almost exclusively."[10] But the tendency to treat the artwork as symptom and its creator as neurotic was subsequently attacked. Otto Rank, for instance, saw the process of sublimation as more of a benign practice. As he writes: "I, for my part, am of the opinion that . . . positively willed control takes the place of negative inhibition, and that it is the masterful use of the sexual impulse in the service of this individual will which produces the sublimation."[11] Other theorists have also expressed reservations about Freud's formulation. As Robert Gorham David remarks: "If art is merely a substitute gratification of repressed desires in such disguised form that they can get by the censor, then art is essentially the same as a dream, even though it may, by its realism and coherence, seem to take account of external reality. And criticism is largely a matter of penetrating the disguises and discovering what is really behind them. It has no criteria for the work of art as such."[12] Nonetheless, even today, one finds articles like a recent one in *Psychology Today* by Susan K. Perry, Ph.D., entitled "How Creative Flow Is Like Sex." To make her point, she quotes Isabel Allende as stating: "Writing is like making love. Don't worry about the orgasm, just concentrate on the process."[13] Elsewhere, a similar statement by Allende is quoted by a different author: "The deep joy I feel after . . . making love is invariably reflected in my work, as if my body, gratified, destines the best of its energy to lend wings to my writing."[14]

It is significant that in *Swimming Pool*, the repressed authoress stands in contrast to a famous male character: Humbert Humbert in Vladimir Nabokov's *Lolita*. He, too, rents a house in order to finish a book and encounters the daughter of its homeowner, Charlotte. But lasciviousness rather than asceticism is his response to the young woman. A diary also figures heavily into Nabokov's plot as it is by surreptitiously reading Humbert's journal that Charlotte learns of his illicit desires for her child. There is also a murder when, many years after his encounter with Lolita, Humbert learns that a man wanted to cast her in pornographic films; in retaliation, Humbert kills him.

Though in *Swimming Pool*, Sarah initially dismisses Julie's ways, they obviously affect her, and we see her loosen up over the course of the narrative. It is here that a sense of doubling between the two women surfaces (as the narrative itself doubles *Lolita*). But the question of surface has other ramifications. Given the film's title, the pool is a central space both physically and metaphorically. With numerous shots of Julie and one of Sarah underwater, there is a sense of the mise-en-scène as echoing the women's psyches, composed of surface and depth, fluidly interconnected. The pool is also a reflective plane that replicates any image that hits it (as when Julie sunbathes and we see her image duplicated on the water). Mirrors are also crucial in the film and are utilized at significant moments. The first such shot occurs one day when Sarah removes Julie's panties from the lawn (but, strangely, takes them to her own room). Once there, she sits at her computer typing. In a shot that follows, we pan to a mirror that reflects her image in second mirror across the room, above the fireplace mantle—so she is doubly framed in a Magritte-like manner that confuses the spectator's perception. Interestingly, it is after this shot that we first see Sarah swim in the pool, followed by a pan up her body as she sunbathes—indicating a new sensuality. The next time a mirror shot occurs, we see Sarah notice that the cross has been mysteriously repositioned above her bed (indicating that someone has been in her room) but, then, decide not to remove it (she finally does so only after she has assisted in hiding the murder). Here, however, it is as though she accepts the bizarre complicity that is materializing between herself and Julie—their pact to avoid acknowledging the other's voyeuristic interest (like Blue and Black spying on one another in Paul Auster's *The New York Trilogy*). The last mirror shot of Sarah occurs at the moment that Julie tells her she is leaving and Sarah asks about the scar on her stomach. Julie inquires: "Is that [information] for your book?"—revealing again that she knows she is its subject. This time, Sarah says, "Yes," admitting for the first time that Julie is her topic. While Sarah may seem the typical spinster/writer, her genre is crime (vs. romance), not the conventional female form (though Agatha Christie is mentioned in the film). Interestingly, Sarah's sexuality has a role in Julie's offense as we assume that the latter has hooked up with Franck specifically to make the older woman jealous. Furthermore, it is only after Julie kills Franck that Sarah engages in sex, though it is passionless and done as a ruse (to divert the old gardener from the burial plot). Significantly, at the moment she "seduces" him, she is wearing the orange floral robe (so unlike her own clothes) that she has found in the bedroom closet. In a variety of ways, the two women's relationship resonates with sadomasochism. Significantly, Franck hails from Lacoste (the home of the Marquis de Sade), and in conversing with Sarah at the café he suggests she visit the touristic site. In the next shot we see her standing by an old, crumbling wall—which could be the locale in question. Of course, Sade was a novelist—like Sarah. Though seen initially as an "old maid," Sarah is later placed in the maternal position—first negatively (when Julie sarcastically responds "Yes, Mother" to Sarah's scolding), then positively (when a panicked Julie seeks Sarah's help after her murderous act), then ambiguously (when Sarah reads and perhaps draws upon Julie's mother's manuscript). Hence, the theme of doubling expands to include mothers as well. This role fits into certain clichés of authorship—often those voiced by men. Kim Greenblatt states: "The best analogy for writing fiction, if you have to do it, is that it is like giving birth. Not having female reproductive equipment I can't vouch for that particular statement but I can see some analogies."[15] Women have used the metaphor too; for instance, Flannery O'Connor (who never bore a child) once quipped: "Writing is like giving birth to a piano sideways."

In the maternal stance, Sarah springs into action—finally besting Julie and gaining control of her fate. Here, we recall what seemed like a gratuitous shot early on of a suggestive, egg-shaped, sculpture in Sarah's bedroom. Also significant is

FIGURE 19. Sarah Morton (Charlotte Rampling) twice reflected in mirrors as she sits at her writing desk in *Swimming Pool* (2003).

the fact that Sarah openly states her interest in Julie's mother when the two dine out, and ultimately may utilize the woman's manuscript in her own book (as she has already mined Julie's diary). Here, we are reminded of the theme of theft we have located in the theories of Roland Barthes, the fiction of Italo Calvino, and the films of Paul Auster, not an unfamiliar topic in literary scholarship or creation. On another level, Sarah is also a kind of vampire (like Calvino's readers) who sucks the life out of others. Here, her uneasiness with the bedroom crucifix seems a central rhetorical figure.

Given that the work of Julie's mother has been suppressed by a man, Sarah can be seen, in a feminist frame, to bespeak the silenced maternal voice. In this regard, our reading of the female writer's work in *Swimming Pool* is consonant with the critical approach that Susan Stanford Friedman suggests for analyzing the writing of real authoresses (significantly, the scenario for the film was co-written by a woman). As Friedman notes: "Adapting Freud to a feminist project, I will propose a psycho-political hermeneutic for reading women's narratives that decodes them as articulations of what has been forbidden to women, that reads them as effects of ideological and psychological censorship."[16] In particular, she finds the maternal trope central to that which is often repressed in women's texts. As she writes,

> "There is," Freud writes in *The Interpretation of Dreams*, "at least one spot in every dream at which it is unplumbable—a navel, as it were, that is its point of contact with the unknown." As the dream's "navel," the unplumbable aporia of the dream-text for Freud is the point of contact with the maternal body, the irretrievable site of origins. Freud's metaphor for the gap or knot in the dream-text and the text of dream interpretation privileges woman—specifically the maternal-as-origin of what is

censored, what is disguised in the grammar of the dream-work. Ultimately, his figurative formulation suggests, the return of the repressed is the return of woman, of that mother/other, to him forever unknown, untranscribable, untranslatable.[17]

Several things are resonant in this quote in relation to *Swimming Pool*. Friedman highlights Freud's use of the term *navel* to signify the incomprehensible element of the dream—clearly a metaphor that associates the maternal with the unknown. In *Swimming Pool*, we are shown a brief (and seemingly gratuitous) shot of Julie's belly-button (as from Sarah's point of view) as the two women sunbathe one afternoon. Furthermore, it is the story of the mother that has been repressed in Julie's narrative (as has the maternal word), and the entire tale of the mother is shrouded in mystery. What is also interesting about Friedman's approach is that (again following Freudian notions of free-association) she "interprets [women's writing] as part of an endless web of intertext."[18] Here, we recall *Swimming Pool*'s connections to such classic works as Nabokov's *Lolita* and Bergman's *Persona*—which also focus on the maternal (the former in Lolita's mother, and the latter in Elisabeth's failed parenthood and in Alma's traumatic abortion). What is also especially interesting about *Swimming Pool* is its vision of writing as linked to murder—a theme we have previously uncovered in *Barton Fink* (1991), *Homicide* (1991), *Adaptation* (2002), and *Basic Instinct* (1992). Interestingly, when Virginia Woolf talks of writing in a solitary room, she says that there, "life is subjected to a thousand disciplines and exercises. It is curbed; it is killed."[19] Clearly, this last phrase has particular relevance to the work of crime writers like Sarah Morton (whose name includes the French word for death, *mort*) and Catherine Tramell (possibly a homicidal sociopath).

When Julie is asked by Sarah why she has murdered Franck, she says, "For you, for the book." Hence, she flippantly asserts that she has done so to provide the writer with provocative material. Of course, there is hostility toward Sarah in her statement and act—especially since she later suggests that the author burn her manuscript to prevent its being used as evidence in her prosecution. (Was that her plan all along? To murder Franck in order to destroy Sarah's novel?) Beyond that, Sarah not only writes detective narratives but seems only to come to life when there is real slaughter in her world. She responds to it clinically and amorally—using all the tricks of her authorial trade to cover up the heinous deed (apparently for no reason). Though her task is to hide someone else's crime (and not to commit one herself), she is again like Catherine Tramell, whose fictional and real-life homicides intermix in a troubling fashion.

Of course, the major way in which the form of the film comes into dramatic play occurs at the end, when Sarah visits her publisher's office and passes by his daughter entering the room. The secretaries call her Julia and she looks very different from the girl we have previously known as Julie. Sarah stares at her through a window in the door, but her expression is hard to read and certainly not one of shock. This shot is followed by a dream-like sequence (rendered in subtle slow motion) in which we are back in France with Sarah on the balcony waving to a young woman down below. In the first close-up of the girl we see Julia, and in the second we see Julie. Thus, if Sarah and Julie are "doubled" throughout, one of the doubles now has a double as well (like the film's mirrors within mirrors). But these sequences also lead us to question the veracity of the narrative we have seen that has been presented as "reality." Was Julie actually at the house, living as an imposter? There is plausibility for this view, as Sarah never manages successfully to speak to John after Julie arrives, so the girl might have been able to get away with the hoax. Sarah does, however, leave an irate phone message for John, which he would have found puzzling if his daughter were not there. In this reading, Sarah accepts Julie's subterfuge at the moment she learns of it (in John's office)—just one more element in the two women's illicit complicity. According to another interpretation, there was no daughter (real or fake) visiting the country home at all. If it had actually been Julia, she and Sarah would have recognized each other as they passed in John's office (which they do not). From this perspective, the film's narrative events are actually occurring within Sarah's novelistic imagination—much in the spirit of the latter half of *Barton Fink* or *Adaptation*. (Ironically, earlier she ordered Julie to stop imagining.) Like the surface and depth of the swimming pool, the two realms have been connected seamlessly—the point at which one becomes the other is entirely unclear. In some sense the insistent prevalence of windows in the film (through which Sarah often gazes at Julie down below) also speaks of a borderless connection between interior and exterior. Here, the camera often marks the tension by assuming two alternating stances—one of Sarah inside looking out (with her body either pictured in the frame or not) and the other of the camera outside looking in at her observing. Thus, the spatial metaphor of interiority and exteriority tends to replicate the psychic poles of fantasy and reality. Ultimately, the film offers no resolution of this enigma and we are left with a puzzle—much like the marble sculpture that adorns Sarah's room.

TANGO LESSON

In shifting from *Swimming Pool* to *The Tango Lesson* (1997), we move from a work directed by a man (though co-written by a female) to one entirely authored by a woman: Sally Potter. We are also veering from a text that posits the female writer as repressed and linked to formulaic fiction to one that depicts the author as desirous and committed to self-expression. We also turn from a fairly conventional work (though one with great stylistic flourishes) to a modernist narrative form.

But first, a word about its maker. When Sally Potter came of age as a filmmaker in London in the 1970s, she did so within the force field of two powerful cultural movements: feminist theory and structural film. From the former, she gained an understanding of the historic suppression of female authorship and the ways in which issues of gender might be integrated into works of art. From the latter, she inherited an appreciation of experimental cinema of a conceptual bent. Her first major film, *Thriller* (1979), was immediately hailed by E. Ann Kaplan as a ground-breaking feminist "theory film," a work "concerned with demystifying representation so as to make women aware that texts are producers of ideology." Such films were said to be both highly self-reflexive and concerned with questions of female subjectivity and women's history.[20] With its deconstruction of traditional melodrama (specifically the libretto of Giacomo Puccini's *La Bohème*) and its analysis of the tragic role assigned to the heroine in literature and theater, *Thriller* clearly conformed to this new genre.

At first glance, *The Tango Lesson* seems a far cry from the stern and ascetic *Thriller*. Rather than dissect a patriarchal form like opera, Potter engages another—tango. Moreover, instead of rejecting melodrama, the director relishes it, since *The Tango Lesson* concerns Potter's passionate and tumultuous love affair with dancer Pablo Veron (as well as her decision to create a film about it). But with a work as sly and complex as Potter's, we should not jump to rash conclusions about its relative conventionality. And with a title like *The Tango Lesson*, we should not precipitously dismiss its pedagogical potential. Ultimately, Potter's movie is a "theory film" for the 1990s—one that teaches us not only the lessons of the tango but of feminism as well. But if it is a revised "theory film," what suppositions does it rework—especially regarding female authorship? If *The Tango Lesson* provides us with lessons in more than dance, what cultural curriculum does it endorse?

Lesson 1: The Female Author

Significantly, Potter made *The Tango Lesson* following the release of her film *Orlando* (1992), an adaptation of a novel by Virginia Woolf, a feminist authorial heroine. As Potter notes: "There was an absolute explosion after I finished doing the press tour of *Orlando*. . . . I got back to my table and sat down and thought, 'Now what?' I reached for my pencil and there was this wild explosion of ideas that had accumulated."[21] As though to raise the issue immediately, *The Tango Lesson* begins with black-and-white footage of a blank sheet of paper on a table. In close-up, Potter (cast as "Sally") lifts a pencil and begins to write. Abruptly, the image shifts to color footage of a female model, dressed in red, who is fired upon by a gun—ostensibly Sally's authorial vision. The image then returns to black and white and depicts a blank page on which Sally writes the word *rage*. Instantly, she crumples the paper and discards it. As though to imply her frustration in writing (and her need for escape), the next sequence depicts Sally entering a theater in Paris where the tango is to be performed. It is here that she first encounters dancer Pablo Veron. What this segment has succinctly communicated is the female author's alleged difficulty with art making—a dread and blockage that propels her toward flight. Significantly, Sally has attempted to compose with a pencil, a more tentative implement than a pen. When she returns to London, she again confronts her *tabula rasa*. As she sharpens the lead to begin to write, the screen once more erupts with Felliniesque color images of the scenario she envisions: a drama in which high-fashion models are shot at during a photography session. The image returns

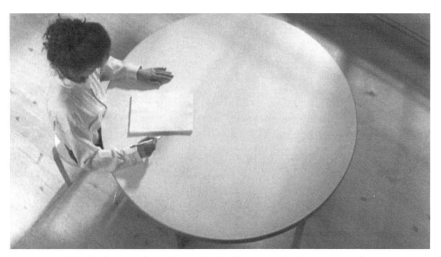

FIGURE 20. Sally (Sally Potter) confronts the blank page in *The Tango Lesson* (1997).

to Sally in black and white, whereupon she again seems discouraged in writing and relaxes by taking a few tango steps. In the next sequence, she enters a London nightspot for ballroom dancing. In a later segment, she returns to the blank sheet of paper and her authorial task but is distracted by a stain on her writing table. As Françoise Sagan once said: "Public enemy number one is the paper!"[22]

After some intervening color footage of her imagined fashion-thriller, Sally kneels on the floor and examines a crack in the wood planking. Her action again suggests writer's block, this time masked by obsessive-compulsive behavior that focuses on the minutia of domestic space. As the drama continues (and Sally's ceiling disintegrates), we are reminded of the Gothic genre and of the decaying house in which the literary heroine often finds herself. We seem to be witnessing "The Fall of the House of Potter," whose collapse appears to be tied to her disquietude with writing. At the suggestion of a contractor, Sally vacates her crumbling London abode (while he deconstructs it). She then travels to Buenos Aires to pursue her "double life" as a tango dancer. Clearly, "a room of her own" has proven a troubled site and her attempt at authorship seems momentarily on hold.

Lesson 2: Writing Pleasure over Pain

In bolting to Argentina, Sally leaves behind an aborted film scenario. Entitled *Rage* (shown to us in fleeting, garish vignettes that contrast with the other black-and-white segments), it seems to be a quasi-experimental work, drawing on themes from a range of films including *The Eyes of Laura Mars* (1978), and concerning a group of models who are murderously pursued by a demented, fashion designer. At a later meeting with Hollywood executives, Sally (with calculated pretension) calls her film a "treatise on beauty and the glamorization of death" (while the studio "suits" crassly deem it "Carnage on the Catwalk"). Although such a scenario might have been novel in the late seventies (bespeaking the newly voiced feminist "rage" at an exploitative culture of female objectification), by the late nineties the idea seems clichéd and hackneyed—which is precisely the point. On some level, Sally has not only abandoned the screenplay for *Rage*, but the very emotion that it signifies. Thus, in trekking around the world in pursuit of the tango, she chooses pleasure over pain—an amorous "last tango in Paris" rather than a grim "dance of death."

In having Sally travel around the world, Potter questions the dominant feminist doctrine of the 1970s, which, suspicious of visual/erotic pleasure, called for the forging of a new minimalist style of art. As Laura Mulvey wrote in her seminal 1975 essay, "It is said that analyzing pleasure or beauty destroys it. That is the intention of this article. The satisfaction and reinforcement of the ego that represent the high point of film history hitherto must be attacked."[23] In the intervening years (between 1975 and 1997), the feminist community had clearly nuanced its stance on this issue. In 1982, a provocative conference entitled "Toward a Politics of Sexuality" was held at Barnard College. It led to publication of an anthology, *Pleasure and Danger*, in which the "puritanical" nature of the contemporary women's movement was questioned—reminding us of the contrast between the characters of Sarah and Julie in *Swimming Pool*. As Carole S. Vance wrote in the introduction to the volume, "To focus only on pleasure and gratification ignores the patriarchal structure in which women act, yet to speak only of sexual violence and oppression ignores women's experience with sexual agency and choice and unwittingly increases the sexual . . . despair in which women live."[24] Vance added that the intent of the conference was "to expand the analysis of pleasure."[25] The titles of several essays in the collection illustrate how this subject was foregrounded: "Seeking Ecstasy on the Battlefield" (by Ellen Carol DuBois and Linda Gordon), "The Taming of the Id" (by Alice Echols), and "No More Nice Girls" (by Brett Harvey). In a similar vein, Lynne Segal, in *Straight Sex*, voices her regret that the women's movement turned away from a validation of "women's rights to sexual pleasure and fulfillment" to embrace a "bleak sexual conservatism."[26]

Not only had Mulvey's essay challenged visual pleasure, it had called for the renunciation of popular narrative in favor of a "politically and aesthetically avant-garde cinema."[27] Once more, in the decade following the publication of her treatise, many feminist critics disputed Mulvey's rejection of classical form and attempted to locate redeeming features of mainstream works that voiced female rebellion, or offered women a position from which to "reclaim" their love of traditional texts. Mulvey herself, in a piece entitled "Afterthoughts on 'Visual Pleasure and Narrative Cinema,'" revised her earlier posture, admitting that the female spectator can assume multiple viewing positions, some of which allow her the satisfaction of identifying with the active male hero. In a related move, Jackie Stacey, in *Star Gazing*, interviewed female movie fans to document their enjoyment at identifying with screen actresses.

In the spirit of such feminist revision, Sally rejects her scenario for *Rage* (a film

Potter admits she did not want to make) and moves from the confines of experimental cinema to the broader realm of modernist narrative. In so doing, she frees herself from her artistic (and, perhaps, sexual) demons. In retrospect, Sally's uneasiness about writing (as depicted in the film) seems reasonable. It is not that the female author has made no progress since the nineteenth century (the era of the Gilbert and Gubar study), but rather that to write one must remain true to oneself rather than craft a text according to cultural expectations (the "ladylike" novel or the "politically correct" screenplay). Clearly, however, the "real" Sally faced no writer's block in conceiving *The Tango Lesson*; it came to her as a "wild explosion of ideas."[28]

Lesson 3: Authoring the Self

Having lived a variant of the love story that she performs and dramatizes in the film (her offscreen romance with Veron), Potter had more than just a theoretical reason to make *The Tango Lesson*. By allowing a version of her affair to be restaged in the film, she squarely enters the autobiographical realm. Critical responses to Potter's gesture varied greatly. On the one hand, Claire Monk saw *The Tango Lesson* as "perilously on the knife edge between reality and fiction" but praised the director for taking a "significant personal risk" to make "a film which is mostly intriguing and affecting rather than embarrassing."[29] David Rooney, on the other hand, thought that the film ran "to self-indulgent extremes" and predicted that people would either "adore" or "abhor" it.[30] In metaphorically violating the "180-degree rule" and moving from behind to in front of the camera, Potter broke the normal pattern for female film artists, who typically move from screen star to director (as did Jeanne Moreau, Ida Lupino, and Barbra Streisand)—and not the other way around. In focusing upon her real-life romance, she also veers away from the stereotype of the repressed, aging authoress who needs to write about the love she has failed to experience. While Sarah Morton can only fantasize about an erotic encounter and Joan Wilder needs to be wilder, Potter lives an erotic adventure and records it.

Lesson 4: Tango Argentino

While all of ballroom dancing has an ideological discourse, the tango has a particular rhetoric. Conceived in Argentina in the late nineteenth century, the form has its roots in the dance of enslaved African exiles in the Rio de la Plata region.[31] Not only was the dance originally associated with the racial Other, it was linked to the lower classes and to the culture of brothels and slums.[32] Moreover, the tango evinced a particular sexual politics that was associated with a male-oriented subculture.[33] As Marta E. Savigliano observes, "The dilemma of macho pride . . . haunts the tango." There are two traditional styles of the art form: the *ruffianesque* and the *romantic*. It is the former and older style that is most tied to the aggressive male posture. In the archetypal tango plot (expressed in the song lyrics), the *compadrito* (a "whiny ruffian") and the *milonguita* ("a rebellious broad") perform "gender stereotypes and heterosexual dynamics that [are] disturbing and unsettling for the bourgeois patriarchy, given its fixation with . . . respectability." Because of its sexual politics, the tango was immediately marked by controversy. As Savigliano continues, "The worldwide popularity of the tango has been associated with scandal: [since it involves] the public display of passion performed by a heterosexual couple, the symbol of which is a tight embrace and suggestive, intricate footwork."[34]

Eventually, the tango gained popularity with the Argentine middle and upper classes, as its disrepute was replaced by a chic aura of exoticism. Its popularity spread to Europe as part of what Savigliano terms the "world economy of passion." Especially struck by the tango's impact was Paris in the early 1900s, where dancers first performed it in Montmartre cabarets. By 1913, civic and religious groups had launched organized protests against the dance. Nonetheless, Paris became the "manager" of the tango; it "reshaped its style and promoted it to the rest of the world as an exotic symbol of heterosexual courtship."[35] London also experienced tango fever. Turn-of-the-century England held "tango teas," and in 1913, Gladys Beattie Crozier published an instruction manual called *The Tango and How to Do It*.

Savigliano says that, given the dance's male orientation, "at first glance, tangos seem to offer women two [unacceptable] positions. They can be either the object of male disputes or the trigger of a man's reflections. In either case, it is hard for a woman to overcome her status as a piece of passional inventory." Yet Savigliano and others have noted that the dance is a qualified assertion of male dominance. In the tango ballad (which is part of a composite aesthetic of song and dance), "teary-eyed men talk about how women (mis)treated them." These lyrics are "male confessions of weakness" and have been called "the lament of the cuckold."[36] Significantly, when Pablo and Sally discuss her directing him in a film, he balks at the notion of playing a melodramatic scene: "Suppose I don't want a tear down my face," he says. "What *else* don't you want to do?" she sardonically replies. What is especially noteworthy here is the focus on male (rather than female) melodrama, since women have often been exclusively associated with the form. For literary historian Peter Brooks, heroines (not heroes) are the classic melodramatic protagonists—symbols of innocence wronged, misprized, and abused.[37] Furthermore, it was precisely this histrionic female role that Potter dissected in *Thriller*. Thus, her interest in the lachrymose male subject of the tango ballad seems logical—challenging, as it does, the melodramatic paradigm.

If men are, ultimately, not that strong in tango discourse, women are not that weak. Savigliano calls the *milonguita* a "femme fatale" and sees "a whole array of manipulative stratagems, deceptive behaviors, and strategies for subversion . . . allocated in tango-women's hands."[38] Hence the art form engages in the "blatant exposure of . . . insurgency on the part of the victimized heroine."[39] Savigliano notes that "women's participation in tango, whether as characters . . . or as audience members, presents a dilemma. Tango has avoided giving any straight answers

FIGURE 21. In a romantic scene, Sally (Sally Potter) and Pablo (Pablo Veron) tango by the Seine (*The Tango Lesson* [1997]).

about women, perhaps because they were/are seen as the pawns of the tangueros' male wars. [I] question the hegemony of the macho message."[40]

Lesson 5: Two to Tango

But what do the history and politics of tango have to do with Sally Potter? It seems significant that her filmic alter ego "Sally" lives in London and first meets Veron in Paris, thus negotiating two European capitals with strong historic ties to the tango. (Interestingly, *Swimming Pool* also shuttles between England and France, with the latter signifying sensuality.) Similarly, as one of many foreign tango devotees in Buenos Aires, Sally joins a long tradition of pilgrims that have come to the city to study the dance.[41]

Clearly, as a contemporary feminist, Potter would be interested in the sexual dynamics of the tango. In the beginning of the film, when Sally first studies with Veron, she seems entirely under his spell—hanging on his every word, capitulating to his every choreographic command. Her subservience, of course, coincides with her growing ardor for him, her teacher. By the drama's end, Sally has come to dismiss Veron's complaint that she "does too much" in dancing and chastises him for "dancing like a soloist." Furthermore, she complains of having to "walk backwards" in executing the tango, a comment that seems to have political as well as spatial meaning. Hence, Sally invokes the rebellious spirit of the *milonguita*, who saves the tango from male domination. Ultimately, Sally extends her power by enlisting Veron for a role in her film, thus reversing the positions of teacher and student, director and performer. As Sally proclaims, "It doesn't suit me to follow; it suits me to lead and you can't deal with that." Significantly, scholar Beatrice Humbert argues that the popularity of the tango in Europe at the turn of the twentieth century promoted women's liberation: "Tango opened a venue for women to exhibit sensuality in public. . . . Tango showed and performed the strong changes in gender roles that were under way at the time, conflictively joining voting demands, dress reforms, and the recent scientific findings in birth control as well as the psychoanalytic incursions in female sexuality."[42]

A certain female power can even be found in the gaze associated with the tango. As Julie Taylor confesses, when she first frequented Buenos Aires dance halls, she was perplexed that no men asked her to tango. Her Argentinean girlfriends finally informed her that her veiled gaze discouraged the men from approaching. Evidently, she immediately lowered her eyes whenever a potential male partner looked at her. She recalls that "in a concerned fashion, the women around me explained that I needed to hold the other person's gaze to transmit acceptance of his invitation. This proved far more easily explained than performed. . . . Dropping my eyes was a reflex I did not know how to control."[43]

This need in the dynamics of the tango for a strong (versus a reticent) female gaze seems especially relevant to Potter, whose craft as filmmaker relies on the act of observation. Indeed, when Sally first witnesses Veron dancing in a Paris theater, the camera focuses on her looking. To make the parallels to cinema even sharper, Veron and his partner throw shadows against a white wall, like projected images on a screen. By the end of the drama, Sally's gaze empowers her to move from the audience to the stage, thus entering theatrical space herself.

Critics who have accused Potter of a certain melodramatic excess in *The Tango Lesson* should know that her stance borrows from the dance's aesthetic. As Savigliano notes, "Tangos . . . are public displays of intimate miseries, shameful behaviors, and unjustifiable attitudes. In tango, intimate confessions are the occasion for a spectacle" since "the personal is the political."[44] Moreover, the pathos of tragic love is also part of the tango's staple rhetoric, for the "tango is . . . a spectacle of traumatic encounters," a story of meetings "between those who should never have met."[45] As though to mock this melodrama, when Sally and Pablo say goodbye at the Paris airport, they execute a series of campy, overblown gestures on parallel moving sidewalks.

Finally, in dividing her film between dance numbers and narrative segments, Potter mimics the tango's dual-track discourse of dance and storytelling song—elements that are separate and contradictory. One does not dance to music with lyrics, and the emotions of a tango ballad run counter to those of the choreography. As Taylor explains, "The passive woman and the . . . physically aggressive man [in the dance] contrast poignantly with the roles of the sexes depicted in the tango lyrics."[46] It is this complexity of both art and romance that Potter attempts to capture in her film.

Lesson 6: Shot/Countershot

In the contemporary cinema, it is no longer the case that the female auteur must address an alien, pre-established canon, for by now their work has entered the mainstream. A year after Potter's film was first shown, a male director made one so similar that it had to be viewed in relation to hers. I am speaking of Carlos Saura, whose *Tango* (1998) was directly compared to Potter's film in a review by Janet Maslin. Saura had already done significant work in the dance-film genre, having made *Carmen* (1983) and *Flamenco* (1995). Like *The Tango Lesson*, *Tango* concerns an author/dancer making a film about the dance. Here, the protagonist is not a literal double of the director but a fictional character named Mario Suarez (Miguel Angel Sola). Mario is divorced from a dancer in his company but is still captivated by her. Soon, however, he falls in love with another performer, a young woman named Elena (Mia Maestro), who is the girlfriend of a gangster. The film toys with the ambience of film noir and with the tensions of love, jealousy, murder, and retribution. Although *Tango* has far more plot than Potter's movie, Saura's film is equally self-reflexive. In the opening, in a scene paralleling that of Sally at her writing table, we see Mario's hands holding a pen (not a pencil) and reviewing pages of the script for his movie. Furthermore, most of the film's dance sequences are shot in a cavernous rehearsal hall and are presented in abstract, shadowed tableaux that are entirely synthetic.

What is perhaps most noteworthy about *Tango* (in relation to Potter's work) is its male orientation; thus, Mario is identified as a *compadrito*. Saura's film is represented as entirely Mario's fantasy, and many of the scenes are superimposed over images of him reclining in bed, as though he were dreaming or imagining the events. While Potter largely eschews the tango lyric (which is identified with the remonstrative *tanguero*), Saura wallows in the music's anguish—a stance that conceives the male as a victim of female perfidy. As an opening song croons, "How could I know that her affection would cause me all the troubles that it did?" Finally, Mario relishes the role of male writer/director/impresario. An opening voiceover queries: "Who is Mario Suarez, the hero of our story? That's not as important as what happens to him." It is clear that Mario has functioned as Svengali to his former wife and happily assumes that role again with the young Elena —launching her dance career by featuring her in his production. While Maslin compares *Tango* to Bob Fosse's *All That Jazz* (1979), we might also liken it to Federico Fellini's *8 ½* (1963)—already discussed as a paradigmatic tale of the male writer/director/lover. While Potter downplays the violent aspects of tango lore in favor of its romantic elements, Saura highlights the dance's cultural associations with machismo and brutality. In one tango number, two *compadritos* fight over a woman (played by Elena). When she is stabbed, we are unsure whether the deed is part of the fictional dance scenario or a bloody retaliatory act that Elena's real mobster beau has ordered.

Lesson 7: Fade Out

Clearly, Potter's *The Tango Lesson* is a highly pedagogical and theoretical work. In the course of its narrative, it provides a treatise on the female author—portraying both the perils and glories of writing. At the same time, the film questions rigid binaries that have haunted feminist creative work—sexual pleasure versus repression, power versus oppression, and male versus female roles. Moreover, the film invokes (in the course of its modernist romance) the history of the tango. Finally, in the intertextual conversation that has developed between Potter's and Saura's work, we find opposing stances on the tango—ones that starkly conform to cultural notions of masculinity and femininity. The two films together constitute the perfect cinematic tango "couple" (*compadrito* and *milonguita*), locked in an inspired embrace. While in the traditional dynamic, the female artist has had to respond to the male's prior authorial statement, now it is the male who must suffer "the anxiety of influence." Thus, in closing, we might return to the opening of *The Tango Lesson* and the image of Sally's dreaded writing desk. It turns out to be not simply a symbol of the problematics of female authorship, but an emblem of how the tables have turned.

EPILOGUE

While in *The Tango Lesson* Sally's alter ego abandons her screenplay for *Rage*, the real Potter ultimately returns to it some twelve years later (after numerous intermediary drafts).[47] In 2009 she released a film of that name (simultaneously distributed to theaters, cell phones, and the web) that confronts the subject she first imagined—"carnage on the catwalk." Rather than utilizing the kind of lush clips of imperiled models that we glanced in *The Tango Lesson*, however, the film consists of a series of interviews with fictional fashion industry personnel (models, designers, critics, managers, investors)—ostensibly videotaped by a student filmmaker working on a school project. The impressive cast (including Judi Dench, Jude Law, Eddie Izzard, John Leguizamo, Steve Buscemi, and Dianne Wiest) is photographed against a "green screen" and then given various "day-glo" colored backgrounds that make their images resemble garish, flattened, Warhol silk screens. Thus, the fashion show and the sensational death of models remain entirely off-screen (a way of refusing a certain visual "pornography," as well as controlling the budget). Rather than focus solely on the exploitation of women, Potter has widened the scope of her social lens here, invoking issues of marketing, consumerism, sweatshop labor, global capital, and illegal immigration—all part and parcel of the fashion world.

What is most interesting of all, however, is that the film incorporates the process of writing into its very making. As the film opens, instead of a blank sheet of paper on a table we see a pulsating cursor, which is soon replaced by words being written onscreen. First we get the phrase "All the rage," which (through deletions) gets transformed into "Rage" (and then bolded and increased in font size). Then the following words appear: "I meet some important [deleted] people the day before the show, who explain why a dress is not just a dress." We come to learn that the first-person pronoun refers to Michelangelo, the ostensible filmmaker within the film, whom we never meet or see.

The trope of words being formed onscreen is repeated for all seven days that Michelangelo conducts his interviews, and often after words appear he backspaces to erase them or to supplant them with others. Hence, we might argue that not only is the act of writing (so important to *The Tango Lesson*) incorporated into *Rage*, but so is the act of revision—a process important to feminist filmmaking and one that explains Potter's move from one version of *Rage* to another.

5 WRITING PAIN
The Infirm Author

> Considering how common illness is, how tremendous the spiritual change
> that it brings ... it becomes strange indeed that illness has not taken its place
> with love and battle and jealousy among the prime themes of literature.
> —Virginia Woolf, *On Being Ill*

    While Virginia Woolf finds the motif of illness rare in literature, it
has certainly not been infrequent in films that feature the writer as protagonist.
Clearly, the most common form that sickness takes is the mental kind—a recurrent cliché in visions of the artist. As Philip Sandblom writes: "The proportion
of individuals with a borderline mental constitution is high among great creators.
Aberrant psychic traits which in ordinary people would seem morbid may add
to the originality and infatuation of artistic creation; they may even constitute its
basis or origin."[1] Already, we have discussed such films as *Adaptation* (2002) and
Deconstructing Harry (1997), in which the writer is a full-fledged neurotic, as well
as *Swimming Pool* (2003), in which the author is sexually repressed. Finally, we
have examined works like *Barton Fink* (1991) and *Stranger Than Fiction* (2006), in
which the protagonist fears he is going mad.

    In this chapter, however, we also discuss illnesses of a more corporeal kind—
in keeping with our focus on authorial incarnation. Here, it is of interest to note
that Virginia Woolf finds verbal discourse inadequate to the task of representing infirmity:

> To hinder the description of illness in literature, there is the poverty of the lan-
> guage. English, which can express the thoughts of Hamlet and the tragedy of Lear,
> has no words for the shiver and the headache. . . . The merest schoolgirl, when she
> falls in love, has Shakespeare or Keats to speak her mind for her; but let a sufferer
> try to describe a pain in his head to a doctor and language at once runs dry. There
> is nothing ready made for him. He is forced to coin words himself, and, taking
> his pain in one hand, and a lump of pure sound in the other . . . so to crush them
> together that a brand new word in the end drops out. Probably it will be some-
> thing laughable.[2]

Aside from the limitations of discourse, Woolf sees literature as selectively preoccupied with consciousness versus the body (despite the former issuing from the
anatomical part known as the brain): "[Literature] does its best to maintain that
its concern is with the mind; that the body is a sheet of plain glass through which
the soul looks straight and clear, and save for one or two passions . . . is null, and
negligible and non-existent."[3] So, we might wonder, can the moving image (with
its requisite corporeal embodiment) do any better than that? According to Sander
Gilman, the tradition of "seeing disease" is a longstanding one. As he notes: "The
idea of representing the diseased through visual images reaches back through
the ages."[4]

THE LONG-SUFFERING ARTIST

Skin Deep

The first text to be considered is a televisual one, *The Singing Detective* (1986), a
six-episode miniseries produced by the BBC, directed by Jon Amiel, and written
by Dennis Potter. It was later adapted unsuccessfully as a 2003 American movie. In
discussing the miniseries, I focus on the first two episodes, which set up the narrative and introduce techniques utilized in the overall program.

The film concerns a mystery writer, Philip Marlow (Michael Gambon), clearly
a misspelled version of Raymond Chandler's detective hero (e.g., *The Big Sleep*
and *The Long Goodbye*). So already we have a merging of author and character figures.[5] Marlow is plagued by chronic psoriasis, a scaly and eruptive skin condition
that requires him to be frequently hospitalized. Basically, the narrative wanders
(without clear delineation) among four levels: Marlow ill in the hospital (the present tense of the film); his writerly, *noir* fantasies (with him pictured as his private-
eye hero and others from his life cast as supporting players); recollections of his
traumatic childhood (marred by his mother's adultery and suicide); and elements
of his world outside the hospital (e.g., his wife and her lover's attempt to swindle
him out of the rights to a film scenario he has written).[6]

The layers of reflexivity in the text are dazzling. Marlow speaks of having
penned a screenplay named *The Singing Detective*, and another patient in the ward
is reading the novel on which it is based. In attempting to gain the rights to his scenario, his wife must literally have him affix his authorial signature to a document.
And as though to emphasize the linguistic realm, in a visit to the psychotherapist
in Episode 5, he is asked to play an association game whereby he must respond to
each word offered by the doctor. When the latter says "writer," Marlow says "liar";
when the latter says "tin," Marlow says "type." As though threatened by language,
after the game Marlow mutters, "Words, just words," and he vows never to visit the
doctor again. Finally, Marlow tells us that "words make [him] hold his breath" and
that (like Barthes's "tissue of quotations") he often "wonders where they've been."

In terms of embodying the author, there could be no better disease with which
to mark him than psoriasis, one that is external and visible (affecting the skin) and

tactilely repulsive (signifying deterioration). As Gilman remarks, popular opinion would have it that "the diseased and the beautiful cannot be encapsulated in one and the same category."[7] *The Singing Detective* gives us numerous disturbing shots of Marlow's raw, irritated epidermis (starting with a close-up of his sore-marked face as he is wheeled into the hospital ward)—making it reasonable that another patient assumes he is a burn victim. The malady makes him feel like an object. When a nurse greases him with salve, he feels like an "axle." Moreover, the disease infantilizes him, since nurses must handle him like a baby with diaper rash—applying creams, turning him over, and changing his dressings. He is not, however, a child, and he becomes embarrassed when, as a nurse massages him, he gets an erection, despite his thinking (as rendered in voiceover), "Poor cock, do not stir!" When his hard-on becomes apparent, he muses regretfully, "Oh, the shame of it!" Finally, the observable nature of his illness makes him feel like a freak or pariah— reminding us that writers in general often feel like misfits or outcasts. Interestingly, Al Alvarez opines that an infirm artist's isolation may help him produce work: "By preventing other activity, disease may be a factor that favours artistic creation."[8]

Significantly, there is a famous real-life author with psoriasis who wrote extensively about the condition—John Updike. In "At War with My Skin," part of his 1989 memoir, he speaks of the volatile nature of the disease and of feeling alternately normal and hideous. (Woolf called the sick body a "monster.")[9] Updike talks both of his self-consciousness (trying to hide his wounds) and his narcissism (constantly consulting mirrors and reflecting glass). He confesses feeling sorry for himself: "I am unfortunate is my prime thought: Nature played a quite unnecessary trick on me." He mentions how the malady haunted his sex life (which requires being naked). He talks of feeling "occupied" by an alien force. He admits to being aggravated by encountering the disabled: "Handicapped people annoy me, in reminding me of myself."[10] Finally, he links his disability to his art (even punning on being "thick-skinned"):

> I self-consciously wondered was not my sly strength, my insistent specialness, somehow linked to my psoriasis? Might it not be the horrible badge of whatever in me was worth honoring: the price, high but not impossibly so, I must pay for being me? Only psoriasis could have taken a very average little boy, and furthermore a boy who loved the average, the daily, the safely hidden, and made him into a prolific, adaptable, ruthless enough writer. What was my creativity, my relentless need to produce but a parody of my skin's embarrassing overproduction? Was not my thick literary skin, which shrugged off rejection slips and patronizing reviews by the sheaf, a superior version of my poor vulnerable own, and my shamelessness on the page a distraction from my real shame?[11]

All these sentiments circulate in *The Singing Detective*, which is authored by another writer who suffers from psoriatic disorder—Dennis Potter. Clearly, the visual nature of its discourse, however, makes the qualities of the disease (as well

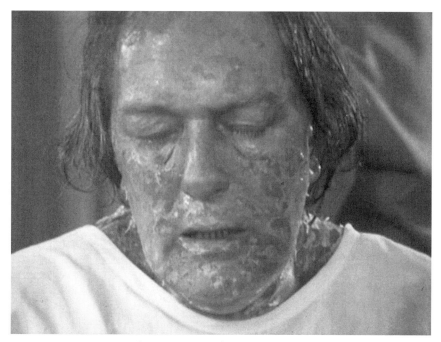

FIGURE 22. Phillip Marlow (Michael Gambon) suffers an outbreak of psoriasis (*The Singing Detective* [1986]).

as its subject's trials) appear more intense than in print—endangering the "thin-skinned" viewer's identification with the hero.

It is interesting that, according to Mary Ann O'Farrell, medical practitioners have spoken of what they deem the "psoriatic personality," which involves many of the traits outlined by Updike. She wants to argue, however, for a form of "psoriatic textuality" in the works of artists so afflicted.[12] This entails a style characterized by excess (like the disease itself), shifts between exuberance and self-loathing (like a patient's mood swings), and reflexivity (like a patient's self-consciousness). Again, we find all these in Potter's narrative.

Excess is everywhere in *The Singing Detective*, but most noticeably in its camp moments. Though most of the hospital scenes are meant to be "real" (though exaggerated), some are entirely fantastic, possibly the result of Marlow's drug-induced visions. At one point, as a doctor and some medical students examine him, the group breaks out in a musical number to the tune of "Dem Bones," a spiritual whose lyrics are appropriate to the setting ("The knee bone's connected to the thigh bone"). There is suddenly a band in the hospital ward, a chorus line of "nurses" dressed in skimpy white outfits, and skeletons whose bones double as xylophone keyboards. On another occasion, an elderly ward-mate sits up in bed and lip-synchs "On the Sunny Side of the Street," a tune that seems hopelessly out of place in the depressing milieu. At one point, Marlow responds to these visions by referencing the movies: "Sometimes hallucinations are better than reality. People sing and dance. I like pictures."

But the major fantasies in the program do not involve the scene of the hospital but rather the terrain of Marlow's imagination—specifically, the detective story he is formulating. In fact, like *Deconstructing Harry*, the first episode of the BBC series begins within the fiction (though the spectator does not know this). The sequence opens on a mysterious urban night scene—the streets wet with rain (a standard image from crime films). An old man plays a harmonica on the street (an atmospheric touch), specifically the tune "After You've Gone" (1918). A bowler-hatted man (Mark [Patrick Malahide]) comes into view under an archway and, when he passes by the musician, throws a coin into his hat. As the musician retrieves it, the camera reveals that the money is wrapped in a slip of paper on which is written the enigmatic word "Skinscapes" (a name with obvious relevance to Marlow's infirmity). We begin to suspect that the two men are some kind of agents. Mark then descends into the basement entrance of the Skinscapes bar, accompanied on the sound track by the Cole Porter tune "I've Got You under My Skin" (1936)—another ironic reference. A narrator (whose voice we have heard intermittently all along) says something about descending into a "rat hole." The entire segment has a retro feel that we place sometime in the 1930s or 1940s. It is at this point that we suddenly move to a contemporary hospital ward into which Marlow, a patient, is being wheeled.

This shifting pattern continues as, throughout the program, we move (in perplexing ways) between levels of fiction and reality—though the visual techniques for doing so vary. Sometimes an image from one level is layered over an image from another, as when water from a fantasized scene of a drowning is superimposed over Marlow's face in bed. Sometimes the sound from one level creeps into the space of another, as when the nurse tells Marlow she must lift his penis to apply salve around it, and we suddenly hear those same words spoken by a seductive femme fatale within the noir drama. (In a later episode, a wonderful acoustic bridge connects the pumping sounds of his mother's illicit lovemaking to the rhythm of respiratory paddles being applied to the chest of a dying patient.) Sometimes Marlow mutters dialogue from his novel while lying in his hospital bed—even noting punctuation marks, as though in the process of dictating text. Significantly, his disease has so deformed his hands that for much of the drama he cannot hold a pen, a sure sign of the relation between infirmity and writing. (When later he finally can write, the first word he forms is "blood.") Sometimes, a detail from Marlow's hospital world "infects" the noir story. When Marlow feels hot in bed (since his skin disease affects temperature regulation), the protagonist of his novel suddenly feels warm too. Finally, sometimes characters we recognize from his fictional plot appear inexplicably in the hospital (e.g., a waitress from the Skinscapes bar). A similar technique is used to link recollections from Marlow's childhood to the present—both harrowing periods in his life. In one sequence, we start with an extreme close-up of Marlowe in bed when suddenly we hear, offscreen, a man's voice shout "Philip"—as though he were in the same room. The image of a tree fades in over Marlow's face and, as the camera pans right, we discover a young boy hiding in its high branches (ostensibly the youthful Marlow). Suddenly, another voice is heard and we cut back to the hospital, and we realize that it is that of one of his ward mates. Thus, both sound overlaps and visual dissolves tie the past and the present together. Throughout the drama, we return to the scene of young Philip in a tree secretly observing the world, an emblem of the author's gaze.

As the camp episodes make clear, there is considerable humor in the program as seen from Marlow's wry perspective. He mentions that "sardonic wit" is his weapon and (using the same metaphor as Updike) that he cultivates a "thick skin." Thus, when having read some of his work a hospital psychiatrist says that his writing is a "pastiche," Marlow responds: "I don't like Italian food." Similarly, when a physician criticizes Marlow's pessimistic attitude toward his disease, Marlowe asks whether they expect him instead "to sing madrigals."

But this light mood alternates with a tragic sense of suffering that seems almost biblical (another instance, perhaps, of thematic excess). The chorus of the song "Dem Bones" warns us to "hear the words of the Lord," and Marlow himself compares his trials to those of Job. He is also asked by hospital staff if he wants to see the "Padre." Marlow curses constantly, using such phrases as "For Christ's sake!" "Christ almighty!" and "Jesus Christ on a bike!" Finally, his psoriatic wounds seem likes forms of stigmata. The often-mocking religious tenor of the hospital scenes contrasts to the more reverent tone of childhood remembrances, as when we hear his youthful self recite "The Lord's Prayer." The topic of artist suffering has been eloquently voiced by Marcel Proust, an infirm, bed-ridden writer portrayed in another work considered in this chapter. As he noted: "They have composed our masterpieces. We enjoy delightful music, beautiful paintings and thousands of small miracles, but we don't consider what they have cost their creators in sleepless nights, rashes, asthma, epilepsy—and, worst of them all, fear of death."[13]

Sensory Deprivation

If *The Singing Detective* is about the surface of illness (disease literally inscribed on the body), *The Diving Bell and the Butterfly* (directed by Julian Schnabel in 2007) is about its interstices. Based on the published memoir of Jean-Dominique Bauby (a French journalist and editor), it tells the story of his life following a massive stroke (at age forty-three) that left him mute, quadriplegic, and with vision and movement in only one eye. When he awoke in a hospital some twenty days after the incident, he could not speak, but his responses (through blinking) to a series of questions made clear that his mind and intelligence were fully intact. He was thus diagnosed with "locked in" (or what the French deem "walled-in alive") syndrome. Though crushed and depressed by the realization of his profound disability, with the help of several therapists he eventually learns to communicate more than simple "yes" and "no" answers through an elaborate and cumbersome system enabling him to spell out words by blinking. This allows him to write an autobiography chronicling the experience of his illness, a project that gives him a reason to survive. Hence Bauby represents the infirm writer par excellence—one who overcomes enormous obstacles in his desire for self-expression. But this kind of writing is no easy task. As Virginia Woolf observes: "To look [illness] squarely in the face would need the courage of a lion tamer; [and] a reason rooted in the bowels of the earth."[14] Bauby has just these qualities.

The film does an excellent and innovative job of representing Bauby's (Mathieu Amalric) coming into consciousness at the hospital. The title sequence begins with the song "La Mer" (introducing us to the theme of water and presaging the fact that Bauby will liken his condition to being trapped in a diving bell). Visually, the segment presents us with X-ray images of skeletal tissue and bones. We soon hear a low sound that we realize is a heartbeat and begin to see (in alternation) blurred images (fading in and out), light flares, and a black screen. We start to hear snatches of dialogue (medical personnel talking) and finally someone telling Bauby to keep his eyes open. As a doctor leans in near Bauby's head, we are so close that we can see the stubble on the man's face. When Bauby is asked to follow a light with his eyes, viewers respond to the medical commands as well. It is the same when his eye (really the camera) is poked and we recoil. When Bauby is asked to say his name, we hear his voiceover utter "Jean-Dominique Bauby," but it soon becomes apparent that others cannot detect his vocalization. "I can't speak," we "hear" him think.

During the first few scenes, the use of partial, indistinct, or shadowed images continues to give us a sense of Bauby's compromised vision and consciousness, but soon other inventive techniques are utilized to render his point of view. Shots are often askew (since his head droops in his wheelchair and is angled in bed). Images are sometimes superimposed (to represent his transitory double vision). Blurry imagery is employed when he cries. As he is moved around the hospital (for example, as when placed in a tub to bathe), a hand-held camera is used to give us a sense of awkward, jerky movement. When he is first asked to blink to signify "yes" or "no," the camera "blinks" by opening and closing its lens (as though the viewer were seeing things from Bauby's vantage point). Sometimes, this is the only way that we understand his response. Furthermore, the speed with which he opens and closes his eye gives us some sense of the tone of his expression.

When doctors determine that his right eye is not irrigated (and will become infected) they sew it closed, and we witness the terrible act as though inside his head looking out. It is after this sequence that we first see his body from the outside (though only his eyes). When aides dress him for a wheelchair ride, his clothes seem to be put on the camera, and a traveling shot replicates Bauby's new mobility. When he first glimpses himself in a mirror (and is horrified by his paralyzed, sagging mouth), we see his full face for the first time too (though distorted and rippled by refraction). Later on, we see a clear close-up of his lips when his physical therapist hands him a mirror—a tool that he rejects. Like Marlow in *The*

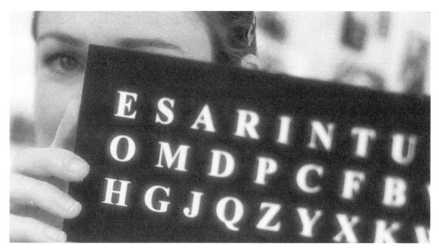

FIGURE 23. Jean-Dominique's therapist holds up a chart of the alphabet organized by letter frequency in *The Diving Bell and the Butterfly* (2007).

Singing Detective, Bauby also feels infantilized by his disability and is embarrassed to have his "ass wiped like a baby." Furthermore, the first time a nurse switches on the TV for him, she leaves it on a cartoon channel as though he were a child.

The portion of the narrative that deals with Bauby as writer, however, begins when he receives lessons on how to communicate more fully. He gets physical therapy, but there seems little hope of his ever moving his lips to utter a sound. However, he also is taught a technique for spelling by blinking his eyes, thus enabling him to form words and sentences. His speech therapist Henriette (Marie-Josée Croze) utilizes a method that entails her calling out letters of the alphabet organized not from A to Z but by how frequently they are used in words (for French, E-S-A-R etc.). When he hears the letter he wants, he blinks once and she notes it down; at the end of the word, he blinks twice. If she makes a mistake, he blinks numerous times to alert her. He is skeptical of the process, which is—as one can imagine—awkward, burdensome, slow, and frustrating. In a sense it is like typing letter-by-letter, key-by-key, without hope of achieving touch-typing speed with practice. For each new letter, Henriette must return to the beginning of the list and go through it all again—and Bauby must wait until she utters the desired vowel or consonant. At first, the technique is used merely for him to converse. When she initially asks him to try it, he does not know what to say and utters only "I" (signifying a focus on his own mind, which is now his only resource). What is especially interesting about these sequences is that the viewer has to go through the process of forming words as well. If the first letter that Bauby needs is "T" we too have to wait until Henriette says it. If he is bored, we are bored. If it is agonizingly time-consuming for him, it is the same for us.

At one point, he shocks and angers Henriette during a session by spelling out

"I want to die." Significantly, here, we do not hear his inner monologue—but must spell the words out with his therapist. Though she initially scolds him (shouting "How dare you?" and calling his statement "obscene" and "disrespectful"), she ultimately understands his position, though she refuses to let him give up on life. Finally, Bauby accedes to her position, but not before he has reached the depths of despair. In a particularly poignant and creatively rendered sequence, we see a shot of a submerged, old-fashioned metal diving bell—a metaphorical image we have seen before (accompanied by breathing sounds)—but here, for the first time, we can see Bauby's face inside it. As his voiceover recites a series of regrets about his life, we see silent flashbacks to personal moments. Eventually, we see a glacier slowly crumbling and falling into the sea—another figurative trope. He wonders, "Did it take a disaster to know this?" Shortly thereafter, his voiceover proclaims that he has decided no longer to feel sorry for himself—having realized that, though his body is frozen, his memory and imagination are not. It is at this moment that we first see a long shot of him as he sits outside in a wheelchair—signaling that his mind is finally ready to accept his corporeal self (and, perhaps, so are we).

His statement is followed by a series of images clearly meant to represent his consciousness and its abstract mode of association (memories and fantasies rendered through montage): shots of the pyramids, mountains, Martinique, women, surfers, bullfighting. He decides to remember himself as he was ("handsome, debonair, glamorous"), at which point we see a picture of Marlon Brando. With humor, Bauby thinks: "That's not *me*; it's Brando!"—making light of the human tendency toward self-glorification and delusion. As we see an extreme long shot of a man skiing the slopes, he thinks, "*That's* me!" and we believe it is. Interestingly, in one sequence, he likens his imagination to the cinema. As he sits outside on a terrace, his voiceover says that it is like being at a film studio. Here is how he describes it in his book: "I often hav[e] myself wheeled to Cinecittà, a region essential to my imaginary geography of the hospital. . . . I could spend whole days [there]. On the town side, I reshoot the close-ups for *Touch of Evil*. Down at the beach, I rework the dolly shots for *Stagecoach*, and offshore I re-create the storm rocking the smugglers of *Moonfleet*. . . . I am the hero of Godard's *Pierrot le fou*."[15] He also notes that the white foam on the ocean looks like "special effects." His reference to movies makes us think of a passage in Woolf's essay on illness in which she speaks of how bed rest often makes us notice aspects of nature we usually ignore—for instance the sky. As she writes: "One should not let this gigantic *cinema* play perpetually to an empty house" (my emphasis).[16] Significantly, part of Bauby's first fantasy involves such natural images as flowers, insects, and trees, and we sometimes see shots of the sky through his open hospital room window, curtains blowing in the wind.

It is after Bauby's epiphany (the refusal of self-pity) that he decides to write. At the time of his accident, he had a contract to pen a modern-day version of Alexandre Dumas's *The Count of Monte Cristo*, but following his stroke he decides to write a memoir. So now, retrospectively, we realize that the voiceover narration we have heard from him throughout actually comprises passages from that book. Hence, of course, the film is adapted from literature into cinema. But, as in Charlie Kaufman's *Adaptation*, that term has a double sense, in that it is only through writing that Bauby adjusts to his tragic situation. His publisher sends an assistant to the hospital to take dictation, utilizing the tortuous, letter-by-letter system that has been previously employed. Significantly, one of his major forms of entertainment (and survival) is having others read to him—especially from the Dumas classic. Sometimes we can hear his voice in the background repeating the words of the speaker.

He also imagines a play he might someday write (to be titled either *The Pressure Cooker* or *The Eye*) with obvious biographical overtones—a work about a man learning to live with distress. He conceives that the drama would entail an off-stage monologue relating the character's inner thoughts. Clearly, there are stylistic parallels to the drama we are watching. There is, however, one major difference. The play ends with the stage going black and the protagonist thinking: "Damn, it was only a dream!" Unfortunately, the life of the real Bauby has no such escapist denouement.

Eventually, Bauby's condition deteriorates (he contracts pneumonia), a process that is represented by a fantasy of him on an operating table in a decrepit room, his diving suit thrown on the floor. He continues, however, to write—evidence of his passion for the craft. As he is whisked away in an ambulance and he thinks about his "past reced[ing]," we finally view the scene of his stroke, which occurred while driving with his son. This is a sequence of pure kinetic movement (as seen from a car)—a complete contrast to the stasis that haunts Bauby afterward. As he slips toward death, we see a reversal of the stylistic trajectory of the film's opening, with clear images becoming blurry and sounds becoming inaudible or asynchronous (except for the interminable beeping of some medical device). Before he succumbs, however, he is shown a published version of his memoir and is read numerous rave reviews. This is consonant with the facts, as Bauby died ten days after his volume was released. Shortly before his final decline, however, he thinks to himself, in hard-wrought acceptance of his fate: "My life is here." And, as he dies, we see a reverse-motion sequence of the glacier seen earlier—this time reassembling itself into a whole (a strangely recuperative image for the moment of death). On some level, we have to believe that writing "saved" Bauby's soul and sanity, if not his life.

September Song

Thus far we have discussed works that depict the infirm author during periods of relative youth (Bauby) or middle age (Marlow). But clearly sickness is more common in the elderly. By far the most interesting film about the ill, aged writer is Alain Resnais's *Providence* (1977), written by David Mercer. It concerns seventy-eight-year-old Clive Langham (John Gielgud), who spends a fretful night without sleep—due to disease and alcoholism. The narrative continually cuts between him in bed or stumbling around the house and scenes of his lawyer son, Claude (Dirk Bogarde); the latter's wife, Sonia (Ellen Burstyn); Claude's mistress, Helen (Elaine Stritch); and Kevin (David Warner), a man that Claude is prosecuting in court. Actually, at the start of the film, we do not know that its protagonist will be Clive, since we perceive him only in partial visual or acoustic flashes (as he drops a glass or mutters offscreen). Instead, the film begins with events depicting the other characters. Specifically, it opens on a shot of a wooden sign bearing the word *Providence* (as though the name of an estate) and then tracks and pans through dense trees. A strange old man (whose hands and face are covered with hair) runs through the forest as militiamen chase him, firing guns. Soon Kevin appears and shoots him, and we abruptly cut to Claude (obviously at a later point) railing against Kevin in court as Sonia watches from the gallery. Suddenly, we begin to hear a disembodied male voiceover (Clive's) characterizing Claude as "a tailored dummy" and asking Sonia, "Why did you marry that son of mine?" Then Clive opines that the events we have witnessed "will have to be rewritten." Beyond commenting on the action, Clive's offscreen voice discusses his compromised physical condition. He tells us that he has found spots of blood on his underwear and talks of his "troubled rectum." Furthermore, he repeatedly speaks of dying and refers to his bedroom as a "coffin." He mentions a physician and complains, "He wants to cut me up." As he utters these words, we shift to a shot of a man dissecting a cadaver, at which point Clive grumbles, "Oh, get out of my mind!"[17]

Clearly, although we have not yet been visually introduced to Clive, we realize that we are listening to someone who can miraculously "observe" and remark on the action we are seeing. That he talks about getting things "out of his mind" —or that, in response to a character appearing onscreen, he says "I'm getting rid of you at once"—makes us realize that we are privy (in cinematic form) to his thoughts (despite the fact that the film also uses the convention of soliloquy for him to communicate them). That Clive speaks of "rewriting" things (and refers to some people as "characters") cues us in to the fact that he is creating a narrative before our eyes. Later, in a similar fashion, he wonders whether Sonia having sex with Kevin would seem too "vulgar" (ostensibly as a narrative ploy), and, when Helen first appears onscreen, he opines that she "*could* be Claude's mistress," a role she ultimately fulfills. Thus, we are not surprised to learn that Clive is a famous writer. He recalls, in fact, that Claude inquired why he had never received a Nobel Prize and revealed that his teacher thought his father a lesser talent than Graham Greene. As a tryst between Sonia and Kevin unrolls before us, we hear Clive's voiceover ask: "But where will the tyrannical lawyer be?" In response to his query, we immediately cut to Claude in his office—Clive's broaching the question having led to its fictional, narrative solution.

In the drama we continue to watch, Claude is a mean-spirited, derisive man with contempt for everyone. He seems to take perverse pleasure in Sonia's sexual interest in Kevin and has no qualms about cheating himself. Speaking to his secretary, he rails against his father, complaining that he is dying "too slowly" and asks why he doesn't "just go to a nursing home." Claude describes his parent as "shout-ing, drinking, and protesting his way through death's dark door" and claims that only a blissful "silence" will signal that he has "actually gone." When later Claude calls his father an "infant," Sonia defends the man as a "visionary." When Claude wonders, "Shall we never be rid of [him]?" we hear Clive crying offscreen—as though in response. As we have seen, Clive's comments about his son are equally barbed—for instance, he judges him an "emotional cripple"—completing the ele-ments of a longstanding Oedipal battle. Added to this psychic mix is mention of the suicide of Claude's mother, and at one point we see a flashback of Clive finding her dead in a bathtub.

The unlikely storyline continues as depicted onscreen. Militiamen intermit-tently reappear, shooting people, dragging them off into somber official buildings, or collecting dead bodies. (Clive [in voiceover] wonders if these figures are not too strident as "fear symbols.") Often, as characters converse, the sound of gunfire or bombs is heard in the background—creating a sense of a fascistic government that they seem to nonchalantly accept. Terry Gilliam later presents a more comic version of this situation in *Brazil* (1985), but here it has a menacing valence. In some sense, the near Surrealist tone of *Providence* reminds us of the work of Luis Buñuel—certainly an inspirational cinematic figure for Resnais. Specifically, one thinks of *The Discreet Charm of the Bourgeoisie* (1972), in which people's meals are repeatedly aborted by the appearance of terrorists, soldiers, firing squads, or po-licemen. In fact, on several occasions in *Providence*, characters talk about whether or not they are "bourgeois" (or if the bourgeoisie is to blame for the carnage sur-rounding them). Reference is also made to Clive's "revolutionary" past (although Claude mockingly says he was only radical "in his mind"). Also threatening are images of wrecking balls demolishing old buildings, reminding us of the smoke-stack that crashes down at the end of *The Blood of a Poet* (1930), Jean Cocteau's Surrealist film.

There are numerous other strange elements in the tale that Clive spins. The hairy old man in the woods is referred to as a werewolf, and later a scene occurs in which Kevin succumbs to the same supernatural syndrome. Throughout the narrative a young footballer (supposedly Kevin's brother) is seen to run through locales at unlikely times (e.g., when Claude and Helen meet in a hotel room). At moments, characters are instantaneously transposed from one place to another, as when Claude and Sonia begin talking in her living room, then suddenly ap-pear at a formal party (much like one in Resnais's *Last Year at Marienbad* [1961]). Characters also shape-shift. At one point Helen asks Claude whether she reminds him of his mother. Then as they sit and talk (with bombs and sirens sounding out-side), she speaks to him as though she *were* his mother. Once, after we hear Clive's voiceover say: "Cross out and transpose" (a reference to literary editing), Kevin seems to "become" Claude, and Claude Clive. Later, the two men's positions alter again and Claude talks to Kevin as though he were his parent, blaming him for mistreating his mother.

Sporadically we return to "reality," as we watch Clive get through the night, drinking, talking to himself, stumbling, coughing, defecating, and moaning in pain. Sometimes he calls out for Molly, whom we surmise to be his dead wife (perhaps a reference to James Joyce's *Ulysses*). In a scene depicting Helen (who has already stood in for Molly), Clive's voiceover mutters: "Will you kindly get out of my mind, Molly?" Often the shots of Clive at night are brief, some being mere flashes. Every now and then, Clive seems to talk about his actual life (versus his literary fantasies). When he envisions a fictional scene of interrupted adultery, he recalls that he was never caught cheating. Once, after considering his own life, Clive says, "Back to business," meaning a return to the craft of writing.

Toward the end of the film, we suddenly see a daylight scene on the lawn of a mansion (which we assume to be Clive's): birds chirping, sun shining, flowers blooming—quite a contrast to the gloomy estate in which we have "spent" the night. A fairly robust (rather than decrepit) Clive sits outside on a chaise longue as his staff lays a table for several guests. Clive briefly picks up a notepad but puts it down (a nod to his profession). He asks a servant, "Are the children here yet?" His employee then reveals that he found Clive on the bathroom floor that morning and the writer admits, in a jocular fashion, that he had gotten "pissed." So, some of what we have witnessed in the night was accurate.

Soon a couple approaches sweetly holding hands. It is the real Sonia and Claude coming to attend Clive's birthday party. They seem happy and content, entirely unlike their aggressive, bickering, fictional selves. Rather than sarcastic, theatrical, and bombastic, Claude is kind, shy, and deferential. Soon, another man approaches. It is the real Kevin, who is Clive's "bastard" son. He, too, seems affectionate to his father, who welcomes him. All seem friendly and pleased to mark the occasion. The children ask Clive about his new book and inquire whom he is "disemboweling this time"—a comment that squares with the vicious story we have seen. A propos, as a gift, Sonia gives Clive a knife that once belonged to Hemingway—the perfect instrument for evisceration. When Clive and Claude are left alone for a moment, Clive muses about his son's disapproval of his treatment of Claude's mother. We now learn, however, that Molly had cancer (seemingly like Clive) and that her illness (not the latter's bad behavior) explains her suicide.[18] Clive does admit his absence as a father, as well as his boozing and marital infidelity. Claude, however, seems at peace with all this. The family sits down to a fancy meal on the lawn (in a scene that looks more like one out of an Ingmar Bergman film than one by Buñuel). Clive says he refuses to die and must finish his book. He toasts to his children's future and says (invoking the theme of providence), "Nothing is written. We all believe that, don't we?"

At one point early on, when Clive envisions his son as an attorney prosecuting Kevin, Claude says: "Surely, the facts are not in dispute." In view of the tenor of the film, however, this is an ironic statement—since everything we observe is "in dispute." Ultimately, what we witness is a transposition of the "facts of life" into fiction—with the latter maintaining certain parallels to the former (Clive is an alcoholic, ill and probably dying, Sonia and Claude are married, Kevin is a person in their lives, there are tensions between Clive and Claude). But in their fantasized version, things are improbably transposed and exaggerated, and characters are composites, not replicas of any single individual. Such is the process of creation.[19]

Aside from Resnais's citation of his own films or homages to his directorial colleagues, there is another interesting self-reference in *Providence*. Resnais, having made an austere, modernist work like *Last Year at Marienbad*, has sometimes been known as a "cinematic intellectual" as well as a virtuosic stylist—this, perhaps, at the expense of emotional depth.[20] Even *Night and Fog* (1955), with its montage of color and black-and-white footage, live action and photograph, word and image, has been viewed as a formal triumph, but a restrained invocation of the Holocaust. In *Providence*, Resnais, through the voice of Clive, remarks at one point: "It's been said about my work that a search for style has often resulted in a want of feeling." And certain critics have claimed this about the film we are watching. John Francis Kreidl, for instance, refers to its tone as "distancing" and calls its characters "devices with voices."[21] Of course, Claude (and perhaps Resnais) has a retort to the charge of affective vacancy: "I'd say style is feeling in its most elegant and economic expression."

Other aesthetic or philosophical debates are conducted in the heady dialogue of the film—about the right to die, justice, morality, and the existence of God. Kevin (in both fictional and "real" segments) is an astrophysicist and retired astronaut who has had a sense of "God's eyes" watching him in outer space. (After he speaks these lines, their author [Clive] opines that there is "nothing in this icy universe.") Fittingly, for his father's birthday, Kevin gives him an antique telescope (as though to help him see those heavenly "eyes"). However, at the celebration, Clive tells his children that he dislikes approaching death because one faces the "temptation of believing in something."

But the only actual source of power we have seen in the film is that of Clive's mind, which, despite his illness, flexes its imaginative muscle, creates characters, and controls the events of their existence (demonstrating providence). Hence, when Clive decides to make a telephone ring in his story, we next hear it sound onscreen. Thus the only rival for the Almighty is the Author—both the fictional one and the real filmmaker who makes the former's (dying) thoughts come alive. Significantly, Kreidl sees a strong reference to the director toward the end of the film. After the birthday meal has been completed, the camera suddenly cranes up (to a "God"-like view) and executes a slow, 360-degree pan that circles around the estate's gardens and grounds. It has started as a shot from Claude's perspective and we expect that, when the camera returns to its initial point, no one will be there —a perfect ending to the story. Instead, it returns to Clive (as seen externally— not from his vantage point), and the film continues for a few minutes. For Kreidl, this reflexive, tour-de-force segment "inform[s] us that we are to take with us an authorial 'I,' first person ending, a literal summation by Renais."[22] He continues:

"Resnais [in this shot] . . . wanted to empty out of the film all its characters but one [the writer]," but also to "usurp" his point of view.[23]

THE PATIENT'S "HELPMEET"

We have already discussed how illness "infantilizes" the writer (as it does all individuals)—but for him, it only confirms the widespread view (advanced early on by Freud) that artists are daydreaming children unready to face the challenges of adult life.[24] As Victor Hugo once remarked, "A great artist is a great man in a great child."[25] Because they are often seen as cases of "arrested development," writers are frequently portrayed as requiring coddling and assistance, especially when infirm. In the films discussed below, rather than focusing centrally on the author, the text splits its attention between him and his helper. In the first case, the relationship is benevolent; in the second, perverse.

Novelist and Nursemaid

In one sense, *Céleste* (1981), written and directed in Germany by Percy Adlon, is a biopic about Marcel Proust, who spent the final years of his life (while completing *Remembrance of Things Past*) plagued by asthma, bed-ridden in a cork-lined room in his Paris apartment. But in truth, it is a portrait of Céleste Albaret, his maid and assistant (whom he employed for nine years), as derived from her 1976 memoir *Monsieur Proust*. So in that sense she has authorial status.

   It is significant that his aide is female—for, as we know, women often make men's writing possible.[26] Much attention has been paid to the case of Bertolt Brecht, who was assisted in the 1920s by Elisabeth Hauptmann on *The Threepenny Opera* and *Happy End*.[27] Later, during his exile period, Margarete Steffin and Ruth Berlau "took similar though less indispensable roles."[28] Recently, following the death of Swedish novelist Stieg Larsson, his partner of thirty-two years (Eva Gabrielsson) claimed that the two often wrote together and that she intends to complete the manuscript he left unfinished when he died in 2004. Because the couple never married (and he left no will), she has been denied any inheritance from the huge profits made on his "Millennium" series, which was published posthumously but written during their years together.[29]

   In *Céleste*, Proust (Jürgen Arndt) is portrayed not only as physically ill but neurotic, a depiction that conforms to details of his life. The ritualized schedule Céleste (Eva Mattes) must keep for him reveals an individual with obsessive-compulsive disorder. She is told that he must have his "breakfast" coffee at precisely 4:30 P.M. every day. She is instructed on how to enter his bedroom as well as how to open his curtains. She can never offer him the same towel twice (even during a single drying of his hands), and he is not to be given a glass if she has touched its rim. Furthermore, she is not to talk to him (unless specifically asked to) and often he will not speak himself, communicating only with hand gestures. She is not to walk around the house (so as not to produce footsteps); to emphasize

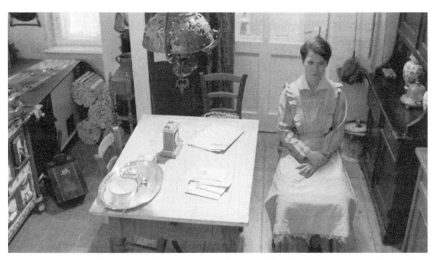

FIGURE 24. Céleste (Eva Mattes) waits in Marcel Proust's kitchen for him to ring the bell for his afternoon "breakfast" in *Céleste* (1980).

this, we hear the creaking of the floor whenever she moves. She must disinfect his mail and change his sheets every day. When he asks whether her life is "sad" being around a sick man, she replies in the negative and explains that she is "eccentric."

We frequently see Céleste sitting motionless in the kitchen for extended periods of time, as rendered in long duration shots. In fact, it is with such a scene that the film opens. She only moves when she hears the ringing of Proust's bell, signaling his need for her attention. If the author's act of writing seems boring and uncinematic to the viewer, so does the behavior of his patient assistant. Sometimes what he requires is a meal, and the camera documents the entire process of Céleste brewing coffee, heating milk, and putting food on a plate. At other times, her chores relate to his wardrobe or personal care, as when she warms his clothes in the oven to make sure he does not get chilled, or sanitizes the instruments for his barber. Finally, his needs are sometimes medical, as when Céleste burns herbs for inhalation therapy when he has an asthma attack. When this occurs her usual stasis is interrupted by panic, as rendered in hand-held camera movement as she races to his room.

Many of her regular tasks are repeated throughout the film, giving the viewer a sense of the routine of his and her lives. Here, the infirm writer's female assistant is also a domestic and the detailed representation of her jobs is reminiscent of Chantal Akerman's focus on housework in *Jeanne Dielman* (1975). Of course, one of Céleste's primary tasks is waiting (an experience heightened by the loud ticking of a clock that is heard in the background throughout the film). This is a role that women have historically been assigned while men go forth to succeed in the world. As Mary Ann Doane has noted: "The iconography is quite insistent: women and waiting are intimately linked and [it] . . . has become a well-worn figure of the classical cinematic text."[30] In direct address to the camera (a technique utilized throughout the film), Céleste informs us that she "didn't get bored." Proust's apartment "was eerie, but [she] felt at home" there. As though to encapsulate the voyaging male and the house-bound female (despite the former's status as an invalid), several scenes show Proust exiting the elevator after a night out and returning to his apartment—Céleste standing there to welcome him home. We never see her in the mobile elevator "cage"—her own cage being the kitchen. When Proust is close to death and Céleste is tearful and exhausted, her husband, Odilon (Norbert Wartha), asks her what she wants to do. "Wait," she replies.

As his primary caregiver, Céleste is also given the job of worrying about Proust. She reveals that her worst days are those in which he fails to ring for her, causing her to go mad with anxiety and to eschew sleep. One such sequence is extraordinarily protracted, making the viewer as tense as Céleste. Because she has been told never to disturb him, she refrains from checking on him, but she stands outside his door and weeps. At one point, we are privy to her nervous fantasy—presented in images of Proust falling down or lying dead. The sequence ends with a close-up of Céleste's eye as Proust's bell finally rings; shocked, she sits still—temporarily frozen. She later tells us (in direct address) that he failed to call because he "wanted to know what it was like to die for his book." Clearly, Céleste has little life of her own; though Odilon does errands for Proust, she hardly sees him. Significantly, in one scene we find Odilon pacing the kitchen floor as Céleste tends to her charge.

Much of what we learn about Céleste's life with Proust she tells us in direct address to the camera—for instance, that she sleeps from 8 A.M. to 3 P.M. to conform to his schedule. Sometimes, we are privy to her visual memories of him, as we see a flash of him comically bowing to her (in pajamas), saying: "Madame, I present you Marcel Proust." Every now and then, her actions or monologues are interrupted by snatches of Proust's voiceover, for instance telling her: "When I've written the word 'end,' we'll go south." Sometimes, as we watch Céleste onscreen, her image is accompanied by her own voiceover. In the flashback of her first meeting with Proust, her offscreen narration says: "I couldn't see his face but his eyes looked at me." Elsewhere the vocal technique is used to recall their trip to the ocean, as we watch images of the sea and the Grand Hotel.

If Céleste barely sees Proust, we are also denied his presence, since he remains behind a closed door or is glimpsed incompletely, through its partial opening. Sometimes his existence is registered only by an offscreen sound—his bell ringing or his cough. In the flashback to the day Céleste was hired, his bedroom is shrouded in shadow, allowing us only a view of his hand or his eyes. His room is kept exceedingly dark, so even when he is pictured onscreen he is barely visible.

Aside from tending to his daily life and health, Céleste is his social secretary, telephoning people with whom he wants to meet and making restaurant reservations. Her voiceover informs us that these excursions were related to Proust's fiction, since he needed to find "models" for his characters. She also plays a more direct role in his writing process—taking dictation and reading passages back to

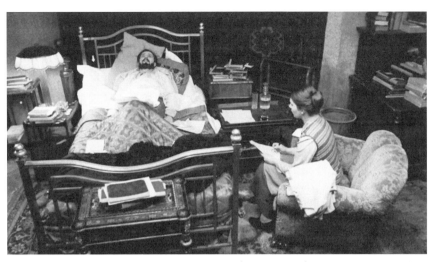

FIGURE 25. Céleste helps an ailing Marcel Proust (Jürgen Arndt) write his novel in *Céleste* (1980).

him. Céleste also assists Proust's authorial work in another way. He often wrote additions to his text on scraps of paper rather than in a notebook, and frequently he lost track of their order. Céleste and Odilon devise a way of attaching them in an accordion-like scroll, which helps Proust establish continuity.

At times, Proust and Céleste seem like good friends, as when he returns from an evening engagement and gives her a witty and copious description of the event and its attendant gossip. Clearly, she already knows something of all the people he mentions. In general, Proust is exceedingly kind to Céleste (despite his rigorous demands on her), but a clear hierarchy remains based on employment and class. He asks her to call him Marcel, but she refuses—referring to him instead as "Monsieur"—despite the fact that (as he points out) she does not know how to use the formal "third person." Similarly, she asks that he call her Céleste, not "Madame," and he finally complies—indicating that his relation to her is more malleable than hers to him.

We have already mentioned Céleste's classic stance of waiting, which gives the film a slow, static quality. In fact, its entire temporal structure bears attention (not surprising for a film about Proust). To some degree, like the author's work, it is a kind of jigsaw puzzle that combines visualized flashes of present, past, imagined, and ambiguous moments. Sometimes, Céleste has pure acoustic recollections, as when we hear Proust's voiceover muse: "When I'm dead you'll think of Marcel." Thus, we must make an audio-visual assemblage of the film, as Céleste does of his literary fragments.

We noted that in *The Singing Detective* and *The Diving Bell and the Butterfly*, the infirm author is often placed in an infantile position, and in this film Céleste certainly takes a maternal stance. As we know, *Remembrance of Things Past* reveals what we might deem Proust's maternal fixation, so it comes as no surprise that, in one night scene, he calls for Céleste and says that he is "pining for Mama." Later, he refers to Céleste as a "mother substitute," and her own voiceover reveals that she often feels like his parent. Moreover, Proust asks Céleste to describe her own mother's funeral—just one of the many narratives he wants to hear about her life. As he says at one point: "Tell me another story." So the film is as much about her tale spinning as his.

In sum, *Céleste* demonstrates the kind of labor (often female) it takes to sustain the life of a great writer. In classic fashion, however, Céleste refuses to be celebrated for assisting Proust. As she notes in her memoir: "There was no sacrifice in pleasing or helping him. For me it was . . . [a] pleasure to be completely drawn into his work."[31] Finally, however (given that the film is based on her memoir), he is also drawn into hers.

Frailty and Fandom

In chapter 8, we consider the author's readers and critics, but here we will touch upon her fans. On the one hand, this group seems a hospitable bunch, in that they profess love for a writer and her oeuvre. However, like any passion, fandom can be overdone and tip toward unhealthy fixation. It is such a condition that we find in *Misery* (1990), directed by Rob Reiner and written by William Goldman.

Rather than concern a historical literary great, the film is about a fictional bestselling author, Paul Sheldon (James Caan), who has just completed his first serious novel. Like Sarah Morton in *Swimming Pool*, he has decided to abandon his series of popular romances (featuring the heroine Misery Chastane) to a more significant and personal project (currently called *Untitled*). He leaves his Colorado writing hideout to return home; however, en route, he crashes his car in a severe snowstorm. He is left unconscious but is rescued by someone that we see only fragmentarily. The Good Samaritan turns out to be Annie Wilkes (Kathy Bates), a former nurse who, rather than take him to a hospital, brings him to her remote house. When he becomes alert, he thanks Annie for saving him and for setting his fractured leg bones (though she has done so with odd pieces of scrap wood and metal). He also asks why he is not getting professional medical attention. She says that the roads are closed from the storm and that, luckily, as a nurse, she can tend to him in the interim. As he comes into consciousness, she says: "You're fine. There's nothing to worry about; I'll take good care of you." When he asks whether he can make a phone call, she tells him that the lines are down. She knows his authorial identity and confesses that she is his "number one fan." Stephen King (who wrote the novel on which the film is based) has called it a story of "fan love," which for him "is the purest love there is."[32] As a sign of this, Annie has collected all of Paul's books and has even named her pet pig Misery.

Up to this point, we might liken Annie to Céleste—a caregiver to a renowned author. But as the film progresses, both the viewer and Paul (who is bed-bound from his injuries) realize that Annie is psychologically unbalanced and holding

Paul captive, lying about the impossibility of moving him to a hospital and the phone being disconnected. Here, we recall that the word *fan* is etymologically related to *fanatical*—a term that implies excess and even psychopathology. Furthermore, we realize that the portrayal of this kind of fan is most often attached to the female. As Kathleen Franz and Susan Smulyan note, in the nineteenth century "women and girls were widely criticized for their frivolous addiction to novel reading . . . more often . . . than were men with similar interests. Women were prominent in the crowds who thronged the engagements of touring celebrities such as . . . literary lions like Charles Dickens, Mark Twain, and Oscar Wilde."[33] When Paul Sheldon's New York agent (who has been expecting his return) calls a local sheriff (Richard Farnsworth) to express concern about his absence, an investigation is opened into her client's disappearance.

The issue of writing is highlighted from the moment the film opens, since during its credit sequence we hear the sound of typing. As the film starts, Paul sits at a table with his (requisite) typewriter and we even see some words on the paper in the carriage ("What else was there?")—perhaps signifying that he has written an "existential" novel. When he finishes his manuscript, however, he writes "The End" in longhand on the final page, as though these words require more human inscription. (Recall that, in *Céleste*, Proust imagines the day that he will write "the end.") It is, of course, Paul's status as an author that gets him kidnapped by Annie, the plot point that sets the drama in motion. We later learn that she has been spying on him during his stay at Silver Lake Lodge and followed him when he departed there. This raises interesting questions about authorship, stalking, and celebrity. King has commented on this topic: "Writers are anonymous. I could walk out here anywhere, and nobody would know who I was. . . . If Paul Newman walked down the street, he would be recognized immediately."[34] We suspect that this is no longer true for King, and clearly not for Paul Sheldon.

In the first part of the film Annie treats Paul very nicely (though her saccharine enthusiasm strikes a false note), clearly impressed by the fact that she is hosting a literary star. Learning that he has just finished a new book, she asks whether she might read his manuscript. Though normally he refuses such requests, he grants her wish. That is when the plot takes a turn for the worse. When she feeds him soup on the morning after reading his book, she chastises him for using "swear" words in it and gets so animated in her hostility that she spills some soup. "See what you made me do!" she shouts punitively. As she leaves the room, we see a close-up of Paul looking shocked and disturbed. Sometime later, she wheels a charcoal grill into his room, places the manuscript on it, saturates it with lighter fluid, and tells Paul to ignite it. Having no choice in the matter, he is forced to do so—destroying the literary work of which he is most proud. By the next day (in a bipolar swing) she is all sweetness and light, telling him what a poet he is. She is excited because she has just purchased *Misery's Child*, the newest (and, for him, the final) book in his romance series, and on subsequent days (as she progresses through it) she compliments him on his brilliant style.

In the middle of one night, however, when Paul is fast asleep, she barges angrily into his room and launches into a tirade: "You dirty bird—how could you do that?" She has come to the end of Paul's novel and learned that her beloved heroine has died (a strategy Paul has used to close the series and free him from future installments). "I don't want her dead!" Annie screams plaintively. Her verbal abuse turns physical as she breaks furniture and throws a chair against the wall, terrifying Paul. "I thought you were good," she says, "but you're no good." She taunts him by revealing that she is holding him prisoner and that no one knows his whereabouts. Clearly, fan love has turned to hate, and intimations of romance have taken a Gothic turn. But—rather than an innocent female being trapped in a menacing man's home—here gender roles are reversed and Paul is feminized in the process. This is a radical about-face from his earlier macho deportment whereby we have seen him smoking, drinking, throwing snowballs, and driving heedlessly into a blizzard with the song "Shotgun" blaring on his car radio.

Beyond emasculating him, illness leaves Paul infantilized—a position familiar to us from earlier portrayals of sick writers. Given that Paul is largely crippled, he is as immobile as a baby and Annie must tend to all his bodily needs: urination, defecation, bathing, dressing, and nutrition. She even ties him down at one point. And in the scene in which he first comes into consciousness after being rescued, his face looks as swollen as a newborn's. After Annie shaves him one day, she coos: "Just like a baby!" In later sequences in which he attempts to escape from her house, he crawls on the floor (like a toddler) or scoots around in a wheelchair (as in a baby walker). As he does so, the shots of the doorknob and lock are taken from a low-angle, as from the view of a small child. His efforts remind us of a youngster's quite natural endeavor to leave or separate from the mother, and Paul's tool for unlocking the door is a stray hairpin, a female accouterment. Finally, Annie praises him extravagantly, as would a doting parent, calling him "perfect," "brilliant," a "genius." Significantly, we learn that, before having her license revoked (for killing babies), Annie was a maternity nurse, and retrospectively her extraction of Paul from his wrecked car seems like a form of mechanical "birth"—with crowbar standing in for forceps, and mouth-to-mouth resuscitation standing in for a physician's attempt to clear a newborn's airway. Here it seems significant that Paul killed off his novelistic heroine in childbirth—hence his is a literary matricidal act.

Clearly, according to this reading, Annie is the archetypal Bad Mother (while Céleste has been the Good)—an awesome, frightening, and punishing figure. When she learns that he has escaped from his room while she is out doing errands, she hobbles him—placing a board between his legs and hitting it with a mallet. Here, as in many other such segments, we focus on Paul's expressions of excruciating pain—screams, facial contortions, perspiration. On numerous occasions she erupts in "maternal" rage: for example, by complaining that he fails to appreciate all she does for him. Sometimes she acts like a glum and morose parent, sensing wistfully that her offspring will inevitably leave.

FIGURE 26. Annie (Kathy Bates) sets up a writing desk for Paul (James Caan) in *Misery* (1997).

From the perspective of authorship and film, however, the most intriguing aspect of the narrative is the fact that, after Annie reads Paul's latest book (*Misery's
Child*) and learns that the heroine expires, she forces him to write a sequel (to be
called *Misery's Return*), with Annie serving as his "number one critic." She buys
an old typewriter (which, given his circumstances, assumes some of the malevo-
lence of the machine in *Naked Lunch*). She also purchases typing paper, though
he remarks that the erasable kind is not best—thus angering her. To reprimand
him for this faux pas, she sadistically smacks his broken leg with a ream of paper.
Her choice of erasable paper seems to stand for her desire for him to "unwrite" his
work. She has already burnt his latest manuscript and now forces him to create a
story that undoes the outcome of *Misery's Child*.

From this point on, the film presents numerous scenes of a crippled Paul sitting at a card table typing away (for his life) as he composes his new volume—
his major problem being how to revive Misery from the death she suffered at his
hands. When Paul tries to take some narrative short cuts, Annie yells at him for
violating the rules of continuity. But she later praises him for naming the gravedig-
ger after her and dedicating the book to her (actually by her demand). Paul solves
the problem of reviving Misery by conceiving that she has been mistakenly buried
alive (while in a coma), thus allowing for her resurrection. We cannot help but
think that Paul was once buried alive (in a snowstorm) before being reanimated
by Annie Wilkes and is now "entombed" in her house.

While Paul, having no choice, plays along with Annie's scheme and permits
Misery to rise from the dead, he is really plotting another death—Annie's. Paul
secretly lifts his typewriter as a free weight to rebuild his strength (and manhood).
He knows that she will be a fierce opponent in any fight, given that she is a large
woman and has already shot the sheriff who came to her house to investigate.

Following that murder, Annie has turned depressive and made clear that she is planning a double "suicide" for them. He asks that he first be allowed to finish *Misery's Return*, and she accedes to his request.

On the night he finishes the book, he asks her to bring him a match and cigarette (his well-known routine when a manuscript is completed). Then, when she leaves the room for a minute, he pours some lighter fluid he has surreptitiously obtained on the pages of the text and, as she returns, sets it afire. When she dives down to put the flames out, he slams her head with his typewriter (a novel use for the object in the history of cinema). She comes to and fires her gun, but he pins her down, stuffing her mouth with the ashes of his book (death by typing paper). She rises up again, but he pushes her down and her skull crashes on the typewriter. More fighting ensues before she actually dies. Like Misery, she has been difficult to kill.

In eventually expunging the maternal figure in the narrative (and with a typewriter), Paul is similar to other writers, according to Wendy Lesser. In *His Other Half: Men Looking at Women through Art*, she notes: "The mother is the initial woman from whom the male artist has literally to sever himself in order to become both a man and an artist. The mother may, in some disguised form, be the female figure animating the work of all male artists."[35] Here, it is intriguing that, in Paul's journey to become a man, the one letter broken on the typewriter he uses is "n"—the letter that separates the words "Ma" and "Man." Furthermore, Annie's sardonic nickname for Paul (at moments of annoyance) is "Mr. Man."

Lesser also claims that male-authored narratives involve a wrestling with empathy. As she remarks: "Whenever a man sets out to write a story about a mother . . . it is also, inevitably, a story about the extortion of sympathy. . . . That is to say, it becomes a story both about the sympathy the author had to feel for his mother and about the sympathy we have to feel for him because that other sympathy was forced from him."[36] Certainly throughout the film we have witnessed Annie's "extortion" of emotion from Paul and we have felt for his entrapment in this malicious dynamic. But at the conclusion (which takes place some months later), he manages to express sympathy for her, admitting to his New York agent (an older woman who might constitute yet another parental figure) that Annie "helped" him complete his latest, acclaimed novel. While the manuscript she burnt could only be named *Untitled*, the one he has finally published is called *The Education of Philip J. Stone*—which seems to place the imagined protagonist in the position of a schoolboy, just done with his studies. (The name of its hero may also indicate that he starts out with the emotions of a "stone" and gains depth as the novel progresses.) As the strains of "I'll Be Seeing You" (sung by Liberace) are heard on the sound track (a song that Annie previously played in her house), we understand that, like a child, Paul will never be free of her. Again, Lesser's words resonate: "In order to become a writer a man must both immerse himself in his mother and free himself from her."[37] Perhaps Paul shares more with Marcel Proust than he or King might realize.

MADNESS AND THE FAMILY

Lesser's insights about authorship and the maternal bring to mind one final film concerning the infirm writer—*The Shining* (directed by Stanley Kubrick in 1980). Here the illness is mental, since read one way, the narrative is about a novelist (Jack Torrance, played by Jack Nicholson) who sinks into insanity. Furthermore, like *Misery*, it is based on a work by Stephen King.

In the drama, Torrance has been hired as winter caretaker of a large, old hotel (the Overlook), which is located in the secluded mountains of Colorado. It is closed for the season since the region is often snowbound and inaccessible. Here, of course, we recognize the icy geographical terrain of *Misery* and the terror of being cut off from civilization (a favored scene for horror). Torrance brings along his wife, Wendy (Shelley Duvall), and his young son Danny (Danny Lloyd). While there, each of them develops the power of "shining," which involves seeing both the future and the past (when a former caretaker savagely murdered his family at the lodge). Obviously, in this regard, the film solicits our belief in the supernatural, and its haunted inn reminds us of the Earle in *Barton Fink*. But on another level (which brackets the occult), the film can be taken as a drama of domestic strife and abuse; and it is on this plane that I wish to consider it.

We learn that Jack is a former teacher, now unemployed, which is why he accepts the position at the Overlook. Clearly, he has not been successful as a novelist or a wage earner, and he takes the hotel job to earn money and gain time to write. In truth, however, it is Wendy, the author's "helpmeet," who does all the work (checking heating levels, electrical fixtures, phone lines, radio communication, etc.) while he sits at his manual typewriter waiting for inspiration. Beyond that, in her role as wife and mother, she does all the "caretaking" of the family— uprooting herself for her husband's job, cooking meals, cleaning, and tending to their child.

Early on, there are signs of trouble. When Wendy asks Jack how his writing is going, he responds that he has "lots of ideas" but "no good ones." Later, a shot begins with a close-up of Jack's abandoned typewriter on a table in a cavernous lounge, beside which there is a burning cigarette, pens, and pencils. Accompanying the shot is a harsh pounding sound, and ultimately we see Jack throwing a ball against the wall—as though to take out his aggression and frustration. When, later on, Wendy comes into the room to ask how his work is proceeding, he lies and tells her things are fine, after which he scolds her for interrupting him and tears up a manuscript page. Finally, he yells, "Get the fuck outta here!" and she meekly departs. On another occasion, Wendy hears Jack screaming and, when she arrives in the lounge, finds him with his head on the typewriter—awakening from a dream in which he has killed and dismembered his family (like his predecessor).

Once at the hotel, Danny (who has earlier shown signs of psychological disturbance by talking to an imaginary friend, Tony) has horrific visions (e.g., of blood surging out from the elevator, like the fire in *Barton Fink*). Soon, he will only talk through his surrogate, who tells Wendy that "Danny's gone away." When Danny tells "Tony" that he has been frightened by an apparition of murder, the latter comforts him by saying that "it's just like pages in a book" and "isn't real" —phrases that tie Danny's visions to his father's craft. Danny also appears one day with unexplained scratches on his neck; Wendy is suspicious since Jack once dislocated the child's shoulder. She becomes alarmed and suggests to Jack that the hotel environment is harmful for Danny and that they should leave (already difficult due to a developing snowstorm). At this, Jack erupts, reminding Wendy of his singular opportunity to write and claiming that she is "fucking up his life."

Ominous tracking shots recur of Jack, seen from behind, sitting motionless at his typewriter, and, in a series of facial close ups, his appearance becomes more and more demonic. Frightened of him and armed with a baseball bat, Wendy enters the lounge at a time when he is not there and peers at his writing machine (she is shot from below with its carriage in view). A reverse angle reveals a page in the typewriter covered by one sentence, repeated ad infinitum: "All work and no play makes Jack a dull boy." As she rifles through the copious sheets in his manuscript box, she finds scores of pages on which the same phrase appears—typed in myriad line arrangements and paragraph styles. As Greg Smith notes, "The sentence mimics various conventional writing forms, including poems . . . [and] (God help us) an academic essay."[38] Suddenly, Jack approaches and perversely inquires: "How do you like it?" As she swings the bat at him, he says: "I won't hurt you. I'm just gonna bash your brains in." She escapes and comes upon Danny shouting an inexplicable word, "Redrum," which he writes on a door with her lipstick (inverting several letters). When the writing is reflected in the room's mirror (and thereby reversed) it spells "murder." The rest of the film details Wendy and Danny's flight from the Overlook, as Jack pursues them. Ultimately, they get away while he freezes in a hedge maze on the hotel grounds.

So what does the film have to say about the writer and his helpmeet? As in *Misery*, the latter is configured as maternal—here the kind mother of Danny and caretaker of Jack—whose function is to make her husband's art possible. At one point he even refers to her viciously as his "sperm bank." Numerous critics (while not focusing on Jack's authorial position) have seen him as a symbol of brutal male control and privilege—abusing both his son and wife.[39] As Walter Metz notes: "Positioned as a melodrama, *The Shining* seems to produce a critique of the patriarchal relations inherent in the American familial structure."[40] This stance becomes clear when, wielding an axe, Jack breaks down the door of the bathroom in which his wife is hiding and shouts cheerfully, "Wendy, I'm home." It is also signaled in an early scene of the couple driving to the hotel, remarking on the journey of the Donner party that resorted to cannibalism.

Critics have also noted how the film evokes the feminine "abject"—both in Jack's attitude toward Wendy and in the pool of blood that repeatedly is seen issuing from the hotel elevator. Robert Kilker remarks that while "the film does make a monster out of the repressive patriarch . . . it also codes the feminine as

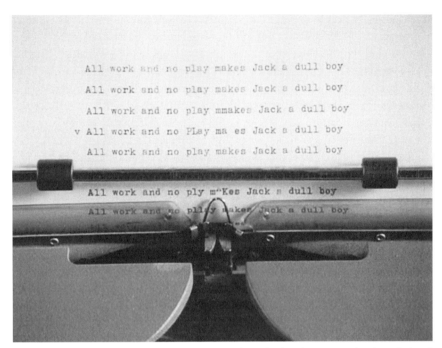

FIGURE 27. A repetitive page from the stalled novel on which Jack Torrance (Jack Nicholson) works in *The Shining* (1980).

monstrous, and equally threatening as the patriarchal forces that would try to contain it."[41] This view is most apparent in a scene in which Jack fantasizes seeing a gorgeous woman in a hotel room emerging naked from a bath. As he embraces her, however, her skin begins to rot as she ages into an elderly hag. Ironically, although authoritarian, Jack also stands in the position of a child (as an ineffectual writer manqué who fails to support his family). Here, it seems significant that, as he is chasing Wendy with an axe, he quotes from "The Three Little Pigs." Furthermore, the sentence he obsessively types is a children's aphorism that utilizes his name ("All work and no play makes Jack a dull boy"). Its moral lesson seems sardonic since Jack appears not to work at all and, likely, his writing problems stem from his dullness (read: lack of talent) and not from the interference of family life. Furthermore, as Smith suggests, "the one-sentence-per-line arrangement [of text is] reminiscent of the wayward student reproducing the same cliché litany on a blackboard as punishment."[42]

While in previous chapters we have discussed numerous troubled writers, few have resorted to violence. While the novelist in *Smoke* (1995) mourns his dead wife, Jack wants his mate dead. Perhaps Jack's greatest parallel is to William Lee in Cronenberg's *Naked Lunch* (1991), who realizes that his status as author depends on having killed his spouse. Jack's hostility also makes us consider the links between his last name, Torrance, and the word "torrents," which can signify "violent, tumultuous, or overwhelming flow[s]: [as in] torrent[s] of abuse."[43] The fact that Jack's sadism erupts in a scene of solitude (he has been warned of "cabin fever") is consonant with the stance of the writer, who must often work alone. The hotel's name, the Overlook, also suggests that, too often, society "overlooks" the foibles of the artist, who is released from bourgeois social mores in the name of genius and creation. Finally, it seems important that the act that haunts the narrative (and the hotel) is spelled out in the alphabet letters that Danny writes on the wall: "Murder." Moreover, they are inscribed with a red lipstick—a female accouterment whose color is that of blood (like that of the victims of the ancient caretaker's carnage—all females—wife and daughters).

EPILOGUE

In all the works we have considered in this chapter, the health of the writer is compromised by diseases of the skin, brain, bones, bowels, lungs, or mind. To this list we might add films in which the author is neurotic and, most especially, plagued by writer's block. This latter issue creeps up (either centrally or peripherally) in numerous movies—not only *The Shining*, but in *Smoke*, *The Tango Lesson* (1997), *Swimming Pool*, *Adaptation*, *Barton Fink*, *Starting Out in the Evening* (2007), *My Effortless Brilliance* (2008), and *Paris When It Sizzles* (1963). If the act of writing is already a static and uncinematic event, how much more so is the act of not writing? Yet it appears ubiquitous onscreen, perhaps because, as Alice Flaherty notes, with "professional writers the syndrome is an obsession, and many writers have transferred [it] to their characters."[44] Like all afflictions the disorder involves torment, for as Flaherty opines: "Someone who is not writing but not suffering does not have writer's block; he or she is merely not writing."[45]

But the question remains (be it a condition of the mind or the body) as to why the infirm writer is such a popular figure (as opposed to the productive author). Sander Gilman offers one answer: that our own fear of illness causes us to project it onto others, thus separating ourselves from it. As he writes: "It is the fear of collapse, the sense of dissolution, which contaminates the Western image of all diseases. . . . But the fear we have of our own collapse does not remain internalized. Rather, we project this fear onto the world in order to localize it, and indeed, domesticate it. For once we locate it, the fear of our own dissolution is removed. Then, it is not we who totter on the brink of collapse, but rather the Other."[46] Alternately, in *The Wound and the Bow*, Edmund Wilson confronts the subject of creativity and illness by returning to ancient Greek tragedy, specifically to a play by Sophocles—*Philoctetes* (first performed in 409 B.C.). It is named for its protagonist who is given a magical bow by Heracles that never misses its mark. Along with Agamemnon and Menelaus, Philoctetes sets forth against Troy. On his way there, however, he gets a snake bite on his foot and the wound becomes infected and malodorous. His cohorts abandon him and he remains marooned for ten years. Finally, Neoptolemus comes back for Philoctetes and his wondrous bow.

Philoctetes is brought back to Troy, where he is healed. Returning to battle, he and Neoptolemus become heroes of the Trojan War.[47]

For Wilson, the ancient tale is significant since "one feels in . . . Philoctetes a more general and fundamental idea: the conception of superior strength as inseparable from disability. For the superiority of Philoctetes does not reside merely in the enchanted bow." Wilson also discusses a modern adaptation of the narrative by André Gide (1898–99), in which Philoctetes is portrayed as an ailing artist. At one point in the play, for instance, he says: "I have learned to express myself better. . . . And I took to telling the story of my sufferings, and if the phrase was very beautiful, I was by so much consoled; I even sometimes forgot my sadness by uttering it." Thus, as Wilson concludes, Philoctetes is "a literary man . . . an artist, whose genius becomes purer and deeper in relation to his isolation and outlawry."[48]

So, on some level, the infirm writer represents all creators—a group for whom "genius and disease, like strength and mutilation, may be inextricably bound up together."[49] Thus when, in a scene from the Reiner film, Paul Sheldon toasts "To Misery"—we suspect he is not simply referencing his fictional heroine but his authorial fate. Furthermore, the seclusion that infirmity brings writers (whether Philoctetes or his modern counterpart) separates them from the mainstream—again validating clichés of their being loners or misfits.

6 CINÉCRITURE: WORD AND IMAGE

> In today's culture we may feel we are the compliant and gratified hostages of a productive interaction of image and writing.
> —Karen Knorr and Tracey Moffat, "When the Photographer"

Throughout the book, in discussing the embodiment of the writer on-screen, we have focused on filmic moments that provoke tensions between word and image—be they shots of a book's page (*Barton Fink*), words on a computer screen (*Rage*), manuscript copy in a typewriter (*Naked Lunch*, *The Shining*), a handwritten text (*The Tango Lesson*), or a screenplay on a table (*Poetic Justice*). In this chapter we pursue the subject head-on by examining works that make this dynamic a primary strategy. Furthermore, we confront the topic in a more theoretical manner.

To that end, we might note that the letters of certain languages (like Egyptian hieroglyphs) were based on pictorial models: for example, the icon for "worship" resembled a person praying.[1] The same obtained for many Asian languages. As Will Eisner remarks: "In the development of Chinese and Japanese pictographs, a welding of pure visual imagery and a uniform derivative symbol took place. Ultimately, the visual image became secondary . . . marking the transition from pictographs to characters." Of course, this is what led filmmaker Sergei Eisenstein to liken the roots of the ideogram to filmic montage.[2] But some have argued that all written language has a pictorial base. As Anne-Marie Martin states: "Writing was born from the image, and whatever the system of writing, whether ideographic or alphabetic, its effectiveness comes from the fact that it is an image."[3] W.J.T. Mitchell agrees. As he states (using a word I employ in this book's subtitle): "Writing, in its physical, graphic form, is an inseparable suturing of the visual and the verbal, the 'imagetext' *incarnate*" (my emphasis).[4]

Second, one might argue that typography (with all the artistic choices involved in its selection) lends a potentially pictorial quality to all printed words. Serif fonts, for instance, are those with decorative accents on the end of alphabetic characters —originating in the brush strokes used for creating early typefaces, eventually becoming standard. Notoriously, the Bauhaus movement (requiring form to follow function) favored typography that was sans-serif, since it was believed to be more practical and legible. As Jan Tschichold wrote in 1925, the New Typography "must not be expression, least of all self-expression. . . . In a masterpiece of typography the artist's signature has been eliminated."[5] More recently, Steven Heller and Karen Pomeroy remark: "The traditional notion that text was to be read (a linear, encoded, left-brained activity) and images were to be seen (a holistic, experimental, right-brained activity) was questioned. Text became cross-functional . . . moving into the realm of the illustrative (type as image), atmospheric, or expressive. Similarly, images could be 'read,' sequenced, and combined to form more complex information patterns."[6] Not surprisingly, one of the earliest contemporary textbooks for film analysis was titled *How to Read a Film*.[7]

Third, beyond the pictorial aspects of typeface, there are numerous art forms (aside from cinema) that frequently combine word and image—for instance, poster art, the illuminated manuscript, the captioned photograph, the picture book. Of the latter, Michel Foucault says: "On the page of an illustrated book, we seldom pay attention to the small space running above the words and below the drawings, forever serving them as a common frontier."[8] There are also works that make pictures out of words, as in concrete poetry. Here, one thinks of Guillaume Apollinaire's "Heart, Crown, and Mirror," with stanzas arranged to create pictures of those three objects.[9]

Fourth, we have earlier made reference to Garrett Stewart's *The Look of Reading*, which deals with paintings depicting people perusing books. Likewise, we have drawn parallels between it and our own project, which, on one level, can be seen as a study of "The Look of Writing." Here, it is worth noting that Stewart mentions how, in regarding pictorial "scenes of reading," the viewer's "eyes are often pulled toward the painted reader's held page to see what it is we are to think she is reading, whether that text appears simulated from a faithless distance by arbitrary squiggles or approximated by potentially shaped words."[10] He concludes: "The deciphering urge is contagious." As Stewart makes clear, there are certain paintings that highlight the verbal sign. This is most common in religious art, where sacred books are pictured open for the spectator to view.[11] Occasionally, a printed text in a painting takes on gargantuan proportions, as in Charles Humbert's *La femme au grand livre* (1919), where a woman is seated against the background of a book's huge pages (bearing Chateaubriand's prose).

Of course, in the cinema, it is also possible to visualize a reader—either showing or not showing that which she sees. In *La Lectrice* (1988), for example (to be discussed in chapter 8), we do not get a glimpse of the page as the heroine regards her book. But, in other films we are privy to a volume's contents. In *The Golem* (1920), when Rabbi Loew consults the tome *Necromancy*, we view the page he reads as an insert shot. In silent film, of course, all intertitles are meant for the spectator to peruse, but some (with text in quotation marks) can signify material that a character is reading. Furthermore, in adapted works, the credit sequence often shows the literary source as a book whose pages flip open. Currently, the

BBC television series *Masterpiece* (which frequently dramatizes adapted works) uses this trope.

Some works go one step further. Jean-Pierre Melville's film *La Silence de la Mer* (1949), based on a 1942 novel by Jean Bruller, opens mysteriously with a man waiting on a bridge as another approaches carrying a briefcase. The latter drops his attaché by the waiting man and moves on without a word. The waiting man then opens the satchel and, below sweaters and newspapers, uncovers a book whose title is the same as the film's. The sense of the volume as smuggled relates to the fact that the novel was published in France, against all odds, during the Nazi occupation. The film's opening credits then appear as pages of a book. At the close of the film, the narrator's voice is heard to say, "Outside a pale sun was shining through the mist. It felt very cold to me." We then cut to an image of a book page on which the same phrase is written. This is followed by views of other pages that describe how the book was published. A final page is turned to reveal the word "Fin" (end).

As modern painting progressed, it gradually abandoned the image of the reader and began to take on print alone as a form in its own right—as in René Magritte's *The Treachery of Images* (1929), which assertively proclaims, "This is not a pipe." As Stewart notes, in such works "any marking associated with writing comes forward as reading matter only, no longer part of reading's narrated event."[12] But, he asks, to whom is such material addressed? He concludes: "With no subject figured on canvas to embody either the strain or the release of interpretation, reading . . . is ineradicably left to [the viewer]." Here we think of such works as Georges Braque's *The Programme of the Tivoli Cinema* (1913), which depicts (among other things) a flyer for the film *La Petite Fifi*. More radically, one considers Joseph Kosuth's *Titled (Art as Idea as Idea) (red)* (1967), which consists only of a verbal definition of the word *red*. Obviously, cinema too has dabbled in the hyper-verbal. We have already discussed Hollis Frampton's *Poetic Justice*, which almost exclusively presents words onscreen (and in the Afterword we examine Frampton's *Zorns Lemma* [1970], which depicts the language of urban street signage). But there is also Marcel Duchamp's *Anemic Cinema* (1926), in which phrases (like "L'enfant qui tête est un souffleur de chair chaude et n'aime pas le chou-fleur de serre chaude") are written in a spiral pattern on the surface of rotating disks.

In such works, filmmakers seem, on one level, to buck the overarching trend of their era. As Jay David Bolter notes, during the twentieth century (which he deems "the late age of print"), "the desire to capture the world in the word has been gradually supplemented by the more easily gratified desire to see the world through visual technologies."[13] This is no doubt what Mitchell means by the era's "pictorial turn."[14] Similarly, Matthew G. Kirschenbaum notes: "For many it has become a truism that the boundaries between word and image have never been more permeable than they are now, in the midst of our 'postalphabetic' era."[15] Yet rather than entirely "put their faith in the image" (to use a Bazinian phrase), the cineastes I have cited foreground language over image (knowing full

well, however, that text onscreen must ultimately be pictured).[16] For, as Stuart
Moulthrop observes: "The word is an image after all."[17] On another level, the
work of these artists is entirely in keeping with an epoch that sees the equaliza-
tion of linguistic and visual realms. Thus, Mitchell "offers the figure of the *image/
text* as a wedge to pry open the heterogeneity of media and of specific representations" (my emphasis).[18] On some level, we might see his trope as one that underscores this entire book.

Film studies experienced the reign of the "imagetext" with the rise of semiotics
in the 1970s, which regarded the visual image (and cinematic discourse) as a sign
system that bore at least some comparison to verbal language. Most known for
this position was Christian Metz, who in 1974 stated: "When approaching cinema
from the linguistic point of view, it is difficult to avoid shuttling back and forth
between two positions: the cinema as a language; the cinema as infinitely different from verbal language. Perhaps it is impossible to extricate oneself from this
dilemma with impunity."[19] Later, writing in 1990, Jean Mitry considers film and
language by returning to Eisenstein's focus on Asian calligraphy. As he notes: "To
some extent, the cinema appears to be a new form of ideographic writing—with
this very great difference: that the artificial and conventional symbols of the latter are replaced, in the cinema, with fleeting symbolic values depending less on
the objects or scenes represented than on the visual context in which they are
placed."[20] Thus, the film image can provide no fixed but only "temporary meaning." While Mitry finds cinema lacking the qualities of logical/discursive language, he deems it a lyrical one, "not the [kind] used in conversation but that used
in a poem or a novel."[21] Thus, film is a "language in the second degree" because its
images only "have the *possibility* of becoming signs. They are not uniquely signs,
like words, but first and foremost objects and concrete reality, objects which take
on (or are given) a predetermined meaning [by the filmmaker]" (my emphasis).[22]
Mitry is also interested in the relation between thought and cinema—how our
brain formulates ideas prior to linguistic expression. Here, he turns to the notion of the "verbal image"—a concept drawn from the work of Joseph Vendryes
and Jean-Martin Charcot—one that signifies "the psychic unit preceding speech,
combining visual, auditory, and oral components."[23] Likewise, in writing about religion and film, Thomas Martin considers the formal hybridity of thought asking:
"Do words give rise to images or are images always required for words? That is
a futile inquiry for which extensive psychological testing or intense reflection on
our experiences cannot give a compelling answer. Rather, the important point is
that all of human thought is interrelated."[24]

Italian author Italo Calvino considers similar issues in a series of lectures given
in the mid-1970s. He discusses two types of imaginative process: "The one starts
with the word and arrives at the visual image, and the one that starts with the visual image and arrives at its verbal expression."[25] The cinema, he opines, begins
with a written text, is visualized in the director's mind, is reconstructed on the set,
and then is realized in a film. However, "during this process, the 'mental cinema'

of the imagination has a function no less important than the actual creation of the sequences as they will be recorded by the camera and then put together on the moviola." For him this mental cinema existed prior to the invention of film and never stops "projecting images before our mind's eye." Significantly, for his own writing, Calvino begins with a mental picture. As he comments, "A visual image [is] at the source of all my stories."[26] He continues: "In devising a story . . . the first thing that comes to my mind is an image that for some reason strikes me as charged with meaning, even if I cannot formulate this meaning in discursive or conceptual terms. I set about developing it into a story; or even better yet, it is the images themselves that develop their own implicit potentialities."[27] His grappling with language is ultimately "a search for an equivalent of the visual image."[28]

In his linkage of visual and verbal registers, Calvino's thoughts take us back to Mitry's reference to "verbal image." Some years later, Noël Carroll adopts this term but uses it in a different sense. While admitting that "cinema is not a language," Carroll asserts that "nonetheless language plays an intimate role in several of the symbolic structures used in cinema."[29] His purpose is to investigate one such trope, the "verbal image," in which we "find . . . words through . . . pictures."[30] As an example, Carroll cites a scene from *The Last Laugh* (1925), in which a fired hotel doorman continues to wear his uniform as he walks through his neighborhood, unaware that its inhabitants know that he is unemployed: "The camera faces him frontally and in the background of this deep focus medium long shot we see people poking their heads out of the windows and jeering riotously. Quite literally they are 'laughing behind his back,' while at the same time this phrase is a cliché connoting slander and humiliation."[31]

Thus, through an image, a linguistic saying comes readily to mind. Extending his inquiry into language and image, Carroll draws upon the theory of "illocutionary acts" advanced by J. L. Austin. As Carroll notes: "Images are not utterances in the normal sense of the word so each of the acts discussed in what follows should be understood as having 'para' as a prefix. . . . I will assume that the acts of inserting verbal images into films are pictorial (para-)illocutionary acts with the (para-)illocutionary force to evoke words or strings of words by means of images that remark upon a subject of the ongoing film."[32]

Having surfaced numerous cultural and theoretical crossovers between language and image as well as the discourses that surround them, we now extend our investigation of this topic by examining two films about writers that highlight this issue, and in our choice of texts we move quite literally from the sublime to the ridiculous.

CHRONICLE AND CHRONOTOPE

The Diary of a Country Priest (1951), directed in France by Robert Bresson, is based on an acclaimed novel by Georges Bernanos first published in 1936. The film tells the story of a young unnamed priest (Claude Laydu) who arrives at his first parish in Ambricourt, a rural town. There is very little action in the pared-down narrative; as Bresson has said, "One does not create by adding, but by taking away."[33] Séraphita (Martine Lemaire), a schoolgirl, is disrespectful to the priest; Chantal (Nicole Ladmiral), the daughter of a local count, is distressed because her father is romancing the governess; the countess (Rachel Bérendt) comes to terms with the loss of her son and dies peacefully; the town doctor commits suicide; and the priest struggles with an illness that we learn is terminal stomach cancer. (So here we have yet another tale of the infirm writer—though his sickness will not occupy center stage.) If the film portrays minimal drama in the external quotidian world, it depicts a profound interior battle (told from a first-person perspective), as the priest wrestles with his reception by the villagers, his limited ability to intervene in people's lives, his wavering faith, and his confrontation with impending death.

Bernanos's text is written as though it were an edited transcript of the priest's diary, though we do not know this initially. Rather, as we begin to read it, the narrative simply speaks of events in the first person and the past tense, as do many other novels. A few pages in, however, we find a partial, interrupted sentence ("Whereas a bishop's remand—"), followed by a graphic break, and the words "I have been looking over the first few pages of my diary without any satisfaction, and yet I considered very carefully before making up my mind to write it."[34] So we understand that what we have read and will read are excerpts from the priest's journal. However, our interest here will not be in comparing novel and film, but in comprehending the manner in which the latter presents the diary—since Bresson has chosen to do so by foregrounding shots of its pages. He was not required to do this, as he could simply have filmed the events of the story (in first person or not), or have shown the priest periodically writing in a notebook. Instead, Bresson follows the more complex and captivating path of picturing words onscreen. In fact it is difficult to find, in the entire history of narrative cinema, another dramatic work that does so as relentlessly. Though in her essay on *The Diary*, Susan Sontag does not dwell on the journal per se, she highlights its status as material artifact: "Bresson's art moves increasingly away from the story and toward documentary. . . . The journal device allows Bresson to relate the fiction in a quasi-documentary fashion."[35] Similarly, Bazin, in speaking about the novel versus movie, says: "When you compare the two, it is the film that is literary while the novel teems with visual material."[36] Finally, for Dudley Andrew, Bresson's interest in language overturns the conventional "primacy of the image" and derives from Alexandre Astruc's notion of cinematic "écriture."[37] In his *Notes on Cinematography*, Bresson makes clear his fascination with word and image. He states emphatically: "CINEMATOGRAPHY IS A WRITING WITH IMAGES IN MOVEMENT AND WITH SOUNDS."[38] He compares images to "words in a dictionary" that gain power "through their position and relation."[39] He speaks of a "language of images," and claims that even a "flood of words" (as in *The Diary*) "does a film no harm"—that it is "a matter of kind, not quantity."[40]

Much of the criticism of *The Diary of a Country Priest* concentrates on its place in Bresson's broader oeuvre (Cunneen, Pipolo, Price, Reader), the nature of its restrained style (Sontag), the subjective mode and complex narrative structure (Feldman), its stance as adaptation (Bazin, Andrew), and its spiritual tone of its discourse (Andrew, Bazin, Cunneen, Price, Sontag, Schrader). Our concern, however, is with its status as a work about an author, and in this regard our perspective offers something new. While we touch on insights offered previously by other scholars, we present them in a different context.[41]

The film begins its concentrated spotlight on writing in the credit sequence, whose background image consists of a standard exercise book, a pen, and a bottle of ink—all on a table (much like the objects in Hollis Frampton's *Poetic Justice*). These are the writing tools the priest will use throughout. In foregrounding his journal, we think of a painting by Roy Lichtenstein entitled *Composition II* (1964), which shows the cover of a traditional black and white speckled notebook—the type that American kids brought to school for generations. The credit sequence of *Diary* also touts its roots in the Bernanos novel, which won the Grand Prize from the Académie française. In the drama's first shot, we see a hand open the pages of the journal, remove a blotter from it, and turn to the latest entry (Keith Reader asserts that it is Bresson's hand that is used throughout, clearly identifying the protagonist with the filmmaker and reminding us of the directorial hand in films by Winsor McCay and the Fleischer Brothers).[42] An offscreen voice reads words that we view on the page and which establish the import of the diary: "I don't think I'm doing anything wrong in writing here from day to day the simplest and most insignificant secrets of a life lacking any mystery."[43] According to Tony Pipolo, there are a total of twenty-five such diary close-ups in the film.[44] This is not surprising, given what Bresson has said about the elements of Bernanos's novel that attracted him: "In my eyes, what was striking was the notebook of the diary, in which through the curé's pen, an external world becomes an interior world and takes on spiritual coloration. My scenario concentrated on that rather than on events that are usually considered more cinematographic."[45] Already, we are enmeshed in a temporal complexity that continues throughout, involving (1) the implied tense of the image, (2) the tense of the voiceover, (3) the tense of the diary entry, and (4) the tense of the film screening.[46] Here, the words on the page are expressed in the linguistic present tense, but they have already been written (thus locating their inscription in the past). Furthermore, they are being shown onscreen in what seems like the diegetic "present," but are viewed at a later moment (the "now" of the film screening). Furthermore, while the tense of the voiceover is marked linguistically as the present, the time of its "utterance" is unclear. Does it represent the writer's consciousness at the past moment of writing? Or is it the author rereading his written material in the diegetic present? All these layers of time circulate at the very start of the film, before we have even seen the protagonist onscreen. As Laura Mulvey writes, "The photograph"—and, we might add, the cinema—"pushes language and its articulation of time to a limit leaving the spectator sometimes with a slightly giddy feeling, reminiscent of a *trompe l'oeil* effect."[47]

This interest in language carries into the second image of the film, which consists of a road sign reading "Ambricourt." Rather than a visual establishing shot (as is common in a movie's expository sequence), we get a word. Actually, we never get a wide view of the town, and much of what takes place there is rendered only by offscreen sound (dogs barking, cars passing, machines whirring, people partying, storms, etc.). In part, this reflects Bresson's view that "when a sound can replace an image, cut the image, or neutralize it."[48] On another level, this technique forwards the theme of the priest's isolation (his elder, the Curé of Torcy, later tells him that he "cuts an odd figure" in town).

As the priest arrives in the village, the camera tracks into a close-up of his face (a device used repeatedly to emphasize his first-person subjectivity), as on the sound track we hear him say: "My parish! My first parish!" Here there is no journal page to accompany the voiceover. So we wonder: Do the words represent those on a page we have never seen? Or do they signify the unrecorded thoughts of the priest at the moment he is pictured? For Andrew, the latter option is not viable, as everything we see must be filtered through the diary. As he notes, any action represented onscreen is merely "a reflection upon an event, not the event itself."[49] The uncertain link between word and image will continue and escalate throughout. For instance, in a later sequence we see the priest eating as his voiceover explains that his stomach problems require a diet of bread and wine (causing some villagers to mistake him for an alcoholic). Once again, we wonder if these are his musings at this moment or a transcription of words he has written (or will write) in his diary. Obviously, these "confusions" between thought and writing underscore the fact that all authors draw upon "internal monologues" (as well as "verbal images") to fashion their texts.

While the first journal entry we encountered has already been written when pictured onscreen, many are seen as they are being manually composed. For instance, the scene of the priest's arrival at Ambricourt is followed by a shot of his diary page as he notes down his refusal to acknowledge his poor health. Before long, the screen dissolves to another entry being written (about how he finds his bicycle very useful), but the temporal relation between the two shots is entirely unclear (since a cinematic dissolve can mean almost anything). On other occasions, after we see words being recorded, we dissolve (or cut) to the scene described, indicating that the secondary image represents not the diegetic present (as do certain other shots) but the past. For instance, after the scene of the priest eating, we see him write about a visit from M. Fabregars (Léon Arvel). We then dissolve to that retrospective scene, which is in fact the first synch sound dialogue we hear (another facet of the film's audio-visual temporal relations).

There is also great variation in how the voiceover is handled (beyond its use to accompany journal composition). While in some scenes, there is no synch sound dialogue (and we hear only the priest's thoughts), in others, after a period of recorded conversation, the camera tracks into the prelate's face and his voiceover is heard, sometimes with another character continuing to speak in the background.

Hence audible as well as visible words are intricately woven into the fabric of the film. Perhaps in creating a complex matrix of language and image, Bresson was ahead of his time. For as Karen Knorr and Tracey Moffat note: "Situations where oral and visual texts combine, in forms that can be generically described as bi-medial presentation, have become increasingly common in the transmission of information, both printed and virtual."[50]

Sometimes in the film, a flashback is sandwiched between two diary entries. At one point, the priest writes that he was "expecting much from catechism class," following which we cut to a scene in which his student, Séraphita, embarrasses him in front of others by complimenting his beautiful eyes. We next return to him writing as his voiceover says: "[The students] had plotted together." Other times, diary composition precedes a scene that seems set in the present. For example, in advance of his visiting the Count's mansion, we see him write: "This visit to the manor has me quite worried." On yet other occasions, the diary entry is written immediately after a scene we have witnessed, as when, following the priest's meeting with the count, he writes that his mention of the governess seemed to upset the man. Finally, there are moments when the temporality of his writing is entirely ambiguous (since it does not refer to an event we have seen or will see), as when he inscribes, "Yes, I scold myself for praying so little." As is clear from these examples, the tenses that the priest employs in his commentary (here, past, pluperfect, and present) vary throughout. This not only adds to the temporal intricacy of the film but, as Alexander Sesonske has noted (in speaking of literature), to its emotional impact: "First-person mixed-tense narratives, where the narrator both describes the past and makes present-tense comments, may combine intimacy of close contact with the greater objectivity of a distanced view. . . . All this suggests that tenses . . . function not merely to indicate temporal relations within [a] work but also to help create and control . . . the degree of felt involvement [by the reader or viewer] in the world of the work."[51]

Given that so many shots of the film involve our reading the priest's diary, we confront the differences between the expression of time in word and image. As Wolfgang Klein and Ping Li note: "All human languages . . . provide their speakers with a range of lexical and grammatical devices to say when something happened and how long it lasted, to say whether it happened, or will happen, for the first time, regularly or very often and to say whether some event or state precedes, overlaps with or follows another event or state."[52] Klein goes on to note how there are six devices that carefully encode time in language: tense (the grammatical category of the verb), aspect (the presentation of a situation from a particular perspective [e.g., as ongoing or completed]), *akionsart* (event types [e.g., sleeping (a state) or running (an action)]), temporal adverbials (e.g., the words *now, soon, often*), temporal particles (somewhere between temporal adverbials and suffixes or prefixes), and discourse principles (how sentences are organized).[53] While the priest's writing can engage all these codes, the images that portray him can be nowhere as specific. Without external markers (like dialogue, intertitles, captions, historic costumes or sets, or positionality), a cinematic shot is imprecise in its temporal placement. Ann Banfield (referencing Barthes) has remarked on the ineffability of photographic versus linguistic media in this regard: "The seeming conjunction of tenses which are distinct in spoken language marks the point at which [an] attempt to name the essence of photography meets the resistance of ordinary language, which fails to offer the appropriate tense to capture the photographic moment."[54] She offers as the paradoxical *noeme* of the photograph: "This was now here." The "now" in her formulation reminds us that, beyond photography, cinema unrolls with an immediacy that some have likened to an "eternal present."[55] Alexander Sesonske has argued that this sense is greatest in films that, like *The Diary*, employ first-person narrators. As he remarks: "Voice-over narration seems not to locate the speaker within the action-space of the film; rather it speaks directly to us in words not heard within the world of the film. Thus its immediacy may establish the present time of the film as its time, thrusting all of the action-space events into the past."[56]

During the first part of *The Diary*, when scenes of writing occur, we see only the hand of the priest as he marks the page; in contrast, at later points we are given long shots of him composing at a table. Sometimes, we see him riffle through pages already filled, as though to ascertain his progress. At other points, as we view journal pages, we notice words or lines that are crossed out.[57] (Here, we think of *Tropos* [1993], a performance piece by Ann Hamilton in which a woman burns through lines of text, sequentially obscuring them.) Often, the obliterations of the priest's notations come at particularly emotional moments. When he writes, "I am seriously ill," we notice that the line above has been eradicated with black ink. Here, we are made aware of the process of authorial creation and revision—how a writer stops and starts, changes her mind, thinks better of a word choice or whether to state something at all. In the novel, in fact, we learn (through editorial notes) that certain sentences trail off in midstream.[58] In the film, we also intermittently see a blotter in his diary, which reminds us of the instability of handwritten language, its propensity to smear (this recalls the shot in *Misery* when Paul writes the word *smudge* on Corrasable paper, then blurs it with his finger to show Annie the problem). The periodic expunging of text in *Diary* adds an expressive layer to linguistic inscription—signifying, perhaps, a desire to suppress one's insights. For example, after one upsetting meeting with the count, we see the priest rip out some journal pages (a gesture communicated in the novel by a note to the reader).[59] The priest's voiceover (relating his thoughts, not the words in the diary) states: "I must destroy these pages written in a moment of delirium." Claire Bustarret in "The Material Surface of Modern Literary Manuscripts" discusses the expressive gestures of writing. As she notes: "It is well known that the writing hand can scrawl things and can cross them out, but it is too often forgotten that the hand can attack the material itself. . . . In this way, paper sometimes reflects the suffering involved in creativity."[60] She even mentions the destruction of pages.

But diary entries are not the only form of writing presented in the film. One

FIGURE 28. The priest (Claude Laydu) sits at a table with wine and ink to write in *Diary of a Country Priest* (1951).

day the priest receives an anonymous letter, which reads: "A well-wisher advises you to seek transfer to another parish." Some days later, when entering his church, he finds a prayer book on the floor; as he retrieves it, a paper slips out. With a shocked expression, he removes the letter from his pocket and compares the handwriting with that of the note he has found (as does the viewer, who sees both documents). Realizing that they were written by the same individual, he returns the book to the pew from which it has fallen. When the governess (Miss Louise [Nicole Maurey]) enters the sacristy, she reaches for the volume, and he realizes that she has authored the threat—presumably because he knows of her affair with the count. (Ironically, the priest later drops the letter from his own Bible on an excursion to the manor.) In another scene, Chantal visits the priest, enraged at the tryst between her governess and her father, and vows she will run away, leaving only a note for her dad. By the end of their conversation, he has convinced her to relinquish the correspondence, and we see him burn it in the fireplace, the words on the envelope ("To My Father") blackening in the flames (like the photographs we will later discuss in Hollis Frampton's (*nostalgia*) [1971]). Beyond epistles, in one sequence, as the priest emerges from the home of a local woman, we view the pages of his memo book in which are listed the parishioners he must visit. He crosses out "Delplanque" and moves on to the next.

Furthermore, a provocative discourse on words occurs in the film's dialogue. When the priest visits the countess who lost faith decades ago with the death of her infant son, she accuses him of spouting "nothing but words," as he quotes from the Bible. When she says that God has "broken" her, he retorts that her utterance is "mere human words." By the end of their meeting, he has reached her, and she chants: "Thy kingdom come. . . ." In a later scene, he receives a letter from her thanking him for his intervention. As his voiceover intones her words, we learn of her insistence that the two never speak of the issue again—silence triumphing over language after all.

Toward the end of the film, after the priest can no longer deny being sick, he consults a doctor in Lille. In readying for the trip, he packs his diaries in his suitcase, indicating that writing is for him a requisite, daily act. When he arrives in the city, we are shown a door whose plaque reads "Dr. Lavigne," followed by a shot in which the priest is ushered out of the same door. All representation of his medical encounter (and its temporal span) has been excised from the narrative (along with the melodrama such a scene would entail). We see only the physician's name (as earlier we saw only the sign for Ambricourt). The prelate's stunned and dejected expression upon exiting, however, communicates that the news has been bad. The first thing he does is to go to a bar where he sits at a table and writes. As we view his diary page, his voiceover states: "Cancer, stomach cancer"—as though he can only admit the fact through writing. In a shot that follows, he continues to compose as his voiceover says: "God, I must write it down."

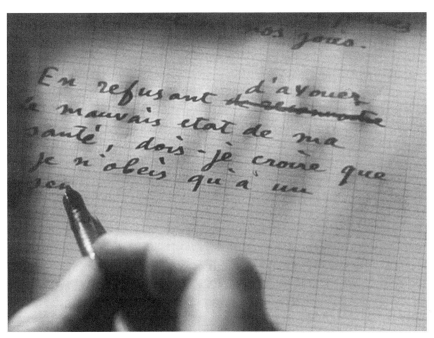

FIGURE 29. A page from the priest's dairy with words crossed out (*Diary of a Country Priest* [1951]).

Instead of returning home (ashamed of having "this thing"), he visits an old seminary friend in Lille, Dufrety (Bernard Hubrenne), who has left the priesthood and lives "in sin" with a woman in a shabby apartment. The priest is now so ill that he must immediately lie down, but even so he begins to write in his diary. The words he inscribes are sloppy, and do not keep to the lines—indicating his terminal condition and the ties between writing and the body. What he records is that Dufrety has agreed to meet with the Curé of Torcy, hopefully leading him back to the ministry. The priest drops the paper and pen, attempts to pick them up, but fails to do so. This is the last we see of him—his expiration tied to the end of his writing.

The final document we view is not composed by the priest, but by Dufrety. It is a typed letter (a first of its kind and, by definition, less personal than the handwritten text we have been reading) addressed to Torcy. It is accompanied by Dufrety's voiceover, signaling the end of the priest's subjective existence (he has died in an ellipsis). Dufrety's communiqué narrates the last hours of the priest's life, when he could only speak, not write. In our realization of his death, we consider again the nature of the photographic image and André Bazin's view that it can both attest to a person's existence and figuratively "mummify" him—foreshadowing his future demise.[61] Hence, there is no need for Bresson to picture the priest's death, since it was already prefigured in every shot of the film (as was the death of actor Laydu). If, according to the priest, his life had no "mystery," there is mystery in the image, as per Bazin's Catholic spirituality. Similarly, Bresson once wrote: "DIVINATION —how can one not associate that name with the two sublime machines I use for my work? Camera and tape recorder."[62] Interestingly, Bresson invoked the issue of death (and resurrection) in his summary of the filmmaking process. As he notes: "My movie is born first in my head, dies on paper; is resuscitated by the living persons and real objects I use, which are killed on film, but . . . projected onto a screen, come to life again like flowers in water."[63]

In general, language (an entirely symbolic medium that is not an index to the material world) does not share the "morbid" qualities of the photograph. But we could argue that the handwritten text (e.g., the priest's diary) does. It bears the trace of a human imprint at a frozen moment of "utterance." In fact, when some critics have sought metaphors for explaining the photograph's link to its human subject, they have drawn on the relation of the fingerprint to the hand.[64] As Dufrety's final words are heard on the sound track, the shadow of a cross appears over his typescript, as the words disappear. Dufrety reports that the priest's final statement was "All is grace." While the entire film has been absorbed with facsimiles of the prelate's written words, here they are replaced by a sign of another order—a cross. We wonder—has picture triumphed over language at last? On the other hand, the cross seems ethereal—not a material crucifix but, almost, the shadow of one—so its status as picture is qualified. As Bazin observes: "There is nothing more the image has to communicate except by disappearing. The spectator has been led, step-by-step, toward that night of the senses the only expression of which is a light on a blank screen."[65]

Clearly, in *The Diary of a Country Priest*, the act of writing takes on a particular significance that we have not encountered previously. While so many of the authors discussed suffer from writer's block, the priest has no such problem. Rather, he has a compulsion to write (if not hypergraphia). While for most fictional writers, authorship has much to do with earning money (Barton Fink), being high (William Lee), or ego gratification (Charlie Kaufman), for the priest it is a reflexive and holy act. He simultaneously scrutinizes himself and communes with God—allowing the spectator to share his process by reading his texts. (Here we recall that in medieval religious art, the Bible was painted with its pages open to the viewer.) In its record of struggle (both of body and mind), the priest's written saga suggests the Passion of Christ (or, as Bazin says, the Way of the Cross)—thus giving it sacred overtones.[66] There are numerous hints of this throughout the film. At one point, the priest thinks to himself: "I was prisoner of the holy agony." Furthermore, his diet of bread and wine recalls the Eucharist, symbolizing the body and blood of Jesus. Moreover, the priest's disease causes him to hemorrhage, a fact he notes in his diary, and the presence of a stained blotter in the volume hints that words too can "bleed." There also seem to be parallels between the wine he drinks and the ink with which he composes—with bottles of each placed side-by-side on his writing table—investing them with a sacramental valence. Finally, in the priest's post-mortem disappearance from screen and his replacement by Dufrety's typescript, we seem to have a demonstration of the "flesh made word."[67]

Interestingly, in discussing the contemporary relation between word and image, Jay David Bolter uses language relevant to Bresson's tale of a man with a terminal illness. Bolter says: "In the late age of print . . . the *death of prose* will never be complete, because our culture will want to keep the *patient* alive, if *moribund*, so that the mutual remediation with digital media can continue" (my emphasis).[68] Here, Bresson is in the vanguard, but takes a different stance. Refusing (in his drama of a dying writer) to consider print "moribund," he "remediates" in the opposite direction—reestablishing the right of language to vie with image for our attention in pictorial art.

SUPERHEROES AND SCHLUBS

While *The Diary of a Country Priest* speaks of the ethereal and the sacred, *American Splendor* reeks of the material and the profane. While the tone of the *Diary* is hushed and reverent, that of *American Splendor* is bellicose and sacrilegious.

Specifically, the film (directed in 2003 by Shari Springer Berman and Robert Pulcini) tells the real-life story of the late Harvey Pekar, a file clerk for the Cleveland Department of Veterans Affairs who becomes a famous writer of underground comics (aka graphic novels). Clearly, the kind of manuscript that Pekar authors (seen as frivolous popular culture) contrasts with that penned by the fictional country priest, who composes a literary autobiography charting his struggles with illness, loneliness, and religious faith. On the other hand, the two documents are not as opposed as one might think, since Pekar's journal (in comic book form) records his vocational and romantic sufferings, as well as his battle with cancer (yet another infirm writer). Furthermore, the movie that chronicles Pekar's life involves the same tension between word and image that we found in Bresson's film.

The challenge facing Berman and Pulcini (in their inventive "biopic") is to deal simultaneously with Pekar's life and the graphic novels that issued from it: the *American Splendor* series (first published in 1976), *Our Cancer Year* (1994), and *Our Movie Year* (2004). For this reason, many of the "characters" in the film are doubled: giving us both their authentic and fictional selves. But their fictitious representations are further split, leading to a tripling of personae. Hence, to cite one example, we see the "real Pekar," Pekar as drawn in his comics, and Pekar as played by Paul Giamatti (to be called "Pekar" throughout). So here we have both the author and his multiple embodiments in dialogue with one another in the same work. Clearly, in this proliferation of authorial selves we are reminded of Spike Jonze's *Adaptation* and Woody Allen's *Deconstructing Harry*.

The multiplication of identities in the film is handled in a multifaceted and creative fashion. Sometimes we see the real Pekar sitting in a faux white studio among miscellaneous objects related to his life (records, books, papers, furniture), all artfully strewn about. He speaks into a microphone while being interviewed off-screen by Berman. At other times, as we watch Giamatti play Pekar or view Pekar's cartoon image (animated or still), we hear the real Pekar narrating on the sound track. At one point, he makes direct allusion to the confusion of identities. As we watch Giamatti's screen incarnation of Pekar, the real Pekar's voice is heard to say: "Here's our man or here's me or the guy playing me though he don't look like me." Most often, as one might expect, the real Pekar narrates in the first person. But sometimes he takes a third-person perspective, as when we see a shot of Pekar frustrated at work, as the real Pekar says in voiceover: "He can't quit his day job. He'd be lost without his routine." Sometimes, the real Pekar is visually and acoustically absent and we watch only Pekar or his comic book self. On one occasion, both the real Pekar and the filmic one appear in the same shot. Significantly, in a drawn frame of Pekar, a dialogue bubble reads: "If you're wonderin' how a nobody guy like me ended up with so many incarnations, pay attention . . ."

The proliferation of Pekar's authorial selves is made even more multifarious by the fact that numerous artists have drawn him. In fact, when his wife-to-be Joyce Brabner (Hope Davis) first comes to Cleveland to meet him and waits in a bus depot, she imagines all the cartoon versions of him embedded in the live-action shot (some handsome and some unattractive). Toward the end of the film, in an inventive sequence that places Pekar in a white void (save a cartoonish line drawing for the floor), he talks of how he once discovered two other Harvey Pekars in the Cleveland phone book, and later learned (from a published death notice) that they were father and son. After solving that mystery, however, he found a listing for yet another Harvey Pekar. Nonplussed, he inquires: "Who are these people? Where did they come from? What's in a name? Who *is* Harvey Pekar?"

Other individuals in Pekar's life are multiplied in a similar fashion in the film: Brabner and Pekar's co-workers Toby Radloff (Judah Friedlander) and Mr. Boats (Earl Billings). In one instance, Pekar and Mr. Boats are walking down a hall at work as they discuss jazz recordings. We then cut to a cartoon frame with Mr. Boats asking (in a dialogue bubble): "Say, what kinda junk you sellin' there?" Another time, as the real Toby silently poses for the camera (having become something of an MTV geek celebrity), we hear his voiceover describing his loneliness. At the very end of the film, at the real Pekar's retirement party, we see his actual family and co-workers (as well as the desk at which he has toiled all these years).

But the most interesting aspect of the film is its articulation of language and picture. Obviously, comic books are an art form that draw on this dynamic; as Will Eisner notes, they are an "image-word mix."[69] Though they present a pictorial series, they are read left to right and top to bottom, as is Western prose.[70] Significantly, Eisner uses the cinematic term "montage" to reference the conjunction of word and image, and argues that to "read" comics is to "exercise both visual and verbal interpretive skills."[71] Furthermore, drawing on a photographic concept, Eisner asserts that in comics, "the regimens of art (e.g., perspective, symmetry, brush stroke) and the regimens of literature (e.g., grammar, plot, syntax) become *superimposed* upon each other" (my emphasis). Furthermore, like many theorists of cinema, Eisner argues for a "grammar" of the comics. As he notes: "In its most economical state, comics employ a series of repetitive images and recognizable symbols. When these are used again and again to convey similar ideas, they become a language."[72]

Many scholars have seen comics as a precursor to the cinema, one of the earliest being John Fell in *Film and the Narrative Tradition*, in which he examined how turn-of-the-century strips utilized certain "cinematic" techniques.[73] Others have investigated direct ties between the comics and film. Alex Kupfer, for instance, discusses a comics-based movie from the primitive era, *Happy Hooligan* (1897).[74] Similarly, Donald Crafton mentions Edison's *The Rivals* (1907) as being derived from a T. E. Powers strip, and *Dream of a Rarebit Fiend* (1907) from one by Winsor McCay.[75] Likewise, Charles Musser references the *Buster Brown* series of 1904.[76] While these films are all live-action, there are also examples of early animation, including *Little Nemo* (1911) and *Gertie the Dinosaur* (1914)—both based on McCay strips.

But aside from historical ties, there are also important formal parallels between comics and movies. Like film, comics are a "sequential art" composed of conjoined "frames," "boxes," or "panels."[77] Moreover, the process of comic construction sounds a bit like film editing: "The task . . . is to arrange the sequence of events (or pictures) so as to bridge the gaps in action. Given these, the reader may fill in the intervening events from experience." While most comics involve the combination of word and image, there are some that tell their story without dialogue, invoking comparisons to the "silent film." Like the cinema, the depiction of duration is important in comics, as is the rhythm of image presentation. Eisner suggests, for instance, that to mimic compressed time one might use a larger number of panels, increasing the action's segmentation. Equally important in comics and movies is the artist's choice of point of view. As Eisner notes, one must decide both the perspective from which an action or object is seen (like camera angle) as well as the portion of that action or object seen (like shot distance). Furthermore, much as filmmakers can control the aspect ratio of the screen (and, through matting, its configuration), so can comic artists vary the shape of the panel.[78] Early on, Fell discussed the means by which comics simulated physical movement—a property of cinema.[79] When static, however, the comic frame can also suggest filmic "freeze motion."[80] While graphic perspective always provided comic artists a means of showing depth, certain uses of the panel can heighten 3D effects (as when a border "becomes" an open door). For Eisner, even the font and size of the words within the comic frame can imply the human voice (as in film dialogue): "Letters of a written alphabet, when written in a singular style . . . [are] not unlike the spoken word, which is affected by the changes of inflection and sound level." Finally, both comics and the movies (as collaborative arts) raise questions about authorship. As Eisner asks: "Who is the 'creator' of a comic page which was written by one person, penciled by another and inked, lettered (and perhaps colored or had backgrounds created) by still others?"[81]

Eisner, of course, also notes numerous differences between the comics and the movies. While the former tend to have a very limited number of images at their disposal (due to publishing constraints), the latter have considerably more.[82] While the maker of comics must constantly fight the spectator's "wandering eye," traditional film exhibition controls that urge. As Eisner remarks: "The viewer of a film is prevented from seeing the next frame before the creator permits it because these frames, printed on strips of transparent film, are shown one at a time. So film, which is an extension of comic strips, enjoys absolute control of its 'reading.'"[83] Finally, while the cinematic screen generally presents a single frame to the viewer, comics generally have multiple frames—the individual panels and the page that contains them. There are exceptions, of course, as when a comic artist uses "frameless" boxes. Similarly, cinematic "split screen" or other multiplications of frames-within-frames can bring the two media closer together.

Berman and Pulcini exploit the connection between comics and the movies from the very start of *American Splendor*. The credit sequence puts Pekar in a drawn frame while a printed legend says: "From off the streets of Cleveland comes . . ." In another drawn frame we see urban streets overlaid with the title *American Splendor*. The camera then pans down (as though scanning a page of a comic book) to another frame containing a drawing of Pekar and a printed dialogue bubble that says, "My name is Harvey Pekar." In a subsequent image from

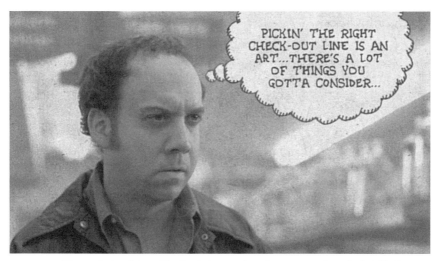

FIGURE 30. Harvey Pekar (played by Paul Giamatti) with a cartoon thought bubble (*American Splendor* [2003]).

the same ersatz comic book, we see a drawn picture of Pekar with a dialogue bubble that introduces us to "the guy playin' [him] in the movie." Pekar's cartoon hand points screen-right, and the camera moves there to reveal a live-action shot of Giamatti (as Pekar) shown walking down a Cleveland street. Shortly thereafter we get a shot of Pekar (absent the drawn frame) walking in the city while a male voiceover talks of the lack of romance in his life. We then cut to the real Pekar sitting in a studio speaking and retroactively identify the voice as his. Thus, the credit sequence has played with word and picture (by utilizing the expository and dialogue boxes deployed in graphic novels), real author and faux, as well as moved us between shots framed like comics and those presented as conventional movie images.

Other elements of comic book discourse are utilized. Sometimes the bubble shown emerging from a character's head is meant to signify thought rather than speech. In one scene we see a drawn image of Pekar in a comic book frame with a thought bubble reading: "No matter how many records I get I'm never satisfied. This is like being a junky." At other times, however, we get a live image of Pekar with a drawn thought bubble attached to him. In one particularly humorous episode he is in a supermarket trying to determine which checkout aisle will be the quickest. Suddenly the shot of him freezes and a thought bubble reads: "Pickin' the right checkout line is an art . . . There's a lot of things you gotta consider. . . ." He selects the line at which an old Jewish lady is unloading groceries. In a live-action shot of Pekar impatiently waiting, an animated version of him looks over his shoulder and complains about how elderly Jewish women always slow things down. The same animated Pekar uses the situation to talk to his live-action self more broadly about how he is wasting his life.

FIGURE 31. The real author, Harvey Pekar, in a cartoon strip (*American Splendor* [2003]).

Clearly, language in comics must take a particular form. After Pekar is diagnosed with cancer (relating him, against all odds, to Bresson's priest) and Brabner collaborates with him on a graphic novel about his treatment, Pekar is upset that her first attempts put "too many words in the frames." We also notice that all the verbiage contained in legends as well as in thought and dialogue bubbles is written in caps, in defiance of normal linguistic convention. Furthermore, many phrases (e.g., "TREATMENT BEGINS, TIME PASSES STRANGELY . . .") end with ellipses, as though signaling the continuation of the narrative and movement to the next frame. Related to this is the fact that some of the shot changes proceed almost like slideshow transitions — another common form of articulating sequential images.

Up until now, our only sense of Pekar as a writer comes from the comics that we see representing his vocation in an *ex post facto* manner: the comics about his life exist, so he must have written them. However, after his animated self impels him to reconsider his dull, grim existence, we find Pekar sitting at a table, actually drawing comic cells on a sheet of paper — clearly, his first attempts at this mode of authorship. A legend in one of the frames reads: "Standing behind old Jewish ladies . . ." — and we realize that he is writing about his recent mundane encounter, hardly the typical subject for a graphic novel. Day turns into night and he remains at the table composing—clearly passionate about the process. In an earlier scene, at a used jazz record sale, he had met a guy with similar musical interests—Robert Crumb (James Urbaniak). At the time, Crumb was illustrating greeting cards for Hallmark but later became a famous underground comic author and illustrator, known for such series as *Fritz the Cat* (whose comic pages we also see onscreen). The two men become and remain friends and, after Pekar experiments with comic book writing (utilizing only crude stick figures for pictures), he shows it to the now-successful Crumb. The latter likes what he sees and volunteers to illustrate it. It is this work that initiates the *American Splendor* series in 1976—an ironic title given Pekar's banal and gritty lifestyle. Prior to writing the comic, Pekar has suffered a voice problem due to a node on his vocal cords. He jokes that he had to take "a vow of silence" (which makes us think again of the country priest). Immediately after Crumb praises his work, however, Pekar's hoarseness disappears and he declares himself "cured." Surely, this is an innovative (if literal) way to depict a writer "finding his voice." What is even more intriguing is that, in writing about *The Diary of a Country Priest*, Keith Reader claimed that the curé's journal-keeping was a kind of "writing cure."[84]

Now a bona fide graphic novelist, we view Pekar in various live-action scenes with comic thought bubbles emerging from his head. In one, he sits on a bus and we read: "Takin' the bus saves time, but it don't lengthen your life." In another, he looks into a mirror at his less-than-handsome face and we read: "Now that's a reliable disappointment." In his Semitic self-deprecation, we hear echoes of Woody Allen (as well as in Pekar's neuroses, which Brabner diagnoses as involving depression and OCD); but his persona is quite different. He does not live in fabulous Manhattan and hang out with artists and intellectuals (save Crumb). Rather, he lives in the Rust Belt, has a "dead-end job," and socializes with losers. Neither does he have any facility with women (as does Allen does, despite his looks). When we first meet Pekar, a woman with whom he has cohabited is moving out of his apartment—sick of his "plebeian lifestyle." When he initially invites Brabner to Cleveland, he brings her to a cheesy "family restaurant" for their first date. Woody Allen and Pekar do share a love of film; Pekar tells Crumb, "The words and pictures [of comics] could be more of an art form—like those French movies" (perhaps *The Diary of a Country Priest*). The linguistic manner with which Pekar expresses himself also makes clear his working-class roots—a background he shares with Allen (who, however, got over it). Pekar, on the other hand, still drops the 'g' in the gerund (*takin'* versus *taking*) and frequently uses the wrong verb form (*don't* versus *doesn't*). Rather than eat gourmet foods, he consumes Macaroni-O's. Furthermore, in many respects, Pekar (who admits to being a "Yid") is a classic Jewish *schlub*—a slang term for a boorish, unpolished person, usually male.[85] Obviously, such a figure is nothing like a "superhero," the usual protagonist of comics. As though to foreshadow this deficiency, in the opening scene of the film we see Pekar as a young child on Halloween night trick-or-treating with friends. While the others are dressed up as Superman, Batman, and the like, he comes as himself.

Aside from print forms associated with comic book discourse (thought and dialogue bubbles, expository legends), other types of print appear in the film. When Brabner, then a Delaware comic store owner, wants more copies of an issue of *American Splendor*, she writes a letter to Pekar with her voice (Hope Davis's) narrating offscreen. We then see him retrieving the letter and eventually responding to it (tearing up various versions), as Pekar's (Giamatti's) voice narrates on the sound track (here we have instances of actor-voiceovers versus those by "real" personages). Brabner, in fact, is a creative writing teacher who instructs prisoners —so the proliferation of authors continues. Eventually, we will see a comic book version of her, as the real one discusses her marriage on the sound track.

Success changes Pekar's life. In one scene, we see a close-up of the colorful *American Splendor* comic book cover and pull away to find his colleagues making a fuss about it at work. An elderly clerk says: "We have a regular Hemingway here" —proudly proclaiming Pekar's *bona fides* as a writer. This is not the only indication that we should take Pekar seriously as an author. We learn that, even before composing comics, he penned local jazz reviews. Furthermore, when he encounters an old college friend in a bakery, they discuss Theodore Dreiser's novel *Jennie Gerhardt*, and later the real Pekar praises it in a voiceover. Moreover, in response to the publication of an *American Splendor* anthology, some compare Pekar to Mark Twain. Finally, his comics bring him a variety of book awards.

What is also particularly intriguing is the fact that Pekar (along with others) published *The Beats: A Graphic History* in 2009, which concerns the famous American bohemian writers of the post–World War II era. Pekar (with art by Ed Piskor) is responsible for the chapters on Kerouac, Ginsberg, Ferlinghetti, and numerous others. Essentially, the text is biographical, noting the major details of each author's life. The illustrations are done in comic book style. For example, a frame that depicts Kerouac drinking has as its legend, "Already he was drinking heavily. He struggled with an alcohol addiction throughout his life." A word bubble shows Kerouac saying (or thinking): "Down the hatch!"[86] Significantly, the section Pekar composes about William Burroughs touches on numerous issues raised in the film *Naked Lunch*. One frame shows Burroughs with a gun and reads, "The only sport he enjoyed was shooting," while another depicts him killing his wife.[87] We learn as well that he worked as an exterminator and visited Tangier, where he enjoyed both the drugs and the boys. One frame shows him at a typewriter with the legend: "While in Tangier, Burroughs worked on *Naked Lunch*. He described to [Allen] Ginsberg his method of writing: 'This is almost automatic writing. I often sit high on hash for as long as six hours, typing at top speed.' "[88]

While, in general, Pekar's life (holding down a bureaucratic job) bears little comparison with the wild, exotic experiences of the Beat writers, there are similarities. Pekar tells us in *The Beats* that "Burroughs and his wife lived in filthy conditions," a frame illustrated by someone standing in the writer's apartment asking him: "Isn't your kid shitting in the Revereware?"[89] Clearly, Pekar and Brabner's digs are similar to Burroughs's. But despite Pekar's apparently "bourgeois" job, his attitude toward the world shares much with the Beats. The title *American Splendor* mocks what he sees as the wasteland of U.S. society, and when his colleague Toby (a geek) is impressed by the movie *Revenge of the Nerds* (1984), Pekar calls it "Hollywood bullshit"—pointing out that it concerns college kids, not a guy like Toby —living in an ethnic ghetto with his grandmother. Furthermore, upset at being diagnosed with cancer and with Brabner's leaving for a trip abroad, Pekar decides he has been "selling out" and explodes during a guest appearance on *Late Night with David Letterman*—railing against NBC, General Electric, and corporate capitalism. Interestingly, in prior appearances on *Letterman* pictured in the film, real footage of the TV show was used. Here, however, perhaps because NBC did not want to promote the damning material, we see only a reenactment (with a Letterman stand-in shot from the back in silhouette). Finally, Pekar has repeatedly been accused of spouting "doom and gloom" and advocating that "misery loves company." When, at the close of the film, we seem to have an agreeable denouement (the cancer treatment has worked; he and Brabner have adopted a child), the voice of the real Pekar warns that there will be no "happy ending"—that his life remains "total chaos"—just like the Beats. His graphic novel about them also raises issues of biography. Clearly, Pekar feels that such information is helpful to the reader (or why write about the writers' lives?). Furthermore, he has no qualms about using his own existence as fodder for his creative work, which would not exist without it.

Pekar's authorial chops are further expanded when a producer from Los Angeles calls and tells him that he would like to do a dramatic version of *American Splendor*. We then cut to a theater marquee announcing the play and to Pekar and Brabner in the audience. We next shift to the stage and see further incarnations of Pekar and Brabner in the form of other actors and realize that they are dramatizing a scene we have earlier witnessed from "real" life (Brabner vomiting on her first evening with Pekar). As the couple waits in the airport on their way home, the real Pekar's offscreen voice is heard to say: "If you think readin' comics about your life seems strange, try watching a play about it." Then, referencing the film we are now viewing (and for which we have observed him record sound), he continues: "Who knows how I'll feel when I see this movie?" Here, his diary-like thoughts approach the temporal complexity of those of the priest in Bresson's film.

While, on the one hand, the real Pekar's voice tells us that the comics "brought [him] a life," the film is replete with intimations of mortality. Early on, when Pekar is disgusted with his empty existence, he opens a file drawer at work whose label reads "Deceased." Flipping through some papers, he finds the death record of a clerk (a man ostensibly just like himself). It is after this that he gains the courage to experiment with comic book writing. His demise is also invoked in his treatment for cancer and, even though he is ultimately proclaimed disease-free, the real Pekar admits that "eventually [he will] lose the war." (He died in 2010.)

While death does not faze Bresson's country priest because he realizes "all is grace," Pekar finds no such comfort (as grace, either physical or divine, is unavailable to him). At one point in the film, Toby (a devout Catholic) tells him: "I am a very spiritual person. You should try believing in something other than yourself." Pekar clearly does not heed this warning. During his chemotherapy, as he stares at himself in a mirror, he wonders aloud: "Am I the guy who writes comic books or am I just a character in them?" Probing even further (and indicating his earthbound narcissism), he inquires: "If I die will *he* keep going or just fade away?" It is not a good sign that he faints immediately thereafter. The Death of the Author (and the Character) seems assured.

7 CORPUS AND OEUVRE
Authorship and the Body

THE PROBLEM BODY

A recent book on disability and film is called *The Problem Body*.[1] One might argue that this could also suffice for the title of a volume on authorship and film. What the "death of the author" suggests is that we let "expire" (if only figuratively) the human agent responsible for creating a work and, along with it, her body—the site of human existence. Rather than a flesh and blood individual, the author is to be treated as an "effigy" or, worse yet, an "effect." Such a program seems at odds with the notion of *corpus* as signifying a writer's collected work—a term with clear reference to the body. On the other hand, its dictionary definition states its special meaning as pertaining to the remains of the dead.

Throughout this book, we have alluded to the authorial body: in the titular notion of the author "incarnate" and the film persona as a "body double." We have also singled out instances in which the author's hand (the part that writes) is visible—be it that of the filmmaker (as in Fleischer cartoons) or of the author-character who writes or types onscreen (as in *The Tango Lesson* or *Naked Lunch*). Furthermore, we have invoked the biblical notion of the "flesh made word" in our discussion of *The Diary of a Country Priest*. Moreover, in examining the female writer, we have mentioned pernicious associations between the pen and the penis —a notion that French feminists countered in their vision of écriture féminine —by which women would compose in a style that mirrored their sexed carnality. Finally, in the chapter on the infirm author, the suffering body has been repeatedly invoked.

In all these instances the emphasis has been on the body of the author as the site of art production—a corporeal entity refusing to vanish or dematerialize. In this chapter, however, the stress will be placed on the body as a *surface of writing* rather than as the locus of authorial agency. In our emphasis here on skin, we recall that one of the first inscription media was parchment, made from animal hide. We also think of a statement by Maya Deren: "[A] work of art is skin for an idea."[2]

Drawing upon the connections between image and language developed in the previous chapter, we examine works that highlight writing on the body (with both pictorial and linguistic signs)—the first arising in the Japanese film *Irezumi* (1982) and the second in the British film *The Pillow Book* (1996). Interestingly, both works are set in Asia and draw upon that region's cultures and arts.

IREZUMI: TATTOO, TABOO, AND THE FEMALE BODY

Adventures in the Skin Trade

> Only in Japan is tattooing an art; that is, only here has the craft of pigmentation become so skilled that it becomes an act of creation; and only here does this have the artistic dimensions of a long consecutive history.
>
> —Donald Richie, "Introduction"

Questions of authorship, eroticism, and female corporeality circulate in *Irezumi* (*Sekka Tomura Zashi*) made by Yoichi Takabayashi.[3] It concerns Akane (Masayo Utsunomiya), a modern Japanese woman who is having an affair with Fujeda (Yuhsuki Takita), an older library administrator who can only be aroused by women who are tattooed. He is, in fact, on the verge of leaving his middle-aged tattooed lover Haruna (Naomi Shiraishi) when his relationship with Akane begins. Bowing to his wishes, Akane meets with Kyogoro Yamato (Tomisaburo Wakayama)—a master tattooist who has not practiced his craft in many years (and is now a kimono designer). After he apprises her of the perils of the process and questions her intent, he agrees to give her a full back tattoo in the form of the image of Lady Tachibana as painted by Kuniyoshi. As the two begin their tattoo sessions (which last for months) and Akane makes weekly pilgrimages from Tokyo to Kyoto, Akane realizes that Kyogoro has a strange and unique method. Ostensibly in order to mute the pain of his hand-tapped needles or awls, he employs a young male apprentice, Harutsune (Masaki Kyo), to make love to Akane during the process. Kyogoro's aberrant technique also stems from his conviction that "a woman's skin is most beautiful in the act of love." Although Akane completes her tattoo (thus fulfilling Fujeda's desires and expectations), she becomes alienated and distant from him (despite their decision to marry). When Kyogoro dies, she honors his wish and returns to his home to have the "final cut" performed by his daughter, Katsuko—an act that will supposedly liberate his spirit from Akane's body. Clearly, in *Irezumi* issues are raised around the female body as *tabula rasa*, and questions are entertained about the intersection of authorship, eroticism, fetishism, and gender politics.

The Japanese Tattoo

> Tattooing is still done in Japan today, and the same themes are in demand. Taken from religion and popular mythology, they are chosen to help the bearer gain strength, health, wisdom and various magical powers.
>
> —John Thayer, "Tattoos"

In *Irezumi*, the issue of tattooing is immediately apparent but not easy to comprehend. Perhaps this explains some of the Western critical impatience and perplexity with the film. Writing in the *Village Voice*, Carlos Clarens sees it as part of a "tradition of kinkiness" in the Japanese cinema. As he mockingly notes, all the "cryptic motivations" of the characters "are merely a hangover from reading too much Georges Bataille."[4] L. L. Cohn in *Variety* asserts that the film uses "the tattooing ritual as a springboard for tortured passion."[5] On a more philosophical note, Vincent Canby states in the *New York Times* that the "film provides us with a glimpse into an ancient cultural system as it survives, in kinky shards, in contemporary Japan."[6] But it is important to have more than a "glimpse" of the tradition of *irezumi* in order to understand the film. For without such a perspective, the movie is reduced to mere "erotica for export."[7] As we shall see, the cultural interrogation of the Japanese tattoo stresses more the recipient of the mark than the author/artist who creates it—this despite the fact that *irezumi* literally means "insertion of ink"—the latter substance tying tattooing to writing.

According to experts, the earliest evidence of the practice of tattooing in Japan dates back to the Jomon period (10,000 B.C.–300 B.C.), when facial markings were common.[8] As for the written record, early Chinese chronicles of travel in Japan (A.D. 238–247) describe tattooed men.[9] It is also known that the indigenous Ainu people of Hokkaido tattooed women (between puberty and nubility) for ritual purposes—favoring marks on the backs of their hands and around their mouths. Such tattoos were believed to have magical powers, for example, "to ward off the demons of menstruation."[10] According to anthropologists, "some [Ainu] women, spurred by competition or subservience, even sported imitation tattooed beards" to mimic their men.[11] Furthermore, the legend of Japan's first emperor, Jimmu Tenno, is replete with references to his "opulent tattoos."[12] As early as the fifth century A.D., tattooing was used to mark and punish criminals. According to Amy Krakow: "First offenses were marked by a tattooed line across the forehead. A second crime added an arch, a third crime another line, with the three-mark tattoo forming the Japanese character meaning 'dog.' "[13] Here, the practices of writing and tattooing converge. As the procedure of tattooing outlaws developed, "the *Gojogaki Hyakkajo* ('One Hundred Articles of the Criminal Code') codified a great number of patterns, each indicating a separate offense."[14]

For David McCallum, the contemporary Japanese tattoo is a product of the Edo period, which lasted from 1600 to 1868.[15] During this era, courtesans of Edo and Osaka frequently had the name of their lover tattooed on a hidden body part: the upper thigh or inner arm. Typically, the practice was associated with the so-called "floating world"—the plebeian and marginal segments of society. The vogue for tattooing in this age (and its move from limited imagery to full-scale pictorial mode) was, however, associated with the fate of a particular work of literature —a fact that ties the art to writing and will link it to Greenaway's *The Pillow Book* (whose title also derives from a work of Asian literature). In 1727, ten volumes of a famous fourteenth-century Chinese novel were released in a Japanese version as the *Suikoden*. In 1839, the novelist Takizawa Bakin (1767–1848) translated and published a more popular edition of the text, illustrated by the wood block prints of artist, Katsushika Hokusai (1760–1849). Another volume of more flamboyant illustrations was released by Utaway Kuniyoshi (1797–1861) in 1827—entitled "108 Heroes of *Suikoden*."[16] The *Suikoden* tells the tale of a band of rebels who sport full-body tattoos. As Victoria Lautman notes: "A tattoo craze based on these illustrations and heroic characters ensued, particularly among members of Japan's more raucous and often bareskinned trades, such as the fire brigades, carpenters and palanquin bearers."[17] During this period, there were many edicts restricting the merchant class from wearing fine clothing. Some have theorized that *irezumi* was popular with them because they "could, however, wear an expensive tattoo, displaying it only to trusted confidants. So while a rich merchant might wear a plain kimono, vividly embroidered with gold threads on the inside, the merchant's son might sport an equally expensive tattoo on his arm."[18] With the Meiji Restoration (after the revolution of 1868), tattooing was forbidden by the government. This interdiction was tied to the opening of Japan to the West and to the fear that Americans and Europeans would find tattooing barbarous. According to Felman: "The police raided the mansions of tattoo masters, seized their paraphernalia, and destroyed their 'pattern books."[19] Ironically, however, many Westerners found tattooing irresistible, and the practice remained available "to foreigners only."

Tattooing became legal again only after the end of World War II. While the electric needle had come into vogue in the West as early as the turn of the century, hand-wrought methods prevailed in Japan[20]—with machines employed only occasionally, for the broad figural outline. Colors continued to be applied with steel needles bound to bone or ivory handles by silk thread.[21] Tattooing remained associated with the underground. Its modern clients tended to be "laborers and hangers-on at the fringes of society" and, especially, the *yakuza*: criminals engaged in gambling, shakedowns, prostitution, drugs, and murder.[22] As McCallum has observed, tattooing is "considered to be an entirely inappropriate practice for members of 'decent' society."[23] Some have theorized, however, that it can be attractive to mainstream individuals who wish to rebel against oppressive elements in Japanese society. As Thomas asks: "Do the *irezumi* defend themselves against their emotions? Against the technology, consumerism, and conformism of modern Japan?"[24]

Transgression and Obsession

> In nature you find the male animals with the brightest plumage and the most attractive colours, in order that they can attract the female of the species. This is why most men get tattooed. But I would be strongly suspicious of women who get tattooed. Since they would be offensive to men, they must have some other idea in mind.
> —Male tattoo fancier, quoted in Scutt and Gotch, *Art, Sex, and Symbol*

It is clear how a reading of *Irezumi* benefits from historical knowledge of Japanese tattoo tradition. Only such a background provides the context for understanding the level of trespass that Akane's act (allowing a man to inscribe her body) represents. Generally, of course, it has been Japanese men who are tattooed. Scutt and Gotch, for example, estimate that in 1986 only some fifty Japanese women had extensive body tattoos.[25] The few who engage in the ritual are prostitutes, bar maids (like Haruna), or women tied to the *yakuza*. Obviously, as a middle-class, educated woman, Akane would have no connection to the underworld that circulates around tattooing. Significantly, Takabayashi names his film *Irezumi* (a term linked to tattooing as punishment) rather than *horimono* (another, more neutral, word for the practice).[26] Evidently, the only other class of tattooed women is that associated with tattoo artists or devotees: "It would be fair to state that most women who possess tattoos gained them under or through the influence of their men-folk."[27]

A historical sense also allows us to appreciate how important it is that Kyogoro lives in Kyoto, the seat of traditional Japanese art and culture. (Ironically, at one point Fujeda tells Akane: "Kyoto isn't what it used to be.") Furthermore, Kyogoro's second name, Yamato, refers to a province that was the cradle of ancient culture from the fifth to the eighth centuries. Knowing history also permits us to comprehend Kyogoro's reluctance to resume his tattooing craft: when he picks up his needle, after many years, he cries, "How sinful am I!" It is an art with a legacy of strong censorship in Japan, and his abandonment of the trade (and its brand of authorship) replays the destiny of tattooists in the Meiji Restoration. Furthermore, tattooing remains abhorrent to most Japanese. As McCallum notes, "Beauty is in the eye of the beholder, and the normal Japanese response to a tattooed individual —whatever the subject—is revulsion."[28] Other details of the film are replete with documentary resonance: Kyogoro's hand-wrought tattooing method (done by hammering awls or needles), the pattern books he consults, his choice of a Kuniyoshi print for Akane's back.

What is also apparent from the history of tattooing in Japan is the cultural fascination that obtains around the practice—both in the East and in the West. As McCallum notes, "The fact that edicts [against tattooing] were repeated at frequent intervals [during the Edo period] suggests that they were not entirely effective."[29] While *Irezumi* does not invoke tattooing's broad social appeal, it does focus on its potential to obsess particular individuals. Clearly, both Fujeda and Kyogoro have (what we would term) a "fetish" for tattooed women. Only through the mediation of the tattoo is a female made sexually desirable to them. Furthermore, Kyogoro also has the obsession *to* tattoo (a pictorial form of hypographia, perhaps). After his first meeting with Akane (when he contemplates resuming his craft), he falls on his knees, confesses his desire, and cries, "Please help me!"—a vain attempt to resist his impulses.

On the one hand, critics like Vincent Canby refuse to invoke Western psychoanalytic models to explore the implications of *Irezumi*. As he notes: "Mr. Takabayashi is more interested in esthetics than psychology. Freud has no place in this world."[30] On the other hand, Canby falls back upon such a framework to describe how Kyogoro interviews Akane about her desire to be tattooed: "As a psychiatrist might examine someone who wants a sex change operation, the old man questions Akane at length about her motives, repeatedly making the point that the tattoo can't guarantee happiness and may possibly ruin her life." Experts on Japanese culture validate a psychological approach to the tattoo process. McCallum, for example, proposes the issue through his discussion of an important modern Japanese story—"The Tattooer," written in 1910 by Tanizaki Junichiro (1896–1965)—a work that establishes ties between tattooing and literature. While the tale's relation to *Irezumi* is tangential, it was the source for the 1966 Japanese film *Tattoo*, directed by Yasuzo Masumura.[31] "The Tattooer" is set in the pleasure quarters of Edo in the 1840s. Seikichi has a secret desire to create a tattoo masterpiece on the body of a beautiful woman. Having searched for a proper subject for four years, he spies the foot of a young woman entering a palanquin and realizes that she is the individual he has sought (more fetishism, perhaps). He brings her to his tattoo studio and shows her lurid, pornographic Chinese paintings. He then sedates her and executes a tattoo of a black widow spider upon her back. When she awakens, he declares that "all men will be [her] victims" (as though the tattoo has invested her with perverse power). By the story's end, he is one of them. McCallum sees Tanizaki's work as "characterized by decadent, erotic fantasy."[32] As he observes: "Tanizaki's short story . . . must . . . be analyzed on a dee[p] psychological level. It is quite apparent that erotic and sado-masochistic impulses motivated Tanizaki's writing and [it] is unlikely that such motivations are unique to him. Rather, I would suggest that the very deviance of the tattoo—its perversity—has exerted an influence on conventional society."[33] Hence, for McCallum, a drama like *Irezumi* (which bears much similarity to "The Tattooer") is not (as Clarens would have it) mere "erotica for export," but a work that invokes themes that are fundamentally Japanese. While McCallum is loath to imagine "a specific genre of 'tattoo literature,'" he notes that "the theme has a place of some importance in modern Japanese writing."[34]

It is significant that Tanizaki is the author of "The Tattooer" (and the source for *Tattoo*), because an entire genre of Japanese movies began with the adaptation of two of his other literary properties. The films in question were *Daydream* and *Dream of the Red Room*—both directed by Takechi Tetsuji in 1964.[35] According to David Desser, they ushered in the Japanese "pink film," a brand of soft-core pornography (made for a land where hard core is illegal). According to Desser: "Shochiku, Mikkatsu and, soon after, Toei [Studios], began the production of pink films, which quickly came to dominate the home market. By the mid-1960s, pink films accounted for fully one-half of domestic production."[36]

Clearly, *Irezumi* has a peripheral relation to this genre—a film form that peaked in 1982, the year it was made. Though more an art film than a pink film, it willfully blurs such borders (as did Oshima's *The Realm of the Senses* [1976]). Takabayashi had earlier worked in the pink film genre. In 1978, he made *Ojo Anrakukoku* (*In the Realm of Death and Pleasure*), a work that explicitly portrays a sexual encounter.

Thus, Carlos Clarens calls him a director who "made his name with experimental erotica and soft core commercial features."[37] Following *Irezumi*, Takabayashi went on to make *Red Scandal: Love Affairs*, for Nikkatsu. It falls within the "romance pornography" genre, one that Desser deems a "radical extension" of the pink film.[38] As evidence, however, of *Irezumi*'s recognition outside the soft-porn ghetto, it was exhibited in the United States in 1983 as part of the renowned New Directors/New Films series in New York City.

Writing the Female Body

> Just as women's sexuality is bound up with touch, so too women use words as a form of touching. Words join in the same way as do muscles and joints. Sex and speech are contiguous: the lips of the vulva and the lips of the mouth are each figures of and for each other.
>
> —B. Freeman, quoted in Dallery, "The Politics of Writing"

While rife with local cultural associations, there is an aspect of *Irezumi* that also transcends them—that seems to invoke broader questions of gender and sexual dynamics. For on some level, we might regard the dynamics between Akane and the composite Fujeda/Kyogoro/Harutsune as emblematic of all male/female relations. Clearly, our mention of Fujeda's "fetishism" invokes Freudian theories regarding man's fear of the female genitalia. For the fetishist, woman's bodily absence, her phallic lack, can only be compensated for by the substitution or coordination of a symbolic object—be it underwear, shoes, or a tattoo. While Freud sees this as a limited pathology, film theorist Laura Mulvey has famously viewed the syndrome as widely applicable to mass cultural forms—as in the male spectator's stance in watching the female screen persona. As she has noted: "The structure of looking in narrative fiction film contains a contradiction in its own premises: the female image as a castration threat constantly endangers the unity of the diegesis and bursts through the world of illusion as an intrusive, static, one-dimensional fetish."[39]

The notion of tattoo as fetish—of tattoo as "replacing" woman herself—is foregrounded in the remarks of D. M. Thomas (who introduces a volume of photographs of tattooees). He writes: "Looking at the woman's back in this book, I know that making love to her would be making love to the tattoo more than to the woman. . . . It is not unlike the fetishist's need to interpose a symbol—fur or leather, garter belt or high-heeled shoes—between himself and his naked lover. Both fetishism and *irezumi* are largely the preserve of men."[40] In addition to serving as a fetishistic "supplement" for genital lack, the tattoo (as the insertion of ink) is a kind of "deformity" of the skin, which also works to literalize deep-seated male fantasies of the female sexual organ as "wound." This association of tattoo and defect is at the root of society's aversion to the process. As Lautman suggests: "Most people will start to squirm just imagining the tattoo process. The suggestion of needles, blood, and pain can cause profound discomfort among the untattooed.

. . . Such squeamishness often disguises an even more primal fear—namely alter-
ing the body forever."[41]

But there are other aspects of the tattoo process that seem "over-determined"
from a gendered perspective. Clearly, its method of penetrating skin with needles
has a decidedly phallic cast to it—literalizing the feminist notion of equating pen
with penis. While, in the usual configuration (of male tattooist and male subject),
this has homosexual overtones, in the case of *Irezumi* it replays the standard male/
female sexual dynamic. The fact that while Akane is tattooed by Kyogoro (on orders of her male lover) she has intercourse with Harutsune only makes the inherent paradigm more obvious. Furthermore, because the tattoo process results in
piercing and bleeding, it has obvious parallels to the act of sexual deflowering.

The film insistently presents the heterosexual dynamic (of tattooing or lovemaking) as laced with sadism for the male and masochism for the female—the
culturally "standard" paradigm. The close-ups of Akane (as she is simultaneously
written upon and ravished) willfully conjoin the grimaces of pain and ecstasy.
Again, this confusion (of suffering and euphoria) seems signaled in the words
of Tanizaki, writing about his master tattooer. For Seikichi admits that his pleasure lay in the agony his subjects feel from his carnal authorship "as he drove his
needles into them, torturing their swollen, blood-red flesh." Evidently, "the louder
they groaned, the keener was Seikichi's strange delight."[42] Takabayashi augments
this sense of tattooing's cruelty in *Irezumi* by highlighting the sound that Kyogoro's hammers make as they tap the awls or needles into Akane's back (much as
other films we have examined emphasize the noise of typewriter keys).

While this focus on questions of male fetishism and sadism makes *Irezumi* a
hyperbolic work from a gendered perspective (either retrograde or self-conscious,
depending on one's perspective)—the main issue it raises is one of "writing the female body" (a term coined by French feminist critics). Obviously, what concerns
them is the fact that established literature has been authored by men (as have been
tattoos). In wondering what a true *écriture féminine* would read like, they invoke
the configuration of the female body as a model for feminine writing. As French
theorist Hélène Cixous declaims: "Write yourself, your body must be heard. . . .
To write an act which will not only realize the decensored relation of woman to
her sexuality, to her womanly being; it will give her back her goods, her pleasures,
her organs, her immense bodily territories which have been kept under seal."[43] In
Irezumi, we get no such subtle (or feminist) notion of "writing the female body."
Rather, in classic patriarchal fashion, a woman's body is etched and authored by
men. Furthermore, it is important just how it is detailed: with a graphic representation of another female (Lady Tachibana). Thus, the film literalizes not only
some perverse brand of "writing the female body," but a cliché sense of the naked
female form as "spectacle." Akane's back is, quite concretely, transformed into a
picture. As though her naked body were not sufficient for the male gaze, a painting
of another woman is superimposed upon it. In possessing Akane, Fujeda not only
collects a female but an artwork. The gorgeous, colorized portrait on her back also

literalizes the sense of woman as decorative object; here she is layered with yet a second-order level of ornamentation.

In this respect, *Irezumi* is reminiscent of a classical work of the Japanese cinema — Kenji Mizoguchi's *Utamaro and His Five Women* (1946). Set in eighteenth-century Tokyo, the film concerns Utamaro, a woodblock artist, known for his vibrant portraits of women. At one point, he visits a courtesan who is about to receive a tattoo. Instead of finding the process under way, he ascertains that the tattooist has been so overwhelmed by the beauty of his subject's skin that he has been artistically paralyzed. No design, he feels, will do justice to her perfection. Here, Utamaro leaps in, offering one of his own designs. He then proceeds to paint an image on the woman's back, using her body as a literal canvas or page for writing.

It is significant that in *Utamaro* the woman's back is ornamented. That this embellishment is for the eyes of another is made clear by its bodily location. As McCallum has remarked: "It is interesting to note that normally the most significant part of the [tattoo] design is at the back, presumably because this area allows the broadest canvas for the tattooist's art. An important result of this format is that the individual cannot see his or her tattoo, except in a mirror, suggesting that the function of the tattoo is display."[44] Thus, Akane's tattoo would be unknown to her except as seen through the looking glass — an object that only presents it indirectly (and reversed) and is pejoratively associated with female vanity.

Clearly, Takabayashi's prior work in the pink film genre has prepared him for his subject in *Irezumi*. As Desser notes: "Rape and torture are prevalent components in the pink films. . . . It takes no staunch feminist to claim that pink films, which cater to overwhelmingly male audiences, fulfill repressed male desires to rape and torture women."[45] He also notes that such movies favor innocent heroines who fall in love with their rapists. In *Irezumi*, one might claim that Akane falls in love with three.

Citizen Kyogoro

> [Women are] inscribed in hero narratives, in someone else's story, not their own; so they figure as markers of positions — places and topoi — through which the hero and his story move to their destination and to accomplish meaning.
>
> — Teresa de Lauretis, *Alice Doesn't*

In addition to presenting, in almost textbook fashion, certain archetypal notions of the male perception of woman (through the actions of the tattooist/author), *Irezumi* also adopts a standard patriarchal narrative form — as written by screenwriter Chino Katsura (based on a novel by Baku Akae). While, on some level, the film is about the character of Akane and her "adventures in the skin trade," her story is entirely embedded within the tales of several masculine characters. Most noticeable, of course, is that of the tattooist, Kyogoro, who is the paternal center of the film. Like the opening of *Citizen Kane*, *Irezumi* begins with (what seems to be) a deathbed stream-of-consciousness meditation, as we hear Kyogoro's voice

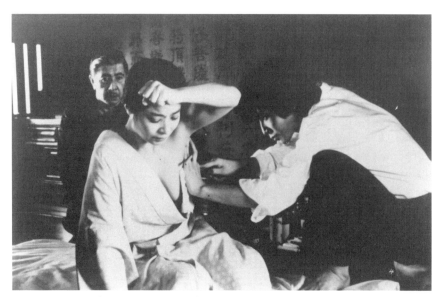

FIGURE 32. Akane (Masayo Utsunomiya) is tattooed by Harutsune (Masaki Kyo) as master practitioner Kyogoro (Tomisaburo Wakayama) looks on (*Irezumi*, 1982).

(in interior monologue) utter the words: "Akane, I'm glad you came—you kept the promise to come to my house when I die." As it turns out, he is speaking post-humously about Akane's return to have the final cut executed by his daughter Katsuko. Not only is Akane's drama bundled within that of Kyogoro, he is able to enfold it from the grave (like the hero of *Sunset Blvd.*)—giving the dead author continuing powers. Adding to the magical sense of the sequence (and to its parallels with the Welles film), snow falls across the image, as though escaped from Kane's glass ball. Clearly, the flakes function on another level as well. It is through his discovery of Kyogoro's volume of snowflake tattoo patterns that Harutsune learns, to his shock, that he is the tattooer's son. Evidently, his mother (who left Kyogoro) gave Harutsune the matching companion volume—which she took from Kyogoro when she fled their marriage. When Kyogoro completes Akane's tattoo, Harutsune (turning from authorial assistant to creator) asks if he can make his own small image, to be rendered on a hidden part of her body—a "promise engraving" or *kisho bori*.[46] The icon he chooses is a snowflake—taking us back to the Wellesian opening of *Irezumi*.

Beyond the snowflake's link to Harutsune's Oedipal drama (reminiscent of Kane's triangular family romance), it is symbolically associated with Akane's purity and with the fetishized whiteness of her skin (the preferable blank page).[47] At moments, Kyogoro refers to the snowflake tattoo pattern as a snow "flower" —reminding us of the associations between tattooing and defloration. Ironically, even snow's frigidity references tattooing. As Thomas notes: "The irezumi's skin, which has borne the fiery pain of the needles, becomes cool, reptilian."[48] Snow also has ties to death in Japanese culture—an issue linked to Kyogoro's desire for Katsuko to perform a posthumous final cut. Significantly, the Japanese title for the film (*Sekka Tomura Zashi*) means "Funeral Tattoo of Snowflake Flowers"—making clear the ties between the image and fatality. Finally, snow is an index of the ephemeral within Buddhist thought—a figure for the vulnerability of beauty. As the snowflake is perishable, so is the tattoo—which dies when its host expires (the death of the text versus the author).[49]

The second dominant hue in the film is red—one that can be associated with impurity within Japanese culture. The name "Akane" means "dark red"—and when she dresses in a kimono, it is white with a red sash. Furthermore, as she begins to undergo the tattoo process, she glances at some scarlet flowers in Kyogoro's studio. Clearly, this color has associations to blood—a fluid that can link sex (menstruation, defloration) and tattooing. As though to stress this, as Akane and Harutsune make love during one of the tattoo sessions, her blood drips onto his full-body tattoo. When he later stabs himself (the demise of a second author), his blood flows onto the pages of the snowflake tattoo pattern book—joining the color red to notions of death. This semantic nexus is extended further because red tattooing pigment is "made of material so lethal [mainly lead] that the client can tolerate only a few new spare inches a week."[50]

Like *Citizen Kane*, *Irezumi* is postulated as a grand "flashback," but its temporality has further complexities. Within the overall flashback, there are smaller ones, as several male characters are allowed to relate their stories. Most prominent are the recollections of Kyogoro, whose first reverie occurs when he is discussing the perils of tattooing with Akane. As he describes how his encounter with a prostitute initiated his obsession with tattoos, we see a series of abstract images in montage. Some of them seem illustrative of his words, but others are less semantically anchored. The flashback continues, as he recounts incidents concerning his tutelage with a tattoo master; his adoption of Katsuko (whom he found upon his doorstep); the forced tattooing of his wife and her subsequent flight; his meeting Harutsune (who Kyogoro secretly realizes is his son). The narrative ends with the fulfillment of Kyogoro's quest: to have his spirit released from Akane's body (the author banished from the text).

At other times in the film, the narrative flashes back to signal events in Fujeda's relationship with Akane: for instance, the moment when he confesses his love of her smooth white skin and his desire to have it tattooed. In all cases, it is the male who has the privilege of reminiscence. Furthermore, the drama of *Irezumi* is overlaid with a sense of patriarchal tension: Kyogoro's attempts to achieve the standards of his tattoo master; Harutsune's anger at discovering Kyogoro is his abusive father. In Harutsune's Oedipal angst (which ends in suicide), we are again reminded of the plight of Charles Foster Kane—whose self-destructive tendencies date back to childhood separation and trauma.

Lady Tachibana's Revenge

> When I make myself imagine what it is like to be one of those women who live at
> home, faithfully serving their husbands—women who have not a single exciting
> prospect in life yet who believe they are perfectly happy—I am filled with scorn.
> —Sei Shōnagon, *The Pillow Book*

While on one level *Irezumi* seems a classic case of patriarchal cinema (with a passive heroine who endures pain and degradation to become a spectacle and writing
surface for her man), on another level it offers some resistance—contributing to
the film's strange and unsettling tone. While it is true that Akane allows herself to
be violated by Harutsune, she soon grows to enjoy their sexual encounters. Ultimately, she manages to use her tattoo sessions to "cheat" on Fujeda—cuckold-
ing him at his own expense in the very act of fulfilling his desires. There is also
an implicit "sexual" relation between Kyogoro and Akane as well—which, given
their age, has the taint of incest. Kyogoro even removes his kimono and works on
Akane bare-chested—straddling her and Harutsune in a grand orgy, or *ménage à
trois*. As Thomas notes: "It would not surprise me if for most *irezumi*, the deep-
est relationship is with the master, so tirelessly penetrating them."[51] Akane also
agrees (like an Edo-era prostitute) to have one of Harutsune's tattoos inscribed on
a hidden body part. When she chooses her armpit, Kyogoro cautions her against
that location, asserting that she will be unable to tolerate the pain. Countering his
warnings, she insists on the spot—demonstrating that she is more courageous
and stoic than he has imagined—beating him at his own game. In the perverse
strength Akane derives from submitting to *irezumi*, we are reminded of notions of
the tattoo as a kind of "shield."[52]

The narrative also makes abundantly clear the violence that Fujeda and Kyogoro have perpetrated on women (saving the film from pure masculine romance).
In one flashback, the tattooist reveals that he forced his wife to undergo the procedure at his own hands—both to inscribe her with the fetish mark and to practice
his trade ("If I tattoo her now, I'll have a tattoo as great as my master's," he thinks,
revealing his desire to possess the corporeal text that he authors on the body
of another). As part of Kyogoro's reverie, we see his wife's pained and incensed
face staring straight at the camera and learn that she soon abandoned him. As he
muses, "I didn't know what she felt."

In some respects, Akane gradually takes on the rage of Kyogoro's wife (as in
Swimming Pool, Sarah Morton takes on that of Julie's mother). Thus, it is significant that the image tattooed upon her back is that of Lady Tachibana carrying a
sword—an icon of fierce femininity.[53] Rather than make Akane more compliant,
the tattooing process makes her bolder. (We recall that she told Kyogoro at their
first meeting: "I don't want to be defeated. . . . My life is what I have chosen. . . . I
will not lose.") One day, when she meets Fujeda after an appointment with Kyogoro, she refuses her lover's voyeuristic urge to see the tattoo. Instead, she walks,

fully clothed, into the river—affronting his sense of propriety. She claims that her skin is "burning" and that the water will cool it down. We sense, however, that it is her anger that is inflamed. Here, we are also reminded of the last line of Tanizaki's story, in which the back of the Seikichi's client "caught a ray of sunlight and the spider was wreathed in flames."[54] On another occasion, Akane meets Fujeda in a train station and begins to strip off her clothes to reveal the tattoo. Again, there is a rebellious and aggressive tone to her gesture—as though her primary purpose is to humiliate rather than to please him. Significantly, she jokes about being "possessed by Lady Tachibana." Another time, Fujeda asks to witness one of Akane's tattoo sessions, a request she refuses. When she asks him whether the tattoo process has changed her, he reluctantly admits that it has.

Skin Flicks

> I think the cinema is a woman. . . . This uterus which is the theater, the fetal darkness, the apparition—all create a projected relationship, we project ourselves onto it— just as we do with women.
>
> —Federico Fellini, quoted in Bachmann, "Federico Fellini"

In the same way that *Irezumi* highlights questions of woman and the *corpus*, it can be imagined as foregrounding questions of body and cinema. For upon thought, there are parallels not only between the processes of tattooing and writing, but between it and filmmaking—similarities that were sparked in my mind by the use of the term "final cut" in the English subtitles to represent Katsuko's incision of Akane's body following her father's death.

While this may be a mere accident of translation, it foregrounds how both tattooing and traditional filmmaking involve the creation of an image through a process of cutting—one of skin, the other of celluloid. Both can be seen to involve the "burning in" of a picture—tattooing, through the insertion of ink and needles; film, through the exposure of photographic material to light. Both are "alive"— the tattoo through its embodiment on a human being, the cinema through its animated illusions. While the tattooist interjects pigment into a layer of the human epidermis, the photographer renders color through manipulation of the filmic emulsion—a kind of "skin" on the celluloid strip.

The fact that, in *Irezumi*, it is the skin of a female that is written upon reminds us that when theorists have imagined parallels between screen and body, they have done so around the figure of woman. For example, in writing about the primitive American film *Uncle Josh at the Moving Picture Show* (1902), Judith Mayne compares the screen image (which Josh sees) of a Parisian dancer lifting her skirts to that of Josh lifting the movie screen, hoping to find the showgirl embodied behind it.[55] While I would not wish to press the metaphorical links between tattooing and filmmaking too far, it is abundantly clear how the Japanese tattoo process at least relates to the broader subject of art. (Some tattooists actually include their authorial signature as part of the tattoo design.)[56] Beyond being a skilled craft in itself, there are the pictures of tattoos by Kunisada (1786–1864), Yoshitoshi (1839–1892), and Kunichicka (1836–1900), which illustrate the *Suikoden*—demonstrating how the craze for tattooing was tied to the woodblock genre. (As McCallum observes, there was a "reciprocal relationship" between the two.)[57] There is also the prominence of the tattoo as a theme in Japanese literature and drama. We have already discussed the case of Tanizaki, but other writers (like Okamoto Kido, Kunieda Kanji, Hirabayashi Taiko, Takagi Ashimitsu, and Mishima Yukio) have also taken on the topic.[58] Furthermore, there is the case of the Kabuki play, *The Scarlet Princess of Edo* (by Takao I and Tamasaburo V), which forecasts the story of *Irezumi*. It concerns a princess who is raped by a scoundrel on whose arm she notices a tattoo. When the rapist later reencounters her, he discovers that she has had her limb tattooed with the identical image as his. As Felman notes: "She had undergone this pain as proof and pledge of her passion and, according to the power of tattoos, as amulets, as magical assurance that she would meet him once again. They resume their love affair but do not live happily ever after. They join the society's dregs, and live miserably but lovingly in Japan's lower depths. At the end of the play . . . [he] sells her to a house of prostitution so that they may live in comfort."[59] Clearly, this narrative bears parallels to *Irezumi* (with its passive heroine who allows herself to be tattooed and degraded for the love of an abusive man). What it also makes clear is that Takabayashi's film (despite its flirtation with "erotica for export") is an indigenous product—tied, in a profound manner, to ancient motifs within Japanese culture.

Finally, it is crucial to recall that, with a back tattoo, it is only a looking glass that can provide the subject a view of that bodily adornment. Significantly, in *Irezumi* it is women who sport this form of tattoo and several scenes exist in which they are portrayed in front of a mirror. The first instance occurs in one of Kyogoro's flashbacks—as we see the prostitute who first captivated him seated at her dressing table. The second instance depicts Akane at a mirror, as she rebuffs Fujeda's advances and endures his tearing the kimono from her back to caress her tattoo. Both scenes are fraught with tension and, on both occasions, the woman is refused the image she desires—the hidden view of her back and the text for which she has served as medium.

Given the parallels that exist between screen and mirror, it is tempting to read these shots as emblems of woman's position in traditional cinema: "authored" by a man, posed before the screen as spectacle, but refused an image that reflects her "back."

THE PILLOW BOOK: CARNAL KNOWLEDGE

The Pillow Book is the second film I've made which has the word "book" in its title. So I'm certainly very interested in metaphors like "the body is a book, the book is a body."
    —Peter Greenaway, quoted in Chua, "Peter Greenaway"

While *Irezumi* concerns authorship and "writing" on the body in the form of the pictorial tattoo, Peter Greenaway's *The Pillow Book* returns us to the linguistic form (while keeping the focus on corporeal inscription). Moreover, like *Irezumi*, it is set in Asia (Kyoto and Hong Kong) and references aspects of the region's literature, deriving its title from a tenth-century Japanese journal written by a courtesan, Sei Shōnagon. In its focus on this literary genre, we are, of course, reminded of Bresson's *Diary of a Country Priest*.

In Greenaway's film, Nagiko (Vivian Wu), a contemporary Japanese woman (whose father [Ken Ogata] has had the eccentric practice of writing her name on her face each birthday), attempts to recapture the excitement of that paternal gesture by encouraging her calligrapher-lovers to inscribe her body. (Here, we recall that in the film *Utamaro*, the protagonist painted a woman's skin instead of tattooing it.) Eventually, Nagiko meets Jerome (Ewan McGregor), a bisexual English translator, who suggests that, instead, she mark the body of her male lovers, becoming the "pen" rather than the "paper" (a notion that never occurred to Akane). Nagiko then enacts this rite with a host of men, including Jerome, with whom she has a romantic liaison. While Greenaway's film seems initially only about calligraphy, Nagiko ultimately is tattooed when Jerome dies (though the act occurs off-screen). After Jerome's death, his male lover (a publisher) has his inscribed skin flayed, cured, and transformed into a human parchment book in a manner reminiscent of how some Japanese preserve the skins of tattooees.[60]

As should already be clear, *The Pillow Book* is of interest in a variety of ways. Like other texts considered here, it engages in the multiplication of embodied authorial figures: Nagiko, her father, her numerous lovers, her maid, and even Shōnagon (who appears periodically to Nagiko [and us] as a haunting historical vision). Like many films we have examined, it also privileges the tension between pictorial and verbal discourses. As Greenaway has noted: "In Asian calligraphy, we have the possibility of an image being a text, a text being an image at one and the same time. Wouldn't this be a good way to consider the possibility of a reinvention of cinema?"[61] Finally, even more than *Irezumi*, the film is about writing and the body. As Greenaway has remarked: "The calligraphic text is essentially made by the body. . . . If the body makes the text, then the best place for the text is back on the body."[62]

Like *Irezumi*, it is impossible to contemplate *The Pillow Book* without considering its gender politics. Since much has been written on this, we do so here briefly —stressing only elements relevant to our perspective.[63] That Nagiko's special form of hypographia begins with her father's inscription of her name upon her brow makes clear the notion of patriarchy writing itself upon the bodies of women (as well as legitimating their very identity). Furthermore, whenever Nagiko's father does this, he says: "When God made the first clay model of a human being, He painted in the eyes and the lips and the sex," a statement that tends to equate paternal authority with the deity (and God with the author). The letters he writes

on her extend below Nagiko's forehead to her mouth—demonstrating how patriarchal language will mark woman's organ of speech and expression. After painting
her face, her father continues: "If God approved of His own work he brought the
painted clay model to life by signing His name." He then autographs her neck (in
black letters that magically turn red, as though searing themselves into her skin).
Thus, he is not only a writer in the conventional sense, but the God-like author
of his child. This linguistic complexity is made even denser due to the fact that
Nagiko's father speaks in Japanese while his words are translated into English subtitles. This alternation of English-subtitled spoken Japanese (and later Chinese)
versus English dialogue is continued throughout the film, making it an audio-
visual verbal crazy salad.

While in writing about *The Pillow Book*, Douglas Keesey emphasizes Nagiko's
childhood birthday ritual as a kind of lost paradise and only entertains the notion
of its disturbing valence quite late in his analysis, the perversity of her father's act
seems immediately blatant.[64] If Nagiko wishes to return to this primal scene, she
is like an incest victim destructively craving a repetition of sexual abuse. That the
deviance of her early familial experience makes her a passive text for male inscription is made more apparent by the fact that, on one of her early birthdays, she
witnesses her father (a writer) prostituting himself to his publisher (Yoshi Oida)
in order to get his book in print. The latter is the same man who will become Jerome's lover and preserve his "calligraphed" skin after his demise. So throughout,
writing is, in every respect, tainted by aberrance and corruption. Moreover, in
adulthood, when Nagiko moves to Hong Kong, she becomes a model, a classic
profession in which the female body becomes spectacle—a corporeal work designed, controlled, and displayed (largely) by and for men. Her choice of profession also reminds us that, in the statement her father made each birthday, he
talked of God bringing a clay "model" to life. Interestingly, the first time we see her
father write on Nagiko's brow, a relative holds up a mirror for her to admire her
male-authored countenance.

Unlike the heroine of *Irezumi*, however, Nagiko quickly learns to "turn the tables" on patriarchal authority and authorship—much as Sally does in *The Tango
Lesson*. On her sixth birthday, she decides to keep a handwritten diary. When she
turns twenty-one and moves to Hong Kong, she decides to learn to type. We see
her in a dingy apartment straining at the machine. Ultimately, she rips a typed
page from the carriage and glues it to her chest—obviously trying to gain the experience of corporeal inscription. Finding this unsatisfactory, she tears it off and
throws the typewriter in the toilet. In Nagiko's world, only being marked by another's human hand is adequate.

Ultimately, however, she decides that rather than remain the writing surface,
she will become its agent—marking the bodies of men. This feminist gesture is
qualified, however, because it is Jerome who suggests it to her. On the other hand,
a second female writer has a strong place in the film—Sei Shōnagon, the author of
The Pillow Book, a work given to Nagiko as a child by her aunt (Hideko Yoshida),

and which continually inspires her. Thus, periodically we get quotes (read in her aunt's voice) that are attributed to the ancient text, for example: "Elegant Things: Shaved ice in a silver bowl. Wisteria blossoms." Greenaway says that he first read Shōnagon's book in 1972 and was intrigued by its organization around a series of lists—not surprising for a filmmaker whose work is more structural than dramatic. As he has said, "I don't think the cinema is a particularly good narrative medium. . . . If you want to be passionately attached to narrative, then be a writer."[65] Shōnagon's book inspired him to plan a film entitled *26 Facts about Flesh and Ink*, to be arranged by the letters of the alphabet. Here, Greenaway was clearly influenced by Hollis Frampton's *Zorns Lemma* (1970), a work to be discussed later, that takes a similar approach.[66] Already, the topic of Greenaway's never-to-be-realized movie invokes the corporeal subject matter of *The Pillow Book*, and a treatment for it is published along with the screenplay for the film he finally made. Under the letter *A*, he writes: "The most suitable flesh to write on must be very white, perhaps the flesh of a body whose jet-black hair suggests the shine of black ink."[67] Here, we can envision an Asian individual, and later Greenaway refers directly to the character of Nagiko, who is said to love literature and writing implements but whose "body is paper." Interestingly, there is nothing in Shōnagon's *The Pillow Book* that mentions carnal inscription—so Greenaway's "adaptation" is entirely quirky and original. As he admits, Shōnagon "would not have recognized the narrative of [my] film project or its characters."[68]

But it is the formal conjunction of word and image that is most interesting in *The Pillow Book*, especially as it pertains to questions of authorship and writing —an aspect that has received less critical attention than its complex psychology, sexual politics, and resonant themes. Clearly, Greenaway has made a conscious choice in the film to foreground Asian languages, since (as he has noted) their characters are ideograms that incorporate pictures into linguistic signs. But Anne-Marie Christin has made the point that all languages mix the two registers. As she notes: "Writing was born of a hybrid process."[69] Another pictorial element of Asian calligraphy is the fact that it was traditionally executed with a brush, a tool that links it to painting.

Long before Greenaway, of course, film theorist Sergei Eisenstein had seen the pictogram as not only relevant to the cinema, but to the specific technique of montage. In discussing Chinese pictograms, he notes that the symbols for *dog* and *mouth* had been combined to make the word *bark*, as the symbols for *child* and *mouth* had been combined to make the word *scream*.[70] As he continues: "It is exactly what we do in the cinema, combining shots that are *depictive*, single in meaning . . . into *intellectual* contexts and series." The opening credits of *The Pillow Book* begin, in fact, with a scroll of pictograms, with the camera panning down the page in the manner of someone reading a Japanese or Chinese text. The film must be one of the only movies for which calligraphers receive screen credit.

Like Eisenstein, Greenaway engages in every variety of assertive montage: shot-to-shot editing, audio-visual collision, juxtaposition within the frame—all of which call attention to his status as offscreen auteur (joining the ranks of those within the narrative). Given the intricacy of the film's assembly, we can only give representative examples of the varied types of shots he constructs. In the first scene of the adult Nagiko modeling in Hong Kong, the image is overlaid with a scroll of Japanese pictograms, which is labeled "*The Pillow Book* Section 150." Then, at the center of the frame, a rectangle opens up and depicts Shōnagon (in ancient garb), as a female voice speaks in Japanese and subtitles translate her words into English: "The empress wore a robe of green Chinese silk." So in essence, we are watching three shots at once and have three representations of language—written Japanese, spoken Japanese, and written English. (Later, we learn that Jerome can translate six languages.) Greenaway was able to achieve this visual effect through an early use of digitalization. As he notes: "The original film-stock used was super-35mm and the rushes were converted to tape and edited on an Avid tape-editing system, where the possibilities of maneuvering the imagery were far more considerable that originally envisaged."[71] In another scene (that reverts back to childhood and is shot in black and white like other such segments), Nagiko's aunt reads to her from *The Pillow Book* for the first time. A page of Japanese writing fills the screen, as her aunt enumerates Shōnagon's list of "elegant things," mentioning "duck eggs." A colorful picture of the latter captioned with words appears in a rectangle center-screen, then opens up to a full-frame image—like the page of a children's book. Ironically, it is at this moment that Nagiko witnesses her father sodomized by his publisher, hardly something that counts as "elegant." This sequence's use of ma-nipulated images, its reference to a book page, its employment of language on-screen, all attest not only to the author characters within the narrative but to the creator behind the scene. In future episodes, as Shōnagon's words are read and illustrated, some of the images (e.g., a picture of "a large garden covered in snow") seem timeless, while others (a shot of "an imperial procession") represent pre-cise historical moments (gleaned by costume and setting). Other types of word/image juxtapositions occur in the film. In one scene, as the young Nagiko and her father walk on the street and her adult voiceover discusses her marriage, a page of Japanese writing is superimposed over the image—though it is unclear what the document represents.

Authorship is also referenced in the film through shots of the publishing house that is printing the manuscript by Nagiko's father—and we see black-and-white multi-screen images of the presses rolling or men binding books by hand. Here once again, Nagiko experiences childhood trauma when her father emerges from the publisher's office just as the latter hitches up his pants. Again, authorship and prostitution seem to go hand in hand. Significantly, Nagiko's adult voiceover in-forms us that it was on this day that she first met her husband (then also a child) —a marriage marred by the publisher's intervention. We learn as well that it was then that she started to keep a diary, one characterized by emotional distress at its very inception.

Her anguish becomes worse when, as a grown-up, she marries the man—an

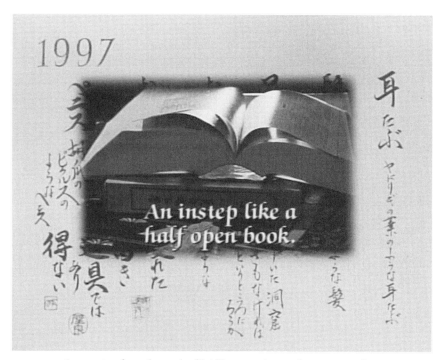

FIGURE 33. A quotation from the work of Sei Shōnagon inserted into a page of contemporary writing in *The Pillow Book* (1996).

individual who mocks her love of literature, and, while practicing archery, shoots arrows through her books. On her birthday, he refuses to reenact the paternal inscription, calling it "childish." She goes to a mirror and tries to write on herself but gives up in frustration. We then see, for the first time, a page of her diary as she composes it (while a rectangular image of her grim, stilted marriage ceremony comes into view center-frame). Soon an English subtitle translates for us: "Things that irritate: Boorish sportsmen," while a rectangular image of archers (including her husband) opens up in the middle. Clearly, like Shōnagon's, Nagiko's "pillow book" comprises lists, but, in her case, they will all be "negative." (Another thing that "irritates" her is "prejudice against literature"—a clear foible of her mate.) Later, her husband admits that he reads her diary (a decided breach of trust), and we see a page of it (stamped with her *hanko* seal). This reminds us of the fact that, as Béatrice Fraenkel notes, such pictorial marks originally stood in for the writer's signature and were "the sign of identity and validation *par excellence*."[72] The page Nagiko is writing reads (in English): "I don't like this house." Her spouse inquires rudely: "What's all this English?" He then sets fire to her diary and we see a close-up of its pages with flames superimposed over them. A center rectangle soon opens up with an image of pages actually (not virtually) being immolated—reminding us of a similar act in *Misery*. The scene of her marital breakup is followed by a shot of Shōnagon's *Pillow Book* with a female voiceover reading about sad farewells (hardly the case in Nagiko's break with her spouse). But the sequence also superimposes black-and-white footage of Nagiko leaving her home as a bride, truly a poignant goodbye.

It is after her marriage collapses that Nagiko first asks men to write on her body. In one scene, we watch a man inscribe her back with pictograms, as her voiceover says that the scent of paper reminds her of skin. In another instance, she is calligraphed by an old man as she reads passages from *The Pillow Book;* we then cut to a shot of Shōnagon, who recites the following line: "If writing did not exist, what terrible depressions we would suffer." Nagiko asks the elderly man to sign his name to the text (and offers the sole of her foot), although he has already stamped her with his *hanko* seal. Then, desiring a replay of the paternal act, she asks him to write her name on her body. She also hires professional calligraphers to inscribe her, including one who writes in Arabic (a language she cannot understand), and another who specializes in mathematical symbols (inscribing addition problems on her back and subtraction problems on her front).

Eventually, she meets Jerome in a café and has him write in four languages on her back. Following this, she leans on a white sofa pillow and "prints" the words on its surface. Here, of course, we are reminded of André Bazin's notion of the photographic image as a kind of "transfer" of reality onto celluloid.[73] When Nagiko rejects Jerome, accusing him of scribbling versus writing, he retorts that she should train him by "using [his] body like the pages of a book—[her] book." She runs off, but that night, while taking a bath, she writes the following on her fogged up bathroom mirror in Japanese: "Treat me like the page of a book."[74] She then picks up a brush and writes ideograms on her midriff. (Interestingly, the walls of her room are decorated in huge, seemingly projected, Japanese letters.) Later, we see a close-up of black ink running down the drain of her white tub like the blood in *Psycho* (1960)—an association that reminds us of the parallel between ink and blood in *The Diary of a Country Priest*. This sequence is followed by images of Nagiko's diary pages containing comparisons like those made by Shōnagon: "an instep like a half open book" (the latter portrayed as an image center-screen), or "a belly like an upturned saucer"—thus, she links literary and bodily metaphors. Significantly (given Gilbert and Gubar's notion of the historic prevalence of male authors), Nagiko writes: "A penis like a pickled cucumber or sea slug—not a writing instrument at all."

She then finds numerous men to mark: the first being an English gent whom her friend Hoki (Yutaka Honda) photographs. He lies in bed with words on his torso and an open book covering his face. In this particular instance, her body is inscribed as well and she reclines next to him and snapshots of the two are taken (rectangles open within the frame to show us the captured images). Hoki suggests that she try to publish her writing and that he transcribe her words from skin to paper (literalizing the notion of "flesh made word"). When a publisher rejects Nagiko's manuscript, she decides to try to seduce him (ironically modeling herself on her father). When she goes to his office, however, she recognizes him as the man who, years ago, prostituted her father, and she sees Jerome emerging from his inner sanctum, clearly more sexual prey.

She then decides to seduce Jerome in retaliation. He drives away from the publishing house and she uses her palm to write down his license plate number (here, her body functioning as notepad), hailing a cab to follow him. She finds him in a café and a complex frame shows us the scene, with his license plate pictured in a box, center-screen, and the French words (as subtitles) of a song that is playing.[75] When it comes time to pay the tab, Jerome has no money so she covers the cost herself, but she writes an IOU on her hand. She then photocopies it and gives him the paper—her skin now acting as a bill and a template for printing.

Although Nagiko continues to inscribe men, she periodically succumbs to the practice herself. Significantly, at one point, Jerome writes the Lord's Prayer on her arms and torso: "Our father who art in heaven hallowed be thy name . . ."—an act that returns her (through text) to her father's discourse on God signing His creations. Here it is she, however, who controls the Holy Scripture. On the other hand, although male genitalia have been frequently visible in the film, when the camera pans Nagiko's body here, her hands cover her sex—as though it were threatening or lacked visuality. Later, she tells Jerome that she would like him to perform her father's birthday ritual. He complies, though it is she who repeats the verbal incantation as he inscribes her body—assuming some authority. As we watch the scene, a rectangle opens up center-frame with a monochrome image of Nagiko as a child (thus mixing color and black-and-white as well as past and present).

It is at this point that Jerome suggests that Nagiko write on him and that he take that corporeal text to his publisher, urging him to print it. Thus, a second man (the first being Hoki) serves as intermediary to her authorship. As she shaves his body (to prepare it as a writing surface), she first inscribes letters in the cream she has applied. Soon we see him covered with ink—and labeled "The First Book of Thirteen." When Jerome appears before the publisher, the man is ecstatic: he begins to kiss the symbols on Jerome's body and command his assistants to transcribe them. (Twelve other men will be similarly marked and sent to the publisher—Books of: The Innocent, The Exhibitionist, The Idiot, The Impotent, The Seducer, The Youthful, The Secret, The Silent, The Betrayed, The False Start, etc.) Unfortunately, Jerome also has sex with the publisher despite the fact that Nagiko expects him to return to her apartment. She becomes violently jealous and refuses ever to see him again. Distraught, Jerome takes Hoki's advice and feigns death (like Romeo), and Hoki provides him with medicine to accomplish the ruse. Jerome goes to Nagiko's apartment, ingests numerous pills (as screens-within-the-screen show written numerals), and dies on her bed, with Shōnagon's *The Pillow Book* covering his genitals. When Nagiko discovers him, she inscribes him with The Book of the Lover, and then burns her library, diaries, and papers. Eventually, the publisher exhumes Jerome's body, flays his skin, and makes a book from it that he fetishistically embraces as though a living man. We also see his workers dump

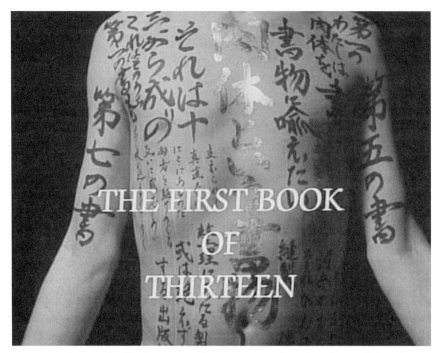

FIGURE 34. The inscribed body of Jerome (Ewan McGregor) in *The Pillow Book* (1996).

Jerome's internal organs in the garbage—reminding us of the deceased's full corporeal being. When Nagiko's final human "book" is delivered to the publisher (that "Of the Dead"), the camera focuses on the inscribed man's body, while Nagiko's voiceover translates the message, which chastises the publisher for having violated her father, desecrated her beloved, and lived too long. The inscribed man takes out a razor and slashes the neck of the publisher, who immediately expires. We assume that the man will return "The Book of the Lover" to Nagiko.

When, earlier, another of Nagiko's "human books" arrived at the publisher's to display its textual body, a series of intriguing titles were superimposed over the man's image, asking the following questions about authorship:

Where is a book before it is born?
Who are a book's parents?
Does a book need two parents—a mother and a father?
Can a book be born inside another book?
Where is the parent book of books?
How old does a book have to be before it can give birth?

Talking about the "birth" of books clearly likens them to humans (specifically children), as do all the references to a book's "parents." Asking whom the latter might be gives a human face to the author (rather than constituting her as an "effect"). Asking whether an artistic work can only issue from the conjunction of male and female forces raises questions about the gendering of creation. Inquiring whether a "book can be born inside another book" reminds us of Greenaway's technique of opening up one frame within another. On the other hand, several queries imply that books (not humans) beget books—raising the issue of literary influence and shoving the author back into the closet or grave.

This talk of "birthing" connects with the final episode of the film in which Nagiko returns to Japan, pregnant (ostensibly by Jerome). She takes The Book of the Lover (comprised of his skin) and puts it in an urn, topping it with a plant, and adding water—thus preparing to glean life from death. There is a flashback to the childhood birthday at which her aunt first read to her from Shōnagon's text, and we learn that Nagiko turns twenty-eight today. Her voiceover declares herself ready to write her own pillow book. As a page of her calligraphy fills the screen, a center frame depicts a flashback to Nagiko showering, accompanied by the title "Warm falling rain." Other such words and inserted images follow (Nagiko in a tub with the caption "Quiet water"). Rather than listing negative items, she is finally ready to highlight "that [which] make[s] the heart beat faster." Now, it is her maid (played by the actress who depicted her aunt) who inscribes her body—specifically her belly—with greetings of good fortune for the fetus.

Later, Nagiko will write birthday greetings on her baby's face; although, as she does this, an image of her father appears within the frame and his voice intones the traditional incantation. Despite his reentry, female authorship has gained strength, as evidenced by Nagiko's calligraphic act, and her creation of a child. As Nagiko breastfeeds her infant, she lowers her kimono and we see that her body is now covered by a tattoo (mixing calligraphic and pictorial icons)—returning us to the bodily discourse of *Irezumi*.

EPILOGUE: INTIMATIONS OF MORTALITY

But embodied authorship and extended works of corporeal writing are not limited to fictional dramas like *Irezumi* or *The Pillow Book*. In 2003, Shelley Jackson launched her "Ineradicable Stain" project, by which she voiced the intention of composing a story, word by word, on the skin of different people. Her interest in the body was already clear from *The Melancholy of Anatomy*, a collection of stories bearing titles like "Heart," "Nerve," "Hair," and "Blood." Her solicitation of volunteers for the "Ineradicable Stain" project read as follows:

> Writer Shelley Jackson invites participants in a new work entitled "Skin." Each participant must agree to have one word of the story tattooed upon his or her body. The text will be published nowhere else, and the author will not permit it to be summarized, quoted, described, set to music, or adapted for film, theater, television or any other medium. The full text will be known only to participants, who

may, but need not choose to establish communication with one another. In the event that insufficient participants come forward to complete the first and only edition of the story, the incomplete version will be considered definitive. If no participants come forward, this call itself is the work. . . . Participants must accept the word [or word plus punctuation mark] they are given, but they may choose the site of their tattoo, with the exception of words naming specific body parts, which may be anywhere but the body part named. Tattoos must be in black ink and a classic book font. Words in fanciful fonts will be expunged from the work. When the work has been completed, participants must send a signed and dated close-up of the tattoo to the author, for verification only. . . . Author retains copyright. . . . From this time on, participants will be known as "words." They are not understood as carriers or agents of the texts they bear, but as its embodiments. As a result, injuries to the printed texts, such as dermabrasion, laser surgery, tattoo cover work or the loss of body parts, will not be considered to alter the work.

Jackson's website informs us that, as of April 2010, she had enlisted 1,875 of the requisite 2,095 participants necessary to complete her story. Evidently, librarians signed up in droves.[76]

Several intriguing issues about authorship arise in her "call." Given that it is posted on a website called "Ineradicable *Stain*," the tattoos she solicits seem to be given a negative valence, with overtones of filth or evil. Participants must accept the word and/or punctuation mark they are assigned, and must have it tattooed in an acceptable publishing font. If the word refers to a body part, they cannot have it tattooed on that organ (as did Jerome in *The Pillow Book*, when he wrote the Yiddish word for breast on Nagiko's bosom). Participants will be known as "words"—thus dehumanizing and fragmenting them. Furthermore, "they are not understood as carriers or agents of the texts they bear, but [merely] as its embodiments." Whether or not they decide, at some later point, to remove the tattoo in question from their skin, the words remain as part of Jackson's photographic and narrative archive. Though only participants will ever know the complete text of Jackson's story, she will own the "copyright" to the totality of words emblazoned on their skin.

On her website, Jackson posts photos of the first word inscribed for her project —"skin," tattooed on the inside of her right wrist (the authorial hand) in Baskerville font, also giving credit to tattoo artist Tabare Grazioso. Furthermore, she provides a video "excerpt" of her story thus far, as told by consecutive images of words tattooed on participants' bodies as each voices the word involved. Thus, the viewer/listener can string together sentences of the text-in-progress. It begins: "Skin. After the fall we came to in [*sic*] another place. We don't remember who we are but we are certain that we are not dead." In her project, not only do we have a multiplication of "authors" (though they might be deemed tattoo artists or "words"), but we have an embodiment of text. Furthermore, her mention of "the fall" (if taken biblically) reminds us of the passage in Paul Auster's *New York*

Trilogy that relates this moment to language: "After the fall . . . names became detached from things; words devolved into a collection of arbitrary signs; language had been severed from God. The story of the Garden, therefore, records not only the fall of man, but the fall of language."[77]

Especially interesting is the focus in Jackson's story on death. Jackson claims that her work will never achieve the longed-for immortality of art, since she will allow no adaptations, and it will perish as do the people comprised by it. As she notes in her call for volunteers: "Only the death of words effaces them from the text. As words die the story will change; when the last word dies the story will also have died."

Clearly, the "death of words" will include her own, since the very title of the work is inscribed on her skin. So, here (through embodiment) the dreaded "Death of the Author" is not only anticipated but desired and celebrated. Though, ironically, her website is called "*Ineradicable* Stain," neither the verbal mark nor its literary creator will have proven indestructible.

8 STEALING BEAUTY

The Reader, the Critic, and the
Appropriation of the Authorial Voice

> Books are objects. On a table, on shelves, in store windows, they wait for
> someone to come and deliver them from their materiality.... Made of paper
> and ink, they lie where they are put until the moment someone shows an
> interest in them.
>
> —Georges Poulet, "Criticism and the Experience"

As Georges Poulet notes, the writer does not work in a vacuum. When
a manuscript is completed it enters a broader universe, waiting for someone else
to "show an interest" in it. Among those who do are readers, editors, and critics.
In this chapter, we will examine films that highlight two of these roles. But before doing so, we mention a work that touches on all three—albeit across a temporal divide: Stephen Daldry's *The Hours* (2002), based on Michael Cunningham's novel.

The film tells the tale of three women. First is the historical figure of Virginia
Woolf (Nicole Kidman), who is seen in short segments over a period of some
twenty years, battling mental illness as she composes her work. Here, we often see
close-ups of her hand gripping a pen, scratching words on manuscript pages, or
we view sheets of paper strewn haphazardly on her office floor. Privilege is given
to her writing *Mrs. Dalloway* (1925), a novel that considers twenty-four hours in
the life of an upper-class London housewife preparing for a party she will throw
that evening. In so doing, she encounters an old love and hears of a World War I
veteran's suicide. Both events (and the dull get-together she organizes) make her
doubt her achievement of happiness. The second female character is Laura Brown
(Julianne Moore), a depressed, suburban California 1950s wife and mother who
is struggling to prepare a birthday dinner for her husband—clearly a parallel to
Woolf's heroine. Significantly, she is reading *Mrs. Dalloway*, and, like its protagonist, she has misgivings about the value of her conventional existence, leading her
to consider suicide (echoing Woolf's termination of her life, and that of the veteran
in her novel). The third character is Clarissa Vaughan (Meryl Streep)—whose

FIGURE 35 (*top*). Virginia Woolf (Nicole Kidman) writing *Mrs. Dalloway* in *The Hours* (2002).
FIGURE 36 (*bottom*). Laura Brown (Julianne Moore) reading Virginia Woolf's *Mrs. Dalloway* in *The Hours* (2002).

first name is the same as Mrs. Dalloway's. Clarissa is a New York book editor who is arranging a celebration for poet Richard Brown (Ed Harris)—her ex-lover and (possibly) client—who is receiving a prestigious award. Significantly, his nickname for her is Mrs. Dalloway. Clarissa's contemporary story is interspersed with those of the other two women, adding a third time period to the mix. At any one moment, the tale of one character may switch (through an unanticipated cut) to that of another. To tie the plots together further, we often hear Virginia Woolf's voice (really Kidman's) attached to images of the other women. Moreover, we learn toward the film's end that Richard (who is suffering from AIDS) is the son of Laura Brown. When he jettisons himself from his loft window, we suspect that his suicide is not merely a result of his illness, but of childhood trauma caused by his mother's desertion of her family. The film closes with Clarissa's party cancelled and its shaken hostess left to ponder the cruel and senseless vagaries of life.

What *The Hours* accomplishes is to break the vacuum seal around the author and (as Poulet notes) to "deliver" her work "from [its] materiality" (the manuscript pages viewed in the film)—connecting it to the lives of others—readers, editors (and, by extension, critics). As Poulet observes, the writer must wait "until the moment someone shows an interest in" her work—whether it be hours, years, decades, or centuries later. Thus, Laura Brown in the 1950s is profoundly affected by reading Woolf's novel, seeming to find in it troubling reverberations of her vapid life and justifications for rejecting it. Modern-day editor Clarissa Vaughan is an incarnation of Mrs. Dalloway—a sophisticated social player melancholy about her lost love (Richard), shocked at his suicide, and disillusioned with her future. Thus, the author (Woolf) has been shown to transform lives (Laura) and encapsulate personages (Vaughan), both fictional and real. Of course, the film's vision of the writer is one we have encountered earlier—mentally unstable and haunted by death. As Woolf states in the film (while working on *Mrs. Dalloway*), it is not her heroine that must die, but the poet—the demise of the author proclaimed once more.

THE READER

While not as broad as *The Hours*, Italo Calvino's *If on a Winter's Night a Traveler* does contain a discourse on the reader and the writer. In "From the Diary of Silas Flannery," we enter the mind of a novelist who is obsessed with watching a female reader he views through a spyglass (an image that brings to mind the camera's lens). He says: "Every day, before starting work, I look at the woman. . . . I say to myself that the result of the unnatural effort to which I subject myself, writing, must be the respiration of this reader, the operation of reading turned into a natural process."[1] He remarks that "at times [he is] gripped by an absurd desire: that the sentence [he is] about to write be the one the woman is reading, at that same moment."[2] (Ironically, this is what Daldry accomplishes in *The Hours* by cutting between Woolf composing and Laura reading.) Moreover, Calvino's protagonist asserts that "reading is necessarily an individual act, far more than writing" because the author must compose with a universal eye, while the reader's "mental circuits" are personalized.[3] This contrast of readerly singularity and authorial anonymity is summed up in the enigmatic phrase "*I* read, therefore *it* writes" (my emphasis). Finally, the novelist wonders what it would be like were the reader "to train a spyglass" on him writing—thus making a spectacle of the literary act (like Blue's surveillance of Black in Paul Auster's *New York Trilogy*).[4]

On a more theoretical level, Roland Barthes considers the reader in "The Death of the Author," when he remarks that with the literary artist's "demise" comes "the birth of the reader," a figure ignored in "Classic criticism."[5] Hence for Barthes, reception of the text is inextricably tied to creation. It is the reader, indeed, that marks the "place" where the "multiple writings" that a text comprises come to be "focused"—as through a photographic lens.[6] Like the author, however, the reader should have no "history, biography, [or] psychology" but should simply be "that *someone* who holds together in a single field all the traces by which the written text is constituted." For many, however, Barthes's formulation of the reader is vague and problematic. As Sean Burke remarks, it is "no less ambiguous and mystified than the 'Author' whom it sought to supplant."[7]

Other theorists have commented on the congruence between author and reader—most notably Poulet in "Criticism and the Experience of Interiority." He describes how a reader's mind, in a sense, is "invaded" by the writer's: "I am aware of a rational being, of a consciousness; the consciousness of another, no different from the one I automatically assume in every human being I encounter, except that in this case the consciousness is open to me, welcomes me, lets me look deep inside itself, and even allows me, with unheard-of-license, to think what it thinks and feel what it feels."[8] Thus, the reader is prey to "the thoughts of another, and yet it is [he or she] who [is] their subject."[9] As Poulet continues: "Whenever I read, I mentally pronounce an *I* and yet the *I* which I pronounce is not myself."[10] This process positions the reader within the fiction: "[The reader is] inside it; it is inside [the reader]; there is no longer either outside or inside."[11]

Poulet's observations are stunningly relevant to the French film *La Lectrice* (1988), directed by Michel Deville, which is about the improbable topic of reading books. The subject is unlikely because, as is the case with writing, the act of reading is static and un-cinematic. As stated earlier, Garrett Stewart has considered the portrayal of reading in another visual medium, painting, and notes (in a similar vein) that such pictures involve "stasis, blankness, introversion . . . not normally the stuff of scenic drama."[12] Despite this drawback, he finds the "reading scene" a prevalent and resonant genre of pictorial art. Asking why this is the case, he concludes that "in its most ambitious instances, [the 'reading scene' can] recruit narrative energy even while removing it from view."

Stewart's thoughts are relevant to *La Lectrice*, which begins as a young man, Philippe (Christian Ruché), and a woman, Constance (Miou-Miou), are lying in bed, a book covering the latter's face. We next hear Constance's humming offscreen in the bathroom while Philippe opens the volume. When the camera moves in closer, we see its title: *La Lectrice* by Raymond Jean (the book on which the film is based). When Constance returns to the room, she accuses Philippe of "stealing her book." Philippe responds that he would like to read it but that his eyes are tired. She volunteers to read it to him, boasting that she has a nice voice. He is reluctant, remarking that it will take one and a half hours to complete the narrative (not coincidentally, the approximate running time of the film we are watching). Before beginning, Constance tells Philippe that she is pregnant (a fact that seems to please him), but she also confesses that she has damaged their car (a fact that

does not). Sternly, he orders her to read. She does so and we see the novel's narrative visualized onscreen (as a literary story within a filmic one).

The tale Constance tells is about a woman named Marie who is also played by
Miou-Miou (and so is visually identical to Constance). In a conversation between
Marie and her friend Françoise (Sylvie Laporte), the latter compliments Marie's
voice (further identifying Marie with Constance) and suggests that she use this
asset to be a professional "reader." While Marie is skeptical of this role (in an era of
audio books), she decides to place an ad for her services in the paper. We briefly
cut back to Constance reading in bed to Philippe—to reestablish the fact that the
drama we watch onscreen is, in part, the visualized narrative of a novel (and not
"real life" or the "present" moment—which remain the couple in bed). Intermit-
tently throughout the film, we revisit this scene as a means of restoring the base-
line. Here we find a structure that, perhaps, resembles *How Is Your Fish Today?*
which alternates between scenes of a screenwriter working and visions of the scenario he is imagining.

When we return to the novelistic story, we see Marie place an ad for her services. A male advertising agent is wary of her "ambiguous" notice and suggests
that she replace the words "young lady" with "person" and omit a phone number.
Clearly, he anticipates that individuals will interpret her advertisement as one for
illicit liaisons. Despite his chaste concern, Marie's voiceover informs us that he
stares at her legs as she leaves. Her acoustic commentary will be heard intermit-
tently throughout the film—allowing viewers the same pleasure and experience
of her voice as the people to whom she reads. We are thus gratified by what, in another context (writing about song), Barthes has called the vocal "grain": "the very
precise space (genre) of the encounter between a language and a voice."[13] While,
for Barthes, the reader (like the author) should have no "history, biography, [or]
psychology," in this film she does—but of a fictional kind.

A significant aspect of Marie/Constance's status as reader is that she is female.
For Stewart, the "feminine body" in painting is the "model of a stereotyped readerly stance."[14] Sometimes, she is painted as a nude (as in Theodore Roussel's *The
Reading Girl* [1866–67]); if not naked, she is often "sexualized" or seen as a "liber-
tine." This, of course, squares with the advertising agent's response to the wording
of Marie's newspaper notice. Even more insulting, many art critics argue that the
woman pictured, though holding a book, is not "really" reading—as though she
lacks the intelligence to do so.[15]

Within the novelistic story embedded in the film, Marie has a boyfriend, Jean
(who is played by the same actor cast as Philippe)—so again, for the viewer, there
is an identity between "real" and "fabricated" worlds (as Poulet has told us, in
reading there is no difference between inside and out). Marie asks Jean to choose
a book that she can read to her first customer and he suggests "The Hand" by Guy
de Maupassant, remarking that the writer is "easy and pleasant for all ages." This
is the first of a series of actual authors and texts to be mentioned and quoted in
the film as Marie becomes enmeshed in her new job. As Philippe utters the title,

Constance puts her hand on his lips—a strange gesture, given that Maupassant's story is eerily supernatural and concerns a dismembered hand that appears to have killed a man who has murdered another to acquire it. Clearly, Jean has not been an insightful reader of Maupassant.

Much of the remaining film alternates between shots of Marie cheerfully walking down the streets of an old city (Arles) accompanied by jaunty music, and scenes of her encountering various clients—perhaps establishing a parallel between physical and imaginative journeys (the latter accomplished through literature). In reading to others, Marie assumes the position of those we have encountered in other films: for instance, the friend who reads to Bauby in *The Diving Bell and the Butterfly*. Marie's situation also reminds us of the pictorial works that Stewart calls scenes of "dual reading." One such painting is even called *Reading Aloud* (1884, by Albert Moore), which directly alludes to Marie's job. Stewart sees a loss of subjectivity in the act of reading to others. As he remarks: "Under secular humanism, reading to oneself is the proof of that self. . . . But once this effect is externalized in a second body, the composition stands in danger of surrendering the magnetic aura of text altogether."[16]

Marie's first client is Eric (Régis Royer), a handicapped teenager in a wheelchair who selects "A Tress of Hair" by Maupassant for her to read (significantly, the section of that story she reads aloud begins with the line: "I was sauntering in Paris on a bright, sunny morning"—words that remind us of Marie's urban travels). Like "The Hand," it is a rather sinister tale about a man who buys an antique cabinet and finds within it a secret drawer containing a lock of a woman's hair from which he derives erotic gratification. As Marie reads the story, shots focus on her knees and on Eric gazing at them—making clear that he is more interested in her corporeal presence than in fiction (here we recall that the film began with a couple reading in bed, which already tied literature to sexual intimacy). Of course, the topic of Maupassant's narrative (a man aroused by a female body part) has a clear relation to the scene we are watching. Like the protagonist of the story (who almost loses consciousness after caressing the hair), Eric suddenly faints and is taken to the hospital. A nurse accusingly asks Marie, "What did you read [to him]?" and cautions her to be more "careful." A bizarre doctor informs Marie that Eric has choked and has experienced visions of hair; he reminds her that Maupassant ended up "in an asylum."[17] These statements are the first of many allusions in the film to the "dangers" of literature—both for the writer and the reader. Later, a police detective who interviews Marie (because her advertisement has "aroused his curiosity") warns: "Reading is fine, but look where it leads."

Future encounters with Eric are equally strange. At one point he requests that Marie don a particular dress, indicating a certain fetishistic predilection. Revealing that he is no naïf, he asks Marie to read Baudelaire's *The Flowers of Evil*, a request that makes his mother (Brigitte Catillon) nervous. One poem, "The Jewels," is about a woman lying naked, adorned only with baubles. Baudelaire talks of her belly, breasts, waist, and hips and compares her to a Moorish concubine. Marie also reads "The Cats," which mentions the animals' "fertile loins" full of "magic sparks," and which deems the creatures "ardent lovers" and "friends of sensual pleasure." Again, the relation between the literature read and the lives lived is obvious. Interestingly, Marie now purposely raises the hem of her skirt to show Eric her thighs, aware of his need for physical stimulation (beyond verbal address). Finally, when a blind friend, Joel (Hito Jaulmes), visits Eric, the latter asks Marie to read *The Blind Man and the Parasitic*, a fable by Florian that clearly and perversely mirrors the impaired states of the two young men (shades of Luis Buñuel). Before Marie reads the fable (in an illustrated version), however, the two boys argue about who will enjoy it more, given their varied disabilities. Eric says he will find it more beautiful because he can see (and we suspect his visual object is Marie as well as the book). Joel says it will be better for him because he can imagine. This dialogue raises an issue relevant to the film and to the concept of word versus image, since when Marie reads verbal passages the audience is, like Joel, essentially blind—in that, except for one occasion (described below), the images we see do not represent the story being told. Hence, like those to whom she reads we must imagine events happening (while looking at other things).

The relation between literature and sexuality (a subject broached in our discussions of *Swimming Pool* and *The Tango Lesson*) is further advanced in Marie's encounters with other individuals. In a scene in which she meets with Françoise to discuss her career, the latter suggests she read a book entitled *The Skirt*.[18] Unlike other instances in which we focus on Marie's face as she reads or we hear her offscreen voice, here we get a sudden visualization of the story (actually a visualization-within-a-visualization, like enmeshed Chinese boxes). A husband and wife walk down a winding alley in an urban "red light" district. The man impulsively goes off with a prostitute, as his wife sullenly waits for him outside. Another man (a stranger) comes along and leads her away to a hotel room where the two copulate. Eventually, she returns to her husband who is waiting for her in a café. He advises her to forget about the day's occurrences.

What is significant about this story is that, later, Marie actually prostitutes herself in her meetings with another client, a businessman (played by Patrick Chesnais) who seems interested in learning about literature only so that he will appear cultured.[19] Marie at first rejects him, only to return at a later date with Marguerite Duras's *The Lover* in hand. As she recites a passage about a woman in semi-transparent clothing, he admits to feeling a tremor of desire. On a third visit, she reads to him in bed and the two have awkward and comic sex. Finally, one of Marie's clients is an elderly magistrate (Pierre Dux)—a widower ensconced in a stately apartment.[20] Almost immediately (and inappropriately) upon her entry, he mentions "unsatisfied desires" and asks her to read from the Marquis de Sade's *120 Days of Sodom*. Her voiceover informs us that she is apprehensive about this choice but feels that her profession requires her to proceed. As she recites a rather scandalous passage (involving graphic details of lewd sexual acts), her narration states that she is "pleased with [her]self" since her "voice did not tremble." Later,

FIGURE 37. Marie (Miou-Miou) reads to a client in bed in *La Lectrice* (1988).

however, when he invites two friends to listen to her recite the same novel, she walks out—refusing to be a group spectacle. For her, there is something sacrosanct about the one-to-one relationship of reader and listener, even when the intent is pornographic.

Marie's frequent mention of her vocal abilities draws attention to the issue of the female voice—clearly at the center of a film about a woman who reads aloud for a living. The fact that hers is deemed "pleasant" relates to the fact that research has shown a woman's voice is often preferred to a man's, especially "when the text [being read is] reflective (for example, poetry or abstract passages)."[21] Moreover, it has been noted that the "default" voice for such high-tech tools as cell phones and global positioning devices is female. In a CNN web posting about this phenomenon, Stanford University professor Clifford Nass is quoted as saying, "It's much easier to find a female voice that everyone likes than a male voice that everyone likes." He continues: "It's a well-established phenomenon that the human brain is developed to like female voices" (Griggs).

In feminist film studies, attention has been paid to the female voice in relation to the technique of cinematic narration. As critics like Sarah Kozloff and Amy Lawrence have noted, this use of a woman's voice has been uncommon in dramatic movies, where it has usually been a man who narrates the story (as in the classic films noir of the 1940s). When the female voiceover has been utilized, it has occurred more commonly in avant-garde film (as in Chantal Akerman's *News from Home* [1977] or Rea Tajiri's *History and Memory* [1991]). In *La Lectrice*, however, it is not simply employed but used reflexively since the quality and performance of Marie's voice is remarked on repeatedly (it is "pleasant," it doesn't "tremble"). In one scene, she also stands before a mirror practicing her reading skills, whereupon she thinks (as rendered in voiceover narration), "I'm afraid of hearing my own voice . . . I'm wrong, one does not hear oneself." This sequence tends to underscore the precarious relation of the female voice to the self within a masculine culture, and seems to stage the alienation effect of the "mirror stage" on an acoustic level. This vocal distanciation seems underscored in yet another sequence (unique in the film), in which, as Marie speaks with her former teacher, her lips move silently as her voiceover narration tells us what she said (but not in a synchronized fashion).

Interestingly, attention to the female voice in the film also helps to make sense of a moment in its opening that otherwise is puzzling. Why within the narrative logic of the film "must" Constance be pregnant (when it seems to have no future relation to the plot)? Here we are reminded of the work of Kaja Silverman. In *The Acoustic Mirror* (a title that seems entirely appropriate to the aforementioned scene of Marie at the looking glass), Silverman specifically investigates the maternal aspects of the female voice, since, as she argues, it is the first one a child hears even when it is still within the womb. As she notes: "The maternal voice functions as the first voice-over, and the first voice-off—as the generator of sounds that proceed from beyond the child's range of vision, or that precede its ability to see."[22] In addition, of course, within a traditional culture that assigns childrearing largely to women, mothers are the primary oral storytellers (recall that the film begins with Constance reading to Philippe in bed, like a mother to a son). When not reading to children, however, the female reader becomes suspect and her act is seen as potentially seductive as opposed to nurturing, hence Marie's continued insistence that she be viewed as a "professional." Perhaps this is also the reason that she is so upset when her ad mistakenly runs in the "work at home" section, since reading in a domestic context is for mothers. Significantly, the men in the film are generally poor readers. Philippe is too tired to read; the ad agent misunderstands the intentions of Marie's notice; Jean misreads Maupassant; and Eric's senile grandfather repeats the same verse of poetry over and over. Thus, the seemingly random detail of Constance's pregnancy overlays the film with a stratum of maternal discourse. Clearly, in several cases (those of Eric, Joel, and later the girl Coralie), Marie even stands in for the parent.

While the film is certainly about literature (and the act of its reading), from another perspective it can also be seen as confronting authorship—since particular (and real) writers are matched with specific clients in recognition of the latter's fantasies or needs: sexual or macabre selections for Eric, erotic ones for the businessman and the judge, and whimsical ones for Coralie. In this sense, though Marie is only a reader, she becomes a kind of literary artist herself. As Roger Ebert writes in a review of the film: "As she reads to [people], a curious process begins to take place. *She becomes, in a way, the author of the books*" (my emphasis).[23] What he means by this is that she takes on the coloring of each writer: "The teenager idealizes her as a romantic. . . . And the businessman, of course, wants to sleep with her." Here, Ebert's perceptions about *La Lectrice* echo Poulet's sense of the author taking "possession" of the reader.[24] As he notes: "Reading . . . is the act in which the subjective principle which I call *I* is modified in such a way that I no longer have the right, strictly speaking, to consider it as my *I*. I am on loan to another, and this other thinks, feels, suffers, and acts within me."[25]

In the film, this process of identification between reader and author (as well as listening subject) continues with Marie's other clients, including an old, wealthy Hungarian general's widow (María Casares) to whom she reads Leo Tolstoy's *War and Peace*, passages from Marx, and Maxim Gorki's *Lenin and the Russian Peasant*.[26] For the matriarch, Marie becomes an intellectual and a radical whose support she solicits to mark the anniversary of Lenin's death. With the child Coralie (Charlotte Farran), Marie reads Lewis Carroll's *Alice in Wonderland*, but she gets carried away and allows herself (at the suggestion of the girl) to take her to an amusement park (leading to charges of kidnapping). Of course, in the very act of reading the writer's words aloud, Marie also articulates the "authorial voice," shifting it from metaphor to speech act. In a sense, this can be seen as a gesture of "appropriation" on her part (compensatory, perhaps, for the way in which the reader is alternatively "possessed" by the author—having his or her "innermost subjective being" taken over).[27] This complex question of appropriation is signaled early on in the film when Constance accuses Philippe of "stealing" her book.

Given that the film announces a virtual catalog of canonical authors (Tolstoy, Baudelaire, Maupassant, Gorki, Sade, Duras, etc.) we are reminded of Michel Foucault's essay "What Is an Author?" In it, Foucault extends Barthes's theories to examine "the empty space left by the author's disappearance"—its "gaps and fault lines, its new demarcations, and the reapportionment of this void."[28] What fascinates him is not the personhood of the author but his or her *name*, and he seeks to investigate how it functions. First of all, an authorial name "is a variable that accompanies only certain texts to the exclusion of others"—reflecting the relative value of discourses within a culture (e.g., novels versus e-mails).[29] Second, such a name "can group together a number of texts and thus differentiate them from others"—for example, the collected works of Shakespeare.[30] Third, a name can mark a text as an "object of appropriation," a form of "property" regulated by a "penal code" (e.g., copyright).[31] Finally, in traditional literary criticism an author can be "recovered" from a text by the critic's employment of "devices strongly reminiscent of Christian exegesis."

Significantly, throughout the film there are references not only to books and authors but also to their study—adding a discourse of literary criticism to that of artistic production (here we recall that Baudelaire's poem "The Cats" speaks of the pets as "scholars" and "friends of learning"). This is not entirely surprising given that Raymond Jean (the author of the novel *La Lectrice*) is also a literary scholar.[32] First we surmise that Marie has formerly been a student of literature, as she visits one of her old teachers several times. After hearing of the mishaps with Eric, he tells Marie to avoid Maupassant or "it will be the morgue next time," rather than the hospital. He suggests she read Émile Zola's *The Masterpiece* (a tale of artists in Paris in the late nineteenth century), which she confesses she does not know. He then begins to recite an unidentified passage (but one that seems to issue from *La Lectrice*) about a female reader employed by a general's widow, reflexively referencing Marie and the elderly woman who will be her next client —adding to the self-conscious nature of the film's narrative structure. Here we should note that the film ends with Constance in bed having completed her reading of *La Lectrice*. She informs Philippe that she is "not through yet" and intends to place an ad for reading services herself. So here Constance and Marie finally merge (as did Rao and Hao in *How Is Your Fish Today?*); the story returns to its inception; the novel within the film becomes the film itself; and inside morphs into outside as in a Mobius strip. Moreover, in her last visit to her professor, he suggests that she open a "school for reading." Thus, Marie is, on some level, not only a reader who supplants and embodies the authors of the texts she intones —but a literary expert as well.

THE CRITIC

> You know who critics are? The men who have failed in literature and art.
>
> —Benjamin Disraeli, *Lothair*

The Critic as Character

While, on one level, we have argued that in reading aloud, Constance/Marie quite literally "appropriates" the authorial voice, it is a "respectful" usurpation that does not alter, critique, or construe the writer's words; in fact, it can be seen, alternatively, as an act of ventriloquism by which the reader willingly surrenders agency (in mouthing the author's words). The critic, however, stands in a different relation to the writer—engaging in an active process of evaluation, contextualization, and interpretation. Clearly, this can be viewed as a stronger form of appropriation. As Donald Pease has noted (in referencing Roland Barthes's seminal article): "Whereas Barthes declares that the author is dead, the text he thereby produces is not without an author. In Barthes's criticism the author returns—but in the displaced form of Barthes's [own] metatextual account of the writing activity. *In this view, then, the critic is the real beneficiary of the separation of an author from a text.* It is the critic, rather than the author or reader, who can render an authoritative account of the . . . work" (my emphasis).[33] Moreover, Michel Foucault sees the critic/theorist as merely another kind of author, one whom we might see as competitive with the more traditional type. As Foucault notes: "I have (previously) discussed the author only in the limited sense of a person to whom the production of a text, a book, or a work can be legitimately attributed. However, it is obvious that even within the realm of discourse *a person can be the author of much more than a book—of a theory, for instance*. . . . For convenience, we could say that such authors occupy a 'transdiscursive' position" (my emphasis).[34]

Taking Pease's and Foucault's lead, we now consider the "rise" of the critic in the contemporary intellectual scene, and approach it through a variety of lenses

—the first involving an examination of how the figure has been positioned in filmic narrative. Here, we again investigate a movie that pursues the issue indirectly, by displacing the subject of cinema onto literature (mimicking Barthes's alleged displacement of literature onto criticism).

Before analyzing the film, however, there is a novel that bears consideration. Provocatively entitled *The Death of the Author* (written by Gilbert Adair), it concerns the career of an American critic named Leopold Sfax. The name's improbable spelling hints that identities are entirely constructed, and its resemblance to the word "fax" emphasizes the notion of copying. Sfax has become famous for what other scholars call The Theory (which we recognize as some combination of deconstructionism and anti-auteurism). As Sfax muses about his rise to success, he thinks: "So it was, with the advent of the Theory, that the Author was to find Himself declared well and truly dead. Since I had demonstrated that it was for language to do the thinking . . . the presence of a human sensibility somehow embedded within that language, within that text, had at last been understood for what it truly was: an absence, a void."[35] Already, we perceive a certain irony since, as Foucault has asserted, theories have authors as well.

As we come to learn, Sfax was born in France and came of age during World War II, when, as a young critic, he wrote for a publication associated with the Vichy government; hence, he was a collaborator. Fortunately, he wrote under the pseudonym Hermes (another dilution of the authorial moniker), and, after having immigrated to the United States, buried that part of his literary output. (Significantly, among other things, Hermes was the patron of literature and a guide to the Underworld.)[36] In light of his embarrassing early publications, Sfax thinks it convenient that he has pioneered theories of deconstruction that argue for the likelihood "of texts being . . . 'misread.' "[37] Hence, he comforts himself with the thought that, should some of his early writings be discovered, he can always claim that they do not mean what they say. He recalls that he once published a piece on "the Jewish question" and "specifically on the Judaization" of France (a term that had been used by Goebbels).[38] As he notes: "Oh, for that unsubtle time I could be subtlety itself! Resolved to retain [an] aloofness of trenchancy and tone. . . . I took pains never to use the Term 'anti-Semitism' without first qualifying it as 'vulgar' or 'primitive.' " Hence, he surmises that anyone discovering his wartime essays and knowing his theories of language would be hard-pressed to determine whether he "held anti-Semitism to be vulgar and primitive . . . or else that [he] was holding out for some 'higher' anti-Semitism, one that would be not vulgar but refined."[39]

For a long while, he is confident that his shameful past will not be revealed (here, Hermes's association with the underworld does not go unnoticed). However, Sfax becomes anxious when a graduate student at New Harbor University, where he teaches, informs him that she plans to write his biography. While he tells her that she will "never get [him]" (meaning understand him), he promises to cooperate.[40]

From one perspective, Sfax is a barely disguised double for Paul de Man, a

Belgian intellectual (known for deconstructionist theory) who immigrated to the United States and eventually taught at Yale (in New Haven, evoked by "New Harbor"). After his death, it surfaced that he had written for European collaborationist newspapers, one notoriously anti-Semitic. What Adair's novel does is imagine how one's theoretical work can have biographical roots and serve to ameliorate one's background. Thus the "death of the author" removes the actual writer from the scene (no matter what his dishonorable past), and deconstructionist views of language make it difficult to hold him responsible for the words he has uttered. On another level (and one more apt for the film we consider below), Adair's novel envisions the tense and contested relation between critic and author. By the end of the narrative, Sfax has killed his biographer (in order to prevent her from discovering the very creator whose existence his theory denies). Hence, the real title of the tale should be *The Death of the Critic* (by the Author's hand). Furthermore, Sfax uses aspects of The Theory to mask his transgression—making his homicidal act seem as "senseless" as the language he has sought to deconstruct. So, like Sarah Morton in *Swimming Pool*, his writing instructs him on how to cover up a crime.

The trope of the novelist plagued by a researcher also comes up in Calvino's *If on a Winter's Night a Traveler*, in which the author is visited by a graduate student who is writing a thesis on his work. Viewing her with hostility, he notes: "I see that my work serves her perfectly to demonstrate her theories . . . but my books seen through her eyes prove unrecognizable to me."[41] He is also appalled by her use of digital technology to analyze literary works. As she tells him: "A suitably programmed computer can read a novel in a few minutes and record the list of all the words contained in the text, in order of frequency." She adds: "That way I can have an already completed reading at hand . . . with an incalculable saving of time."[42] Moreover, from the types of words that often arise, she already knows the work's genre (i.e., *blood*, *cartridge*, *commander* in a war novel).

In some respects, we see elements of Adair's and Calvino's charged dramas played out in the film *Starting Out in the Evening* (2007, directed by Andrew Wagner). It concerns aging writer Leonard Schiller (Frank Langella), who, though once successful, is now forgotten within the world of the New York City literati.[43] After his first two well-received novels (now out of print), Schiller has had problems finishing a third (writer's block rears its ugly head again). Despite this, he has settled into a comfortable retirement in his large Manhattan apartment, working for specified hours each day. He seems content, though largely isolated, aside from his warm relationship with his grown daughter Ariel (Lili Taylor). Into Schiller's calm and scheduled life comes a vibrant and attractive Brown University graduate student, Heather Wolfe (Lauren Ambrose), who has decided to write her master's thesis on his work. In a meeting with Schiller at a coffee shop, she requests a series of interviews. He declines, citing ill health and the need to avoid distractions from work. He does, however, let her accompany him to his apartment to see the room in which he writes and to borrow one of his earlier novels, *The Lost City*. This last request is puzzling since, though she claims not to own it, we have seen her open

FIGURE 38. Author Leonard Schiller (Frank Langella) encounters Heather Wolfe (Lauren Ambrose)—a young woman researching his work in *Starting Out in the Evening* (2007).

this very volume before Schiller arrives at the cafe, staring at his photograph on the dust jacket. Already, the viewer is warned not to trust her.

Once in his apartment, we follow as she parts the opaque glass French doors to his office, entering it as though it were a forbidden (but hallowed) space. She sits in his chair and touches his typewriter—gestures that strike us as a bit unseemly, since the opening shot of the film had positioned him in this very spot. More cunningly, however, she rifles through a drawer of old photographs that depict Schiller with his family and in other informal poses. She grabs a portrait of him as a young man, holds it to her chest, and then hides it in her pocketbook. In exiting the apartment, she is flirtatious, telling Schiller that it might improve his health and work to have a "fascinating young woman in his life." For the moment, however, he stands fast with his decision to refuse her access.

In a later scene (of Schiller greeting Heather in his apartment), we surmise that he has reconsidered and will let her interview him, a process that she grandiosely hopes will "reintroduce" him to the world. We learn that he has done so having seen an article she published in a literary magazine, lending her credibility. In a series of conversations, however, he balks at her impudent questions about his novel-in-progress and her views that he uses his age to "mask" his writing problems, and that he mirrors his life in his work. He counters that he draws from life but "in a spirit of objectivity" and exclaims, "Can't a writer [do that] without being accused of autobiography?" She flatters him, confessing that his novels "set her free" by presenting female characters who control their destinies.

Gradually, despite his reticence, she makes inroads into his universe. He invites her to a literary party, where she ignores him to mingle with the younger shakers and movers. Returning to his apartment, she tempts him sexually, smearing honey on his lips and then asking if they can lie down together. While he continues to resist her erotic advances, she becomes more and more presumptuous in her stance toward him: asking to read his manuscript (though he forbids this practice), accusing him of hiding after life "betrayed" him, opining that he now writes "less nakedly and personally" than in the past. Finally, arriving one day at his apartment unannounced during his sacred "writing hours," she seduces him. Later, he gives her the keys to his flat and offers her books of criticism by Lionel Trilling, Irving Howe, and Edmund Wilson—writers important to him but no longer fashionable. When he tries to kiss her, however, she pulls away and departs abruptly, leaving the volumes behind. Clearly, he realizes that while she has been attracted to the Author, she is not attracted to the man, reminding us again of Calvino's novel. There, when writer Silas Flannery tries to beguile a young fan, she says: " 'I could easily make love with you . . . but . . . the one who interested me was the other, the Silas Flannery who exists in the works of Silas Flannery, independently, of you here.' "[44]

When Schiller suffers a stroke, his daughter blames Heather—chastising her for "shaking things up." After Schiller's hospitalization, Heather visits him at home —cajoling him by saying that his new book will be his best, and that his old works may soon be reprinted. He slowly reaches toward her as though to caress her cheek but, instead, slaps her—the first sign that he comprehends that she is devious, selfish, cruel, and arrogant (a predator like the animal referenced in her last name). Here, again, we think of Calvino's novel in which the writer proclaims: "Readers are my vampires."[45] Schiller thanks Heather for giving "an old man some excitement" and says (with irony) that it has been "good to know her" (a phrase that puts their relationship in the past). As he nods off, she returns the book she originally borrowed as well as the photo she stole, and then exits. In the final scene, we see him abandon his mired manuscript and begin another. The last shot of the film matches the first: Schiller sits at his typewriter (the antique icon of his craft).

In one way, the film is of interest because it dramatizes an infrequently staged affiliation between a critic and her subject—presenting it (not surprisingly) as a highly vexed dyad in which the former entices the latter while secretly bearing him ill will. Read this way, the critic exploits the artist both sexually and professionally and, perhaps, seeks to displace him (hence Heather's thrill at sitting in Schiller's chair). Read another way, however, she does him good. We recall that Schiller continually explains how he waits for his characters to do something interesting —signaling that his block may stem not only from fictional but real inactivity— having walled himself off in his literary lair (with his front door full of metal bolts). From this perspective, despite her cruelty, Heather (as critic) shocks Schiller into abandoning his lackluster project and creating anew. Interestingly, the drama of Schiller and Heather is counterpoised to that of Ariel and her lover Casey (Adrian Lester). While Ariel wants children (and resists using a diaphragm), Casey does not, insisting on a personal and material "barrier" between them. By the end of the narrative, Casey has agreed to remove the "obstacle," as has Schiller—though the former is a celebratory act while the latter a melancholy one. So, as in *La Lectrice*, the metaphor of pregnancy once more functions in tandem with the topic of authorship.

While the premise of *Starting Out in the Evening* is intriguing, that is not what makes it of interest to this project. Rather, it is the text's reference both to photography and movies in articulating its themes (interestingly, photography also appears in *La Lectrice* when the suspicious police chief presents Marie with surveillance shots of her). It is significant that the first time we encounter Heather in the film she is looking at a photograph of Schiller in more youthful times on the dust jacket of one of his novels. Later, she rifles through a box of his family snapshots, stealing one of Schiller as a handsome young man. Finally, she hungrily scans a series of framed photos on his piano. Clearly, the images with which she is enamored speak to her search for the romantic author who is no longer there, the young man she might have met (and loved) in an earlier day. From this viewpoint, her seduction of Schiller is a form of critical time-travel that works until the reality of age difference sinks in. On another register, her fascination with these photographs signifies the critic's desire to know the human behind the text, the person behind the author, to connect the fictional narrative to the historical life. But the photographs she views of Schiller are actually those of Frank Langella, resembling headshots from earlier in his career. So they also address the film viewer/critic —urging her to consider Langella's star text and to position him here in relation to his prior work.

Beyond photography, important references to movies crop up on several occasions within the drama. Once when Ariel visits her father, she brings along some DVDs to watch, which he declines to do (of *Notorious* [1946] and *The Shop around the Corner* [1940]). The former film involves an intrigue propagated by a young woman (an undercover agent) on an older man in order to infiltrate a Nazi spy ring. A key to a room (the wine cellar) figures prominently in the story (as it does in the movie we are watching). The latter film involves a "virtual" relationship conducted by a couple through the mail, which explodes when a flesh-and-blood liaison ensues. Clearly both *Notorious* and *The Shop around the Corner* have narrative resonances in *Starting Out in the Evening*—given their tropes of duplicity and fantasy. One particular statement made by Schiller also seems noteworthy from the perspective of film and photographic theory. When Heather presses him by identifying biographical traces in his work, he replies, annoyed, and in a contradictory fashion: "A writer's words are his fingerprints" but "the writer should be forgotten." Here, we are reminded not only of Barthes's theories but of André Bazin's notion that the film image bears the same relation to reality as a footprint—a sign of the latter's existence but not his existence itself.

The Critic as Star

While a film like *Starting Out in the Evening* makes the critic/scholar a fictional persona within the narrative, in recent years real critics have made their way into filmic texts, sometimes displacing the author. In the early days of laserdisc and DVD releases, critical essays (in print form) were sometimes included as part of the special features (and needed to be advanced frame-by-frame to be read). Even now, Criterion Collection's DVD of John Cassavetes's *Shadows* (1959) comes with an essay (in booklet form) by Gary Giddens, and the company's DVD for Mike Leigh's *Naked* (1993) includes an article by Amy Taubin as liner notes. Most commonly, however, a critic's voice is present on DVDs as a secondary audio track layered over the original work. To examine how such commentaries function, I randomly chose one from my university library. On the Criterion Collection DVD for *The Lady Vanishes* (1938, directed by Alfred Hitchcock), the critic is Bruce Eder (a former film reviewer for the *Village Voice* and *Newsday*), who seems to specialize professionally in this kind of project, with commentaries on digital versions of *Henry V* (1944), *The Thief of Bagdad* (1940), *The Most Dangerous Game* (1932), *49th Parallel* (1941), *Green for Danger* (1946), and *The Browning Version* (1951), among others. Curiously, Eder has no published book or scholarly articles on Hitchcock, despite the virtual cottage industry on that topic.[46] Clearly, DVD commentaries are meant only for those who have already screened a film in its "pristine" form, since, as the critic speaks, the audio track of the film is often muted to the level of inaudibility. So this raises the question of at whom such a discourse is aimed. The most likely audiences are film buffs, students (perhaps preparing a presentation or a paper), scholars (writing on the film), and teachers (preparing a class and wanting some assistance beyond print material).

But what does such a commentary actually accomplish? Here are the types of things it does on the first nine "chapters" (twenty minutes) of *The Lady Vanishes*. Over the credit sequence we learn that the film has a "unique place" in Hitchcock's career, that it is "steeped in irony" and "deceptive." When Eder comments on how the film uses minimal music, he directly addresses us to "listen to the tune we're hearing now" and stops talking to allow us to do so. Shifting our attention to later events in the film, he informs us that this music "is going to be important." Similarly, directing us to future films in the Hitchcock canon, he tells us that *The Lady Vanishes* "points the way to [the director's] most popular Hollywood films." We are then told that an "aerial" establishing shot of the first locale in the film (which depicts a train yard and hotel in mountainous countryside) is a "model shot"—thus destroying any illusion we might have. Eder then informs us that "it's time for introductions"—as various characters commence to appear onscreen, inquiring about the arrival of their train and learning that it has been delayed by an avalanche. At a later point Eder says: "Ah, we're meeting Iris Henderson" (Margaret Lockwood)—the heroine of the piece. When the camera focuses in close-up on a cuckoo clock on the wall, we are told that "this is a nice touch" and that its sound (a military bugle call) is interesting. He also advises us that the "foreign" language employed by various characters is a nonsensical one. He lets us know when things are "funny" and when we will be "too busy laughing." We're also informed when we will engage in the "suspension of disbelief." We are told that a character's mention of "England on the brink" is a nod to the film's prewar context. As for style, when a certain shot appears, we learn that it "could be [one] out of a German Expressionist film" and that Hitchcock worked in that country. Soon we hear proleptic comparisons between *The Lady Vanishes* and such subsequent Hitchcock films as *Rear Window* (1954), *The Birds* (1963), *Rope* (1948), and *Strangers on a Train* (1951)—all of which it "influences." Eder puts in a similar category several films by other artists: *The Narrow Margin* (1952, directed by Richard Fleischer) and *Mirage* (1965, directed by Edward Dmytryk). In a shot of Iris Henderson and her friends' dishabille in their hotel room, we learn that the women "are showing a fair amount of leg" for a nonmusical movie of this era. In being introduced to the "cockeyed couple" of Caldecott and Charters, we find out that some critics have viewed them as a "vaguely hinted representation of a gay couple," but that Eder disagrees (seeing them as merely "stereotypical of British reticence about sex"). We then hear that, rather than make *The Lady Vanishes*, Hitchcock really wanted to produce *Rebecca* at this time but could not raise adequate funds. Eder then narrates mini-biographies of the actors who play Caldecott (Naunton Wayne) and Charters (Basil Radford). The latter is "very funny" and personifies "the quintessential Englishman." The former specializes in roles of Englishmen abroad; thus, his part in the film became a "permanent act." Later on, Eder sighs: "Ah—here we have Michael Redgrave [as Gilbert] making his first major appearance onscreen." We are also told that Hitchcock wanted Robert Donat for the role (as he later wished him to play the lead in *Rebecca* [1940]). We learn of details in *The Lady Vanishes* that did not occur in the literary source material, and we are told of one particular scene, "You've got to love this sequence the second time you've seen the movie" (which implies that a "real" second viewing must come after this one). Finally, as we watch another scene, Eder discusses Hitchcock's use of the "Maguffin" —the plot device that seems crucial but is not: "It is a bit of cleverness that one appreciates afterward." Here he also quotes more established critical literature, François Truffaut's famous interview with Hitchcock.

So what are the types of information we have been given and what are their effects? We get a consideration of the place of the film in Hitchcock's *oeuvre* as well as in the careers of various actors (whose bios are also recited). We get evaluative comments ("a unique work") and hints on special effects (a "model shot"). We get remarks on historical context (World War II), sexual innuendo (possible gay portrayals, the amount of female "leg" displayed), world film movements (German Expressionism), film style (the use of sound), and narrative structure (the "Maguffin"). At times we are told what to do (e.g., to listen to the music), what we should find funny, and what we should think on subsequent viewings. Aside from the folly of predicting or dictating the viewer's response, the information seems legitimate.

On the other hand, what one most experiences is a bizarre kind of split attention, multi-tasking, or attention deficit disorder. While watching one film, one is prodded to consider numerous others—both works of Hitchcock and other directors—both movies related to *The Lady Vanishes* and not (but linked only to an actor's separate career). Hence one's concentration is fragmented between the visual and the auditory. Moreover, while listening to Eder speak, one also hears a muted version of the film's dialogue (some words of which one may pick up), so acoustic awareness is bifurcated as well. One's sense of temporality is also rifted: while watching one scene we are told how it will relate to a later one. Furthermore, the density of the commentary (with its copious factual information) makes it difficult to process, since one is watching and listening to something else and does not have control over the pace of apprehension as one does with the written word. It is no wonder that, in recent years, more of the special feature audio commentaries seem to be done by directors, who tend to give more pragmatic background information about production details than critics or can answer (for the ever-curious and naïve viewer) what the director "intended."

But the more interesting form of authorial dislocation by pundits comes in the recent flood of documentary films featuring theorists and critics (versus "creative" artists)—with titles such as: *Zizek!* (2005, directed by Astra Taylor), *Derrida* (2002, directed by Kirby Dick and Amy Ziering), *The Examined Life* (2008, directed by Astra Taylor 2008), or (trumping Spielberg) *Judith Butler: Philosophical Encounters of the Third Kind* (2007).[47] In 1970, Joseph Gelmis published a book, *The Film Director as Superstar*, whose title referenced the spread of auteurism. Perhaps now (to quote a famous film title), a new "star is born" as the old one (like Norman Maine) walks into the Pacific Ocean. Tied to the ascendance of the critic, we might cite an unprecedented 2002–2003 exhibit on Roland Barthes at the Centre Pompidou in Paris.[48] Clearly, it was groundbreaking to honor such an individual in an art museum, which is usually reserved for the work of painters, sculptors, video artists, and the like. A description of the event states: "The show . . . presents a large number of documents (manuscripts, notebooks, index cards, and correspondence) selected from the . . . Roland Barthes collection, as well as sound archives and unique audiovisual documents, mostly contributed by the . . . French library of radio and television archives." To supplement Barthes's written material (not artworks in themselves), the museum commissioned creative pieces inspired by Barthes's writing, including "a musical [composition] by the composer Andrea Cera; an interpretation of the 'punctum' in *La Chambre claire* by the photographer and writer Alain Fleischer; the 'Pneumatheque' by the plastic artists Anne Marie Jugnet and Alain Clairet, and finally, the more educational 'Systeme mode d'emploi' created by the multimedia designer Antoine Denize." So, through this museum exhibit, the Author of "The Death of the Author" is valorized and memorialized as heroic Author himself.

As further evidence of the trend to canonize the critic, we discuss one of the most intriguing filmic works of this type, *The Pervert's Guide to Cinema* (2006), directed by Sophie Fiennes and featuring Slavoj Žižek. In the movie, Žižek is billed as a "philosopher and psychoanalyst," but he has also written numerous books that deal with cinema, for instance *Enjoy Your Symptom: Jacques Lacan in Holly-*

FIGURE 39. Critic Slavoj Žižek (in *The Pervert's Guide to Cinema* [2006]) sits in a hotel bathroom used for filming *The Conversation* (1974) but also mimics Alfred Hitchcock's stance in a trailer for *Psycho* (1960).

wood and Out, Looking Awry: An Introduction to Jacques Lacan through Popular Culture, Everything You Always Wanted to Know about Lacan: But Were Afraid to Ask Hitchcock, and *The Art of the Ridiculous Sublime: On David Lynch's Lost Highway.* The title of the film (*The Pervert's Guide*) stems from Žižek's view that cinema is the ultimate perverse art because (as he will tell us) it "doesn't give you what you desire" but instead "tells you what to desire." This view, of course, reflects Žižek's overall belief that human beings are almost entirely "constructed" by, or interpolated within, the social order—here, mainstream film.

The Pervert's Guide consists predominantly of two types of sequences: (1) Žižek interpreting films and/or making theoretical pronouncements (as he addresses the camera in diverse settings), and (2) clips from the works he references. But within these two modes there is also variety. Sometimes he appears as a tiny, full-bodied figure placed into a huge white background (one that suggests the blank movie screen); at other times he is shown in medium close-up against the same white void. Most often, however, he appears in locales that in some manner mimic (or replicate) those of the films he is analyzing. When he talks about a theater scene in *Mulholland Drive* (2001, directed by David Lynch), he stands in front of a red curtain (like that which appears in the sequence he examines). When he discusses *Blue Velvet* (1986, again Lynch), he sits in an apartment that resembles one in the film. When he talks about a black-and-white movie like *Psycho* (1960, Hitchcock), he appears in monotone in a cellar like that in the home of Norman Bates. In some sequences, Žižek's image is purposefully tinted—as when he is shown on blue film stock while discussing Krzysztof Kieslowski's *Blue* (1993). Sometimes he informs us that he is standing in the actual spot where a film was made, as when he locates himself in the same hotel used to shoot *The Conversation* (1974, directed by Francis Ford Coppola), or by the precise Sequoia tree or vantage point on the Golden Gate Bridge used in *Vertigo* (1958, Hitchcock). What such strategies accomplish is to place Žižek vicariously and symbolically *within the world of the film he discusses rather than outside the work*—the more conventional stance of the critic. Since desire is one of the major issues that Žižek highlights in the film (and in much of his written work), we wonder: what desire motivates him as critic to attempt to "inhabit" a film's fictional universe?

In some cases, Žižek stands in the position of a movie actor or star. While discussing *The Exorcist* (1973, directed by William Friedkin), he is dressed in black like the priests who appear in the scene we watch. While discussing *Vertigo*, he alternately assumes the roles of Kim Novak and James Stewart (through diverse techniques). In the first instance, we see Novak in a silhouetted profile image as she sits in a chair. In a later shot, Žižek sits in a chair lit in the same fashion in a similar room. In another sequence from *Vertigo*, we see alternating shots of Novak entering a room and Stewart looking at her. The latter is followed by an image of Žižek looking (apparently from the same position as Stewart)—as though Žižek himself sees Novak. While in his interpretive discourse on *Vertigo*, Žižek focuses on the fetishistic desire of Stewart's character that "mortifies" the woman he pursues, we wonder: what desire impels Žižek to symbolically enter this film—a motivation he fails to question? Furthermore, while Žižek raises the theme of the "double" in discussing works like *Fight Club* (1999, directed by David Fincher), he does not interrogate his own urge to "double" for Stewart or Novak in *Vertigo*, or for the priests in *The Exorcist*. In a sense, even without such clever editing tricks and matches of mise-en-scène, Žižek has already made himself a "movie star" by simply appearing in the film we are watching. But here, regrettably, his distance from a matinee idol is also apparent: he is not beautiful, he has a noticeable speech defect, and his gestures and movements are choppy and awkward. One is reminded of the cruel but truthful saying that "Politics is Hollywood for Ugly People."[49] Perhaps we might say the same about film criticism.

While many of the topics around which Žižek's exegeses cluster are abstract (the libido, Oedipal dynamics, appearances, bodies without organs, etc.), some are concrete and have more direct application to the cinema. In one segment, he focuses on the human voice, which he claims comes from "in between the body" and which always has an element of "ventriloquism" to it. Not surprisingly, the films he discusses here are those in which vocalization has a disturbing aura: *The Exorcist* (in which the voice of a young girl is suddenly that of an evil monster), *Mulholland Drive* (in which a woman appears to continue singing after she faints), Charlie Chaplin's *The Great Dictator* (1940) (in which the voice of a tyrant controls society and cannot be stopped), or Alberto Cavalcanti's *Dead of Night* (1945) (in which the voice of a ventriloquist's dummy overtakes the puppeteer). But here again we have the urge to highlight Žižek's place within the scene and confront the use of his own vocalization in the film we are watching—in particular, as a frequent voiceover superimposed upon a director's original text—giving us an interpretation of the film, telling us what to think about it. For instance, as we watch a scene from *The Birds* (1963), Žižek opines that the creatures are "outbursts of maternal superego" or signs of "incestuous energy." Similarly, while we view a sequence from a Marx Brothers comedy he tells us that Groucho stands for the superego, Chico for the ego, and Harpo for the id. In only one case (Lars von Trier's *Dogville* [2003]) does the film he references actually have its own voiceover narration.

On some level, the surety and fixity of Žižek's readings contradict an image that punctuates the film—that of the Rorschach ink blot. Clearly, this tool (used by psychologists to draw out a patient's unique fantasies) stands here as a metaphor for the cinema screen. This sense of film (as externalizing our interior consciousness) is highlighted in yet another sequence in which we are shown an excerpt from Curtis Bernhardt's *Possessed* (1947), in which Joan Crawford watches a passing train, looking into its windows as each presents a scene of what transpires within. Žižek comments on how the train windows function as ersatz cinema screens—how what Crawford views is not so much reality as that which she desires. Yet this notion contradicts Žižek's earlier statement that cinema tells us what we desire. Furthermore, if (for the moment) we accept the view that spectators project their wishes onto movies, what is the relevance of Žižek's idiosyncratic readings of them? Might not my sense of a film be entirely different from his, and where would this leave the profession of interpretive criticism? The particularity of Žižek's vision becomes quite obvious in a scene in which he is depicted watering a lawn (paralleling a sequence in *Blue Velvet*). Sparked by a shot in that film in which the camera descends below the surface of a beautiful green lawn to show us a mass of repulsive worms and beetles, Žižek pontificates on how he finds flowers disgusting—rather like *vaginas dentate*. For him, flowers present an obscene "open invitation" for insects to come "fuck" them. I would dare say this, not a common opinion, gives us "too much information."

In some ways, Žižek is a psychological contrarian. He is fond of taking common sense behavioral truisms and turning them on their head, in part, for effect. If most people conceive the eyes as "windows to the soul," Žižek sees them as entryways to the abyss. If most people think they would like their fantasies realized, Žižek sees such fulfillment as a nightmare. While most people think death is horrible, Žižek finds immortality terrifying. While most people think we adopt fictional alter egos to compensate for what we lack, Žižek sees such personae as mirroring our true selves. This oppositional stance also characterizes Žižek's view of the cinema. On the one hand, he sees it as an important art. As he notes: "We need cinema to understand today's world. Only in cinema can we find the critical dimension we can't confront in reality." On the other hand, in a rather shocking sequence (cued by a scene from *The Conversation*), Žižek equates cinema with excrement. In that film, a surveillance expert is in a hotel room in which he thinks a murder has been committed. He checks the bathtub drain for blood or skin, then turns his attention to the toilet, which appears pristine. As he flushes it, however, blood gurgles up from the hole in the bowl, eventually overflowing the basin (reminding us of blood spouting from the elevator in *The Shining*). Through voiceover and direct address, Žižek interprets the scene symbolically as concerning the manner in which humans wish to dispense with that which disturbs them, be it bodily fluids, feces, or upsetting thoughts. For him, the scene, however, shows that we can never accomplish this erasure: the repressed returns and floods its bounds. Žižek then opines that the scene presents parallels to the cinema. He inquires: When we stare at a blank screen in the theater before the movie begins, is it not like staring into a toilet bowl waiting for "things" to reappear? He continues: Is the entire magic of the spectacle shown on the screen a kind of deceptive lure concealing the fact that we are basically watching shit?

Despite this scatological view, Žižek clearly respects the artists who fashion works of cinema. Thus, both *The Pervert's Guide* and his critical writings demonstrate that he has an auteurist bent. In the film, he concentrates on the work of Alfred Hitchcock, David Lynch, and Andrei Tarkovsky (though he excerpts films by countless others as well). In his published work he has written in depth about Hitchcock, Lynch, and Kieslowski. Only one of those cineastes, however, physically appears in *The Pervert's Guide*—Hitchcock. In one sequence, the reference to the director is indirect. In Hollywood slang (that is, as represented in *Variety*

FIGURE 40. Director Alfred Hitchcock in a trailer for *Psycho* (1960).

headlines) a cineaste is called a "helmer"—since he or she is at the "helm" of the filming project. As a verb, *to helm* means "to steer," so this epithet for the film-maker is logical. Significantly, the term comes from the nautical world, since a *helm* is the apparatus on a ship that includes rudder, tiller, and wheel. In *The Pervert's Guide*, when Žižek discusses Hitchcock's *The Birds* (which was shot in Bodega Bay, California), he significantly sits in a small motorboat, which he navigates through the waters. It is also the image that appears on the menu screen of the DVD, where one must choose to play the entire movie or select parts I, II or III. So here Žižek (unconsciously?) depicts himself as a literal "helmer"—mimicking the more celebrated captain of *The Birds*. In another instance, we see Hitchcock himself in a trailer for *Psycho*. He speaks to the audience from a bathroom (supposedly recalling [with feigned horror] the bloody carnage of a murder). Clearly, the trailer seeks to pique the public's interest for the chilling shower scene in his upcoming thriller. The footage of Hitchcock is conjoined with shots of Žižek also located in a lavatory. Here, Žižek not only positions himself in a space similar to that of *Psycho* but, by imitating Hitchcock in the trailer, installs himself in the authorial mise-en-scène as well—taking the director's place, as it were. Perhaps in "stealing the show," Žižek should have cited a different Hitchcock film: *To Catch a Thief* (1955).

Finally, when we actually view an excerpt from *Psycho* (involving Norman cleaning up the scene of his crime), Žižek (through voiceover narration) inserts autobiographical musings into the sequence, as he reminisces about his first screening of the Hitchcock film (clearly, Žižek is not Barthes's ideal reader who has no "history, biography, [or] psychology").[50] Žižek recalls his adolescent fascination and identification with Norman at the moment the character toiled to remove all traces of blood from the bathroom, a task that took an extended period of time. Žižek speculates that all work (rather than being essentially creative) boils down to the project of erasing a stain.

But to what stain might he refer? Given the contemporary dominance of the critic (a phenomenon for which Žižek could be the poster child), and considering Žižek's repeated attempts in *The Pervert's Guide* to control or enter the cinematic frame, we wonder whether his interest in this moment from *Psycho* reverberates with the modern critic's stance toward the author—whose death he broadly proclaims, and whose persistent human "stain" he seeks to eradicate.

AFTERWORD
Signs and Meaning in the Cinema

We propose … a morphology … that views film not from the outside, as
a product to be consumed, but from the inside, as a dynamically evolving
organic code directly *responsive* and *responsible*, like every other code to the
supreme mediator: consciousness.
— Hollis Frampton, "On the Camera"

Limitless (2011, directed by Neil Burger) is a rather silly movie about a
blocked, aimless novelist, Eddie Morra (Bradley Cooper), who gains sudden powers by taking a secret, unlicensed medicine. In one scene, we notice on his book-
shelf a copy of *Barthes by Barthes* (a text that combines memoir, anecdote, and
literary theory). One assumes that the set dresser put it there to signify that Morra
is an informed and intelligent writer interested in literary criticism (although
nothing else in the film suggests this). But we know, of course, that there *are* some
artists who combine creative and analytical skills allowing them to "inhabit" their
own work in the manner of a bona fide critic, and to scrutinize it as carefully as
Žižek does the works of others. One of those is American experimental filmmaker
Hollis Frampton.

THE PAST IS PROLOGUE

It seems fitting that the final chapter of this book should focus briefly on two films
by Frampton—perhaps it is even "poetic justice," the title of a work of his that I have
already discussed. Here I must "come out" as the author of my own book and relate
an incident from the beginning of my scholarly career. One of my first seminars as a
doctoral student in the Department of Cinema Studies at New York University was
American Independent Film, taught by Annette Michelson. I knew nothing about
the topic and was horrified when, during the first class session, she told us that by
the next week we had to decide upon a filmmaker to study and on whose work we
would lead a class session. One day soon thereafter, I was wandering through the
halls of the department (then located in a tenement above the Bleecker Street Cinema), when I happened upon a small projection room as someone was screening

a film. Like a Surrealist, I entered in the middle. I immediately became fascinated with the work—in part because I gleaned that sound and image were purposely out of step (not out of synch) with one another, and I hung around until I understood the system or logic of its composition. That film was (*nostalgia*) (1971), by Frampton, and I came into class the next week enthusiastically proclaiming my term project. As it happens, I was able to contact him at the University of Buffalo, where he was teaching, and he made all his work available to me at no cost and proved to be incredibly generous with his time and remarks (and nonjudgmental about my tentative insights). I went on to complete my class presentation, then write about his later work, *The Magellan Cycle* (1971–1984), after interviewing him.[1] Frampton was one of the most brilliant, witty, and munificent people I have ever known.

I return to him now because (as *Poetic Justice* has already shown) he is a filmmaker who has dealt with questions of authorship, writing, and the relation between word and image—creating what we might deem "theory films" (to borrow a name attached to an early category of feminist cinema).[2] *Poetic Justice*, of course, implicated the historic tensions between scriptwriter and director, allowing the former's (oft invisible) contribution to dominate as subject matter of the film. Likewise, the spectator of *Poetic Justice* found herself simultaneously a film viewer and a word reader—with the never-realized "movie" playing only in her mind. Frampton's use of intermittent first-person address in the handwritten written text —especially with reference to the protagonist being a photographer[3]—forced the spectator to consider the author behind the film (since Frampton worked in that medium early in his professional life).

One of the primary theoretical issues Frampton tackled was the relation between verbal and pictorial discourses (also a major theme of this book and one highlighted in chapter 6), so we begin by discussing his *Zorns Lemma* (1970), which Scott MacDonald has deemed "a phantasmagoria of . . . language."[4] The title refers to a proposition in set theory, that being the branch of mathematics that concerns sets, or collections of objects. (For example, in this book, my "set" is filmic texts about authorship and writing.) In *Zorns Lemma* the primary "objects" collected (in the major segment of the film) are (1) letters of the Roman alphabet (having only twenty-four characters),[5] (2) images containing words beginning with those letters, and (3) images that successively replace those depicted in group 2. The film starts with sequential shots of alphabet letters. Then the screen goes blank and we hear a woman's voice reading from *The Bay State Primer*, an early American schoolbook that provides religious-themed rhymes to introduce children to the alphabet —clearly, the first step in learning to read.

In *Adam's* fall
We sinnéd all

The life to mend,
God's *book* attend

In this immediate conjunction of written and then spoken text, we are reminded of Anne-Marie Christin's claim that "what was truly novel and groundbreaking in the development of the alphabet was not that it *represented* speech, but rather that it made speech *visible*."[6]

Following Part I, we move on to Part II (the longest segment), which involves a series of one-minute, hand-held, live-action shots of words (generally located on New York City signage), arranged from A to Z. When each run-through of the alphabet is complete, we get a minute of black leader as separation; then the process resumes with a series of new "environmental words," which seem almost to be written on the screen.[7] Here, numerous things are brought to mind. First, given the prior citation of a school primer we think of children's books, which teach the alphabet by juxtaposing letters and pictures (e.g., *A* and apple). In Frampton's work, instead of being given a picture of an object starting with a letter, we get an image of a word that does. As we know, picture books are exemplary texts for underscoring the relation between word and image, although volumes for adults have sometimes been illustrated as well (e.g., William Blake's *Songs of Innocence and Experience* [1794]). In Frampton's repeated run-through of the alphabet we also think of the therapy sessions in *The Diving Bell and the Butterfly*, in which to spell out words Bauby had to listen to repeated recitations of letters and blink at appropriate times. We recall as well Shelley Jackson's video "Ineradicable Stain," in which people (tattooed with words) appear sequentially onscreen to formulate sentences for her story. Finally, we think of the art of Jenny Holzer who, years after the release of *Zorns Lemma*, created works consisting entirely of language. What was new about her pieces was that they were posted as signage or projections in the urban landscape. One on a building in Times Square, for instance, bore the following phrases (among others): "MONEY CREATES TASTE," "ABUSE OF POWER COMES AS NO SURPRISE," and "PROTECT ME FROM WHAT I WANT." Holzer calls this series "Truisms," but unlike the wisdom proffered in *The Bay State Primer* (i.e., "The life to mend, God's *book* attend"), hers is agnostic and laced with irony.[8] What is even more interesting from a cinematic perspective is that, at a later point, she used movie theater marquees to post her signs. On one she writes: "A MAN CAN'T KNOW WHAT IT'S LIKE TO BE A MOTHER"; on another she opines, "SLIPPING INTO MADNESS IS GOOD FOR THE SAKE OF COMPARISON." One can only wonder how Frampton might have incorporated her work into *Zorns Lemma*.

There is some variation in how the nearly thirteen hundred words are captured in that film.[9] While most appear on signage, some are written as graffiti, appear superimposed over a wordless live-action shot, or are part of a paper collage constructed by Frampton. In one case ("xylophone"), we watch a word being "unwritten" (as the shot is printed in reverse motion). As Bill Simon points out (in the best article on language-image discourse in the film), the words for each letter also appear in alphabetical order (a mode of organization we would be hard-pressed to perceive), so there is both vertical and horizontal alphabetization.[10]

Eventually, we begin to notice that some shots of alphabetized signage are replaced by other wordless footage. For instance, when we come to X, a shot of a fire is substituted. From that point on, each time we return to X, we see the same image of flames. Gradually, many other letters are replaced: instead of Q we see steam escaping from a sidewalk grill; instead of J, a man painting a wall; and instead of Y, a pan shot of tall weeds. As is clear from these examples, the images that replace letters do not necessarily remind us of a word starting with that letter—so their choice seems rather arbitrary in relation to the alphabet. There are many other complexities of both the signage- and substitution-shots involving movement, temporality, composition, illusionism, and depth, but they are well documented and not especially germane to our subject.[11]

But other aspects are important—the first being the spectatorial response to the film, always a central factor in Frampton's work. While it is expected that the viewer already knows how to read and does not need a review of the alphabet (except that the Roman version trips us up with its omission of two letters), she is continually forced (if attentive to the film) to silently recite her ABCs as the signage shots go by, trying to keep track. Then, as words are replaced by seemingly random everyday images (a child on a swing, a man walking around a city block, construction workers digging a hole), she is impelled to notice what letter they "stand for" (having been substituted for them). This becomes a bit like playing the childhood board game Memory, confirming that there is certainly a ludic element to most of Frampton's work.[12] Beyond reciting the alphabet and identifying the letters that shots stand for, viewers sometimes try to make sense of the order of the words depicted onscreen. When *member* follows *limp*, we get the joke, as we do when *hive* comes before *itch*, or *bore* before *college*. But often there is no such logic. (As Simon points out, this refusal of meaning is a sly reference throughout to the belief by some film theorists that a shot is like a word.)[13] On the other hand, sometimes the words we see have obvious relevance to the film we are watching, as when we discern signs reading *cinema* and *movie*. Similarly, the letter A is replaced by a shot of someone turning the pages of a book—referring us back to issues of reading and writing.

In addition to being a filmmaker, Frampton is a widely published image theorist, and a sense of that project informs all his work. In many ways, *Zorns Lemma* is "ahead of its times" in relation to film criticism. It was only around the period of its release and thereafter that the question of semiotics really came into prominence, with the publication (a year earlier) of Peter Wollen's *Signs and Meaning in the Cinema* (1969), and the translation (four years later) of Christian Metz's *Film Language: A Semiotics of the Cinema* in 1974. In fact, the title of Wollen's book could be used as a wry alternate for *Zorns Lemma* since Frampton photographs urban signage while dealing theoretically with the nature of both verbal and visual signs.[14] (Frampton loved puns, as evidenced by a sculptural piece he once made entitled "A Cast of Thousands" consisting of a plaster block on which the number 1,000 is twice inscribed.) In Wollen's book, he draws upon concepts advanced by Charles Sanders Peirce and his taxonomy of signs as divided into three categories: symbols, icons, and indices (although one might occupy multiple positions).[15] A symbol establishes an entirely arbitrary relation between signifier and signified (e.g., the word "table" has only a conventional tie to the piece of furniture for which it stands). On the other hand, an icon represents its object through similarity (as in a portrait). Finally, an index has an "existential bond" to that which it represents (e.g., a footprint testifies to the fact that an individual once stepped there).[16] The photograph and the cinematic image are generally both symbolic (resembling that which they capture) and indexical (existentially related to its object through the refraction of light onto film stock at a particular moment in time). We have earlier quoted André Bazin on this subject, who spoke of the photograph as a kind of decal or transfer of reality to film.[17] Of course, photographs can also be symbolic (as when a shot renders an image of the U.S. flag). In (*nostalgia*), Frampton makes a joke of such symbolism when he shows us a photo of two toilets, which the voiceover says (in mockery of critical patois) is "an imitation of a painted Renaissance crucifixion."

In *Zorns Lemma*, we have all three kinds of signs—often at once. The words we see on signage (e.g., *joint* or *eat*) are symbolic. On the other hand, they are captured in moving picture images that are simultaneously indexical. That is, the shot of the store window that Frampton photographs to capture the words *joint* or *eat* have an "existential bond" to real sites that existed at particular moments. Furthermore, the shots are iconic, in that they resemble the objects originally photographed (while having a status different from them). As we watch *Zorns Lemma*, we must be aware of these blended but contradictory layers, as we must be cognizant of the difference between the worded and wordless shots (e.g., those of signage and those of "pure" action [like beans falling into a container]). Frampton complicates the situation in several clever ways. While the shots of signs represent symbolic words (entirely crafted by the human mind), the shots depicting them are all documentary and unmanipulated. Conversely, the shots of wordless events (which seem to be more "natural" than those of signs) are often manipulated. For instance, the image of a guy bouncing a ball (which substitutes for the letter *O*) involves superimposition, and the one of the man playing with Tinker Toys (which replaces *R*) utilizes reverse motion.

As we have noted, in 1977 James Monaco published *How to Read a Film*, a textbook for film analysis. Its title was *au courant* at the time since it drew upon the science of semiotics and the alleged parallels between film structure and language (the kind of "codes" to which Frampton refers in the epigraph to this chapter). Again, Monaco's title might function as an alternate for *Zorna Lemma*. Clearly, we must not only see but "read" the film's word-laden signage. Here, Frampton not only anticipates later film theory but broader cultural transformations. As Johanna Drucker noted in 2003: "T-shirts, billboards, electronic marquis, neon signs, mass-produced print media—all are part of the visible landscape of daily life, especially in urban Western culture." In this regard the "boundaries between word and image have never been more permeable than they are now."[18]

But as other scholars have shown, *Zorns Lemma* is not only a work of film theory but a "primer" for film history, rehearsing the progression of cinema from silence to sound, and from black-and-white to color.[19] In fact, both *Zorns Lemma* and Frampton's seven-part epic work *Hapax Legomena* (1971–1972) are (to use his own term) "metahistories" of the cinema—restagings (in cryptic form) of the media's trajectory and genealogy.[20] As Frampton notes: "The metahistorian . . . is occupied with inventing a tradition that is a coherent, wieldy set of discrete monuments, meant to inseminate resonant consistency into the growing body of his art."[21]

PORTRAIT OF THE ARTIST

But what of the status of the author in Frampton's work—given that this book is not only about language, writing, and film, but about the creator "incarnate"? Jenkins quotes Frampton as saying that *Zorns Lemma* can "get along without the artist" and seems to take him at his word.[22] He also believes that in the film's charting of "the birth of cinema in the death of language," there is a reference to Barthes's notion of the "death of the author." But as usual, I suspect that the disappearance of the author in Frampton's work is not all that clear. First of all, Frampton makes some cameo appearances in *Zorns Lemma*—as the man changing a car tire (a shot that substitutes for the letter *T*) and as the person working with Tinker Toys (substituting for the letter *R*). (Note how the first image relates to its letter [*tire* and *T*], but the second does not [*Tinker Toy* and *R*].) But these are not the most compelling self-referential elements of *Zorns Lemma*.

Frampton was a master explicator of his own work—having no problem talking or writing about it extensively, rather than playing the coy, reticent, uncommunicative artist (á la Andy Warhol). (In fact, in working on his films, the challenge for the critic is to think about them for herself rather than take his exegeses for granted.) He left us notes on *Zorns Lemma* that are quite telling. Under a heading that explicitly mentions "Elements of Autobiography," he lists aspects that relate to his life. Ostensibly referencing his use of a school primer, he states: "I received the same Judeo-Christian upbringing as everyone else in my culture: rote learning by authority."[23] Explaining his fascination with language, he observes that his adolescence was "concerned with words and verbal values" and that he "fancied himself a poet." He mentions also that the book opened in the image replacement for *A* is one about Ferdinand Magellan, the subject of his future film.[24] Finally, he explains that years of living in New York City led to a gradual "weaning away of [his] consciousness from verbal to visual interests." He also confesses a series of personal "misfortunes" in the making of *Zorns Lemma*, including "lapses of taste" (his use of the word *fuck*) and instances of "faking" (his construction of collages to include words he did not find in his environment).[25]

Furthermore, he admits that the film is replete with homages to the "stylistic tendencies of other directors, mostly within the narrative canon."[26] Jenkins sees this as illustrating Barthes's idea that the artwork is an author-less "tissue of quotation," but such allusions can also serve to mark a practitioner's place in the history of his craft, thus drawing attention to his own creative status.[27] In *Zorns Lemma*, one suspects that the bisected face of a woman (that substitutes for the letter *E*) is a nod to a scene from Ingmar Bergman's *Persona* (1966), and that the fact that the alphabet terminates on an image of the sea is a nod to Michael Snow's *Wavelength* (1967), which ends on a photograph of the ocean.[28] Jenkins also finds references to various filmic "city symphonies" and to Marcel Duchamp's pun-infused *Anemic Cinema* (1926).[29] Finally, in Frampton's notes for *Zorns Lemma*, he interprets several of his own images, telling us, for instance, that the meat grinder is a trope for the camera.[30]

Beyond "annotating" his works, as we have stated, Frampton composed essays on art, photography, film, and narrative theory. In many of these, he tips the hand that he plays in *Zorns Lemma*. In "Film in the House of the Word" (a title with obvious relevance), Frampton considers Sergei Eisenstein's famous 1928 "Statement on Sound," in which he expressed skepticism about the birth of the "talkie," given its potential to eradicate the type of assertive montage for which he was known. Eisenstein, of course, did not entirely reject sound; rather, he held out for its radical asynchronization with the image, imagining a dynamic of assertive audiovisual editing.

What Frampton focuses upon in Eisenstein's essay, however, is the director's seeming opposition to language. As Frampton observes: "It was not simply sound, then, that threatened to destroy all the 'present formal achievements' of montage, but the dubious gift of speech, the Prime Instance of language, the linear decoding of the terrain of thought into a stream of utterance. Thus film, from its first word, was to be perceived in a double posture of defilement and fulfillment." Frampton deems this "logophobia," a trend he recognizes as continuing in the rhetoric of the contemporary visual arts. As he states: "Only the poetics of the title escaped inquisition, for a time." As for the cause of this antipathy, he says: "The terms of the indictment were clear: language was suspect as the defender of illusion, and . . . must be purged." However, he continues: "To ostracize the word is disingenuous to the degree that it succeeds in concealing from itself its fear of the word—and the source of that fear: that language, in every culture . . . is, above all, an expanding arena of power, claiming for itself and its wielders all that it can seize, and relinquishing, nothing." Returning to Eisenstein and silent film, Frampton concludes that the rejection of language led to a "double illiteracy" of the medium: "Its diegesis was legible to a mass populace that could not read, and its formal strategies were largely illegible to a burgeoning elite that could."[31]

Frampton ends his piece with an attempt to "rescue" Eisenstein from the charge of logophobia, and (perhaps) to offer a rationale for his own brand of filmmaking. He finds in his predecessor's writing a "dim outline of what it is that he is so anxious to protect from language," and, in it, a vision of the kind of system that Eisenstein conceives to accomplish this.[32] As Frampton concludes:

> There are only two hypothetical symbolic systems whose formal descriptions meet such requirements: One is a universal natural language; the other is a perfect machine . . . [Thus] it seems possible to suggest that [Eisenstein] glimpsed, however quickly . . . the construction of a machine, very much like film, more efficient than language, that might, entering into direct competition with language, transcend its speed, abstraction, compactness, democracy, ambiguity, power—a project, moreover, whose ultimate promise was the constitution of an external critique of language itself. If such a thing were to be, a consequent celestial mechanics of the intellect might picture a body called Language, and a body called Film, in symmetrical orbit about one another, in perpetual and dialectical motion.[33]

In fact, we find those "bodies" in the "orbit" of *Zorns Lemma*.

Earlier, we cited Frampton's homage to Michael Snow in *Zorns Lemma*, a friend and artist whom he greatly admired. This reference leads us back to the earlier Frampton film mentioned, (*nostalgia*), and the one that makes most clear his status as "author incarnate." It is Part I of *Hapax Legomena*—which (much to the point) has been deemed "an enigmatic structuralist 'autobiography.'"[34] The film consists of a series of black-and-white photos taken (or collected) by Frampton in New York City during the period in which he practiced the art. Each one of them is placed on a hot plate and soon begins to burn, then disintegrates into ashes. Here, we think of the fact that, in *Zorns Lemma*, one shot constituted a reverse-action image of a man writing. As that shot depicted the "unwriting" of a word, so (*nostalgia*)'s shots of flaming images portray the "untaking" of photographs.

A male voice is heard on the sound track relating personal information about the photographs: what constitutes their subject, when and where they were shot, and what other events attended to their production. The only problem is that voice and image are "out of step." As we hear the man describe one photograph, we watch another (which does not "match up" with his verbal portrayal). It is only when the next photograph arrives onscreen that we realize that it relates to the description the man has previously uttered. So each new image thrusts us back into the auditory past, as its voiceover thrusts us into the imagistic future, our minds literally working at cross-purposes. One sense of the term nostalgia means "a wistful desire to return in thought or in fact to a former time in one's life."[35] Thus, it is a feeling perceived in the present that reinserts the past into the mental flow of time. Perhaps this is the reason why Frampton places his title in parentheses.

(*nostalgia*) is clearly a film about temporality, and this is signaled in the portrait of artist Carl Andre posed with a metronome. But it is also about the human capacity (or lack thereof) to comprehend the dynamics of time. In fact, it has always seemed to me that, as the hot-plated coil burns into each photograph, it approximates the convoluted folds of the brain. Interestingly, Frampton has talked about the brain in the context of *Zorns Lemma*:

> Cortically speaking, we are of distinct and separate minds. . . . Generally, it would appear that, in right-handed persons, the left hemisphere is concerned with language and with linear and analytic language-like deductive activities. The right hemisphere is concerned generally with synthesizing nonlinear inductive activities. . . . My own reading of the forty-five-minute central section of *Zorns Lemma*, in which the image that is statistically before one passes gradually from a language-dominated one to a continuous non-language-dominated one, is a kind of allegory, an acting out of a transference of power from one hemisphere of the brain to the other. Of course, that was nowhere within my thinking of the film when I was making it.[36]

Like *Zorns Lemma*, (*nostalgia*) is also a film about language and picture. As Frampton comments, it "is mostly about words and the kind of relationship words can have to images. I began probably as a kind of non-poet, as a kid, and my first interest in images probably had something to do with what clouds of words could rise out of them."[37]

The words spoken in the film are authored by Frampton and constitute a kind of autobiography (a *Frampton on Frampton*, like *Barthes on Barthes*). But in his "Notes" for the work, he speaks of himself in the third person and claims he can only write his "biography."[38] He is, nonetheless, the true "I" of the piece (despite his claim to speak only "*as if* in the first person" [my emphasis]). The voiceover for one image, for example, states, "I made this image of James Rosenquist the first day we met," and for another states, "I did not make this photograph, nor do I know who did."

However, the voice we hear throughout the film is not that of Frampton, the author, but of Michael Snow (though only those who personally know the men's vocal registers would be aware of this). At the beginning of the film, however, we do hear *two* men preparing to record (one of them Frampton), so there is a hint of his presence. But with the use of Snow's voice in the film Frampton displaces his persona on to another (a move signaled in his "Notes"). Ironically, one of the photographs in (*nostalgia*) shows an image of Michael Snow by Frampton—thus making Snow a faux author incarnate, too. Frampton's self-distancing gesture relates not only to his simultaneous desire to reveal and conceal his identity, but to a broader questioning of the unified subject (long before doing so was so popular in film-theoretical circles). Thus, in talking about his status as a youth, he comments, "He had once been myself."[39]

In (*nostalgia*) and elsewhere, Frampton also seems concerned with the Death of the Author. (He once told me that he would never live long enough to finish *Magellan* [at a time when he had not yet made public the illness that would end his life].) As we know, many have theorized that photographs always portend death

—arresting one moment of life that has already ended (as will all). In (*nostalgia*), Frampton references this in a playful manner by showing us a photograph he took of spaghetti from a series that documented its progressive decomposition—with mold growing ever more present, repulsive, and sculptural.

Death is also a specter in *Zorns Lemma*. Section I (read from *The Bay State Reader*) includes a huge number of alphabet rhymes that speak of the topic (perhaps shocking for a text aimed at very young children):

As runs the *glass*,
Man's life shall pass.

Time cuts down all,
Both great and small.

Xerxes the great must die,
And so must you and I.

Youth forward slips,
Death soonest nips.

Here, the invocation of demise is direct, but in Part III of *Zorns Lemma*, it is far more metaphorical. That segment consists of what appears to be a single long shot / long take of a man, woman, and dog, seen from behind, walking away from us into a snow-filled field toward a distant fence and row of trees.[40] If it were not for the latter (as points of reference), we would barely be able to perceive their making spatial progress. On the sound track, we hear the voices of six women reading a text, word by word, to the beat of a metronome. It is "On Light, or the Ingression of Forms" by Bishop Robert Grosseteste, an eleventh-century metaphysical tract.[41] Aside from referencing light (with obvious import to cinema), the passage speaks of four archetypal elements: earth, water, air, and fire—all of which have had imagistic representation in *Zorns Lemma*. But it is not this that concerns us here, but rather the common associations between snow, cold, and death, as in *Irezumi* and in Robert Frost's famous 1923 poem "Stopping by Woods on a Snowy Evening": "The woods are lovely, dark and deep. / But I have promises to keep, / And miles to go before I sleep, / And miles to go before I sleep."[42] Significantly, at the end of the sequence, the walking figures (who have repeatedly "sunk" into deep mounds of snow) disappear behind the trees and the image morphs to ethereal white light, erasing their presence. As Scott MacDonald notes: "The flare-out to white not only signals the end of the roll and the film, it is suggestive of the widespread observation by those who have had near-death experiences that, at the moment of death, we see a powerful light."[43]

Though the man in this sequence is not Frampton, the filmmaker does twice appear as "author incarnate" in *Zorns Lemma*. He does so in (*nostalgia*) as well

FIGURE 41. Hollis Frampton's photographic self-portrait burns on a hot plate in (*nostalgia*) (1971).

—but more emphatically (albeit virtually). One of the photographs he presents is a self-portrait as a handsome young man. We are told it was shot on March 11, 1959, so he would have been twenty-three. The voiceover relating to (but not coincident with it) states: "The face is my own, or rather, it *was* my own"—the phrasing both distancing himself and marking the passage of time (despite his precision about the date the image was captured). The voiceover continues: "I take some comfort in realizing that my entire physical body has been replaced more than once since it made this portrait of itself." Here, not only do we get a mocking of self-identity, but a sense of the body as transient, fluid, biological matter, with cycles and meta-morphoses (like those of spaghetti) that will ultimately lead to annihilation. Of course, as we ponder this insight, the photograph itself is extinguished on the hot plate—the death (at least) of the author's likeness.

In originally watching (*nostalgia*) (and knowing that Frampton was a rather "old" thirty-five when he made it), we began to have a sense of his vanishing youth and physical beauty. Of course, as we now view it (following his death), we have a far more poignant sense of loss. Here, we think of a statement Frampton made in his "Notes" for the film: "In the end, when I saw the film myself, I felt I had made an *effigy*, at least, of his opaque young man's life, even if I had not wholly entrained its sadness" (my emphasis).[44] That sadness is now "wholly entrained," and entirely ours.

The final passage read by Snow in (*nostalgia*) concerns an image that we will never see (since his voice always speaks of the next photograph—not the one currently onscreen). I quote it at length:

Since 1966 I have made few photographs. . . .

So it was all the more surprising that I felt again, a few weeks ago, a vagrant urge that would have seemed familiar a few years ago: the urge to take my camera out of doors and make a photograph. . . . So I obeyed it.

I wandered around for hours. . . . Half a block from my front door, the receding perspective of an alley caught my eye . . . ; a dark tunnel with the cross street beyond brightly lit. As I focused and composed the image, a truck turned into the alley. The driver stopped it, got out, and walked away. He left his cab door open.

My composition was spoiled, but I felt a perverse impulse to make the exposure, anyway. . . .

When I came to print the negative, an odd thing struck my eye. *Something*, standing in the cross street and invisible to me, was reflected in a factory window, and then reflected once more in the rear-view mirror attached to the truck door. It was only a tiny detail.

Since then I have enlarged this small section of my negative enormously. The grain of the film all but obliterates the features of the image. It is obscure: by any possible reckoning, it is hopelessly ambiguous.

Nevertheless, what I *believe* I see recorded, in that speck of film, fills me with such fear, such utter dread and loathing, that I think I shall never dare to make another photograph again.

Here it is!

Look at It?

Do you see what I see?

Several things are important about this monologue. First, it speaks to the demise of Frampton's career as a photographer (which has already been signified by the burning of prints in the film). Second, it demonstrates the role of contingency in the photographic project. Third, it asserts the difficulty of assigning meaning to an image, playing again with notions of semiotics. Fourth, Frampton directly addresses his spectators, speaking to them in the second person, establishing more

of a bond with them than in previous segments. Finally, the scenario of a photographer shooting an image in a public space, then enlarging it in the darkroom
to decipher a small, mysterious detail, reminds us of a popular art film of the era
—Michelangelo Antonioni's *Blow-Up* (1966). In that movie, it is implied that the
photographer concludes that the detail (shot in a park) is a corpse and the landscape a crime scene.

Blow-Up was notorious for not having solved its narrative enigma, so in (*nostalgia*), Frampton mischievously plays with our own desire to solve the puzzle he has
proffered. But like the corpse in *Blow-Up*, it seems that the photographic specter
he has captured may be associated with death. As he says: "What I *believe* I see
recorded in that speck of film fills me with such fear, such utter dread and loathing, that I think I shall never dare to make another photograph again." Here, of
course, we think once more of theories that have linked photography and fatality.
As we have noted, Roland Barthes claimed that "each photograph always includes
this imperious sign of [a] future death."[45] But beyond his art, Frampton invokes
broader issues of human mortality (as did the rhymes in *Zorns Lemma*—"As runs
the glass, Man's life shall pass"). So when he asks his viewers, "Do you see what I
see?" our only answer can be "yes" (despite the ruse that we will never view the
photograph of which he speaks).

On the other hand, as we earlier had watched the Self-Portrait of the Artist
burn on the hot plate and turn to ash (like dust to dust), we realized that, in the
age of mechanical reproduction, the image (and, in some sense, its subject) can be
"resurrected" by printing a duplicate. As Frampton himself has remarked, cinema
can claim the major feat of "resurrecti[ng] . . . bodies in space from their dismembered trajectories."[46] So his has been a sham execution, after all—like that of Mary
Queen of Scots in Edison's 1895 movie. Hence the joke is on us, and the death of
the author a mere "special effect."

Thus, as George Sand remarked: "The trade of authorship" remains a "violent"
but "indestructible obsession."[47]

NOTES

INTRODUCTION

1. Barthes, "Death," 125.
2. Ibid., 127.
3. Ibid., 128–129.
4. Colin MacCabe, paper delivered at the SCMS conference, March 2011. See also MacCabe, "The Revenge of the Author," in *The Eloquence of the Vulgar* (London: British Film Institute, 2008), 33–41.
5. Quoted in Burke, *Authorship*, 76.
6. Calvino, *If on a Winter's*, 171.
7. Ibid., 176, 180, 179, 195, 196.
8. Burke, *Death and Return*, xv.
9. Here, one thinks of William Luhr and Peter Lehman's *Authorship and Narrative in the Cinema* (1977); John Caughie's *Theories of Authorship* (1981); David Gerstner and Janet Staiger's *Authorship and Film* (2002); Virginia Wexman's *Film and Authorship* (2003); Torben Grodal's *Visual Authorship* (2004); David Kipen's *The Schreiber Theory: A Radical Rewrite of American Film History* (2006); Jack Boozer's *Authorship in Film Adaptation* (2008); Barry Keith Grant's *Auteurs and Authorship* (2008); Rosanna Maule's *Beyond Auteurism: New Directions in Authorial Film Practices in France, Italy, and Spain since the 1980s* (2008); David Wharton and Jeremy Grant's *Teaching Auteur Study* (Teaching Film and Media Studies) (2008); C. P. Sellors's *Film Authorship* (2011); and Jerome Christensen's *America's Corporate Art: The Studio Authorship of Hollywood Motion Pictures* (2012). Of course, beyond these tomes on theory are a host of books on individual filmmakers seen as "auteurs"—be they monographs on Hitchcock, Truffaut, Arzner, Godard, Ray, Campion, Kurosawa, Sembene, Herzog, or Rossellini.
10. Gleick, "Books and Other."
11. Keller, "Let's Ban Books."
12. Updike, "End of Authorship."
13. See Susan D. Blum, *My Word! Plagiarism and College Culture* (Ithaca, N.Y.: Cornell University Press, 2009).
14. Miller, "Plagiarism."
15. Smith, "Aggrieved Publisher."
16. Sante, "Fiction of Memory."
17. Ibid.
18. "Times Business Reporter."
19. "*Washington Post* Suspends."
20. Bolter, *Writing Space*, 35.
21. Ibid., 35–36.
22. Kelly, "Becoming."
23. Jenkins, *Textual Poachers*, 223–224.
24. Pelli and Bigelow, "Writing Revolution."
25. Thanks to Colin MacCabe for reminding me of this in a paper he gave at the SCMS conference in March 2011.
26. Hitchman, "A History."
27. Burke, *Authorship*, 6.

28. Ibid., xix.

29. Hess, *Authoring the Self*, 281.

30. Barthes, *Camera*, 5.

31. Deren, *Essential Deren*, 20.

32. Barthes, *Camera*, 6. This trope is also utilized in the film *The Draughtsman's Contract*, which provides a view of the countryside through the frame of a devise used for composing the scene.

33. Kael, *Raising Kane*, and Carringer, *Making of "Citizen Kane."*

34. Paper delivered at SCMS Conference, March 2011. See also Colin MacCabe, Kathleen Murray, and Rick Warner, eds., *Film Adaptation and the Question of Fidelity* (New York: Oxford University Press, 2011).

35. Robb, "Dispute," 1.

36. Larry Gelbart, Barry Levinson, Elaine May, Don McGuire, Murray Schisgal, and Robert Garland.

37. Ronberg, "Rembrandt or Not?" 56–59.

38. An exception is the work of Peter Decherney.

39. "Even in France, where the idea [of film authorship] started to take shape in the late 1940s, according to the law until 1957 the auteur of the film was none other than the producer." Kovács, *Screening Modernism*, 218.

40. Larsen, "Artists' Rights," 2–3.

41. Goldstein, *Copyright's Highway*, 168–169.

42. Bazin, *What Is Cinema?*, 13.

43. Nesbit, "What Was an Author?" 251. The entire history of copyright and cinema in the United States is a fascinating subject. When early in film history Edison sued someone for copying one of his movies, his suit was denied since works of cinema were not seen as covered by the law. In 1903, however, an appeals court reversed the ruling, citing photography (which was covered) as a cinematic precedent. Finally, the movies were brought under the Copyright Act of 1912. Soon, other questions arose: Did a film version of a literary property impinge on the latter's copyright? Was it the movie that did so, or the screenplay? See Goldstein, *Copyright's Highway*, 62–63.

44. Burke, *Authorship*, 289.

45. Fraenkel, "Signatures," 315.

46. Ibid., 317.

47. Here I could note that other filmmakers do tie adaptations to their original, as in Shakespeare's *Romeo and Juliet*, or using a book to open the film during the credit sequence, as in Duvivier's 1947 *Anna Karenina*.

48. Barthes, "Death," 128; Calvino, *If on a Winter's*, 171.

49. Quoted by Colin MacCabe in a paper given at the SCMS conference of March 2011. See also B. Kite, "*Bigger Than Life*: Somewhere in Suburbia." *Criterion*, http://www.criterion .com/current/posts/1412-bigger-than-life-somewhere-in-suburbia.

50. Buscombe, "Ideas of Authorship," 84.

51. Foucault, "What Is an Author?" 233.

52. Forster, *Two Cheers*, 77.

53. Ibid., 79, 81, 84, 86.

54. McGilligan, *Hitchcock*, 7.

55. Quoted in Burke, *Authorship*, xvi.

56. Borges, "Borges and I," 339.

57. Barthes, "Death," 127.

58. Barthes, *Roland Barthes*, 148.

59. Borges, "Pierre Menard," 91.

60. Calvino, *If on a Winter's*, 177.
61. Auerbach, *Body Shots*, 2.
62. Astruc, "Birth of a New," 18; 22.
63. Ibid., 22.
64. Deren, *Essential Deren*, 33.
65. Smith, *Agnès Varda*, 14.
66. Kovács, *Screening Modernism*, 225.
67. Stewart, *Look of Reading*, 81.
68. *New York Times Book Review*, May 13, 2012, 33.
69. Quoted in Burke, Authorship, 101.

1. TYPECASTING THE AUTHOR

1. Hoffman and Spell, "How to Make."
2. Auster, "Typewriter," 10.
3. Ibid., 15, 16, 17, 21, 27, 32.
4. Wershler-Henry, *Iron Whim*, 24.
5. Ibid., 25.
6. Heidigger, *Parmenides*, 80–81, 85–86.
7. Wershler-Henry, *Iron Whim*, 17–21. Evidently, this kind of collecting is just beginning to happen with old computers. See Jennifer Schuessler, "The Muses of Insert, Delete," *New York Times*, December 26, 2011: 1, 6.
8. Bruder, "Click, Clack," E2.
9. See "The Olivetti Lettera 32 Manual Typewriter" and "1980 Olympia Report de luxe."
10. See "Scrubs: Ted vs. Typewriter."
11. Written by William Kernell, Dave Stamper, Paul Gerard Smith, and Edmund Joseph.
12. "Tintinabulous" seems to be a variation of "tintinabula," which is a tinkling bell.
13. Wershler-Henry, *Iron Whim*, 107.
14. Bangs, *Enchanted*, 1.
15. Ibid., 5.
16. Ibid., 13.
17. Wershler-Henry, *Iron Whim*, 31.
18. Bangs, *Enchanted*, 16.
19. Quoted in Kittler, *Gramophone*, 238.
20. Ibid., 200.
21. Hubbard, *Typewriter*, 11.
22. Ibid., 14.
23. Robbins, *Still Life*, ix.
24. Ibid., 271.
25. Ibid., 271–272.
26. Ibid., 273.
27. It was originally published in *Midnight Graffiti* magazine but later released as a book.
28. Darabont, *Walpuski's*, 18.
29. Ibid., 25–26, 26, 39, 51.
30. Schuessler, "The Muses of Insert, Delete," 6.
31. Wershler-Henry, *Iron Whim*, 10.
32. Ruscha, *Ed Ruscha*, 29.
33. Campbell, "Jeremy Mayer."
34. The former was designed by Ettore Sottsass (Italian, born Austria, 1917–2007) and Perry King (British, born 1938); the latter was designed by Eliot Fette Noyes.

35. See "The Typewriter Song" and "78 rpm Leroy Anderson—Typewriter (Played on a Garrard 4HF."
36. See "Typing."
37. "National Gallery of Canada: Acquisition Highlights."
38. Wershler-Henry, *Iron Whim*, 2.
39. Burroughs, "Statement."
40. Snowden, "Which Is the Fly."
41. All quotes from Cronenberg in what follows are from the commentary track to the 2003 Criterion Collection version of the DVD of *Naked Lunch* or from the documentary on the making of *Naked Lunch* (also on the DVD).
42. He did talk of his dislike of centipedes and how he didn't like the touch of spiders. See Snowden, "Which Is the Fly."
43. Ibid.
44. Burroughs, "Exterminator!" 5.
45. Ibid., 6.
46. Ibid., 8.
47. Evidently, Burroughs does mention "black meat" in his writing.
48. Snowden, "Which Is the Fly."
49. Burroughs, *Interzone*, 57.
50. Ibid., 56, 58.
51. See http://www.brainyquote.com/quotes/authors/w/william_s_burroughs.html.
52. Ibid.
53. Ibid.
54. Burroughs, *Interzone*, 49.
55. Ibid., 55.
56. Ibid., 52.
57. Another typewriter in the film is called the Krupps Dominator—which clearly envisions the machine as dangerous to those who use it as well as suggests an S/M sexual practice.
58. Darabont, *Walpuski's*, 51.
59. Burroughs, *Interzone*, 58.
60. Burroughs, *Naked Lunch*, 79.
61. Burroughs, *Ticket That Exploded*, 159.
62. Burroughs, *Nova Express*, 130, 152.
63. Ibid., 85.

2. BEYOND ADAPTATION

1. Eisenstein, "Dickens, Griffith," 444.
2. See Phebe Davidson, editor, *Film and Literature: Points of Intersection* (1997); Timothy Corrigan, *Film and Literature: An Introduction and Reader* (1999); James Naremore, ed., *Film Adaptation* (2000); and Kamilla Elliott, *Rethinking the Novel/Film Debate* (2003).
3. Arthur C. Clarke's novel was developed concurrently with early drafts of a script for the film but was published after the film opened.
4. Bazin, "*Diary*," 23.
5. He is uncredited on *Smoke*. One of his novels, *The Music of Chance* (1990), was adapted to the screen in 1993 by someone else (Philip Haas).
6. Auster, "Making of *Smoke*," 6.
7. Ibid., 8–9, 9, 14.
8. Ibid., 6, 6–7, 7.
9. Benjamin Sachs autographs the novels of Peter Aaron as though he were the author.

10. Auster, "Making of *Smoke*," 9.

11. Ibid., 6.

12. See Auster, *New York*, 206–207, 294, 341.

13. Almost all the characters in *The New York Trilogy* are described as going to the movies (in "City" Quinn goes; in "Ghosts" both Black and Blue go to movies [see Auster, *New York*, 190, 202, etc.]). The protagonist of "The Locked Room" has written about movies (245); he also goes to movies (26).

14. The plot of this film is described in detail in Auster, *New York*, 191–192.

15. In "Ghosts," Blue wants to murder Black. The hero of "The Locked Room" wants to murder Fanshawe.

16. Auster, *New York*, 9.

17. Auster, "Making of *Smoke*," 5.

18. Auster, *Leviathan*, 89, 111.

19. (1) Paul, (2) Rashid, (3) Ruby, (4) Cyrus, (5) Auggie.

20. Auster, "Making of *Smoke*," 12.

21. The character first gives his name as Rashid but his real name is Thomas Jefferson Cole. At another point in the story, however, he also masquerades as Paul Benjamin.

22. Barthes, "Death," 145.

23. Auster, *Leviathan*, 69, 71.

24. Auster, *New York*, 161–232.

25. Calvino, *If on a Winter's*, 172.

26. Auster, *New York*, 194.

27. This quote is from "Auggie Wren's Christmas Story," in Auster, *Three Films*, 161. The full story runs from 159 to 166.

28. Barthes, *Camera*, 97.

29. Deren, "Cinematography," 192.

30. In truth, it was Auster's published story (a Christmas 1990 op-ed) in the *New York Times* that stimulated Wayne Wang's interest in the project that culminated in the production of *Smoke*. In the film, however, the story is put at the end rather than at the beginning. See Felperin, "Smoke Opera," 6.

31. Barthes, "Death," 146.

32. See http://www.brainyquote.com/quotes/authors/p/pablo_picasso.html.

33. Auster, *Leviathan*, 41. The parables—of Bakhtin "smoking" his manuscript and that of Sir Walter Raleigh weighing smoke—that we find in *Smoke* both come from *The New York Trilogy*.

34. Auster, *New York*, 52—Stillman in "The City" section.

35. Auster, "Making of *Smoke*," 16.

36. Bazin, "Ontology," 166.

37. See Kermonde, *Sense of an Ending*.

38. Auster, *Invisible*, 134.

39. All of the above are sections of *The New York Trilogy*.

40. Cannon, "Reader as Detective."

41. Auster, *New York*, 9.

42. Ibid., 172–173, my emphasis.

43. Ibid., 203.

44. Mamet, *Jewish*, 11.

45. Mamet, *Wicked Son*, 45.

46. Ibid., 46.

47. Auster, *New York*, 173.

48. Bigsby, *David Mamet*, 187.

49. Barton, *Imagination*, 191–193.
50. Mamet, *3 Uses*, 14, 18.
51. Ibid., 19, 15, 16–17.
52. Ibid., 19.
53. Ibid., 18.
54. Mamet, *On Directing*, 72.
55. Ibid., 5.
56. Ibid., 6.
57. See Allen, *Three One-Act Plays*.
58. Allen, *Insanity*.
59. Ibid.
60. Ibid., 180–183, 180–181, 181.
61. For instance, in *Manhattan* (1979), Allen plays a television writer.
62. Allen, *Insanity*, 245–269.
63. "Woody Allen Marries."

3. THE AUTHOR AT THE DREAM FACTORY

1. Boon, *Script Culture*, 193, 6.
2. Ibid., 193.
3. Ibid., 7–9.
4. Ibid., 11.
5. Fine, *Hollywood*, 24.
6. Ibid., 53.
7. Ibid., 3.
8. Davis, *Words into Images*, 41.
9. Fine, *Hollywood*, 8.
10. Davis, *Words into Images*, 42.
11. Fine, *Hollywood*, 14.
12. Ibid., 24, 35, 34, 35.
13. Davis, *Words into Images*, ix.
14. Ibid., 43.
15. Ibid., xii.
16. Boon, *Script Culture*, ix-xi.
17. Fine, *Hollywood*, 16.
18. Davis, *Words into Images*, ix.
19. Goodyear, "Letter from Los Angeles."
20. Carringer, "*Making of "Citizen Kane.*"
21. Polan, *Lonely Place*, 36.
22. Ibid., 30.
23. Thanks to Kyle Stevens for suggesting the film to me.
24. Duvivier died in 1967 and had been making films since the silent era.
25. "Flame-Out."
26. Bart, "Holden."
27. There has been much writing on *Barton Fink* but my own thoughts on the film were developed over years of teaching and lecturing on it and did not benefit from a prior reading of this criticism. No doubt some of it touches on ideas presented in this chapter.
28. Odets worked in Hollywood and wrote the screenplays for such works as *None But the Lonely Heart* (1944), *Humoresque* (1946), and *Sweet Smell of Success* (1957).
29. Calvino, *If on a Winter's*, 179.
30. Palmer, *Joel and Ethan*, 116.

31. Calvino, *If on a Winter's*, 177.

32. Ibid., 197.

33. Here one could also say more about the film's Jewish focus. Aside from the world of the Jewish film executives, we have the LA detectives who ask Fink if he's a Jew and seem anti-Semitic. Also, when Meadows walks down the hall after setting fire to the Earle, he shouts: "Heil Hitler!" During the course of the film it's clear that World War II has broken out. When Fink goes to the GSO and dances with a woman, a sailor tries to cut in and he doesn't let him. He tells the sailor that his mind is his uniform. He gets beaten up and thrown out. The last time we see Lipnick, he wears a military uniform—signaling Hollywood's wartime collaboration with the U.S. government.

34. In April 1932, Faulkner signed a six-week contract with Metro-Goldwyn-Mayer, and in May he began working in Hollywood. Of the six screenplays for which Faulkner received screen credit, five were directed by Hawks, the first of which was *Today We Live* (1933), based on Faulkner's short story "Turn About." He left Hollywood for a while but, in need of money, returned and sold Paramount the rights to his novel *Sanctuary*, which became *The Story of Temple Drake* (1933). Faulkner's MGM contract expired in May 1933. See Padgett, "Faulkner."

35. Carroll, *Theorizing the Moving Image*.

36. See Robbe-Grillet, *Two Novels*, 109–110. In *Jealousy*, a picture on a calendar hanging on a wall is described in great detail.

37. Palmer, *Joel and Ethan*, 110.

38. Orlean, *Orchid Thief*, 24.

39. Kaufman, *Adaptation*, 123.

40. Ibid., viii.

41. Ibid., viii.

42. No other credits are listed for him as writer, director, or actor.

43. Tan, "Freeze!"

44. Guo, "Metaphysical Cinema."

45. Guo, "Further Notes."

46. Mamet, *On Directing*, 5.

47. For an excellent and in-depth analysis of *Poetic Justice*, see Jenkins, "Films of Hollis Frampton," 244–258.

48. The published script for the film is in MacDonald, *Screen Writings*, 70–90.

49. Jenkins, "Films of Hollis Frampton," 258.

4. THE AUTHORESS

1. Gilbert and Gubar, *Mad Woman*, 15, 7.

2. *An Angel at My Table* (1991), *Becoming Jane* (2007), *Impromptu* (1991), *Miss Potter* (2006), *Iris* (2001), *Capote* (2005), *Bukowski: Born into This* (2003), *Shadowlands* (1993), *Céleste* (1980).

3. Schilt, *François Ozon*, 96.

4. Ozon, *Swimming Pool*, 21–22.

5. Schilt, *François Ozon*, 96.

6. Henke, "Woman Alone," 22.

7. Ibid., 23–24.

8. Boynton, "Writing Women," 153.

9. Woolf, *Granite and Rainbow*, 47.

10. Freud, *On Creativity*, 47–48.

11. Rank, "Life and Creation," 309.

12. David, "Art and Anxiety," 446–447.

13. Perry, "Creative Flow."

14. Carvalho, "Serving Up," 209.
15. Greenblatt, "Writing Fiction." Likewise, screenwriter Joe Eszterhas speaks of giving birth to his characters; see "Quotations about Writing."
16. Friedman, "Return of the Repressed," 141.
17. Ibid., 142.
18. Ibid., 141.
19. Woolf, *Granite and Rainbow*, 41–42.
20. Kaplan, *Women and Film*, 138, 138–139, 153–154.
21. MacDonald, "Interview," 218.
22. Quoted in Bustarret, "Material Surface," 334.
23. Mulvey, "Visual Pleasure," 748.
24. Vance, *Pleasure and Danger*, 1.
25. Ibid., 3.
26. Segal, *Straight Sex*, xxi.
27. Mulvey, "Visual Pleasure," 748.
28. MacDonald, "Interview," 218.
29. Monk, "Tango Lesson," 54.
30. Rooney, "Tango Lesson," 78.
31. Savigliano, *Tango*, xiv.
32. Taylor, *Paper Tangos*, 2.
33. Savigliano, *Tango*, 12.
34. Ibid., 44, 47, 11, 111.
35. Ibid., 3, 109, 122.
36. Ibid., 48, 55; Taylor, *Paper Tangos*, 7.
37. Brooks, *Melodramatic Imagination*, 27, 32.
38. Savigliano, *Tango* 109, 57.
39. Ibid., 71.
40. Ibid., 69.
41. Taylor, *Paper Tangos*, 33.
42. Savigliano, *Tango*, 127.
43. Taylor, *Paper Tangos*, 39.
44. Savigliano, *Tango*, 61.
45. Ibid., ix–xv.
46. Taylor, *Paper Tangos*, 10.
47. In an interview with Potter on the *Rage* DVD, she emphasizes how long it took her to write the script and how many versions she discarded in so doing. She cites writing the screenplay as the hardest part of making the film.

5. WRITING PAIN

1. Sandblom, *Creativity and Disease*, 31.
2. Woolf, *On Being Ill*, 6–7.
3. Ibid., 4.
4. Gilman, *Disease and Representation*, 3.
5. Marlow here is spelled without the final "e" of Chandler's Marlowe.
6. This storyline occurs in later episodes.
7. Gilman, *Disease and Representation*, 4.
8. Quoted in Sandblom, *Creativity and Disease*, 25.
9. Woolf, *On Being Ill*, 6.
10. Updike, "At War," 75–76.
11. Ibid., 74–75.

12. Quoted in O'Farrell, "Self-Consciousness," 134, 136, 145.

13. Sandblom, *Creativity and Disease*, 58. Sandblom does not give a source for this quotation.

14. Woolf, *On Being Ill*, 5.

15. Bauby, *Diving Bell*, 29.

16. Woolf, *On Being Ill*, 14.

17. Emma Wilson discusses the issue of pain, corporeality, and death in *Providence*. See Wilson, *Alain Resnais*, 139.

18. Among other things, the film is a treatise on the right to suicide or assisted suicide. Aside from this reference to Molly having taken her life rather than face a terminal illness, in the "fictional" narrative Kevin kills the werewolf to put him out of his misery, having been shot. Later, we see him putting up a political banner about the right to die while soldiers march past.

19. In her book on Resnais, Wilson quotes William Van Wert as stating that *Providence* is about "fabricating a work of art" (131).

20. Monaco, *Alain Resnais*, 206.

21. Kreidl, *Alain Resnais*, 195, 205.

22. Ibid., 207.

23. Ibid., 208. Wilson also discusses this shot (143).

24. See Freud, *On Creativity*.

25. See http://www.brainyquote.com/quotes/authors/v/victor_hugo.html.

26. Aside from the cases I cite, collaboration with (often uncredited) women marks the careers of Theodor Adorno and John Stuart Mill as well.

27. Thanks to Dan Morgan for bringing Brecht to my attention here.

28. Kuhn, "Bertolt Brecht," 8–9.

29. Page, "Stieg Larsson's Partner."

30. Doane, *Desire to Desire*, 2.

31. Albaret, *Monsieur Proust*, 278.

32. King, *On Writing*, 165.

33. Franz and Smulyan, *Major Problems*, 178.

34. Underwood and Miller, *Bare Bones*, 135.

35. Lesser, *His Other Half*, 23.

36. Ibid.

37. Ibid., 30.

38. Smith, "Real Horrorshow," 303.

39. Walter Metz does, however, consider Jack's position as a financially disenfranchised person (because of being a writer) in the American capitalist system. See Metz, "Toward a Post-Structural Influence," 51.

40. Ibid., 52.

41. Kolker, "All Roads," 56.

42. Smith, "Real Horrorshow," 303.

43. Definition of "torrent" via Dictionary.com.

44. Flaherty, *Midnight Disease*, 79.

45. Ibid., 82.

46. Gilman, *Disease and Representation*, 1.

47. Wilson, "Philoctetes," 275–276.

48. Ibid., 287, 288, 289.

49. Ibid.

6. *CINÉCRITURE*: WORD AND IMAGE

1. Eisner, *Comics*, 8.

2. Eisenstein, "Cinematographic Principle."

3. Quoted in Maia, "When What You See," 381.
4. Mitchell, *Picture Theory*, 95.
5. Quoted in Heller and Pomeroy, *Design Literacy*, 106.
6. Ibid., 150.
7. See James Monaco, *How to Read a Film* (New York: Oxford University Press, 1979).
8. Foucault, *This Is Not a Pipe*, 28.
9. Apollinaire, *Calligrammes*, 88–89.
10. Stewart, *Look of Reading*, 8.
11. Ibid., 152.
12. Ibid., 329.
13. Bolter, *Writing Space*, 48, 58.
14. Mitchell, *Picture Theory*, 11.
15. Kirschenbaum, "Word as Image," 137.
16. Bazin, "What Is Cinema?" 24.
17. Quoted in Kirschenbaum, "Word as Image," 137.
18. Mitchell, *Picture Theory*, 100.
19. Metz, *Film Language*, 44.
20. Mitry, *Aesthetics*, 14.
21. Ibid., 16.
22. Ibid., 15.
23. Ibid., 23.
24. Martin, *Images*, 13.
25. Calvino, *Six Memos*, 83.
26. Ibid., 89.
27. Ibid., 88–89.
28. Ibid., 89.
29. Carroll, *Theorizing*, 187.
30. Ibid., 187.
31. Ibid., 189.
32. Ibid., 194.
33. Bresson, *Notes*, 48.
34. Bernanos, *Country Priest*, 11.
35. Sontag, "Spiritual Style," 43.
36. Bazin, "Diary," 11.
37. Andrew, "Desperation and Meditation," 24–25.
38. Bresson, *Notes*, 2.
39. Ibid., 5.
40. Ibid., 33, 14.
41. Among the writers who have discussed the issue of the priest's diary writing in some detail are Andrew, "Desperation and Meditation" (28–30), Price, "Word and Image" (50–51, 53–54, 55), Cunneen, "All Is Grace" (45–46, 55), and Pipolo, "Author, Author" (80–82).
42. Reader, "*Journal*," 33.
43. Of course, the English-language version of the film has the words on the page written in French and the voiceover subtitled, the latter of which adds a second confusing level of print onscreen to the mix. My transcriptions of the voiceover narration throughout is approximate but catches the drift of the meaning.
44. Pipolo, "Author, Author," 81.
45. Quoted in Cunneen, "All Is Grace," 45.
46. Bazin ("Diary," 21) and Sontag ("Spiritual Style," 33) talk of a general redundancy or doubling between word and image, though not specifically in regard to written diary entries.
47. Mulvey, "Index," 143.

48. Bresson, *Notes*, 28.

49. Andrew, "Desperation and Meditation," 28.

50. Knorr and Moffat, "When the Photographer," 259.

51. See Sesonske, "Time and Tense," 423. Pipolo, "Author, Author," discusses issues of temporality in the film (81–82), as does Browne, "Film Form" (216–217).

52. Klein and Li, *Expression of Time*, 2.

53. Ibid., 40–41.

54. Banfield, "*L'imparfait*," 75.

55. Sesonske, "Time and Tense," 419.

56. Ibid., 425.

57. In the Bernanos novel, on certain occasions we get an editorial note telling us that certain words have been erased (96) or crossed out (112, 129, 187).

58. Bernanos, *Country Priest*, 174. Price, "Word and Image," uses this term (55).

59. Bernanos, *Country Priest*, 99.

60. Bustarret, "Material Surface," 333.

61. Bazin, "What Is Cinema?" 9.

62. Bresson, *Notes*, 72.

63. Ibid., 7.

64. Mulvey, "Index," 146.

65. Bazin, "Diary," 21.

66. Ibid., 16.

67. This is a reversal of the biblical notion of the word made flesh as in John 1:14. "And the Word became flesh and dwelt among us, and we have seen his glory, glory as of the only Son from the Father, full of grace and truth."

68. Bolter, *Writing Space*, 56.

69. Eisner, *Comics*, 7.

70. Ibid., 42.

71. Ibid., 8.

72. Ibid., 80.

73. Fell, *Film and the Narrative Tradition*, 92–113.

74. See Kupfer, "Anything Can Happen."

75. Crafton, "Comic Strips."

76. Musser, *Emergence of Cinema*, 357.

77. Eisner, *Comics*, 7.

78. Ibid., 39, 10, 23, 30, 30, 42, 30.

79. Fell, *Film and the Narrative Tradition*, 93–104.

80. Eisner, *Comics*, 39.

81. Ibid., 51, 9, 128.

82. Ibid., 20.

83. Ibid., 41.

84. Reader, "*Journal*," 41.

85. See Yiddish Dictionary Online and Dictionary.com.

86. Pekar, *Beats*, 6.

87. Ibid., 79, 85.

88. Ibid., 87.

89. Ibid., 19.

7. CORPUS AND OEUVRE

1. Sally Chivers and Nicole Markotic, eds., *The Problem Body: Projecting Disability on Film* (Columbus: Ohio State University Press, 2010).

2. Nichols, *Maya Deren*, 55.

3. It is also known as *Spirit of Tattoo*.

4. Clarens, "Erotica for Export," 58.

5. Cohn, "Review of *Irezumi*."

6. Canby, "New Directors."

7. Clarens, "Erotica for Export," 58.

8. McCallum, "Historical and Cultural Dimensions," 109.

9. Felman, *Japanese Tattoo*, 16.

10. Scutt and Gotch, *Art, Sex, and Symbol*, 41–42.

11. Ibid., 42.

12. Lautman, *New Tattoo*, 11.

13. Krakow, *Total Tattoo Book*, 20.

14. Richie, "Japanese Art," 50.

15. McCallum, "Historical and Cultural Dimensions," 119.

16. Ibid., 121.

17. Lautman, *New Tattoo*, 12.

18. Richie, "Japanese Art," 50.

19. Felman, *Japanese Tattoo*, 17.

20. The tattoo machine was invented by Samuel O'Reilly in the United States in 1891. See Krakow, *Total Tattoo Book*, 22.

21. Thayer, "Tattoos," 351.

22. McCallum, "Historical and Cultural Dimensions," 128.

23. Ibid., 121.

24. Thomas, "Introduction," 8.

25. Ibid., 48–49.

26. Richie, "Japanese Art," 50.

27. Scutt and Gotch, *Art, Sex and Symbol*, 143.

28. McCallum, "Historical and Cultural Dimensions," 130.

29. Ibid., 120.

30. Canby, "New Directors."

31. Desser, *Eros Plus Massacre*, 119.

32. McCallum, "Historical and Cultural Dimensions," 125.

33. Ibid., 132–133.

34. Ibid., 128.

35. Takabayashi made the film *Naomi* (1980) based on Tanizaki's novel *A Fool's Love*.

36. Desser, *Eros Plus Massacre*, 98.

37. Clarens, "Erotica for Export," 58.

38. Desser, *Eros Plus Massacre*, 98.

39. Mulvey, "Visual Pleasure," 757.

40. Thomas, "Introduction," 9.

41. Lautman, *New Tattoo*, 7.

42. Tanizaki, "Tattooer," 162.

43. Cixous, "Laugh of the Medusa," 250.

44. McCallum, "Historical and Cultural Dimensions," 129–130.

45. Desser , *Eros Plus Massacre*, 101.

46. Felman, *Japanese Tattoo*, 16.

47. The sense of Akane's association with purity is also advanced by the picture of Lady Tachibana tattooed on her back. According to Keiko McDonald, Lady Tachibana was a devoted Buddhist who worshiped at the famous Horyuji Temple house. McDonald also remarks that "the image tattooed upon Akane's back—that of Lady Tachibana with a sword—is a strange mixture of the holy (spiritual) and the carnal." Via e-mail, January 19, 1998.

48. Thomas, "Introduction," 8.

49. Keiko McDonald helped me to understand the symbolism of the snowflake in Japanese culture.

50. Richie, "Japanese Art," 59.

51. Thomas, "Introduction," 9.

52. Ibid., 8.

53. In the *Kodansha Encyclopedia of Japan*, the Tachibana family is described as a "noble family (Uji) of ancient Japan who distinguished themselves particularly during the Nara period" (710–794). It also states that the Tachibana became one of the " 'Four Great Surnames' together with the Fumiowara, Taira and Minamoto families." Lady Tachibana was the consort of minister Fujiwara-no-fuhito in the eighth century, when Nara was the capital of Japan. See Bunji, "Tachibana Family," 292.

54. Tanizaki, "Tattooer," 169.

55. Mayne, "Limits of Spectacle," 7.

56. Richie, "Japanese Art," 55.

57. McCallum, "Historical and Cultural Dimensions," 122.

58. Takabayashi made a film in 1976 based on a Mishima novel: *Kinkakuji* (*The Temple of the Golden Pavilion*).

59. Felman, *Japanese Tattoo*, 18.

60. Lautman notes: "A macabre point of interest is that Japan possesses the only collection of modern tattooed human hides, preserved at the Medical Pathology Museum of Tokyo University. The hundred-plus skins were all collected as masterpieces of the art form with the complete cooperation of the tattooees and their families." See Lautman, *New Tattoo*, 12. Also discussed by Felman, *Japanese Tattoo*, 18, and Scutt and Gotch, *Art, Sex, and Symbol*, 47 (the latter refer to it as the Anatomy Museum of the University of Tokyo Medical School).

61. Chua, "Peter Greenaway, "178.

62. Ibid., 180.

63. See Keesey, *Films of Peter Greenaway*, 148–181.

64. Ibid., 150.

65. Chua, "Peter Greenaway," 177.

66. See "Zorns Lemma."

67. Greenaway, *Pillow Book*, 6.

68. Ibid., 5.

69. Christin, *History of Writing*, 10.

70. Eisenstein, *Film Form*, 30.

71. Greenaway, *Pillow Book*, 12.

72. Fraenkel, "Signatures," 316.

73. Bazin, *What Is Cinema?*, 14.

74. It is translated in a subtitle.

75. That is, rather than subtitling the French words in English, they appear as French words on screen.

76. Pink, "4th Annual Year."

77. Auster, *New York Trilogy*, 52.

8. STEALING BEAUTY

1. Calvino, *If on a Winter's*, 169.

2. Ibid., 170.

3. Ibid., 176.

4. Ibid., 170.

5. Barthes, "Death," 130.

6. Ibid., 129.

7. Burke, "Introduction," xix.

8. Poulet, "Criticism and the Experience," 102.

9. Ibid., 104.

10. Ibid., 105.

11. Ibid., 102.

12. Stewart, *Look of Reading*, 3.

13. Barthes, "Grain of the Voice," 181.

14. Stewart, *Look of Reading*, 5.

15. Ibid., 12, 11.

16. Ibid., 138, 243.

17. In his later years he developed a constant desire for solitude, an obsession for self-preservation, and a fear of death and crazed paranoia of persecution, which came from the syphilis he had contracted in his early days. On January 2, 1892, Maupassant tried to commit suicide by cutting his throat and was committed to the celebrated private asylum of Dr. Esprit Blanche at Passy, in Paris, where he died on July 6, 1893.

18. I have not been able to locate the actual book to which this refers.

19. The name of the businessman is not given in the film or in the credits.

20. The name of the magistrate is not given in the film or in the credits.

21. Kreiman and Sidtis, 381.

22. Silverman, *Acoustic Mirror*, 86.

23. Ebert, "*La Lectrice* Review," my emphasis.

24. Poulet, "Criticism and the Experience," 106.

25. Ibid., 105.

26. The woman's name is not given in the film or in the credits.

27. Poulet, "Criticism and the Experience," 105.

28. Foucault, "What Is," 233.

29. Ibid., 235.

30. Ibid., 234.

31. Ibid., 235.

32. For example, he is the author of *Lectures du désir: Nerval, Lautréamont, Apollinaire, Éluard* (Paris: Éditions du Seuil, 1977).

33. Pease, "Author," 272. This despite the fact that Barthes, himself, claims that the reign of the author has been the reign of the critic! See "Death," 129. Maybe Barthes is thinking of the traditional critic who interprets the meaning of the work, whereas Pease is speaking of the critic/theorist—who is more interested in the process of reading than the "meaning" of the work but the boundaries tend to be blurred.

34. Foucault, "What Is," 240.

35. Adair, *Death*, 27.

36. See Mastrocinque, "Hermes."

37. Adair, *Death*, 25.

38. Ibid., 58.

39. Ibid., 59.

40. Ibid., 3.

41. Calvino, *If on a Winter's*, 185.

42. Ibid., 186.

43. Perhaps his name is a reference to the great German writer Friedrich Schiller. Furthermore, the word *schiller* in German means "iridescent."

44. Calvino, *If on a Winter's*, 191–192.

45. Ibid., 170.

46. I found only three articles by Eder (brief ones in *Films in Review*), none on Hitchcock. Amazon lists one book co-written by him on another subject. I found no extended critical pieces that he has written on Hitchcock. *Film Literature Index* listed a host of his film reviews in the *Village Voice* and one piece on the video rights for *Rear Window*. A short bio for Eder can be found at Answers.com.

47. *The Examined Life* features Judith Butler and Cornel West.

48. See "Roland Barthes — Centre Pompidou."

49. Karlgaard, "Politics Is Hollywood."

50. Barthes, "Death," 129.

AFTERWORD

1. Lucy Fischer, "Frampton and the Magellan Metaphor."

2. See Kaplan, *Women in Film*, 138.

3. In Shot #179, for instance, we read, "Bedroom. Love Making. Outside the window, I am aiming a camera."

4. Quoted in "Zorns Lemma."

5. In the Roman alphabet, U and V and I and J are considered the same letters. Scott MacDonald, in "Hollis Frampton," thinks he chose this alphabet because sound film runs at twenty-four frames per second.

6. Christin, *History of Writing*, 10.

7. This is Scott MacDonald's term for them in "Hollis Frampton."

8. The series was originally created in 1977–1979. At first, she put up posters with her Truisms on city walls, but later she posted them in a more sophisticated manner (as illuminated urban signs or as art works in museums).

9. Jenkins, *Films of Hollis Frampton*, 200.

10. Simon, "Reading," 41.

11. See Sitney, *Visionary Films*, 367–370; Jenkins, *Films of Hollis Frampton*, 190–234.

12. Windhausen, "Words into Film," 82.

13. Simon, "Reading," 48.

14. Simon makes this pun in "Reading," 48.

15. Wollen, *Signs and Meaning*, 122–125.

16. Ibid., 122.

17. Bazin, *What Is Cinema?*, 14.

18. Quoted in Kirschenbaum, "Word as Image," 137.

19. MacDonald, "Hollis Frampton"; Simon, "Reading," 42–44, 47–48.

20. Jenkins, *Films of Hollis Frampton*, 210–218.

21. Frampton, *On the Camera*, 136.

22. Jenkins, *Films of Hollis Frampton*, 206.

23. Frampton, *On the Camera*, 197.

24. Ibid., 200.

25. Ibid., 198.

26. Ibid., 196.

27. Jenkins, *Films of Hollis Frampton*, 206.

28. He also mentions *Wavelength* (in another context) in his notes for *Zorns Lemma*. See *On the Camera*, 197.

29. Jenkins, *Films of Hollis Frampton*, 211–212, 213.

30. Frampton, *On the Camera*, 200.

31. Ibid., 166, 167, 168.

32. Ibid.

33. Ibid., 168–169.

34. See "*Hapax Legomena.*"

35. As defined on Dictionary.com.

36. Quoted in MacDonald, "Hollis Frampton."

37. See "(*nostalgia*)."

38. Frampton, *On the Camera*, 224.

39. Ibid.

40. Evidently, it is a not a continuous take, since a film magazine had to be changed in the middle of the event. This is covered over as best as possible in the film.

41. Frampton, *On the Camera*, 194.

42. Frost, "Stopping by Woods," 35. Scott MacDonald has referred to Frost's poem in his discussion of this section of the film.

43. MacDonald, "Hollis Frampton."

44. Frampton, *On the Camera*, 224.

45. Barthes, *Camera*, 97.

46. Frampton, *On the Camera*, 135.

47. See http://www.brainyquote.com/quotes/authors/g/george_sand.html.

FILMOGRAPHY

FILMS DISCUSSED IN DETAIL

Note: Since this is a book about the author as a figure in cinema, it seems only fitting that for these works I provide a list of the writers—although some names have already been supplied within the text itself. In honor of the writer's role in film production, I have placed this credit first.

8 ½. Written by Federico Fellini and Ennio Flaiano (story); Ennio Flaiano, Tullio Pinelli, Federico Fellini, and Brunello Rondi (screenplay). Directed by Federico Fellini. Rome: Cineriz, 1963.

Adaptation. Written by Charlie and Donald Kaufman. Adapted from Susan Orlean's book *The Orchid Thief.* Directed by Spike Jonze. Los Angeles: Sony Pictures Entertainment, 2002.

An Alan Smithee Film: Burn Hollywood Burn. Written by Joe Eszterhas. Directed by Alan Smithee (Arthur Hiller). Los Angeles: Hollywood Pictures, 1997.

American Splendor. Written by Shari Springer Berman and Robert Pulcini. Adapted from Harvey Pekar's comic book series *American Splendor* and Pekar and Joyce Brabner's comic book series *Our Cancer Year.* Directed by Shari Springer Berman and Robert Pulcini. New York: Good Machine, 2005.

The Auteur Theory. Written by Evan Oppenheimer. Directed by Evan Oppenheimer. Theoretical Films, 1999.

The Bad and the Beautiful. Written by George Bradshaw (story); Charles Schnee (screenplay). Directed by Vincente Minnelli. Beverly Hills: Metro-Goldwyn-Mayer, 1952.

Barton Fink. Written by Joel and Ethan Coen. Directed by Joel Coen. Los Angeles: Circle Films, 1992.

Basic Instinct. Written by Joe Eszterhas. Directed by Paul Verhoeven. Los Angeles: Carolco Pictures, 1992.

Bombay Talkie. Written by Ruth Prawer Jhabvala and James Ivory. Directed by James Ivory. Mumbai: Merchant Ivory Productions, 1970.

Boy Meets Girl. Written by Samuel and Bella Spewack. Adapted from their play. *Boy Meets Girl.* Directed by Lloyd Bacon. Burbank, Calif.: Warner Bros. Pictures, 1938.

Céleste. Written by Percy Adlon. Adapted from Céleste Albaret's book *Monsieur Proust.* Directed by Percy Adlon. London: Artificial Eye, 1980.

Citizen Kane. Written by Herman J. Mankiewicz and Orson Welles. Directed by Orson Welles. Los Angeles: RKO Radio Pictures, 1941.

Deconstructing Harry. Written by Woody Allen. Directed by Woody Allen. New York: Jean Doumanian Features, 1997.

Diary of a Country Priest (*Journal d'un curé de campagne*). Written by Robert Bresson. Adapted from Georges Bernanos's novel. Directed by Robert Bresson. Neuilly-sur-Seine, France: Union Générale Cinématographique (UGC), 1951.

The Diving Bell and the Butterfly. Written by Ronald Harwood. Adapted from Jean-Dominique Bauby's book. Directed by Julian Schnabel. Paris: Pathé Renn Productions, 2007.

His Girl Friday. Written by Charles Lederer. Adapted from Ben Hecht and Charles MacArthur's play *The Front Page.* Directed by Howard Hawks. Burbank, Calif.: Columbia Pictures Corporation, 1940.

Homicide. Written by David Mamet. Directed by David Mamet. Baltimore: Triumph Releasing Corporation, 1991.

The Hours. Written by David Hare. Adapted from Michael Cunningham's novel. Directed by Stephen Daldry. Hollywood: Paramount Pictures, 2002.

How Is Your Fish Today? (*Jin tian de yu zen me yang?*). Written by Xiaolu Guo and Hui Rao. Directed by Xiaolu Guo. London: British Documentary Foundation, 2006.

I Could Never Be Your Woman. Written by Amy Heckerling. Directed by Amy Heckerling. Los Angeles: I Could Never Ltd., 2007.

In a Lonely Place. Written by Andrew Solt and Edmund H. North. Adapted from Dorothy B. Hughes's novel. Directed by Nicholas Ray. Burbank, Calif.: Columbia Pictures Corporation, 1950.

Irezumi. Written by Chiho Katsura. Adapted from Baku Akae's novel. Directed by Yoichi Takabayashi. Tokyo: Daiei Studios, 1984.

La Lectrice. Written by Michel Deville and Rosalinde Deville. Adapted from Raymond Jean's novel. Directed by Michel Deville. France: Eléfilm, 1988.

Limitless. Written by Leslie Dixon. Adapted from Alan Glyn's novel. Directed by Neil Burger. Beverly Hills: Relativity Media, 2011.

Misery. Written by William Golden. Adapted from Stephen King's novel. Directed by Rob Reiner. Beverly Hills: Castle Rock Entertainment, 1990.

My Brilliant Career. Written by Eleanor Witcombe. Adapted from Miles Franklin's novel. Directed by Gillian Armstrong. New South Wales, Australia: Greater Union Organisation, 1979.

My Dear Secretary. Written by Charles Martin. Directed by Charles Martin. Cardinal Pictures, 1949.

My Effortless Brilliance. Written by Basil Harris, Jeanette Maus, Sean Nelson, Calvin Reeder, and Lynn Shelton. Directed by Lynn Shelton. Seattle, 2008.

Naked Lunch [*David Cronenberg's Naked Lunch*]. Written by David Cronenberg. Adapted from William S. Burroughs's novel. Directed by David Cronenberg. Toronto: Film Trustees Ltd., 1991.

(*nostalgia*). Written by Hollis Frampton. Directed by Hollis Frampton. 1971.

Paris When It Sizzles. Written by George Axelrod. Adapted from Julien Duvivier and Henri Jeanson's screenplay for *La fête à Henriette*. Directed by Richard Quine. Los Angeles: Paramount Pictures, 1964.

The Pervert's Guide to Cinema. Written by Slavoj Žižek. Directed by Sophie Fiennes. Virginia: Amoeba Film, 2006.

The Pillow Book. Written by Peter Greenaway. Adapted from Sei Shōnagon's book. Directed by Peter Greenaway. Kasander & Wigman Productions, 1996.

Poetic Justice. Written by Hollis Frampton. Directed by Hollis Frampton. 1972.

Providence. Written by David Mercer. Directed by Alain Resnais. Action Films, 1977.

Rage. Written by Sally Potter. Directed by Sally Potter. London: Adventure Films, 2009.

Ready, Willing, and Able. Written by Richard Macaulay (story); Jerry Wald and Sig Herzeig and Warren Duff (screenplay). Directed by Ray Enright. Los Angeles: Warner Bros. Pictures, 1937.

Romancing the Stone. Written by Diane Thomas. Directed by Robert Zemeckis. Los Angeles: Twentieth Century-Fox Film Corporation, 1984.

She-Devil. Written by Barry Strugatz and Mark R. Burns. Adapted from Fay Weldon's novel. Directed by Susan Seidelman. Los Angeles: Orion Pictures, 1989.

The Shining. Written by Stanley Kubrick and Diane Johnson. Adapted from Stephen King's novel. Directed by Stanley Kubrick. Burbank, Calif.: Warner Bros. Pictures, 1980.

Le Silence de la Mer. Written by Jean-Pierre Melville. Adapted from Vercors's novel. France: Melville Productions, 1949.

The Singing Detective. Written by Dennis Potter. Directed by Jon Amiel. London: British Broadcasting Corporation, 1986.

Smoke. Written by Paul Auster. Directed by Wayne Wang and Paul Auster. Los Angeles: Miramax, 1995.

Starting Out in the Evening. Written by Fred Parnes and Andrew Wagner. Adapted from Brian Morton's novel. Directed Andrew Wagner. New York: Cinetic Media, 1997.

State and Main. Written by David Mamet. Directed by David Mamet. Los Angeles: Filmtown
Entertainment, 2000.

Stranger Than Fiction. Written by Zach Helm. Directed by Marc Forster. Burbank, Calif.: Columbia Pictures, 2006.

Sunset Blvd. Written by Charles Brackett, Billy Wilder, and D. M. Marshman Jr. Directed by Billy
Wilder. Los Angeles: Paramount Pictures, 1950.

Swimming Pool. Written by François Ozon and Emmanuèle Bernheim. Directed by François
Ozon. Paris: Fidélité Productions, 2003.

Tango. Written by Carlos Saura. Directed by Carlos Saura. Buenos Aires: Adela Pictures, 1998.

The Tango Lesson. Written by Sally Potter. Directed by Sally Potter. London: Adventure Pictures,
1997.

Utamaro and His Five Women (*Utamaro o meguru gonin no onna*). Written by Yoshikato Yoda.
Adapted from Kanji Kunieda's novel. Directed by Kenji Mizoguchi. Tokyo: Shôchiko Eiga,
1946.

Zorns Lemma. Written by Hollis Frampton. Directed by Hollis Frampton. 1970.

FILMS MENTIONED IN PASSING

All That Jazz. Directed by Bob Fosse. Burbank, Calif.: Columbia Pictures Corporation, 1979.

An Angel at My Table. Directed by Jane Campion. Sydney: Australian Broadcasting Corporation,
1990.

Atonement. Directed by Joe Wright. London: Universal City: Universal Pictures, 2007.

Avatar. Directed by James Cameron. Los Angeles: Twentieth Century-Fox Film Corporation, 2009.

Becoming Jane. Directed by Julian Jarrold. London: Ecosse Films, 2007.

The Birth of a Nation. Directed by D. W. Griffith. Los Angeles: David W. Griffith Corp., 1915.

Blow-Up. Directed by Michelangelo Antonioni. London: Bridge Films, 1966.

Blue in the Face. Directed by Wayne Wang and Paul Auster. Los Angeles: Miramax, 1995.

Bukowski: Born into This. Directed by John Dullaghan. New York and Austin: Magnolia Pictures,
2003.

Carmen. Directed by Carlos Saura. Madrid: Televisión Española, 1983.

Close Encounters of the Third Kind. Directed by Steven Spielberg. Burbank, Calif.: Columbia Pictures Corporation, 1977.

Day for Night. Directed by François Truffaut. Paris: Les Films du Carosse, 1973.

Death of a Gunfighter. Directed by Alan Smithee [Don Siegel and Robert Totten]. Los Angeles:
Universal Pictures, 1969.

The Draughtman's Contract. Directed by Peter Greenaway. London: British Film Institute, 1982.

E.T.: The Extra-Terrestrial. Directed by Steven Spielberg. Los Angeles: Universal Pictures, 1982.

The Eyes of Laura Mars. Directed by Irvin Kershner. Burbank, Calif.: Columbia Pictures Corporation, 1978.

Flamenco. Directed by Carlos Saura. Madrid: Canal + España, 1995.

From the Manger to the Cross. Directed by Sidney Olcott. New York: Kalem Company, 1912.

Funny Face. Directed by Stanley Donen. Los Angeles: Paramount Pictures, 1957.

The Great Train Robbery. Directed by Edwin S. Porter. West Orange, N.J.: Edison Manufacturing
Company, 1903.

Impromptu. Directed by James Lapine. France: C.L.G. Films, 1991.

Iris. Directed by Richard Eyre. London: British Broadcasting Corporation, 2001.

The Lady Vanishes. Directed by Alfred Hitchcock. DVD commentary by Bruce Eder. New York:
Criterion Collection, 1998.

Laura. Directed by Otto Preminger. Los Angeles: Twentieth Century-Fox Corporation, 1944.

Little Nemo [*Winsor McCay, the Famous Cartoonist of the N.Y. Herald and His Moving Comics*]. Directed by Winsor McCay and J. Stuart Blackton. New York: Vitagraph Company of America, 1911.

The Merry Widow. Directed Erich von Stroheim. Los Angeles: Metro-Goldwyn-Mayer, 1925.

A Midsummer Night's Dream. Directed by Charles Kent and J. Stuart Blackton. New York: Vitagraph Company of America, 1909.

Miss Potter. Directed by Chris Noonan. Los Angeles: Phoenix Pictures, 2006.

Music of Chance. Directed by Philip Haas. New York: IRS Media, 1993.

My Fair Lady. Directed by George Cukor. Burbank, Calif.: Warner Bros. Pictures, 1964.

Ordet. Directed by Carl Theodor Dreyer. Stockholm: Palladium Film, 1955.

Orlando. Directed by Sally Potter. London: Adventure Pictures, 1992.

Persona. Directed by Ingmar Bergman. Stockholm: Svensk Filmindustri, 1966.

Queen Kelly. Directed by Erich von Stroheim. Los Angeles: Gloria Swanson Pictures, 1929.

The River. Directed by Jean Renoir. Oriental International Films, 1951.

La Roue. Directed by Abel Gance. France: Films Abel Gance, 1923.

Shadowlands. Directed by Richard Attenborough. Oxford: Price Entertainment, 1993.

Shattered Glass. Directed by Billy Ray. Santa Monica: Lions Gate Films, 2003.

The Story of Temple Drake. Directed by Stephen Roberts. Los Angeles. Paramount Pictures, 1933.

Thriller. Directed by Sally Potter. London: Arts Council of Great Britain, 1979.

Titanic. Directed by James Cameron. Los Angeles: Twentieth Century-Fox Film Corporation, 1997.

Today We Live. Directed by Howard Hawks and Richard Rosson. Los Angeles: Metro-Goldwyn-Mayer, 1933.

Tootsie. Directed by Sydney Pollack. Burbank, Calif.: Columbia Pictures Corporation, 1982.

Trip to the Moon [*Le Voyage dans la Lune*]. Directed by Georges Méliès. Paris: Star Films, 1902.

Twilight Zone: The Movie. Directed by Joe Dante, John Landis, George Miller, and Steven Spielberg. Burbank, Calif.: Warner Bros. Pictures, 1983.

Wavelength. Directed by Michael Snow. 1967.

Who's Minding the Store? Directed by Frank Tashlin. Los Angeles: Jerry Lewis Pictures, 1963.

Wild Strawberries. Directed by Ingmar Bergman. Stockholm: Svensk Filmindustri, 1957.

Woman Wanted. Directed by Alan Smithee [Kiefer Sutherland]. Winnipeg: Phoenician Entertainment, 2000.

BIBLIOGRAPHY

"78 rpm Leroy Anderson—Typewriter (Played on a Garrard 4HF)." YouTube, February 19, 2007. http://youtu.be/9vuDMInQMYQ.

"1980 Olympia Report de luxe." YouTube, February 19, 2009.http://youtu.be/EEEh-MN4pD8.

Adair, Gilbert. *The Death of the Author*. London: Heinemann, 1992.

"Adventures in Typewriterdom." http://typewritersite.blogspot.com.

Albaret, Céleste. *Monsieur Proust*. Edited by Georges Belmont. Translated by Barbara Bray. New York: McGraw-Hill, 1976.

Allen, Woody. *The Insanity Defense: The Complete Prose*. New York: Random House, 2007.

———. *Three One-Act Plays*. New York: Random House, 2003.

Andrew, Dudley. "Desperation and Meditation in Bresson's *Diary of a Country Priest*." *Modern European Films and the Art of Adaptation*. Edited by Andrew Horton and Joan Magretta. New York: Ungar, 1981. 20–37.

Apollinaire, Guillaume. *Calligrammes: Poems of Peace and War (1913–1916)*. Translated by Ann Hyde Greet. Berkeley: University of California Press, 1980.

Astruc, Alexandre. "The Birth of a New Avant-Garde: La Camera-Stylo." *The New Wave*. Edited by Peter Graham. London: Secker & Warburg, 1968. 17–23.

Auerbach, Jonathan. *Body Shots: Early Cinema's Incarnations*. Berkeley: University of California Press, 2007.

Auster, Paul. "Auggie Wren's Christmas Story."*Three Films*. New York: Picador, 2003. 159–166.

———. *Book of Illusions*. New York: Picador, 2002.

———. *Invisible*. New York: Henry Holt and Company, 2009.

———. *Leviathan*. New York: Penguin, 1992.

———. "The Making of *Smoke*." Interview by Annette Insdorf. *Three Films*. New York: Picador, 2003.3–20.

———. *Music of Chance*. New York: Penguin, 1990.

———. *The New York Trilogy*. New York: Penguin, 1990.

———. *Travels in the Scriptorium*. New York: Henry Holt and Company, 2006.

Auster, Paul, and Sam Messer. *The Story of My Typewriter*. New York: D.A.P., 2002.

Bachmann, Gideon. "Federico Fellini: The Cinema Seen as a Woman . . ." *Film Quarterly* 34.2 (1980–1981): 2–9.

Banfield, Ann. "*L'imparfait de l'objectif*: The Imperfect of the Object Glass." *Camera Obscura* 8 (3 24) (September 1990): 64–87.

Bangs, John Kenrick. *The Enchanted Type-Writer*. New York and London: Harper Brothers, 1899.

Bart, Peter. "Holden: All-American Boy?" *New York Times*, December 12, 1965: X11.

Barthes, Roland. *Camera Lucida: Reflections on Photography*. Translated by Richard Howard. New York: Hill and Wang, 1981.

———. "The Death of the Author." In Burke: 125–130.

———. "The Grain of the Voice." *Image Music Text*. Translated by Stephen Heath. London: Fontana Press, 1977. 179–189.

———. *Roland Barthes*. Translated by Richard Howard. London: Macmillan, 1995.

Barton, Bruce. *Imagination in Transition: Mamet's Move to Film*. Brussels: Peter Lang, 2005.

Bauby, Jean-Dominique. *The Diving Bell and the Butterfly: A Memoir of Life and Death*. New York: Vintage, 1998.

Bazin, Andre. "*Diary of a Country Priest* and the Stylistics of Robert Bresson." In Cardullo: 9–24.

———. "The Ontology of the Photographic Image." In Braudy and Cohen: 41–53.

Bazin, André. *What Is Cinema?* Vol. 1. Translated by Hugh Gray. Berkeley: University of California Press, 2005.

Bernanos, Georges. *The Diary of a Country Priest.* Translated by Pamela Morris. New York: Macmillan, 1970.

Bigsby, Christopher, ed. *The Cambridge Companion to David Mamet.* Cambridge and New York: Cambridge University Press, 2004.

Bolter, Jay David. *Writing Space: Computers, Hypotext and the Remediation of Print.* 2nd ed. London and Mahwah, N.J.: Lawrence Erlbaum, 2001.

Boon, Kevin Alexander. *Script Culture and the American Screenplay.* Detroit: Wayne State University Press, 2008.

Borges, Jorge Luis. "Borges and I." In Burke: 339.

———. "Pierre Menand, Author of the *Quixote.*" *Collected Fictions.* Translated by Andrew Hurley. New York: Viking, 1998. 88–95.

Boynton, Victoria. "Writing Women, Solitary Space, and the Ideology of Domesticity." In Malin and Boynton: 147–164.

Braudy, Leo, and Marshall Cohen, eds. *Film Theory and Criticism.* 6th ed. New York: Oxford University Press, 2004.

Bresson, Robert. *Notes on Cinematography.* Translated by Jonathan Griffin. New York: Urizen Books, 1977.

Brooks, Peter. *The Melodramatic Imagination: Balzac, Henry James, and the Mode of Excess.* New Haven, Conn.: Yale University Press, 1976.

Browne, Nick. "Film Form/Voice-Over: Bresson's *Diary of a Country Priest.*" *Cinematheque Ontario.* Edited by James Quandt. Toronto: Toronto International Film Festival Group, 1998. 215–221.

Bruder, Jessica. "Click, Clack, Ding! Sigh . . ."*New York Times,* March 31, 2011: E1–2.

Buhle, Paul, ed. *The Beats: A Graphic History.* New York: Hill and Wang, 2009.

Bunji, Kitamura. "Tachibana Family." In Itasaka: 292.

Burke, Sean, ed. *Authorship: From Plato to Postmodern: A Reader.* Edinburgh: Edinburgh University Press, 1995.

———.*The Death and Return of the Author: Criticism and Subjectivity in Barthes, Foucault, and Derrida.* Edinburgh: Edinburgh University Press, 1992.

Burroughs, William S. " Exterminator!" New York: Penguin, 1979.

———. *Interzone.* Edited by James Grauerholz. New York: Viking, 1989.

———. *Naked Lunch, The Restored Text.* Edited by James Grauerholz and Barry Miles. New York: Grove Press, 2001.

———. *Nova Express.* New York: Grove Press, 1992.

———. *Queer.* New York: Penguin, 1987.

———. "Statement at the 1962 International Writer's Conference." *Reality Studio: A William S. Burroughs Community.* http://realitystudio.org/texts/burroughs-statements-at-the-1962-international-writers-conference.

———. *The Ticket That Exploded.* New York: Grove Press, 1967.

Buscombe, Edward. "Ideas of Authorship." *Screen* 14.3 (Autumn 1973): 75–85.

Bustarret, Claire. "The Material Surface of Modern Literary Manuscripts." In Christin: 333–339.

Calvino, Italo. *If on a Winter's Night a Traveler.* Translated by William Weaver. New York, London, and San Diego: Harcourt Brace, 1981.

———. *Six Memos for the Next Millennium.* Translated by Patrick Creagh. Cambridge, Mass.: Harvard University Press, 1988.

Campbell, Wendy. "Jeremy Mayer: Typewriter Sculpture." *Dailyartfixx,* August 7, 2009. http://www.dailyartfixx.com/2009/08/07/jeremy-mayer-typewriter-sculpture.

Canby, Vincent. "New Directors/New Films. Screen: Japanese 'Spirit of Tattoo.'" *New York Times,* March 19, 1983. http://www.nytimes.com/1983/03/19/movies/japanese-spirit-of-tattoo.html.

Cannon, J.A. "The Reader as Detective: Notes on Gaddo's *Pasticciaccio.*" *Modern Language Studies* 10.3 (1980): 41–50.

Cardullo, Bert, ed. *The Films of Robert Bresson: A Casebook.* London and New York: Anthem Press, 2009.

Carringer, Robert. *The Making of "Citizen Kane."* Berkeley: University of California Press, 1986.

Carroll, Noël. *Theorizing the Moving Image.* Cambridge: Cambridge University Press, 1996.

Carvalho, Susan. "Serving up Sex: The Writing of Desire in Allende's 'Afrodita.'" *South Atlantic Review* 67.4 (Autumn 2002): 10–26.

Christin, Anne-Marie, ed. *A History of Writing.* Paris: Flammarion, 2001.

Chua, Lawrence. "Peter Greenaway: An Interview." In Gras and Gras: 176–185.

Cixous, Hélène. "The Laugh of the Medusa." *New French Feminisms.* Edited by E. Marks and I. de Courtivron. Translated by K. Cohen and P. Cohen. New York: Schocken Books, 1986.

Clarens, Carlos. "Erotica for Export." *Village Voice*, May 15, 1984: 58.

Cohn, L.L. Review of *Irezumi. Variety*, March 30, 1983: 15, 133.

Corliss, Richard. *The Hollywood Screenwriters.* New York: Discus Books, 1972.

———. *Talking Pictures: Screenwriters in the American Cinema.* New York: Overlook, 1974.

Corrigan, Timothy. *Film and Literature: An Introduction and Reader.* Saddle River, N.J.: Prentice-Hall, 1999.

Crafton, Donald. "Comic Strips." *Encyclopedia of Early Cinema.* Edited by Richard Abel. London and New York: Routledge, 2005.

Cunneen, Joseph. "All Is Grace: *Diary of a Country Priest.*" *Robert Bresson: A Spiritual Style in the Film.* New York and London: Continuum, 2003. 44–57.

Dallery, Arleen B. "The Politics of Writing (the) Body." *Gender/Body/Knowledge: Feminist Reconstructions of Being and Knowing.* Edited by Alison M. Jaggar and Susan R. Bordo. New Brunswick, N.J.: Rutgers University Press, 1989. 52–67.

Darabont, Frank. *Walpuski's Typewriter.* Baltimore: Cemetery Dance Publications, 2005.

David, Robert Gorham. "Art and Anxiety." In Phillips: 440–453.

Davidson, Phebe, ed. *Film and Literature: Points of Intersection.* Lewiston, Maine: Edwin Mellen Press, 1997.

Davis, Ronald. *Words into Images: Screenwriters on the Studio System.* Jackson: University Press of Mississippi, 2007.

deLauretis, Teresa. *Alice Doesn't: Feminism, Semiotics, Cinema.* Bloomington: Indiana University Press, 1984.

Decherney, Peter. "Copyright Dupes: Piracy and New Media in Edison v. Lubin (1903)." *Film History* 19.2 (2007): 109–124.

Deren, Maya. "Cinematography: The Creative Use of Reality." In Braudy and Cohen: 187–198.

———. *Essential Deren: Collected Writings on Film by Maya Deren.* Edited by Bruce R. McPherson. Kingston, N.Y.: Documentext, 2005.

Desser, David. *Eros Plus Massacre: An Introduction to Japanese New Wave Cinema.* Bloomington: Indiana University Press, 1988.

Disraeli, Benjamin. *Lothair.* London: Longmans, Green, and Company, 1870.

Doane, Mary Ann. *The Desire to Desire: The Woman's Film of the 1940s.* Bloomington: Indiana University Press, 1987.

Ebert, Roger. "Review of *La Lectrice.*" *Chicago Sun-Times*, October 6, 1989. http://rogerebert.suntimes.com/apps/pbcs.dll/article?AID=/19891006/REVIEWS/910060302.

Eisenstein, Sergei. "The Cinematographic Principle and the Ideogram." *Film Form: Essays in Film Theory.* Translated by Jay Leyda. New York: Harcourt, 1969.

———. "Dickens, Griffith, and the Film Today." In Braudy and Cohen: 436–444.

Eisner, Will. *Comics & Sequential Art.* New York and London: W. W. Norton, 2008.

Elliot, Kamilla. *Rethinking the Novel/Film Debate.* Cambridge: Cambridge University Press, 2003.

Feldman, Ellen. "Character-Centered Narrative." Ph.D. dissertation, New York University, 1981.

Fell, John. *Film and the Narrative Tradition*. Norman: University of Oklahoma Press, 1974.

Felman, Sandi. *The Japanese Tattoo*. New York: Abbeville Press, 1986.

Felperin, Leslie. "Smoke Opera." *Sight and Sound* (April 1996): 6–9.

Fine, Richard. *Hollywood and the Profession of Authorship, 1928–1940*. Ann Arbor, Mich.: UMI Research Press, 1985.

Fischer, Lucy. "Frampton and the Magellan Metaphor." *American Film* 4.7 (May 1979): 58–63.

Flaherty, Alice W. *The Midnight Disease*. Boston and New York: Houghton Mifflin, 2004.

"Flame-Out." *Time*, April 17, 1964. http://www.time.com/time/magazine/article/0,9171,875847,00.html.

Forster, E. M. *Two Cheers for Democracy*. New York: Homes and Meier, 1972.

Foucault, Michel. *This Is Not a Pipe*. Translated by James Harkness. Berkeley: University of California Press, 1982.

———. "What Is an Author?" In Burke: 233–246.

Fraenkel, Béatrice. "Signatures." In Christin: 315–317.

Frampton, Hollis. "Film in the House of the Word." *October* 17 (1981): 61–64.

———. *On the Camera Arts and Consecutive Matters: The Writings of Hollis Frampton*. Edited by Bruce Jenkins. Cambridge, Mass.: MIT Press, 2009.

———. *Poetic Justice: A Film by Hollis Frampton*. New York: Visual Studies Workshop, 1973.

Franz, Kathleen, and Susan Smulyan. *Major Problems in American Popular Culture*. Boston: Wadsworth, 2012.

Freud, Sigmund. "Fetishism." *The Standard Edition of the Complete Psychological Works of Sigmund Freud*, vol. 21. Edited by James Strachey. 3rd ed. London: Hogarth Press, 1953–1966.

———. *On Creativity and the Unconscious: Papers on the Psychology of Art, Literature, Love, Religion*. New York: Harper & Row, 1958.

Friedlaender, Salomo. *Gray Magic* (*Graue Magic: Berliner Nachshlussel-roman*). Dresden, 1922.

Friedman, Susan Stanford. "The Return of the Repressed in Women's Narrative Author(s)." *Journal of Narrative Technique* 19.1 (Winter 1989): 141–156.

Frost, Robert. "Stopping by Woods on a Snowy Evening." *American Poetry: Poetry for Young People*. Edited by John Hollander. New York: Sterling Publishing, 2004. 35.

Gelmis, Joseph. *The Film Director as Superstar*. Garden City, N.Y.: Doubleday, 1970.

Gilbert, Sandra M., and Susan Gubar. *The Madwoman in the Attic: The Woman Writer and the Nineteenth-Century Literary Imagination*. New Haven, Conn.: Yale University Press, 1979.

Gilman, Sander L. *Disease and Representation: Images of Illness from Madness to AIDS*. Ithaca, N.Y.: Cornell University Press, 1988.

Gleick, James. "Books and Other Fetish Objects." *New York Times*, July 17, 2011: 4.

Goldstein, Paul. *Copyright's Highway: From Gutenberg to the Celestial Jukebox*. New York: Hill and Wang, 1994.

Gonzales, Jesus Angel. "Words versus Images: Paul Auster's Films from *Smoke* to *Book of Illusions*." *Literature-Film Quarterly* 37.1 (2009): 28–48.

Goodyear, Dana. "Letter from Los Angeles: Hollywood Shadows—A Cure for Blocked Screenwriters." *New Yorker*, March 21, 2011. http://www.newyorker.com/reporting/2011/03/21/110321fa_fact_goodyear.

Gras, Vernon, and Marguerite Gras, eds. *Peter Greenaway: Interviews*. Jackson: University Press of Mississippi, 2000.

Greenaway, Peter. *The Pillow Book*. Abbeville, France: F. Paillart, 1997.

Greenblatt, Kim. "Writing Fiction Is Like Giving Birth." Kim Greenblatt's Blog, August 10, 2008. http://www.kimgreenblatt.com/wordpress/writing-fiction-is-like-giving-birth.

Guo, Xiaolu. "Notes toward a Metaphysical Cinema Manifesto." *Guo Xiaolu Official Website* (March 2010). http://www.guoxiaolu.com/WR_MANIFESTO_1.htm.

———. "Further Notes toward a Metaphysical Cinema Manifesto." *Guo Xiaolu Official Website* (July 2010). http://www.guoxiaolu.com/WR_MANIFESTO_2.htm.

Hegemann, Helene. *Axolotl Roadkill.* Berlin: Ullstein, 2010.

Heidegger, Martin. *Parmenides.* Translated by Andre Schuwer and Richard Rojcewica. Bloomington: Indiana University Press, 1992.

Heller, Steven, and Karen Pomeroy. *Design Literacy: Understanding Graphic Design.* New York: Allworth, 1997.

Henke, Suzette A. "Woman Alone: The Spinster's Art." In Malin and Boynton: 21–37.

Hess, Scott. *Authoring the Self: Self-Representation, Authorship, and the Print Market in British Poetry from Pope through Wordsworth.* New York: Routledge, 2005.

Hitchman, Simon. "A History of French New Wave Cinema." *New Wave Film* (2008).http://www.newwavefilm.com/about/history-of-french-new-wave.shtml.

Hocks, Mary E., and Michelle R. Kendrick, eds. *Eloquent Images: Word and Image in the Age of New Media.* Cambridge, Mass.: MIT Press, 2003.

Hoffman, Carrie, and Rusty W. Spell. "How to Make a Movie about a Writer." WeLikeMedia, July 11, 2003. http://welikemedia.com/howtomakeamovieaboutawriter.html.

Hollis Frampton Official Website. http://hollisframpton.org.uk.

"Hollis Frampton's Hapax Legomena." *Museum of the Moving Image.* http://www.movingimagesource.us/events/hollis-framptons-hapax-legomena-20090325.

The Holy Bible: English Standard Version. Wheaton, Ill.: Good News Publishers, 2001.

Homem, RuiCarvalho, and Maria de Fatima Lambert, eds. *Writing and Seeing: Essays on Word and Image.* New York: Rodopi, 2005.

Hubbard, L. Ron. *Typewriter in the Sky.* Los Angeles: Bridge, 1995.

Hughes, Dorothy B. *In a Lonely Place.* New York: Feminist Press at CUNY, 2003.

Itasaka, Gen, ed. *Kodansha Encyclopedia of Japan,* vol. 7. Tokyo: Kodansha, 1983.

Jackson, Shelley. *The Melancholy of Anatomy.* New York: Random House, 2002.

———. "Shelley Jackson's Ineradicable Stain." http://ineradicablestain.com.

Jenkins, Bruce. "The Films of Hollis Frampton: A Critical Study." Ph.D. dissertation, Northwestern University, 1984.

Jenkins, Henry. *Textual Poachers: Television Fans & Participatory Culture.* New York and London: Routledge, 1992.

Kael, Pauline. *Raising Kane and Other Essays.* London: Marion Boyars Publishers, 1996.

Kaplan, E. Ann. *Women and Film: Both Sides of the Camera.* New York: Methuen, 1983.

Karlgaard, Rich. "Politics Is Hollywood for Ugly People." *Forbes,* June 25, 2009. http://www.forbes.com/sites/digitalrules/2009/06/25/politics-is-hollywood-for-ugly-people.

Kaufman, Charlie. *Adaptation: The Shooting Script.* New York: Newmarket Press, 2002.

Keesey, Douglas. *The Films of Peter Greenaway: Sex, Death, and Provocation.* Jefferson, N.C.: McFarland, 2006.

Keller, Bill. "Let's Ban Books, or at Least Stop Writing Them." *New York Times,* July 13, 2011: MM9.

Kelly, Kevin. "Becoming Screen Literate." *New York Times,* November 23, 2008: MM46.

Kermode, Frank.*The Sense of an Ending: Studies in the Theory of Fiction.* New York: Oxford University Press, 1967.

Kolker, Robert. "All Roads Lead to the Abject: The Monstrous Feminine and Gender Boundaries in Stanley Kubrick's *The Shining.*" *Literature/Film Quarterly* 34.1 (2006): 54–63.

King, Stephen. *On Writing.* New York: Scribner, 2000.

Kirschenbaum, Matthew G. "The Word as Image in an Age of Digital Reproduction." In Hocks and Kendrick: 137–158.

Kite, B. "*Bigger Than Life:* Somewhere in Suburbia." *Criterion,* March 18, 2010. http://www.criterion.com/current/posts/1412-bigger-than-life-somewhere-in-suburbia.

Kittler, Friedrich A. *Gramophone, Film, Typewriter*. Translated by Geoffrey Winthrop-Young and Michael Wutz.Stanford, Calif.: Stanford University Press, 1999.

Klein, Wolfgang, and Ping Li, eds. *The Expression of Time*. Berlin and New York: Mouton de Gruyter, 2009.

Knorr, Karen, and Tracey Moffat. "When the Photographer Chooses the Words in Order to Photograph the Images." In Homem and Lambert: 257–266.

Kovács, András Bálint. *Screening Modernism: European Art Cinema, 1950–1980*. Chicago: University of Chicago Press, 2007.

Kozloff, Sarah. *Invisible Storytellers: Voice-over Narration in American Fiction Film*. Berkeley: University of California Press, 1988.

Krakow, Amy. *The Total Tattoo Book*. New York: Warner Books, 1994.

Kreidl, John Francis. *Alain Resnais*. Boston: Twayne, 1977.

Kreiman, Jody, and Diana Van Lancker Sidtis. *Foundations of Voice Studies: An Interdisciplinary Approach to Voice Production and Perception*. West Sussex: Wiley-Blackwell, 2011.

Kuhn, Tom. "Bertolt Brecht and Notions of Collaboration." *Bertolt Brecht: Centenary Essays*. Edited by Rodney Livingstone and Steve Giles. Amsterdam and Atlanta: Rodopi, 1998.1–18.

Kupfer, Alex. "Anything Can Happen in a Cartoon: Comic Strip Adaptations in the Early and Transitional Periods." Los Angeles: UCLA Film and Television Archive.http://www.cinema .ucla.edu/sites/default/files/kupfer.pdf.

Larsen, Randall. "Artist's Rights vs. Copyright Owner's Rights: Conflict Resolution when the Logic of Intellectual Property Law Is Articulated with Motion Picture Production, A Collaborative Mode of Production." Ph.D. dissertation, University of Hawai'i, 2005.

Lautman, Victoria, with Vicki Berndt. *The New Tattoo*. New York: Abbeville Press, 1994.

Lawrence, Amy. *Echo and Narcissus: Women's Voices in Classical Hollywood Cinema*. Berkeley: University of California Press, 1991.

"Leopoldo Maler: Hommage, 1974 Modified Typewriter." *Hess Collection Catalogue*. http://www .hesscollection.com/art/maler.html.

Lesser, Wendy. *His Other Half: Men Looking at Women through Art*. Cambridge, Mass.: Harvard University Press, 1991.

Lethem, Jonathan. "The Ecstasy of Influence—A Plagiarism." *Harper's* (February 2007). http:// harpers.org/archive/2007/02/0081387.

MacDonald, Scott. "Hollis Frampton: Zorns Lemma." *Hollis Frampton Official Website*. http:// www.hollisframpton.org.uk/zlessay.htm.

———. "Interview with Sally Potter." *Camera Obscura: A Journal of Feminism, Culture, and Media Studies* 12 (2 35) (May 1995): 187–221.

———. *Screen Writings: Scripts and Texts by Independent Filmmakers*. Berkeley: University of California Press, 1995.

Maia, Gil. "When What You See Is What You Read." In Homem and Lambert: 377–385.

Malin, Jo, and Victoria Boynton, eds. *Herspace: Women, Writing, and Solitude*. Binghamton, N.Y.: Haworth Press, 2003.

Mamet, David. *3 Uses of the Knife—On the Nature and Purpose of Drama*. New York: Columbia University Press, 1998.

———. *On Directing Film*. New York: Viking, 1991.

———. *Three Jewish Plays*. London, Hollywood, and Toronto: Samuel French, 1987.

———. *The Wicked Son*. New York: Schocken, 2006.

Martin, Thomas M. *Images and the Imageless: A Study in Religious Consciousness and Film*. Lewisburg, Pa.: Bucknell University Press, 1981.

Maslin, Janet. "With Sizzling Tangos, Who Needs a Plot?" *New York Times*, February 12, 1999: E1, E29.

Mastrocinque, Attilio. "Hermes." *Encyclopedia of Religion*. Edited by Lindsay Jones. Vol. 6. 2nd ed. Detroit: Macmillan Reference USA, 2005. 3936–3938.

Mayne, Judith. "The Limits of Spectacle." *Wide Angle* 6.3 (1984): 4–15.

McCallum, Donald. "Historical and Cultural Dimensions of the Tattoo in Japan." In Rubined: 109–134.

McDonald, Keiko. E-mail to the author, January 19, 1998.

McGilligan, Patrick. *Alfred Hitchcock: A Life in Darkness and Light*. New York: HarperCollins, 2003.

Metz, Christian. *Film Language: A Semiotics of the Cinema*. Translated by Michael Taylor. Chicago: University of Chicago Press, 1974.

Metz, Walter. "Toward a Post-Structural Influence in Film Genre Study: Intertextuality and *The Shining*." *Film Criticism* 22.1 (1997): 38–61.

Miller, Laura. "Plagiarism: The Next Generation." *Salon*, February 16, 2010.http://www.salon .com/'books/laura_miller/2010/02/16/hegemann.

Mitchell, W.J.T. *Picture Theory*. Chicago: University of Chicago Press, 1994.

Mitry, Jean. *The Aesthetics and Psychology of the Cinema*. Translated by Christopher King. London: Athlone Press, 1998.

Monaco, James. *Alain Resnais*. New York: Oxford University Press, 1978.

Monk, Claire. "The Tango Lesson." *Sight and Sound* 7.12 (December 1997): 54–55.

Morris, R.N. "The Writer as Detective: My Investigation." Guardian Books Blog, January 10, 2008. http://www.guardian.co.uk/books/booksblog/2008/jan/10/thewriterasdetectivemyinv.

Mulvey, Laura."Afterthoughts on 'Visual Pleasure and Narrative Cinema' Inspired by King Vidor's *Duel in the Sun* (1946)." *Visual and Other Pleasures*. Edited by Laura Mulvey. Bloomington: Indiana University Press, 1989. 29–38.

———. "The Index and the Uncanny." *Time and the Image*. Edited by Carolyn Bailey Gill. Manchester and New York: Manchester University Press, 2000. 139–148.

———. "Visual Pleasure and Narrative Cinema." *Film Theory and Criticism: Introductory Readings*. Edited by Gerald Mast, Marshall Cohen, and Leo Braudy. New York: Oxford University Press, 1992. 837–848.

Musser, Charles. *The Emergence of Cinema: The American Screen to 1907*. Berkeley: University of California Press, 1994. .

Naremore, James, ed. *Film Adaptation*. New Brunswick, N.J.: Rutgers University Press, 2000.

"National Gallery of Canada: Acquisition Highlights: Rodney Graham." *Cybermuse*, http:// cybermuse.gallery.ca/cybermuse/enthusiast/acquisitions/2004-2005/Graham_text_e.jsp.

Nesbit, Molly. "What Was an Author?" In Burke: 233–262.

Nichols, Bill. *Maya Deren and the American Avant-Garde*. Berkeley: University of California Press, 2001.

"(*nostalgia*)." *Hollis Frampton Official Website*. http://hollisframpton.org.uk./nostalgia.htm.

O'Farrell, Mary Ann. "Self-Consciousness and the Psoriatic Personality: Considering Updike and Potter." *Literature and Medicine* 20.2 (2001): 133–150.

"The Olivetti Lettera 32 Manual Typewriter." YouTube, July 19, 2009. http://youtu.be/kPys -RbfwCY.

Orlean, Susan. *The Orchid Thief: A True Story of Beauty and Obsession*. New York: Ballantine, 2000.

Ozon, François. *Swimming Pool*. Paris: Archeediteur, 2003.

Padgett, John. "William Faulkner." *The Mississippi Writers Page*. http://www.olemiss.edu/mwp/ dir/faulkner_william.

Page, Benedicte. "StiegLarsson's Partner Plans to Complete Final Millennium Novel." *The Guardian*, January 14, 2011.http://www.guardian.co.uk/books/2011/jan/14/stieg-larsson-partner -finish-millennium-novel.

Palmer, R. Barton. *Joel and Ethan Coen*. Urbana: University of Illinois Press, 2004.

"Paul Smith's Typewriter Art." *LivingEachDay.com* (2008). http://www.livingeachday.com/ a-PaulSmith-typewriterart.

Pease, Donald E. "Author." In Burke: 263–276.

Pekar, Harvey. *Best of American Splendor*. New York: Ballantine, 2005.

Pekar, Harvey, with Ed Piskor. "Jack Kerouac." *The Beats: A Graphic History*. Edited by Paul Buhle. New York: Hill and Wang, 2009.3–50.

———. "William Burroughs." In Buhle: 78–94.

Pelli, Denis G., and Charles Bigelow. "A Writing Revolution." *Seed Magazine*, October 20, 2009. http://seedmagazine.com/content/article/a_writing_revolution.

Perry, Susan K. "How Creative Flow Is Like Sex." *Psychology Today* (March 8, 2010). http://www.psychologytoday.com/blog/creating-in-flow/201003/how-creative-flow-is-sex.

Phillips, William, ed. *Art and Psychoanalysis*. New York: Criterion Books, 1957.

Pink, Daniel. "The 4th Annual Year in Ideas: Skin Literature." *New York Times*, December 12, 2004. http://www.nytimes.com/2004/12/12/magazine/12SKIN.html.

Pipolo, Tony. "Author, Author: *Journal d'un curé de campagne*." *Robert Bresson: A Passion for Film*. New York: Oxford University Press, 2010. 69–97.

Polan, Dana. *In a Lonely Place*. London: British Film Institute, 1994.

Poulet, George. "Criticism and the Experience of Interiority." In Burke: 101–107.

Price, Brian. "Word and Image, World and Nothingness: Logocentrism and Ironic Reversal in *Procés de Jeanne d'Arc, Diary of a Country Priest,* and *Les Anges du péché*." *Neither God nor Master: Robert Bresson and Radical Politics*. Minneapolis: University of Minnesota Press, 2011. 40–68.

"Quotations about Writing and the Creative Process."http://uncabaret.com/node/55.

Rank, Otto. "Life and Creation." In Phillips: 306–332.

Reader, Keith. "*Journal d'un curé de campagne*." *Robert Bresson: French Film Directors*. Manchester: Manchester University Press, 2000. 30–52.

Richie, Donald. "Introduction." *A Hundred Things Japanese*. Nihon Bunka Kenkyūjo. New York: Japan Culture Institute, 1975.

———. "The Japanese Art of Tattooing." *Natural History* 8.10 (1973): 50–59.

Robb, David. "A Dispute by WGA and DGA over Film Credit." *Hollywood Reporter*, August 2, 1999.1–5.

Robbe-Grillet, Alain. *Two Novels by Robbe-Grillet*. Translated by Richard Howard. New York: Grove Press, 1965.

Robbins, Tom. *Still Life with Woodpecker*. New York: Bantam, 1980.

"Roland Barthes—Centre Pompidou—27.11.2002–10.03.2003." *Euromuse*. http://www.euromuse.net/en/exhibitions/exhibition/view-e/roland-barthes.

Ronberg, Lene Bogh. "Rembrandt or Not? Works by Rembrandt and His School at Statens Museum for Kunst." *The Master and His Workshop*. Edited by Ronberg and Eva de la Fuente Pedersen. Copenhagen: Statens Museum for Kunst, 2006. 56–59.

Rooney, David. "The Tango Lesson." *Variety*, September 8, 1997.

Rubin, Arnold. *Marks of Civilization: Artistic Transformations of the Human Body*. Los Angeles: Museum of Cultural History, 1988.

Ruscha, Ed. *Ed Ruscha: Fifty Years of Painting*. London: Hayward, 2009.

Sandblom, Philip. *Creativity and Disease: How Illness Affects Literature, Art, and Music*. Philadelphia: J.B. Lippincott, 1989.

Sante, Luc. "The Fiction of Memory." *New York Times Book Review*, March 14, 2010: 17.

Sarris, Andrew. *The American Cinema: Directors and Directions, 1929–1968*. New York: Da Capo Press, 1996.

Savigliano, Marta E. *Tango and the Political Economy of Passion*. Boulder, Colo.: Westview Press, 1995.

Schilt, Thibaut. *François Ozon*. Urbana: University of Illinois Press, 2011.

Schrader, Paul. "Bresson." In Cardullo: 145–153.

Schuessler, Jennifer. "The Muses of Insert, Delete." *New York Times*, December 26, 2011: 1, 6.

"Scrubs: Ted vs. Typewriter." YouTube, January 27, 2008. http://youtu.be/7TMObBJM1AY.

Scutt, R.W.B., and Christopher Gotch. *Art, Sex, and Symbol: The Mystery of Tattooing*. York: Cornwall, 1986.

Segal, Lynne. *Straight Sex: Rethinking the Politics of Pleasure*. Berkeley: University of California Press, 1994.

Sesonske, Alexander. "Time and Tense in Cinema." *Journal of Aesthetics and Art Criticism* 38.4 (1980): 419–426.

Shields, David. *Reality Hunger*. New York: Knopf, 2009.

Shōnagon, Sei. *The Pillow Book*. Translated by Meredith McKinney. London and New York: Penguin, 2006.

Silverman, Kaja. *The Acoustic Mirror: The Female Voice in Psychoanalysis and Cinema*. Bloomington: Indiana University Press, 1988.

Simon, Bill. "'Reading' Zorns Lemma." *Millennium Film Journal* 1.2 (1978): 38–49.

Sitney, P. Adams. *Visionary Film: The American Avant-Garde 1943–2000*. New York: Oxford University Press, 2002.

Smith, Alison. *Agnès Varda*. Manchester: Manchester University Press, 1998.

Smith, Dinitia. "Aggrieved Publisher Rejects Young Novelist's Apology." *New York Times*, April 26, 2006. http://www.nytimes.com/2006/04/26/books/26book.html.

Smith, Greg. "'Real Horrorshow': The Juxtaposition of Subtext, Satire, and Audience Implication in Stanley Kubrick's *The Shining*." *Literature/Film Quarterly* 25.4 (1997): 300–306.

Snider, Grant. "Behind Every Great Novelist Is . . ." *New York Times Book Review*, May 13, 2012, 33.

Snowden, Lynn. "Which Is the Fly and Which Is the Human? Interview with William S. Burroughs and David Cronenberg." *DavidCronenberg.de* (February 1992). http://www.david cronenberg.de/burrcron.html.

Sontag, Susan. "Spiritual Style in the Films of Robert Bresson." In Cardullo: 29–44.

Springer, Carsten. *A Paul Auster Sourcebook*. New York: Peter Lang, 2001.

Stacey, Jackie. *Star Gazing: Hollywood Cinema and Female Spectatorship*. London: Routledge, 1994.

Stewart, Garrett. *The Look of Reading Book, Painting, Text*. Chicago: University of Chicago Press, 2006.

Strain, Ellen, and Gregory Van Hoosier-Carey. "Eloquent Interfaces: Humanities-Based Analysis in the Age of Hypermedia." In Hocks and Kendrick: 257–281.

Tan, Tiffany. "Freeze! You're in Mohe." *China Daily*, January 6, 2011. http://www.chinadaily.com .cn/cndy/2011–01/06/content_11800824.htm.

Tanizaki, Junichiro. "The Tattooer." *Seven Japanese Tales*. Translated by Howard Hibbett. New York: Knopf, 1963. 160–169.

Taylor, Julie. *Paper Tangos*. Durham, N.C.: Duke University Press, 1998.

Thayer, John E. III. "Tattoos." In Itasaka: 350–351.

"Times Business Reporter Accused of Plagiarism Is Said to Resign." *New York Times*, February 16, 2010: B2.

Thomas, D. M. "Introduction." In Felman: 8–9.

"Typewriter—The Ultimate Wireless Laptop." Youtube, August 22, 2007. http://youtu.be/ 4NGV4YB9UWY.

"The Typewriter Song." YouTube, May 28, 2007. http://youtu.be/0ohpL3RgyV4.

"Typing." YouTube, September 9, 2009. http://youtu.be/QulmWgv1h-k.

Underwood, Tim, and Chuck Miller, eds. *Bare Bones: Conversations on Terror with Stephen King*. New York: McGraw-Hill, 1988.

Updike, John. "At War with My Skin." *Self-Consciousness: Memoirs*. New York: Knopf, 1989.

———. "The End of Authorship." *New York Times Book Review*, June 25, 2006.

Vance, Carole S. *Pleasure and Danger: Exploring Female Sexuality*. Boston: Routledge and Kegan Paul, 1984.

Variety Staff. "Paris When It Sizzles." *Variety*, December 31, 1963.http://www.variety.com/review/VE1117793876/.

"The Virtual Typewriter Museum." http://www.typewritermuseum.org/collection/index.php3?machine=rem2&cat=ku.

Viswanathan, Kaavya. *How Opal Mehta Got Kissed, Got Wild, and Got a Life*. New York: Little, Brown, 2006.

Waits, Tom. "You're Innocent When You Dream." *Smoke: Original Soundtrack*. CD. Hollywood Records, 1995.

Wallace, Amy. "Name of Director Smithee Isn't What It Used to Be." *Los Angeles Times*, January 15, 2000.http://articles.latimes.com/2000/jan/15/entertainment/ca-54271.

"*Washington Post* Suspends Journalist Sari Horowitz for Plagiarism." *Daily Beast*, March 16, 2011. http://www.thedailybeast.com/cheats/2011/03/16/washington-post-suspends-journalist-sari-horwitz-for-plagiarism.html.

Wershler-Henry, Darren. *The Iron Whim: A Fragmented History of Typewriting*. Ithaca, N.Y.: Cornell University Press, 2005.

Williams, Mason, Edward Ruscha, and Patrick Blackwell. *Royal Road Test*. Los Angeles, 1967.

Wilson, Edmund. "Philoctetes: The Wound and the Bow." *The Wound and the Bow: Seven Studies in Literature*. Cambridge, Mass.: Houghton Mifflin, 1941. 272–295.

Wilson, Emma. *Alain Resnais*. New York: Palgrave, 2006.

Windhausen, Federico. "Words into Film: Toward a Genealogical Understanding of Hollis Frampton's Theory and Practice." *October* 109 (2004): 76–95.

Wollen, Peter. *Signs and Meaning in the Cinema*. Bloomington: Indiana University Press, 1969.

"Woody Allen Marries Soon-Yi in Venice." CNN, December 24, 1997.http://www.cnn.com/SHOWBIZ/9712/24/woody.weds.

Woolf, Virginia. *Granite and Rainbow: Essays*. London: Hogarth Press, 1958.

———. *Mrs. Dalloway*. London: Hogarth Press, 1925.

———. *On Being Ill*. Ashfield, Mass.: Paris Press, 2002.

Žižek, Slavoj.*The Art of the Ridiculous Sublime: On David Lynch's Lost Highway*. Seattle: University of Washington Press, 2000.

———. *Enjoy Your Symptom: Jacques Lacan in Hollywood and Out*. New York: Routledge, 2001.

———. *Everything You Always Wanted to Know about Lacan: But Were Afraid to Ask Hitchcock*. London: Verso, 1992.

———. *Looking Awry: An Introduction to Jacques Lacan through Popular Culture*. Cambridge, Mass.: MIT Press, 1992.

Zola, Emile. *The Masterpiece*. Translated by Roger Pearson. New York: Oxford University Press, 1993.

"Zorns Lemma." *Hollis Frampton Website*. http://hollisframpton.org.uk/zornslemma.htm.

INDEX

ABOUT THE AUTHOR

Lucy Fischer is Distinguished Professor of English and Film Studies at the University of Pittsburgh. She is the author or editor of nine other books: *Jacques Tati* (G. K. Hall, 1983), *Shot/Countershot: Film Tradition and Women's Cinema* (Princeton University Press, 1989), *Imitation of Life* (Rutgers University Press, 1991), *Cinematernity: Film, Motherhood, Genre* (Princeton University Press, 1996), *Sunrise* (British Film Institute, 1998), *Designing Women: Art Deco, Cinema, and the Female Form* (Columbia University Press, 2003), *Stars: The Film Reader* (coedited with Marcia Landy, Rutgers University Press, 2004), *American Cinema of the 1920s* (Rutgers University Press, 2009), and *Teaching Film* (coedited with Patrice Petro, MLA, 2012).

She has published extensively on issues of film history, theory, and criticism in such journals as *Screen, Sight and Sound, Camera Obscura, Wide Angle, Cinema Journal, Journal of Film and Video, Film Criticism, Women and Performance, Modernism/Modernity, Frauen und Film*, and *Film Quarterly*. Her essays have been anthologized thirty times in volumes of film history, criticism, and/or theory.

She has held curatorial positions at the Museum of Modern Art (New York City) and the Carnegie Museum of Art (Pittsburgh), and has written catalog essays for exhibits at the Wight Gallery (Los Angeles) and the Neuberger Museum (Purchase, New York). She has been the recipient of a National Endowment for the Arts Art Critics Fellowship as well as a National Endowment for the Humanities Fellowship for University Professors.

She has lectured internationally in Tel Aviv, Israel; Lausanne, Switzerland; Lisbon, Portugal; Amsterdam, Holland; Vienna, Austria; Glasgow, Scotland, London, Great Britain; and Adelaide, Australia,and has taught abroad in Augsburg, Germany; Stockholm, Sweden; and on the Semester at Sea program of the University of Pittsburgh (which traveled around the world).

She has served as president of the Society for Cinema and Media Studies (2001–2003) and in 2008 received its Distinguished Service Award. As its Conference Program Committee chair, she has twice hosted and organized its annual national conference in Pittsburgh. Furthermore, she has served as chair of the Film Executive Committee of the Modern Language Association and has been a delegate to the American Council of Learned Societies.